All of Shakespeare

Maurice Charney

Columbia University Press
New York

Columbia University Press
New York   Chichester, West Sussex
Copyright © 1993 Columbia University Press
All rights reserved

Library of Congress Cataloging-in-Publication Data

Charney, Maurice.
    All of Shakespeare / Maurice Charney.
        p.   cm.
    Includes index.
    ISBN 0–231–06862–X
    1. Shakespeare, William, 1564–1616—Criticism
and interpretation.
    I. Title.
    PR2976.C44   1993
    822.3'3—dc20
                                                        93–6660
                                                        CIP

⊗

Casebound editions of Columbia University Press books
are printed on permanent and durable
acid-free paper.

Printed in the United States of America

c 10 9 8 7 6 5 4 3 2 1

822.33
C HA
3/94

for
Hanna

"Did you not name a tempest,
A birth and death?"

Contents

Contents

Contents

Preface

This project began with the idea of updating Mark Van Doren's little book *Shakespeare*, first published in 1939, then reprinted in the influential Doubleday-Anchor paperback series in 1953. I have always been a great admirer of this book and of Mark Van Doren as a teacher of Shakespeare. I remember visiting his class at Columbia in the mid-forties, while I was an undergraduate at Harvard. When I came home to Brooklyn, I thought it an intellectual lark to go up to Columbia and sit in on the classes of Mark Van Doren and Meyer Shapiro. Van Doren spoke directly to students about Shakespeare without the weighty intervention of scholarship—at least that's what I thought then, although I now know that he was much more learned than he appeared to a callow adolescent. *Shakespeare* seemed to me a wonderfully personal and idiosyncratic book.

All of Shakespeare is by no means a sequel to *Shakespeare* (as if Van Doren spoke only tentatively of Shakespeare), but I discuss *all* of Shakespeare. My book is much longer and more comprehensive than Van Doren's. I have tried to write a substantial chapter on each of the plays and poems without taking too much account of my personal preferences (although these have not been ignored). Unlike Van Doren, I have not avoided plays and poems that don't especially appeal to me, because I want readers to go to *All of Shakespeare* with their own specific needs in mind. If my hypothetical reader wants to find out more about the second part of *Henry VI*, or *The Merry Wives of Windsor*, or *Timon of Athens*, I am ready.

All of Shakespeare is written with the desires of students in mind, especially students in large lecture classes who don't have the opportunity to ask questions. It is, I hope, a user-friendly and self-teaching book, designed as a series of minilectures with plenty of examples from the plays and poems that are discussed in some detail. I have followed my inclination to pursue topics thoroughly, although not to engage all topics, even some obvious ones. The book is not intended as a series of introductions in the sense that each chapter includes all relevant, preliminary information. Instead, I take a strong point of view that the reader may or may not agree with but one that might provoke argument.

All of Shakespeare is conceived as a play-by-play and poem-by-poem commentary on Shakespeare's works, including plays that may be only partly by Shakespeare, such as *The Two Noble Kinsmen* and *Pericles*, and poems such as *A Lover's Complaint*, whose authorship is uncertain. The book is directed not only to students but also to people outside an academic setting who read and study Shakespeare for pleasure. The mythical "general reader," much revered by publishers and book clubs, may want to read a chapter from this book before seeing a Shakespeare play, watching a Shakespeare movie or videotape, or undertaking a fresh reading of the *Sonnets*. Ideally, my chapters are intended to be stimulating or controversial and call the reader's attention to lines and passages not noticed before and to interrelations among the plays.

In the chapters on individual plays and poems, I quote from the separate paperback volumes of the Signet Shakespeare, under the general editorship of Sylvan Barnet, but for general citation I use the single-volume *Complete Signet Classic Shakespeare* (1972). I also occasionally quote from the First Folio in the Norton facsimile edition by Charlton Hinman (1968). I have made profitable use of all of the volumes in the New Arden Shakespeare, as well as David Bevington's edition, *The Complete Works of Shakespeare* (3d ed., 1980). For the intricate details of the history plays, I have found Peter Saccio's *Shakespeare's English Kings* (1977) invaluable. For the poems, I have benefited from the notes in Edward Hubler's edition of *Shakespeare's Songs and Poems* (1959) and from J. C. Maxwell's New Cambridge edition of *The Poems* (1969). Marvin Spevack's *The Harvard Concordance to Shakespeare* (1973) has been my constant companion, as well as *The Oxford English Dictionary*—the *OED*—especially in its condensed Shakespearean form prepared by C. T. Onions under the title *A Shakespeare Glossary* (2d ed., 1958). I quote various pieces of contemporary information from E. K. Chambers, *William Shakespeare: A Study of Facts and Problems,* (2 vols., 1930). Elizabethan and Jacobean plays are quoted from appropriate Revels or Regents editions, and the dates of these plays are taken from *Annals of English Drama, 976–1700,* by Alfred Harbage, revised by S. Schoenbaum (1964). For proverbs I refer to the magisterial book by Morris Palmer Tilley, *A Dictionary of the Proverbs in England in the Sixteenth and Seventeenth Centuries* (1966).

My own interest in Shakespeare is strongly focused on matters of style rather than ideology. I am not so much oriented to Shakespeare as a Renaissance thinker or to Shakespeare seen in relation to Renaissance ideas and assumptions as to Shakespeare the dramatist and poet, a creator of fictions. This doesn't mean that I have ignored the context of ideas in my interpretations of the plays and poems but only that I have not accorded them primary importance. Shakespeare's politics, for example, inform all the plays, but the literal politics found in any individual work takes precedence over larger concepts that Shakespeare may or may not have had. I am fascinated by the means of expression in the plays and poems, both verbal and theatrical, or perhaps by some combination of verbal and theatrical resources. This kind of criticism is sometimes called "performative." I am committed to the idea of Shakespeare as a dramatist whose plays are performed in the theater. I am especially interested in dramatic characters as they develop at different points in the play, which comes not so much out of a concern with characterization for itself as in the distinctive ways a character is presented in relation to an unfolding action.

Shakespeare's own writings are his most important source, and I believe that his works really do constitute a single comprehensive imaginative unit. His large body of work is inherently intertextual, with early plays anticipating later ones and later plays echoing earlier ones. This is also true for the connection of Shakespeare's poems with his plays. I call attention to specific words and images that anticipate later developments or to recollections of earlier plays in more mature works. I am convinced that Shakespeare's imagery and his important words express his preoccupations as a dramatist and as a poet, although they may tell us tantalizingly little about him as a person.

All of Shakespeare is divided into conventional genres: comedies, histories, tragedies, romances, and poems. The poems do not appear in the first collected edition of Shakespeare's works, the First Folio of 1623, and the romances are included with the comedies (except *Cymbeline*, which is the last of the tragedies). We are coming to realize that Shakespeare's conception of these genres was much more mixed than ours. The tragedies, for example, contain a good deal of comic material, just as the late romances, in their exploitation of tragico- medy, closely skirt tragic materials. The history plays are a puzzling genre, although they constitute a distinct group different from com- edies and tragedies in Shakespeare's First Folio. Some of the histories, such as *Richard II*, are clearly tragedies, but the *Henry IV* plays present us with Falstaff, Shakespeare's most notable comic protagonist. These generic divisions are clearly a convenience. If one took them too seriously, they would require complex qualifications and justifica- tions.

In the matter of dating I have generally followed accepted assump- tions, although it is clear that there is almost no evidence at all on which to date certain plays. If we pay attention to larger chronolog- ical sequences, it is evident that relationships between groups of plays and poems have not been sufficiently explored. Early Shake- speare, for example, extending a year or two beyond the death of Christopher Marlowe in 1593, would probably include *The Comedy of Errors, Love's Labor's Lost, The Taming of the Shrew, The Two Gentlemen of Verona, Titus Andronicus*, the Minor Tetralogy of History Plays (the three parts of *Henry VI* plus *Richard III*), *Venus and Adonis, The Rape of Lucrece*, and many of Shakespeare's *Sonnets*. The generic implications of this grouping still needs to be worked out.

I have profited from extensive reading in the almost endless schol- arly literature on Shakespeare, but I have not considered it appropriate in this book to pursue scholarly matters or to make footnote references. In drawing on the experience of more than thirty-five years of teaching and writing about Shakespeare, I have tried to present matters freshly, as if for the first time. This may be an illusion, but it is a pleasant illusion that dispenses with pedantry. I think I remember points made by students as vividly as many scholarly articles I have read.

I am deeply indebted to the undaunted Jim Shapiro for providing fourteen single-spaced pages of practical suggestions for revision. I hope that Richard Marienstras will recognize something familiar in the discussion of Timon, which first took place in his country house. I am grateful to Rutgers University for a leave during the fall semester of 1991.

All of Shakespeare

COMEDIES

The Comedy of Errors

$\mathcal{T}$*he Comedy of Errors* is probably Shakespeare's first comedy, if not actually the first play he ever wrote. Shakespeare seems proud of his classical learning, as he is in his first tragedy, *Titus Andronicus*. It is not so much that both plays are loaded with classical allusions as the fact that they are meant as models of what a classical play should be. *The Comedy of Errors* has a remarkably well constructed plot, which follows a strict unity of time. Egeon is condemned to death before noon, and he is scheduled to be executed at 5 P.M.

In the final scene of the play, Adriana and her sister, Luciana, are waiting to complain to the Duke that the Abbess has sequestered Antipholus at the very moment that the Merchant and the Goldsmith are also waiting for the Duke:

To see a reverend Syracusian merchant,
Who put unluckily into this bay
Against the laws and statutes of this town,
Beheaded publicly for his offense. (5.1.124–27)

Suddenly, "*Enter the Duke of Ephesus and [Egeon] the Merchant of Syracuse, barehead, with the Headsman and other Officers*" (129 s.d.). At this point the plot is ingeniously unknotted: the Abbess proves to be the long-lost mother of Antipholus and wife of Egeon, who is the father of the Antipholus twins. Unity of time endows *The Comedy of Errors* with a logical propulsion it could not have if the plot were more episodic.

This play also insists on a unity of place that is rare in Shakespeare. All the action occurs in Ephesus and is concentrated in three locations: the house of Antipholus of Ephesus, which is called the Phoenix; the house of the Courtesan, or the Porpentine (Porcupine in modern English); and the priory, in which the Abbess lives. In front of these three localities is the street or mart, which is the main playing area of the stage. These localities strikingly resemble the arcade staging of Latin comedy, which was illustrated in Renaissance editions of Terence and Plautus. In other words, we can imagine a Vitruvian architectural set in which each of the fixed locations was represented by a Roman arcade. This kind of set may have been used for a performance of Shakespeare's play during the Christmas Revels at Gray's Inn in 1594, which is described in the *Gesta Grayorum* (1688).

In its extreme formality, *The Comedy of Errors* imitates what Shakespeare imagined to be a classical style. What Adriana says to her sister might almost be taken as a motto for the entire play: "Come, sister. I am pressed down with conceit: / Conceit, my comfort and my injury" (4.2.64–65). *Conceit* means literally what is conceived by the mind, but it was commonly used as a rhetorical term for the powers of the imagination, especially in an ingenious and overly clever figure of speech, what the Metaphysical poets of the seventeenth century would call *strong lines*. The play attests to its author's being "pressed down with conceit," especially in its witty wordplay; its cultivation of lyric forms in couplets, quatrains, and other kinds of patterning; its hyperbole; and its elaborate stichomythic dialogue. In act 3, scene 1, for example, there is a formal dialogue in old-fashioned, seven-beat fourteeners in the exchange between Antipholus of Ephesus and Dromio of Syracuse:

Antipholus: What art thou that keep'st me out from the house I owe?
Dromio: The porter for this time, sir, and my name is Dromio. (42–43)

Although not exactly brilliant verse, it is clever in its self-conscious archaism.

Once act 3, scene 1 gets under way, it is almost entirely in couplets, which are generally designed to answer each other. Shakespeare wants to call attention to his skill as a versifier, expressed with daring cleverness. For example, when Antipholus of Ephesus says: "But soft, my door is locked; go, bid them let us in," Dromio of Ephesus calls out the names of serving girls: "Maud, Bridget, Marian, Cicely, Gillian, Ginn!" (30–31). Dromio of Syracuse answers from within: "Mome, malt-horse, capon, coxcomb, idiot, patch! / Either get thee from the door or sit down at the hatch" (32–33). We are tickled by such a blatant display of verbal vituperation.

In the next scene we move suddenly into the sonnetlike quatrains of Luciana's complaint to Antipholus of Syracuse, whom she imagines to be her brother-in-law:

> And may it be that you have quite forgot
> A husband's office? shall, Antipholus,
> Even in the spring of love, thy love-springs rot?
> Shall love in building grow so ruinous? (3.2.1–4, Arden edition)

The lilting effect of these quatrains is continued in Antipholus of Syracuse's moving love speech. The variety and unpredictability of the verse in *The Comedy of Errors* is noteworthy.

One final example of the extraordinary test flights of verse in this play is the long, hyperbolic description launched by Dromio of Syracuse of the officer who has arrested his master:

> A devil in an everlasting garment hath him;
> One whose hard heart is buttoned up with steel:
> A fiend, a fairy, pitiless and rough:
> A wolf, nay worse, a fellow all in buff:
> A back-friend, a shoulder-clapper, one that countermands
> The passages of alleys, creeks, and narrow lands . . . (4.2.33–38)

The hyperboles continue for a few more lines, then are taken up again in the next scene for another sixteen lines (4.3.17ff.). The Officer, who is described so elaborately, has no real role in the play but only acts as the vehicle of hyperbole. Shakespeare seems to be enjoying himself with verbal pyrotechnics, which he imagined to be an intrinsic part of a classical style. In later comedies this kind of display is more controlled and more dramatically functional, and the sheer exuberance of *The Comedy of Errors* is notably absent.

This play is Shakespeare's most conscientious attempt to imitate the Roman comic dramatist Plautus (ca. 254–184 B.C.), and especially his *Menaechmus Twins*. The word *errors* in the title extends beyond "mistakes" to "illusions, imaginings, or suppositions," as in George Gascoigne's play *Supposes* (1566), translated from Ludovico Ariosto. A "knight errant" is a wandering knight, presumably subject to chance, fortune, and mere happenstance, and *error* is much closer to the Latin sense of *errare*, to wander, stray, rove, or roam, especially if one thinks of the wanderings of the mind.

Error is used four times in the play in ways that help to define the word. The most important example is in Antipholus of Syracuse's aside in act 2, scene 2. Without any ambiguity at all, Adriana is treating him as her husband, and Antipholus can only be filled with astonishment:

> To me she speaks, she moves me for her theme;
> What, was I married to her in my dream?
> Or sleep I now, and think I hear all this?
> What error drives our eyes and ears amiss? (182–85)

Everything that is happening is essentially incomprehensible; it is the product of error or illusion. The answer in this play is, of course, not tragic. One doesn't do battle with error by considering it in its psychological manifestation of the double, the buried self, or the secret sharer. Instead, one accepts it joyously in celebration of all the good things that error is offering. Antipholus's concluding couplet in this aside accepts error as the essential postulate of the comic hero: "Until I know this sure uncertainty, / I'll entertain the offered fallacy" (186–87). In other words, you don't refuse "the offered fallacy" even though you are sure that it is mistaken.

Later in the play, Antipholus of Syracuse woos Adriana's sister, Luciana, and begs her to be his tutor:

> Teach me, dear creature, how to think and speak;
> Lay open to my earthy-gross conceit,
> Smoth'red in errors, feeble, shallow, weak,
> The folded meaning of your words' deceit. (3.2.33–36)

Antipholus readily acknowledges that he is "smoth'red in errors," but he is not very active in trying to emerge from incertitude. Despite his servant Dromio's fears, Antipholus seems to be enjoying himself.

In the last scene of the play, the errors are resolved and Antipholus of Syracuse begins to understand what has happened:

> I see we still did meet each other's man,
> And I was ta'en for him, and he for me,
> And thereupon these errors are arose. (5.1.387–89)

No deeper explanation is sought, and the Abbess at the end promises the long-awaited resolutions of the happy ending:

> And all that are assembled in this place,
> That by this sympathizèd one day's error
> Have suffered wrong, go, keep us company,
> And we shall make full satisfaction. (397–400)

What more can one ask for in comedy than full satisfaction?

Shakespeare understood the requirements of comic stupidity in farce, but his characters lack the cunning and streetwise cleverness of Plautus's. In this sense, the cynical Machiavelli in *Mandragola* (1518) is much closer to the feeling of Plautus than Shakespeare is. Antipholus of Syracuse is searching the world for his lost twin, but despairs of finding him. In a moving, lyric image totally unlike Plautus, Antipholus declares:

> I to the world am like a drop of water
> That in the ocean seeks another drop,
> Who, falling there to find his fellow forth,
> Unseen, inquisitive, confounds himself. (1.2.35–38)

The last thing Antipholus seems prepared for is actually to find his brother, so he steadfastly refuses to acknowledge any of the revealing signs that surround him.

Even at the end of the play, neither the twin brothers nor the twin servants are eager to throw themselves into each other's arms. The conventional tokens of recognition, spoken about at such length by Aristotle in his *Poetics*, are trundled out and examined carefully. One

7

feels the frustration of proofs of identity, like a person trying to cash a check at a distant branch of his regular bank. We feel that the characters don't really want the play to end. There is something supremely ambiguous in Adriana's immediate declaration: "I see two husbands, or mine eyes deceive me" (5.1.332). Are two husband better than one? Dromio of Ephesus looks upon his brother as a mirror: "Methinks you are my glass, and not my brother; / I see by you I am a sweet-faced youth" (418–19), and in the last couplet, there is a ceremony of democratic twinship: "We came into the world like brother and brother: / And now let's go hand in hand, not one before another" (426–27).

Shakespeare doesn't seem comfortable with the rollicking, high-energy farce of Plautus in either this play or *The Taming of the Shrew*. There are many romantic and lyric elements in *The Comedy of Errors*, such as Antipholus of Syracuse's wooing of Luciana and the marriage debate between Luciana and her sister. Beginning the play with the impending death of the old father, Egeon, is a wistful and melancholy method of exposition, unlike Plautus, although we are sure from the Duke's sympathy that Egeon is unlikely to be executed. Dr. Pinch, the schoolmaster and exorcist, is an exaggerated, grotesque figure as is Luce or Nell, the fat kitchen wench, in whom Dromio of Syracuse "could find out countries" (3.2.116–17) as part of his formulaic comic routine.

Adriana's drop of water image, when she is wooing her husband in a long oration, is moving in a style foreign to Plautine farce. She cannot understand why her husband is estranged from her and from himself:

> For know, my love, as easy mayst thou fall
> A drop of water in the breaking gulf,
> And take unmingled thence that drop again
> Without addition or diminishing
> As take from me thyself, and not me too. (2.2.126–30)

This echoes Antipholus's earlier declaration that his quest for his twin is like one drop of water in the ocean seeking another drop (1.2.35–38).

It is interesting that in Shakespeare's play all of the errors that occur are attributed to magic, witchcraft, dreams, and madness. Ephesus is a dangerous country even for Antipholus of Syracuse because all of the gifts he receives by error could easily be taken away from him and he could at once be made to suffer for his fortuitous good fortune. This is what Dromio of Syracuse keeps reminding his master and why he is more than eager to flee:

> This is the fairy land. O spite of spites!
> We talk with goblins, owls, and sprites;
> If we obey them not, this will ensue:
> They'll suck our breath, or pinch us black and blue. (2.2.190–93)

But Antipholus of Syracuse is more tentative. He keeps asking himself questions:

> Am I in earth, in heaven, or in hell?
> Sleeping or waking, mad or well-advised?
> Known unto these, and to myself disguised? (213–15)

He resolves to continue his mysterious good fortune: "I'll say as they say, and persever so, / And in this mist at all adventures go" (216–17).

Metaphorically, this is the same mist in which Flamineo is confounded in John Webster's tragedy, *The White Devil* (1612): "O I am in a mist" (5.6.260). Antipholus, however, is committed to the idea of "this mist" as an expression of comic indeterminacy. Once favored by Fortune, he cannot tear himself away from his dreamlike existence. He accepts without question the golden chain meant for his twin, and he expresses himself with breezy optimism:

> But this I think, there's no man is so vain
> That would refuse so fair an offered chain.
> I see a man here needs not live by shifts,
> When in the streets he meets such golden gifts. (3.2.185–88)

Meets also means "dreams" in Elizabethan English, and it would be "vain," in the sense of silly, foolish, and doting, for any comic adventurer to refuse "such golden gifts." There is an element of obtuseness built into the play because Antipholus never once suspects that the errors of the play have anything to do with his earnest quest for his twin brother.

Something practical and material about *The Comedy of Errors* is expressed in the array of stage properties that are either lost or misdirected, then recovered in the end. The final scene is not just a recognition scene but also a restoration scene, in which everyone gets back what he or she has lost. A key character in all of this is the Courtesan, whose role is much reduced from what it was in Plautus. In Shakespeare she has a long soliloquy at the end of act 4, scene 3, in which she resolves to tell Antipholus's wife that he is mad and that, "being lunatic, / He rushed into my house and took perforce / My ring away" (95–97). We know that she gave him the ring of her own free will in exchange for a gold chain that Antipholus of Ephesus promised her at the end of act 3, scene 1. Now the Courtesan is genuinely worried that Antipholus has a diamond ring of hers worth forty ducats and that she has nothing in return. She chooses to fib about Antipholus's madness: "For forty ducats is too much to lose" (98). The ring is not just a material object in a play in which objects are of great importance, but it is an object with a price tag on it. We sympathize with the Courtesan because we implicitly agree that, even in a farce, "forty ducats is too much to lose."

The Two Gentlemen
of Verona

This play is the first of Shakespeare's comic romances and is one of the first comedies that Shakespeare wrote (possibly right after *The Comedy of Errors*). *The Two Gentlemen of Verona* establishes the love theme as the basis for comedy, but it also uses a lot of wit and banter to undercut the worst excesses of romantic love. Right from the beginning Shakespeare insists on the doubleness of love: it is grand, transcendental, godlike, lyric, and sweet; but it is also highly conventional, frozen, mechanical, impersonal, and downright silly. We see both extremes in this play. It is useless to try to deal with the characters as if they were sensitive, intelligent, highly developed and psychologized persons. By being votaries of love, they act in strange and seemingly inhuman ways.

There is no more conventionalized wooer than Thurio, who is called "a foolish rival to Valentine" in the Folio list of all the actors. Throughout the action he goes through all the right romantic motions of a lover, including his wooing of Silvia with poetry and music (on the advice of Proteus). But by the end of the play he has had enough of romantic pretense, and when the earnest Valentine threatens him, he gives up immediately:

> Sir Valentine, I care not for her, I.
> I hold him but a fool that will endanger
> His body for a girl that loves him not.
> I claim her not, and therefore she is thine. (5.4.132–35)

There is something touching about this speech, like Sir Andrew Aguecheek's lack of forwardness in *Twelfth Night*. The Duke's comment is entirely irrelevant:

> The more degenerate and base art thou,
> To make such means for her as thou hast done,
> And leave her on such slight conditions. (136–38)

The Duke doesn't understand the gamelike quality of romantic conventions, which can collapse in a moment without any sense of psychological perturbation.

This can take us part of the way toward explaining the workings of comic villainy. Proteus, as the name indicates, is a protean character, who abandons friendship and good faith for the sake of love almost without a qualm. He is impelled by some mysterious and nonhuman force, like the lovers in Ovid's *Metamorphoses* and very much like the lovers under the influence of love-juice in *A Midsummer Night's Dream*. Proteus betrays his sworn friend, Valentine, abandons his troth-plighted lover, Julia, deals falsely with Thurio in his suit to Silvia, tries to make his new love, Silvia, believe that Julia is dead and so is Valentine (this is never pursued very far), tricks the Duke into thinking that he woos for Thurio, and becomes thoroughly contemptible to himself through all these wiles. At the end of the play, he threatens to rape Silvia, but is immediately put off by Valentine. Proteus then, in extraordinarily few words, confesses his shame and guilt and is completely forgiven by Valentine, who offers him Silvia as a love token of true friendship.

How are we to take all of this? Nothing can be interpreted in psychological terms, and it seems pointless for critics to excoriate Proteus and Valentine—and Shakespeare, too—for their superficiality. The lovers act according to the Petrarchan conventions of romantic love and not according to common sense. Comic villainy is a fictional assumption to ensure that "The course of true love never did run smooth" (*A Midsummer Night's Dream* 1.1.134). If Proteus can extricate himself from such deep-dyed villainy—he even slanders Valentine and betrays him to the Duke in order to get him out of the way—then it is a proof of the power of love, or at least of love as a fictional motif.

Proteus doesn't really mean any harm by what he does, but is merely impelled by the irresistible force of love. He doesn't want to make Silvia yield to his desire, but he will woo her "like a soldier, at arms' end, / And love you 'gainst the nature of love" (5.4.57–58) if he has to. Critics who exonerate Proteus by saying that his bad intentions are never realized have the ethical issue upside down, since Proteus does a great deal of harm until he is stopped, but he is impelled by the bewitchment of romantic love and not by any moral, psychological, or ethical considerations. In that sense he is hardly a villain at all, unlike Iago or Richard III, who don't ever mean well and feel impelled to do things against their better judgments. They do exactly what they intend to do.

Although it is never mentioned specifically, love is one of the proper occupations of a young man, who should go abroad to avoid "living dully sluggardized at home," wearing out his youth with "shapeless idleness" (1.1.7–8). In *Love's Labor's Lost*, the King of Navarre's Academy is organized specifically to avoid the idleness of love (but it eventually becomes exclusively devoted to love). In *Romeo and Juliet*, which has many resemblances to *The Two Gentlemen of Verona*, Romeo is first seen as a foolishly infatuated lover much like Proteus. Antonio wants his son Proteus to travel in order to escape from love to some worthier occupation such as "the wars," "to discover islands far away," or "to the studious universities" (1.3.8–10), but all these idealized manly occupations are only a pretext for Proteus. He is a lot like the willful and spoiled boy, Bertram, of *All's Well That Ends Well*. Proteus's statement at the end of this scene establishes Love as a capricious and uncertain power like Fortune:

> O, how this spring of love resembleth
> The uncertain glory of an April day,
> Which now shows all the beauty of the sun,
> And by and by a cloud takes all away! (84–87)

The play doesn't stray much outside these romantic commitments, and the limpid, lyric style of this passage is characteristic of the writing.

Critics take seriously the friendship theme in this play, which is discussed in relation to sources in the story of Titus and Gisippus in Sir Thomas Elyot's *The Governor* (1531), the story of Palamon and Arcite in Chaucer's *The Knight's Tale* (which is also the basis of Shakespeare's *The Two Noble Kinsmen*), Richard Edwards's play, *Damon and Pithias* (1571), and many variations of this popular theme. In *The Two Gentlemen of Verona* love is a considerably stronger motive than friendship, as Proteus says: "In love, / Who respects friend?" (5.4.53–54), but Proteus is constantly aware that he is betraying an ideal of friendship and feels guilty about it. In the end, of course, friendship triumphs, as we expect it to, since it is accepted as a higher ethical ideal than erotic love (as it is in the *Sonnets*).

In this scheme, therefore, it comes as no surprise that Valentine forgives his friend so easily and offers his beloved Silvia to him: "And, that my love may appear plain and free, / All that was mine in Silvia I give thee" (5.4.82–83). *Free* means "generous," and Valentine's generosity is demonstrated by his offering, selflessly, to his friend all that is most dear to him. It won't do to ask why Valentine considers that he has a chattel right—"All that was mine"—in Silvia because he assumes automatically and without any forethought that she is his to give away. Thus friendship is ostensibly victorious in the end as the male lovers are restored to their appropriate women and the play can end happily.

Although *The Two Gentlemen of Verona* is the first in a long series of romantic comedies that are superior to it in wit, expansiveness, lyricism, and the development of female characters that are both charming and intelligent, it nevertheless establishes possibilities that can be exploited later. In the representation of love Shakespeare is already insisting on a multiplicity of points of view, and the gently mocking and ironic tone of *The Two Gentlemen of Verona* is never abandoned. Lovers are always foolish in some way, extravagant and glorying in an excess that needs to be curbed. This opens the way for a continual undercutting of love and its conventions and expectations. Why does Julia, like Helena in *All's Well*, pursue a man who flees her? This is the necessary *perturbatio* (perturbation) in comedy

14

that Donatus spoke of in his medieval treatise on comedy that appeared regularly in Renaissance editions of the Latin comedies of Terence. It is what Prospero is talking about in *The Tempest,* one of the latest of Shakespeare's comedies, when he interposes difficulties for Ferdinand in his wooing of Miranda, "lest too light winning / Make the prize light" (1.2.454–55). Julia appreciates Proteus better when she has to take to the road, like a picaresque heroine, to win her man.

The scene of Julia's preparation for her journey as a disguised page is perhaps the most engaging in the play (and clearly anticipates a similar scene in *As You Like It* of Rosalind disguising herself as Ganymede in act 1, scene 3). Lucetta insists bawdily that Julia must have a codpiece, the exaggerated padding in the trousers in front of a man's genitalia, which Julia needs at least "to stick pins on" (2.7.56)— a very feminine explanation. Shakespeare delights in playing on transvestite implications in his romantic comedies, and it also offers an easy way of mocking male pretensions.

Julia speaks of "the inly touch of love" (2.7.18) with a wistful intensity. She does not anticipate the unfaithfulness of Proteus, yet there is already a seed of doubt and melancholy. The fire of love cannot be quenched with words: "The more thou damm'st it up, the more it burns" (24). Love is idealized as a powerful abstract force, like love in the early *Sonnets,* which seems to come out of the pages of Ovid:

> But when his fair course is not hinderèd,
> He makes sweet music with th' enameled stones,
> Giving a gentle kiss to every sedge
> He overtaketh in his pilgrimage . . . (27–30)

Shakespeare could certainly write better than this—more lyrically and more dramatically—yet Julia's convictions about love help to carry us through a forest of perturbations.

The Clowns in the play do a great deal to undercut love, especially by endless wordplay, or what Speed, the servant of Valentine, calls "mistaking" the word (3.1.282). Speed isn't really a clown but more a witty page in the style of the court comedies of John Lyly. Launce is a full-fledged Shakespearean clown, who establishes the homely, domestic fool afterward seen in Costard in *Love's Labor's Lost,* Dogberry in *Much Ado About Nothing,* and Launcelot Gobbo in *The Merchant of Venice.* Launce, undoubtedly played by the celebrated comic actor Will Kempe, is inseparable from his lovable dog, Crab. Shakespeare later uses dog imagery in a very different and consistently pejorative way, especially in such plays as *Troilus and Cressida* and *Timon of Athens.* In *The Two Gentlemen of Verona,* Launce takes moral responsibility for his dog when he is whipped out of the Duke's chamber for a deed done by Crab: "When didst thou see me heave up my leg, and make water against a gentlewoman's farthingale?" (4.4.38–39). This all has subtle associations with the main action.

Launce in love is a direct parody of Valentine and Proteus in love, and it anticipates the homely courtship of Touchstone and Audrey in *As You Like It.* Launce's beloved is a milkmaid, who, although not strictly a virgin, has "more qualities than a water spaniel" (3.1.271–72). Launce and Speed engage in a long, formulaic account of the milkmaid's qualities represented in the form of a "cate-log," or catalogue, with possible puns on Kate (her name), cat (a familiar term for a whore, as in *cathouse*), or cate (a dainty, usually something to eat). The final specification, that she has "more wealth than faults" (349), is enough for Launce, as it obviously wouldn't be for Valentine or Proteus.

The band of outlaws Valentine joins when he is banished in act 4, scene 1 provides a refreshing pastoral aspect for *The Two Gentlemen of Verona.* The outlaws resemble Robin Hood and his merry men free from the troubles of the court and leading their natural, carefree life in the woods. The Third Outlaw even swears "By the bare scalp of Robin Hood's fat friar [Friar Tuck], / This fellow were a king for our wild faction!" (36–37). All this anticipates the banished Duke Senior and his court in *As You Like It.* Valentine's adoption by the outlaws as their captain is full of a charming improbability, as when they insist that he is not only "beautified / With goodly shape," but also "A linguist" (55–57). We hear nothing further about Valentine's qualifications as a linguist. The outlaws are from different cities in Italy and they wander over a large area, but they all presumably speak the same language.

There are also amusing details about how Valentine seeks to curb the lawless activities of his companions. He accepts the captainship with the proviso "that you do no outrages / On silly women or poor passengers" (4.1.71–72). Presumably all women are "silly," or innocent, and the outlaws in their inherent nobility "detest such vile base practices" (73). In the last scene of the play, Valentine, in his expansive soliloquy on the virtues of the pastoral life, still indicates his moral leadership of the outlaws: "yet I have much to do / To keep them from uncivil outrages" (5.4.16–17). This leads directly to Valentine's request to the Duke to pardon his merry band: "They are reformèd, civil, full of good, / And fit for great employment, worthy lord" (156–57). Idealizing the outlaws gets us ready for the happy ending. There are no loose ends blocking the Platonic fulfillment of "One feast, one house, one mutual happiness" (173).

Love's Labor's Lost

$\mathcal{L}$ove's Labor's Lost is a formal and cere-
monious play that shamelessly imitates and
parodies the witty, courtly, highly sophisticated tone of John Lyly, a dramatist and
prose writer who flourished in the decade
immediately preceding Shakespeare. Love's
Labor's Lost has a relatively simplified action
in both the main plot and the subplot, but it
is extremely verbal and witty and devotes a
great deal of attention to figurative display.
Berowne, who is the spokesman for the King
of Navarre, Longaville, and Dumaine, has a
lengthy oration on Love that is entirely
characteristic of the rhetoric of this play. It
is almost eighty lines long (although about
twenty lines—from 295 to 316—may be a
duplicate version intended to be cut), and it
is a bravura acting piece meant to impress
Berowne's friends and the audience with the
sincerity of the new commitments of the
members of the Academy. They have abandoned their original plan "To fast, to study,
and to see no woman" because it is "Flat
treason 'gainst the kingly state of youth"
(4.3.291–92). Now Berowne celebrates the
power of love in hyperboles: "It adds a precious seeing to the eye" (332); "Love's tongue
proves dainty Bacchus gross in taste" (338);
"And when Love speaks, the voice of all the

gods / Make heaven drowsy with the harmony" (343–44). These are wonderful declarations but strikingly impersonal. We can understand why the ladies think that the courtiers are only playing at love, and especially only amusing themselves in the self-indulgent language of love. In later comedies by Shakespeare, the feeling of love is more personal and more acute, particularly with regard to what the women say.

Love's Labor's Lost is not only very verbal but also very histrionic, in the sense that much attention is devoted to characters who come on stage to do their witty solos without advancing the plot—and the amusement is so striking that who would be foolish enough to insist on plot development? In the subordinate action we have a remarkably rich assembly of characters: Don Armado, Holofernes, Sir Nathaniel, Costard and Moth, and even Dull, the constable. No other comedy of Shakespeare has so many buffoonlike characters who speak so many witty (and unconsciously witty) lines.

Costard, the clown, is typical as a mediator between seriousness and mirth. He more or less takes over as the presenter and master of ceremonies for the play of the Nine Worthies. Unlike the other actors, he is unflappable by the insulting comments of the courtiers. Modestly, he is to play Pompey the Great: "It pleased them to think me worthy of Pompey the Great" (5.2.505–6). He recites his part to the end in a confidential manner without in any way being taken up into the dramatic illusion: "If your ladyship would say, 'Thanks, Pompey,' I had done" (553–54). Costard anticipates Bottom in the Pyramus and Thisby play of *A Midsummer Night's Dream*: both are completely at ease in the world of the theater. When Sir Nathaniel cannot complete his role as Alexander the Great, Costard is sympathetic:

> There, an 't shall please you, a foolish mild man; an honest man, look you, and soon dashed. He is a marvelous good neighbor, faith, and a very good bowler; but for Alisander—alas! you see how 'tis—a little o'erparted. (578–83)

This gets to the heart of the dramatic illusion.

The encounter of Holofernes and Don Armado matches in comedy the tragic meeting of King Lear and the blind Gloucester on the heath. Holofernes and Don Armado play gingerly around each other and negotiate their hesitations by elaborate compliment. As Moth, the witty and diminutive page of Don Armado, says: "They have been at a great feast of languages and stol'n the scraps" (5.1.39–40). Costard, the clown, cannot resist the punning possibilities of Moth / mote:

> I marvel thy master hath not eaten thee for a word; for thou art not so long by the head as *honorificabilitudinitatibus*. Thou art easier swallowed than a flapdragon. (42–45)

A flapdragon is a burning raisin or plum floating in liquor, and *honorificabilitudinitatibus* is supposedly the longest word in the English language. Costard is making fun of Don Armado's substitution of words for persons.

Both Armado and Holofernes are masters of circumlocution and their colloquial English is remarkably bookish and stilted. Armado begins his discourse: "Arts-man, preambulate" (5.1.81), as if he were speaking an invocation to the Muse of poetry, and Holofernes can only congratulate the Spaniard on his refinement:

> The posterior of the day, most generous sir, is liable, congruent, and measurable for the afternoon. The word is well culled, chose, sweet and apt, I do assure you, sir, I do assure. (91–94)

Armado is preened up by such compliments and he accomplishes his errand with bravado: to present the Princess of France and her ladies "with some delightful ostentation, or show, or pageant, or antic, or fire-work" (112–13). Like Holofernes, Armado's speech is laved in synonymy, as if he were reading out all the definitions from a dictionary. He acknowledges that the curate and Holofernes "are good at such eruptions and sudden breaking out of mirth" (114–16). And so the play of the Nine Worthies is decided on.

Constable Dull is a classic foil in this scene. He says nothing until the end, although Holofernes is proposing to play three worthies himself. Holofernes turns to Dull as if to solicit his participation: "*Via*, goodman Dull! Thou hast spoken no word all this while" (5.1.150–51). But Dull can only protest his noncomprehension: "Nor understood none neither, sir" (152). He offers to "make one in a dance, or so; or I will play on the tabor to the Worthies, and let them dance the hay" (154–56). Shakespeare delights in the simpleton, who becomes a stock character in the comedies (like Dogberry and Verges in *Much Ado About Nothing*). Holofernes ends the scene with mock praise: "Most dull, honest Dull!" (157). There is no one else like him in the play.

Well before Marcade appears to announce the death of the Princess of France's father and the comic "scene begins to cloud" (5.2.723), the uneasy suitors, only recently assertive Muscovites in their masque, begin to be penitent about their wooing rhetoric. In a play preoccupied with rhetoric, Berowne forswears his affected discourse:

> Taffeta phrases, silken terms precise,
> Three-piled hyperboles, spruce affectation,
> Figures pedantical—these summer flies
> Have blown me full of maggot ostentation. (407–10)

He resolves that his

> wooing mind shall be expressed
> In russet yeas and honest kersey noes.
> And to begin, wench—so God help me, law!—
> My love to thee is sound, sans crack or flaw. (413–16)

Kersey is a coarse woolen fabric, and russet is the reddish-brown color of peasants' clothes—not spruce or over-elegant, not silken, not taffeta, nor three-piled velvet.

Despite the firmness of his outspoken declaration, Berowne slips up on the word *sans*, which Rosaline takes as the sign of continuing affectation: "Sans 'sans,' I pray you" (5.2.417). That is truly a memorable line. *Sans* is Holofernes' stilted French word from the previous scene: "I do, *sans question*" (5.1.86), and we remember Jaques' self-consciously stylish conclusion to his Seven Ages of Man oration:

> Last scene of all,
> That ends this strange eventful history,
> Is second childishness and mere oblivion,
> Sans teeth, sans eyes, sans taste, sans everything.
> (*As You Like It* 2.7.162–65)

21

So Rosaline is an acute observer of stylistic pretension (which goes hand in hand in this play with male bravado) when she insists on her "sans 'sans'." Rosaline is like Queen Gertrude in *Hamlet* in trying to curb the wandering and self-satisfied rhetoric of Polonius: "More matter, with less art" (2.2.95). It is striking how closely art and artful discourse are associated with male wooing in Shakespeare. *Love's Labor's Lost* seems delightfully devoted to expressing, and thereby dissipating, the "Sweet smoke of rhetoric!" (3.1.64).

The "wooing doth not end like an old play; / Jack hath not Jill" (5.2.875–76), and the year-long penances that are set for all the male wooers are an attempt to curb their extravagance of expression, which seems shallow and insincere. Berowne attempts to apologize for all: "Honest plain words best pierce the ear of grief" (754), and his meandering discourse touches on the "unbefitting strains" of love, "All wanton as a child, skipping and vain," "Full of straying shapes" and the "parti-coated presence of loose love" (761–62, 764, 767). But the Princess is unimpressed and sees all the wooing merely as a "merriment," a "courtship, pleasant jest, and courtesy, / As bombast and as lining to the time" (781–82). *Bombast* is both the cotton stuffing in a jacket and a rhetorical term, as in Iago's complaint that Othello's discourse is "Horribly stuffed with epithets of war" (*Othello* 1.1.13).

Berowne is specifically enjoined to curb his scoffing humor (as we have abundantly seen in his reaction to the "Play of the Nine Worthies"). Rosaline judges him "a man replete with mocks, / Full of comparisons and wounding flouts" (5.2.844–45), a "wormwood" that he must weed from his "fructful brain" (848). Berowne cannot believe the penance that has been cast upon him: "To move wild laughter in the throat of death?" (856), but he agrees with Rosaline's serious plan of reformation. She speaks the essential wisdom of comedy:

> A jest's prosperity lies in the ear
> Of him that hears it, never in the tongue
> Of him that makes it. (862–64)

This social theory of comedy is essentially confirmed by Holofernes' earlier comment to Berowne, who is carried away by his own sophomoric and solipsistic wordplay: "This is not generous, not gentle, not humble" (630). It is strange to see Rosaline and Holofernes allied in attacking Berowne's "idle scorns" (866).

For all his fatuous literalness, Holofernes the Pedant or Schoolmaster is not entirely foolish. His criticism of Berowne's affected and pointless wooing sonnet to Rosaline is well taken. The poem has been delivered to Jaquenetta in error by Costard—both obviously illiterate—and she brings it to Nathaniel the Parson to read. It is written in old-fashioned hexameter quatrains. Holofernes understands immediately that the poem is merely a mechanical exercise without any inspiration: "Here are only numbers ratified; but, for the elegancy, facility, and golden cadence of poesy, *caret*" (4.2.123–24). "*Imitari* is nothing" (127) without some kind of poetic fire, and Shakespeare, who was a great imitator of Ovid in his early work, manages to pay a gracious compliment to his master: "Ovidius Naso was the man; and why indeed 'Naso' but for smelling out the odoriferous flowers of fancy, the jerks of invention?" (125–27). Berowne's clumsy poem is utterly unlike Ovid, whom the courtier mechanically imitates. Holofernes drives his point home with Nathaniel, the curate, whom he invites to dinner at the house of a pupil of his to "prove those verses to be very unlearned, neither savoring of poetry, wit, nor invention" (160–61). Holofernes may be a pretentious pedant, but he takes his poetry seriously, which is more than can be said for Berowne.

The pedantry in the subplot mocks the rhetoric of love in the main plot, yet in both actions Shakespeare is surprisingly tolerant. We laugh indulgently at male boasting expressed in language games or in love games. It is all rather abstract, as is the original founding of the Academy:

> Navarre shall be the wonder of the world;
> Our court shall be a little academe,
> Still and contemplative in living art. (1.1.12–14)

Of course, the point of the comedy is that this ideal proposition cannot hold in the real world. As Berowne protests immediately: "O, these are barren tasks, too hard to keep, / Not to see ladies, study,

23

fast, not sleep!" (47–48). They are barren tasks because they violate human values, and the purpose of the comedy is to show that natural impulses will triumph over moral and ethical formulations.

Notice how practical Berowne is in adding his protest against "to sleep but three hours in the night, / And not be seen to wink of all the day" (1.1.42–43). This is hardly an abstruse proposition, and it is comforting to us that right from the beginning the movement of *Love's Labor's Lost* is toward asserting human frailty. Love's arduous rhetorical labors are hardly lost in this play, even though the witty and chauvinistic lords are temporarily confuted and have to wait a year and a day for proper fulfillment.

One comic truth the play establishes both for the lords and for Don Armado is that you need to talk about love at some length before you can feel love as an imperious entity. This is like the concept of the title story in Raymond Carver's collection, *What We Talk About When We Talk About Love*. Being in love is not necessarily the same thing as talking about love, a truth that lies near the periphery of this intensely rhetorical play. The ladies are trying to convert their men into real lovers rather than talkers about love. The penances have an antirhetorical function. Presumably the King of Navarre, Longaville, Dumaine, and especially Berowne need at least a year to recover from the witty extravagances of *Love's Labor's Lost*. Readers and spectators of the play can do this much more quickly.

The Taming
of the Shrew

Like *The Comedy of Errors*, *The Taming of the Shrew* experiments with farce, as Shakespeare found it highly developed in Plautus. The play is also influenced by folktale motifs. In farce, not a great deal of attention is paid to psychological subtleties of character as the action presses forward to fulfill its mechanistic assumptions. Petruchio, the fortune-hunter, will tame his shrew, the curst Kate, as a function of the successful farce that we watch with fascinated interest. The play uses the archetypal image of the wild hawk or haggard painstakingly trained to accept the lure and to become a sophisticated hunter. Everything turns on obedience, which enters importantly into Katherine's last speech. This conventional oration echoes the marriage debate in *The Comedy of Errors* between Adriana, the wife of Antipholus of Ephesus, and her sister, Luciana. The educational and gender doctrine in both plays is equally simple, if not simplistic. These are not the sorts of plays in which we expect original thinking, nor will it do to postulate elaborate character relations between Kate and her sister, Bianca, or between Kate and her father, Baptista, who seems excessively eager to get his daughters off his hands, especially to the highest bidder (there is only one bidder for Kate, who is considered temperamentally unmarriageable).

Once everything is said about the demands of the farce form, however, we realize that we have not yet begun to speak about the play as it presents itself to us either in the theater or in reading. Shakespeare doesn't suddenly write a comedy in which he demeans women, entirely different from his other comedies in which the women lead the love game by virtue of their intelligence and wit. Petruchio and Kate are not entirely unlike Beatrice and Benedick in *Much Ado*, Rosalind and Orlando in *As You Like It*, or even Romeo and Juliet. Whatever plot assumptions are made in *The Taming of the Shrew*, they need to be worked out in the confrontation of Petruchio and Kate. In *The Merchant of Venice*, Bassanio is a fortune-hunter like Petruchio, who finances an extravagant expedition to Belmont to woo Portia properly, which doesn't mean that he doesn't really fall in love with her. Similarly, everything in *The Taming of the Shrew* depends upon the enormous attraction between Petruchio and Kate. They fall in love with each other without actually knowing it and certainly without acknowledging it, as is customary in Shakespearean comedy.

Before we actually see her, the folktale motif of Kate as a shrew is firmly established. Hortensio describes for Petruchio "Her only fault": "that she is intolerable curst / And shrewd and froward" (1.2.87–89). These adjectives are repeated over and over again as if Kate were a mythical Xanthippe, the wife of Socrates. Petruchio knows "she is an irksome, brawling scold" (187), a "wildcat" in the words of Gremio (196), but he sees this only as a challenge to his manliness: "Have I not in my time heard lions roar?" (200). Petruchio's speech is full of hyperbolic bravado: "Have I not in a pitchèd battle heard / Loud 'larums, neighing steeds, and trumpets' clang?" (205–6). This sounds like a parody of the military imagery in *Othello*.

Our first sight of Kate is in the first scene, where she appears as an angry, ill-used, and ill-tempered older sister, much given to violence in speech and perhaps also in action. She thinks her father ridiculously prejudiced in favor of her younger sister, and she reacts with rage to his exit speech: "Katherina, you may stay, / For I have more to commune with Bianca" (1.1.100–101). Baptista's patronizing is intolerable:

Why, and I trust I may go too, may I not?
What, shall I be appointed hours, as though, belike,
I knew not what to take and what to leave? Ha! (102–4)

"Ha" is the insinuating interjection of Iago, as when he first plants
the seed of doubt in Othello: "Ha! I like not that" (*Othello* 3.3.35).
At the beginning of act 2, we see Kate abusing her sister. She has
tied her hands and strikes her and promises to be revenged, presumably both on Bianca and her father, who calls her "hilding of a
devilish spirit" (2.1.26). In her frustration, Kate "will go sit and weep"
(35).

The first meeting with Petruchio comes later in this scene, and
everything that has gone before prepares us for an explosive encounter. Petruchio has a specific battle plan, which he describes to us in
a soliloquy. He expects to woo her "with some spirit" (2.1.169) and
to show his mastery by speaking exactly the opposite of what occurs:
"Say that she rail, why then I'll tell her plain / She sings as sweetly as
a nightingale" (170–71). This is not subtle, but Petruchio is prepared
for all eventualities: "Say she be mute and will not speak a word, /
Then I'll commend her volubility" (174–75). Luckily, the scene
doesn't take place exactly the way Petruchio plans it. Kate is sharp-
tongued but also witty, and she manages to return all of Petruchio's
clever retorts, if not to top them. The banter is like that of Shakespeare's early clowns, but it has a strongly sexual tone.

Petruchio calls her an angry wasp and Kate warns him to beware
her sting, but he reminds her that a wasp wears his sting in his tail,
which opens the way for a bawdy pun. Kate bids him farewell and
Petruchio pleads the inappropriateness of the moment: "What, with
my tongue in your tail?" (2.1.216). It is at this point that Kate strikes
him out of frustration, but he warns her: "I swear I'll cuff you if you
strike again" (218). Kate doesn't leave nor does Petruchio, and their
wooing scene is animated and witty like other wooing scenes in
Shakespeare's early comedies. Petruchio doesn't succeed in patronizing her as much as he tries, and they seem like intellectual peers. In
relation to the scenes that precede, Kate is transformed in the sense
that she has met her match. Everything seems to point to the fact
that she is as fascinated with him as he is with her, and that they
wind up being strongly attracted to each other. Kate seems to be

flattered by the fact that Petruchio is so determined to marry her, even though he keeps speaking of marriage as a form of taming.

I won't speak about the farcical operation of taming, which has proved to be good fun for prefeminist audiences, who operated on different gender assumptions from ours. One thing to keep in mind is that Petruchio is playing a deliberate role that he explains to us meticulously in his soliloquy in act 4. It is sexual politics, and he has "politicly" begun his "reign" (4.1.182) by turning the tables and playing the willful shrew, but he participates in Kate's experience not to eat, not to sleep, and not to celebrate their wedding night. This is all expressed, with self-satisfied pedantry, in the images of falconry:

> My falcon now is sharp and passing empty,
> And till she stoop she must not be full gorged,
> For then she never looks upon her lure. (184–86)

There is more than a trace of boasting in this scene, as Petruchio celebrates in advance his certain success with Kate: "This is a way to kill a wife with kindness" (202), which proverb provides the title for Thomas Heywood's later sentimental play, *A Woman Killed with Kindness* (1603).

Still, there is something ambiguous in all this. Who is taming whom and who emerges triumphant? John Fletcher, Shakespeare's later colleague as chief writer for the King's Men, wrote a sequel to *The Taming of the Shrew* called *The Woman's Prize; or, The Tamer Tamed* (1611), which reverses the Shakespearean roles. It is obvious that Fletcher already saw this reversal as inherent in Shakespeare's play. At the end of act 3, Bianca expresses an opinion of her sister that promotes ambiguity: "That being mad herself, she's madly mated," to which Gremio completes the couplet: "I warrant him, Petruchio is Kated" (3.2.244–45). He could equally well have said that Kate is Petruchioed, but this formulation suggests that Petruchio receives as good as he gives and that the tamer is in some sense tamed himself.

Act 4, scene 5 is a crucial scene in the interplay of Petruchio and Kate and may help to explain inherent ambiguities. They are on the road to Padua to visit Kate's father, when Petruchio decides to test his mastery:

Petruchio. Good Lord, how bright and goodly shines the moon.
Kate. The moon? The sun. It is not moonlight now.
Petruchio. I say it is the moon that shines so bright.
Kate. I know it is the sun that shines so bright.
Petruchio. Now, by my mother's son, and that's myself,
    It shall be moon or star or what I list,
    Or ere I journey to your father's house. (2–8)

Hortensio advises Kate to go along with Petruchio or they will never complete their journey: "Say as he says or we shall never go" (11), a line that literally echoes Antipholus of Syracuse in *The Comedy of Errors*: "I'll say as they say, and persever so, / And in this mist at all adventures go" (2.2.216–17). Kate, then, for the first time in the play, understands the game and becomes a player: "Forward, I pray, since we have come so far, / And be it moon or sun or what you please" (4.5.12–13). Later, Kate has an amusing, histrionic exchange with old Vincentio, the father of Lucentio, who is also on the road to Padua: "Young budding virgin, fair and fresh and sweet" (37), which can be immediately altered to "Pardon, old father, my mistaking eyes" (45). Reality is malleable, words express desire, and that is the secret. Kate is not the same person as she was earlier in the play.

It is certainly not clear now who is taming whom or whether Petruchio can claim only a Pyrrhic victory over Kate. What is essential is that Petruchio and Kate take pleasure in each other's company, "Kiss me, Kate" is the motto of this stage in their relationship, and they even, to Kate's surprise, kiss "in the midst of the street" (5.1.143). This is the context for the folktale motif of the wager in the last scene. Petruchio bets on Kate's obedience because he is sure of her and she is sure of him. Bianca and the Widow are more unpredictable wives who know nothing of the love game and scorn to play it. The Widow, of course, is right when she refuses to come because "you have some goodly jest in hand" (5.2.91), but Kate comes immediately and delivers a long oration on the standard Renaissance doctrine of wifely obedience.

This speech has astounded many critics because it is so tedious and so unoriginal—as if Kate has learned nothing. Since it comes as Kate's climactic statement on gender issues it is disappointing that she seems so subservient. It is as if the spirited sexual play of previous scenes has been forgotten. I don't think the speech is meant ironically, as if Kate is shrewd enough to say what is expected of a model wife but to mean something quite different. The ironic interpretation implies a perfunctory relation of husband and wife on the assumption that all that a perfect marriage needs is to say the right thing. In the context of the previous scenes, and especially of act 4, scene 5, I think that Kate is playing a prepared role in the games that she and Petruchio have devised to test their marriage. Kate says what she is expected to say—in fact, she overdoes it and says quite a bit more than she is expected to say. She overplays her part of the transaction and anticipates sharing the large wager that she and her husband will surely win. This role-playing and game-playing is not quite the same thing as irony.

Kate's sentiments of "true obedience" (5.2.153) exactly echo those of *The Comedy of Errors*, where Adriana vows to her husband—the wrong one, of course—endless fealty:

> Thou art an elm, my husband, I a vine,
> Whose weakness, married to thy stronger state,
> Makes me with thy strength to communicate. (2.2.175–77)

Kate, too, advances the traditional argument of women's weakness joined symbiotically with man's strength:

> Why are our bodies soft and weak and smooth,
> Unapt to toil and trouble in the world,
> But that our soft conditions and our hearts
> Should well agree with our external parts? (5.2.165–68)

The game ends abruptly with the victory celebration: "Come, Kate, we'll to bed" (184). This seems like the consummation of the marriage that the lovers have so long postponed.

The Taming of the Shrew is a comedy of transformation and metamorphosis, of suppositions and illusions like *The Comedy of Errors*. We should not forget the elaborate induction that precedes the main play and introduces us to the theme of identity that can be so masterfully altered by histrionic means. In *The Taming of a Shrew*, a later, "bad quarto" version of Shakespeare's play, the framing action of Christopher Sly is considerably extended, so that Sly ends up where he began, outside the alehouse, with memories of a wonderful dream like Bottom's in *A Midsummer Night's Dream*. But the transformation of Sly into a great lord is an experiment in acting, and the whole of *The Taming of the Shrew* is a play within a play intended to operate on Sly's imagination like the "wanton pictures" (ind. 1.47), the music, and the appurtenances of upper-class life.

Notice how specifically the pictures recall Ovidian subjects in the *Metamorphoses* and the *Art of Love*:

> Adonis painted by a running brook
> And Cytherea all in sedges hid,
> Which seem to move and wanton with her breath
> Even as the waving sedges play with wind. (ind. 2.50–53)

This is not a scene from Shakespeare's own erotic poem, *Venus and Adonis*, although the spirit of seduction is there. In some sense, Sly is being seduced into accepting the fact that he is a great lord and has finally awakened from his fifteen years' dream that he was Christopher Sly, the tinker. This has obvious analogies with the radical transformation of Kate and with the role-playing of Petruchio, the wife-tamer. It is also linked with *The Comedy of Errors*, especially at the moment when Antipholus of Syracuse, after some questioning of himself, agrees to accept "the offered fallacy" (2.2.187).

As recognition of a new identity comes upon Sly, he suddenly shifts from a racy prose into a high-flown poetry (or partly high-flown, like Bottom's): "I see, I hear, I speak, / I smell sweet savors and I feel soft things" (ind. 2.70–71). The "pleasant comedy" that will be presented by the lord's players is meant to frame Sly's mind "to mirth and merriment, / Which bars a thousand harms and lengthens life" (135–36), but Sly wants to know: "Is not a comontie [a comedy in Sly's idiom] a Christmas gambold or a tumbling trick?" (137–38). Sly's practical conception of drama is endearing, but we are still left to wonder how the induction connects with the play-within-a-play. Is *The Taming of the Shrew* a pleasant comedy, one that will cure Sly's settled melancholy (combined with a convincing hangover)?

Seeing the main play as an expression of the induction is a useful change of perspective. If Sly is transformed, then aren't Kate and Petruchio transformed too? And what about Hortensio and his widow,

Bianca, and Lucentio? Aren't they all transformed by love and marriage? Isn't that the point of comedy? The Lord coming from hunting and discovering the drunken Sly anticipates the drunken Stephano and Trinculo finding Caliban in *The Tempest*: "O monstrous beast, how like a swine he lies!" (ind. 1.34). Aren't Kate and Petruchio, too, "swinish" in their own stubborn way until they undergo a metamorphosis in the name of love? The Lord's lines about the powers of dramatic illusion look forward to Duke Theseus's speech on the lunatic, the lover, and the poet in *A Midsummer Night's Dream* (5.1.7ff.). The heart of the matter is that Sly should be persuaded "that he hath been lunatic, / And when he says he is, say that he dreams" (ind. 1.63–64). That makes the play within a play look very much like the dream of the taming of the shrew.

A Midsummer
Night's Dream

his play, probably dating from 1595
or 1596, around the time of *Romeo and Juliet*,
has the most fully articulated plot of any
play that Shakespeare had yet written. It has
four distinct actions, with a fifth from the
Pyramus and Thisby play. Overarching the
play is the marriage of Theseus and Hippolyta, which will occur in four days. Both
these characters, who reappear in *The Two
Noble Kinsmen*, have strong roots in mythology, especially as presented by Ovid, and
this does much to broaden the scope of the
play. As Hippolyta, Queen of the Amazons,
says in response to the music of Theseus's
hunting dogs:

> I was with Hercules and Cadmus once,
> When in a wood of Crete they bayed the bear
> With hounds of Sparta. Never did I hear
> Such gallant chiding . . . (4.1.115–18)

Crete is where Theseus slew the Minotaur
and escaped from the labyrinth thanks to a
thread provided by Ariadne. Theseus and
Hippolyta in the play have a dual status as
dramatic characters and as mythological personages, which links them with the role of
the fairies at the other end of the spectrum.

The action of the fairies is highly developed, focusing on the quarrel between Ob-

eron and Titania, the King and Queen of the fairies, over the Indian boy Titania is keeping from Oberon. The world of the fairies lends itself to music and dancing, as Mendelssohn understood so well, and to lyric expression both in pentameter couplets and other free forms suitable for song. In Puck, or Robin Goodfellow, Shakespeare develops a figure from English rustic folklore. As a fairy points out,

> Are not you he
> That frights the maidens of the villagery,
> Skim milk, and sometimes labor in the quern [= hand mill for
> grinding grain],
> And bootless make the breathless housewife churn? . . . (2.1.34–37)

Puck loves "jangling" (3.2.353) and to see things "befall prepos-t'rously" (121), but it is hard to say whether he engages in error deliberately (although he is overjoyed to see things go wrong).

The fairies seem ubiquitous and ever-present, and we are not surprised that the quarrel of Oberon and Titania should affect the weather. As Titania complains in a long speech:

> The spring, the summer,
> The childing [= fruitful] autumn, angry winter, change
> Their wonted liveries; and the mazèd world,
> By their increase, now knows not which is which.
> And this same progeny of evils comes
> From our debate . . . (2.1.111–16)

So we are doubly anxious to see the quarrel settled in order to reestablish universal concord before the marriage of Theseus and Hippolyta.

If these represent the overplot and the underplot of *A Midsummer Night's Dream*, then the main plot presents the complications in the wooing of Demetrius and Helena, Lysander and Hermia. Here some of the mix-ups are engendered by Puck's putting the love juice in the wrong eyes (then later, with a different herb, removing the error). Throughout the play we notice that love is an absolute; the characters are either entirely in love or entirely out of love—there is no middle state. It doesn't make much difference whether love is chemically induced by the juice of the mythological love-in-idleness blossom or produced internally by strong passion. The effects are the same. Two postulates of the play are that "The course of true love never did run smooth" (1.1.134) and that "quick bright things come to confusion" (149). So Lysander and Hermia vow to

> teach our trial patience,
> Because it is a customary cross,
> As due to love as thoughts and dreams and sighs,
> Wishes and tears, poor Fancy's followers. (152–55)

It is interesting that Demetrius and Lysander are not sharply distinguished from each other, but Helena and Hermia are, as if the male lovers are interchangeable but the women are not. Helena is the tall girl, but Hermia is short and fierce. Both parts were, of course, played by boy actors and this distinction in stature comes up often in later comedies by Shakespeare. The quarrel between Hermia and Helena is charmingly girlish and both go to it with energy. Hermia says: "How low am I? I am not yet so low / But that my nails can reach unto thine eyes" (3.2.297–98), and Helena is resolved to escape: "Your hands than mine are quicker for a fray, / My legs are longer though, to run away" (342–43).

The mechanicals are the most endearing figures of *A Midsummer Night's Dream*. They are simple working men: Peter Quince, a carpenter; Snug, a joiner; Nick Bottom, a weaver; Francis Flute, a bellows mender; Tom Snout, a tinker; and Robin Starveling, a tailor. They are not unlike the figures that Christopher Sly, "old Sly's son of Burton-heath," mentions in the induction to *The Taming of the Shrew*: "Marian Hacket, the fat alewife of Wincot" (2.21–22), "Stephen Sly and old John Naps of Greece, / And Peter Turph and Henry Pimpernell" (93–94). These names can all be verified in the current Coventry telephone book. Like the medieval guild members who offered plays on biblical themes (and continued to offer them well into Shakespeare's lifetime), the mechanicals are busy rehearsing a classical play, "The most lamentable comedy, and most cruel death of Pyramus and Thisby" (1.2.11–13), like Thomas Preston's *Cambises* (1561), described on the title-page as "A Lamentable Tragedie mixed full of plesant mirth." The mechanicals are set against the figures from Duke Theseus's court and the lovers, who escape to the same wood outside Athens where the mechanicals are rehearsing their play. They are drawn into the play in unexpected ways when Titania, the Queen of the Fairies, falls madly in love with Bottom, the weaver, who has been transformed into an ass.

Many critics have pointed out that the Pyramus and Thisby play is a parody of *Romeo and Juliet,* which either just preceded *A Midsummer Night's Dream* or just followed it. The two plays have many stylistic similarities, especially in their intense and self-conscious lyricism. The Pyramus and Thisby play is represented as "very tragical mirth" (5.1.57) and is played before the lovers who have escaped amorous perturbations in the wood outside Athens and have been restored to each other. The play in some sense enacts again the difficulties of true love that have been overcome by the magic intercession of Oberon. Shakespeare had already experimented with the Show of the Nine Worthies in *Love's Labor's Lost,* and he would soon carry the displacement effect of two old plays even further in *Hamlet* (the Dido and Aeneas play and *The Murder of Gonzago*). Thus the Pyramus and Thisby play in *A Midsummer Night's Dream* serves as a transition.

The archaism of the play-within-the-play sets it apart from the main play, and we can conveniently mock its antiquated style:

Anon comes Pyramus, sweet youth and tall,
    And finds his trusty Thisby's mantle slain:
Whereat, with blade, with bloody blameful blade,
    He bravely broached his boiling bloody breast . . . (5.1.144–47)

The passage gives us an exaggerated example of alliterative emphasis, but we don't hear the alternating, jingling rhyme. This is a grotesque and also poignant reminder that "The course of true love never did run smooth" (1.1.134). In the light of the Pyramus and Thisby play, all three pairs of lovers are made aware of how fortunately things have turned out for them.

Midsummer day is June 24 and it celebrates the feast of the nativity of St. John the Baptist. Midsummer night, or St. John's Eve, is June 23, about the time of the summer solstice, associated with pre-Christian fertility rites and supernatural beings. The date establishes a folklore basis for *A Midsummer Night's Dream* (compare *Twelfth Night,* which occurs on the twelfth day after Christmas on the Christian calendar). In other words, the doings of the play are appropriate for midsummer night, as they are in Woody Allen's movie, *A Midsum-*

mer Night's Sex Comedy, which draws on Bergman's *Smiles of a Summer Night.* The background in folklore and mythology validates the celebratory character of Shakespeare's play, and brings together Theseus and Hippolyta, the fairies, and the mechanicals, preparing their ritualistic play as part of the wedding revelry. It has been postulated that *A Midsummer Night's Dream* was first presented to grace a wedding in a noble household. Harold Brooks, in the Arden edition, thinks the occasion was the marriage of Elizabeth Carey and Thomas, the son of Henry, Lord Berkeley, on February 19, 1596, at a time when Queen Elizabeth was likely to be present. This special performance is set apart from the regular presentation of the play at the Globe theater.

Nick Bottom, the weaver, is part of the folkloric and rustic background of *A Midsummer Night's Dream.* He is at once a practical and realistic character and also eminently a creature of fantasy. He is quintessentially and hyperbolically himself, although he clearly descends from comically self-sufficient characters such as Costard in *Love's Labor's Lost.* The point is that Bottom is histrionically conceived. We don't except to see him weaving on stage with instruments of his art, just as we don't expect to see Francis Flute mending a bellows or Snug engaging in joinery. Once Bottom is identified as a weaver, that is the last we hear of the weaver's trade. We see him primarily as an actor.

In act 1, scene 2, Bottom is so enthusiastic about the play that he tries genially, but without success, to take over the direction from Peter Quince, the carpenter. He has obviously acted before because he proclaims that "his chief humor is for a tyrant" (1.2.29–30). He "could play Ercles [Hercules] rarely, or a part to tear a cat in, to make all split" (30–31). Shakespeare is nostalgically remembering the craft guild plays of his youth. Like Hamlet, Bottom recalls a poignant snatch of verse from an old play to illustrate "Ercles' vein, a tyrant's vein" (41):

> The raging rocks
> And shivering shocks
> Shall break the locks
> Of prison gates;
> And Phibbus' [Phoebus Apollo's] car

Shall shine from far,
And make and mar
The foolish Fates. (32–39)

This is an excellent sample of the style of the Pyramus and Thisby
play that is to follow.

Bottom is bubbling over with eagerness. He wants to play all the
parts, especially the lion: "I will roar that I will do any man's heart
good to hear me" (1.2.71–72). He has no false modesty about his
skills. He can also roar "as gently as any sucking dove; I will roar you
an 'twere any nightingale" (82–84). Bottom shows a surprising
knowledge about the technical details of costume: "I will discharge it
in either your straw-color beard, your orange-tawny beard, your
purple-in-grain beard, or your French-crown-color beard, your perfit
yellow" (93–96). How does it happen that Bottom knows so much
about what color beards are available to amateur actors?

Bottom becomes the likely victim of Puck's mischief when he
places an ass's head on Bottom and "translates" him into an animal
with whom Titania, Queen of the Fairies, will instantly fall in love.
Jan Kott, in *Shakespeare Our Contemporary*, has called our attention to
the fact that the ass (and the zebra, too) are the most generously
endowed sexually of all male beasts, but Bottom is wondrously deco-
rous in his scene with Titania. He tries to ignore graciously all her
blatant sexual suggestions and to establish himself in a cozy domes-
ticity. Despite his ass's head, he is never anything but Bottom the
weaver, scrupulously polite and wondering about his new condition,
like Christopher Sly in the induction of *The Taming of the Shrew*.
Neither of them is ever really translated at all, although they both
make a good pretense of being easy in their new roles. Bottom is
justly proud of the fact that he knows how to make conversation
with the Queen of Fairies, although his speech is homely: "Nay, I
can gleek upon occasion" (3.1.147–48). *Gleek* means to gibe or make
a satirical jest, as in *Romeo and Juliet* 4.5.113. When presented with
four fairies to execute his every wish, Bottom has only humble
requests: "I shall desire you of more acquaintance, good Master
Cobweb: if I cut my finger, I shall make bold with you" (3.1.180–
82). Bottom is emphatically no Dr. Faustus.

Bottom is marvelously comfortable in his role as Titania's paramour, and he doesn't for a moment protest about his guise as an ass. He adapts to his new identity without ever straying from a sense of himself as bully Bottom the weaver: "I must to the barber's, mounsieur; for methinks I am marvail's hairy about the face; and I am such a tender ass, if my hair do but tickle me, I must scratch" (4.1.25–28). In this way, his metamorphosis is in no way different from that of Christopher Sly, the drunken tinker in *The Taming of the Shrew*. Sly calls for "a pot o' th' smallest ale" (ind. 2.75), while Bottom, who claims "a reasonable good ear in music," calls for "the tongs and the bones" (4.1.31–32). He also has "a great desire to a bottle of hay" (35–36). When he awakes and the ass's head is gone, Bottom remembers his wonderful midsummer night's dream, "a most rare vision . . . past the wit of man to say what dream it was" (208–9). Characteristically, he will get Peter Quince to write a ballad of his dream, which he will insert into the Pyramus and Thisby play and sing at Thisby's death. Bottom's main concern is not with himself and his wonderful adventures but with the play that the mechanicals will put on before the court.

Duke Theseus's speech at the beginning of the last scene of *A Midsummer Night's Dream* has often been misunderstood as a defense of poetry; it is just the reverse. The noble Theseus equates lovers, madmen, and poets as "of imagination all compact" (5.1.8). Like the lunatic and the lover,

> The poet's eye, in a fine frenzy rolling,
> Doth glance from heaven to earth, from earth to heaven;
> And as imagination bodies forth
> The forms of things unknown, the poet's pen
> Turns them to shapes, and gives to airy nothing
> A local habitation and a name. (12–17)

Shakespeare seems to delight in presenting aesthetic truth ambiguously. Imagination is set against "cool reason," which doesn't have "seething brains" and "shaping fantasies," nor any "tricks" at all. Hippolyta adds that the "story of the night," or what has really happened in the play, "More witnesseth than fancy's images" (23–25). This is what "grows to something of great constancy" (26), or self-consistency, rather than the fanciful images of lunatics, lovers, and poets.

The play has a bittersweet ending, with the fairies taking over the house when everyone has gone to bed after midnight. This is the fairies' time to enter their domain. Puck's epilogue apologizes to the audience for the "visions" that have appeared, "And this weak and idle theme, / No more yielding but a dream" (3.1.429–30). Shakespeare takes the image of a midsummer night's dream seriously right through to the end.

Recent productions of the play remind us that the dream may also have aspects of a nightmare, at least of an erupting nightmare that is finally and imperfectly contained. The world of the fairies and the folklore traditions of Midsummer Night are much more chaotic and disruptive than we would like to believe. However decorously Bottom behaves when he is transformed into an ass, Titania's lust for a forbidden coupling with an animal is very real. There are all sorts of frightening aspects of the nocturnal forest that must have been taken up by Hawthorne in *The Scarlet Letter*. The wood as a symbolic locale is definitely not benevolent, as it is established in Ovid's *Metamorphoses*. It is the place of the Id, the amoral, perturbations of the unconscious, darkness, lawlessness, and uncontrollable impulse. All these baleful assumptions lie behind Shakespeare's seemingly placid *Midsummer Night's Dream*.

The Merchant of Venice

*T*he *Merchant of Venice* is an odd sort of comedy, probably written in the period 1596–1598, after *A Midsummer Night's Dream*, around the time of *The Merry Wives of Windsor*, and shortly before *Much Ado About Nothing*, *As You Like It*, and *Twelfth Night*. It is unlike any of these plays except that the comic villainy of Shylock bears some resemblance to the machinations of Don John in *Much Ado*. The Shylock action, however, threatens to take over the play and to swamp the romantic and folkloric Portia action in Belmont. Although the last act is devoted specifically to reasserting that *The Merchant of Venice* is a comedy, most readers and spectators feel a falling off of intensity after the departure of Shylock in act 4.

Shylock, the Jewish money-lender, is a grotesque figure in the play, costumed in a recognizably Jewish way in a long gown of gabardine, probably black, with a red beard and / or wig like that of Judas and a hooked putty nose or bottle-nose, and the sort of black skull cap that the Puritans also fancied. He speaks a suspended, grammatically elliptical discourse full of emphatic repetitions, which tends to make him dire and threatening rather than comic.

The Venetian setting contrasts sharply with

that of Belmont, and the play is about equally divided between the two. The Venice of the play is the corrupt, international, commercial city that fascinated Shakespeare and the Elizabethans. Shylock's Venice anticipates the Venice of Iago in *Othello* and there are many ways in which Iago borrows from Shylock. One of the first things Shylock says, in a scathing aside, is that he hates Antonio "for he is a Christian" (1.3.39), and the word *hate* echoes in the play. Antonio knows that Shylock "hates me" (3.3.24) and that there is nothing he can do against his settled malice. When Shylock is "bid forth to supper," he goes not as a friend but as an implacable enemy:

> I am not bid for love—they flatter me.
> But yet I'll go in hate, to feed upon
> The prodigal Christian. (2.5.13–15)

These kinds of feral, ferocious images are characteristic of Shylock. They reach their climax in the trial scene, when Shylock can only plead his irrational humor to have a pound of "carrion flesh" from Antonio. This sounds like a parody of Corporal Nym's "humor" in *The Merry Wives* and *Henry V*. Shylock can give no reason "More than a lodged hate and a certain loathing / I bear Antonio" (4.1.60–61), although elsewhere Shylock, like Iago, gives so many reasons that they tend to cancel one another.

The climax of this sequence comes in Shylock's frightening answer to Bassanio's question "Do all men kill the things they do not love?" (4.1.66). In other words, is killing a necessary act to those who hate? Shylock replies with another question that is diabolical: "Hates any man the thing he would not kill?" (67). This defines the intensity of Shylock's passion, which is not unlike Iago's, who has often told Roderigo that he hates the Moor, "and I retell thee again and again, I hate the Moor" (*Othello* 1.3.359–60). It is repeated as a kind of slogan, but Iago like Shylock uses hate like a passe-partout to justify any sort of action. "I hate the Moor," says Iago,

> And it is thought abroad that 'twixt my sheets
> H' as done my office. I know not if't be true,
> But I, for mere suspicion in that kind,
> Will do, as if for surety. (*Othello* 1.3.375–79)

Shylock hates Antonio with an irrational wildness that goes beyond interest rates and commercial conflicts. Whatever sympathy we are made to feel for Shylock—and we never feel any for Iago—we should not forget his homicidal hatred. Ultimately, Shylock shares in Iago's motiveless malignity.

It is made painfully clear that Shylock, like Othello, is a stranger in Venice, an alien, an outsider without the rights of Venetian citizens. Toward the end of the trial scene, Portia has another tricky pronouncement about the laws of Venice:

> If it be proved against an alien
> That by direct or indirect attempts
> He seek the life of any citizen,
> The party 'gainst the which he doth contrive
> Shall seize one half his good; the other half
> Comes to the privy coffer of the state . . . (4.1.348–53)

Unlike Venetian citizens, Shylock foolishly depends upon the letter of the law—the technicalities of his bond or contract—because he has nothing else to fall back on.

Antonio expresses this in a roundabout way:

> For the commodity that strangers have
> With us in Venice, if it be denied,
> Will much impeach the justice of the state,
> Since that the trade and profit of the city
> Consisteth of all nations. (3.3.27–31)

In other words, Venice depends on international trade and therefore offers strangers and foreigners a special commodity or convenience or commercial benefit that can just as easily be withdrawn if circumstances demand it. In *King John tickling commodity* (2.1.573) is a key phrase emphasizing the equivocal commercial meaning of "Commodity, the bias of the world" (574). Portia catches Shylock on the hip with procedural matters that violate equity and fairness, but nobody complains or remembers the special commodity "that strangers have / With us in Venice." Shylock is always on the defensive and is never comfortable in Venice, just as Othello is never at home among the

Venetians. We remember how shocked Brabantio is that his daughter is not going to marry one of "The wealthy curlèd darlings of our nation" (*Othello* 1.2.67).

Shylock scorns the hypocrisy of the Venetian Christians, and he constructs clever arguments to attack them where they are most vulnerable. In the trial scene, which is a kind of cultural debate, Shylock points out that the Venetians are slaveholders:

> You have among you many a purchased slave,
> Which like your asses and your dogs and mules
> You use in abject and in slavish parts,
> Because you bought them. (4.1.90–93)

In Marlowe's *Jew of Malta* (1589), which strongly influenced Shakespeare's play, act 2, scene 3 takes place at a slave auction in the Venetian marketplace, where Barabas purchases Ithamore. Shylock taunts the Venetian court with impertinent questions:

> Shall I say to you,
> "Let them be free! Marry them to your heirs!
> Why sweat they under burdens? Let their beds
> Be made as soft as yours, and let their palates
> Be seasoned with such viands"? (4.1.93–97)

These are not ethical questions but matters of property that are protected by law. The Venetians will answer: " 'The slaves are ours,' " and Shylock answers them in exactly the same mode: "The pound of flesh which I demand of him / Is dearly bought, is mine, and I will have it" (99–100). Shylock is masterfully sardonic and sarcastic; he knows that his arguments are unanswerable.

Belmont is the other setting of *The Merchant of Venice*, and it is intended to be the typical pastoral place of Shakespearean comedy. Portia is the rich heiress of Belmont like the Countess Olivia in *Twelfth Night*. Bassanio begins the play as a poor but doughty fortune hunter, not unlike Petruchio in *The Taming of the Shrew*, but Portia falls in love with him and wants him to choose the casket that will make him her husband. Although she is tempted to make him "pause a day or two / Before you hazard" (3.2.1–2), she is nevertheless sure, by all the certain prescriptions of folklore, "If you do love me, you will find me out" (41). Portia is like Penelope with a house full of suitors, but among them Bassanio is the lowest in social rank. His very humility gives him a leading clue to finding the right casket.

Belmont is not so different from the commercial city of Venice as is at first postulated. It is clear that Portia is rich, and this comes out quite spontaneously in the way she throws around large sums when she learns of Antonio's indebtedness to Shylock and the danger he now is in. Bassanio says that the sum owed is three thousand ducats, to which Portia replies without any hesitation:

> What, no more?
> Pay him six thousand, and deface the bond.
> Double six thousand and then treble that . . . (3.2.298–300)

These hyperbolic sums must impress her auditors, and she caps it all with: "You shall have gold / To pay the petty debt twenty times over" (306–7). This is the first time that anyone in the play calls three thousand ducats a "petty debt." There is an unmistakable money reference in Portia's final statement to Bassanio: "Since you are dear bought, I will love you dear" (313).

This more or less answers Gratiano's declaration: "We are the Jasons, we have won the Fleece" (3.2.241). It is abundantly clear that Portia is the golden fleece and that Gratiano thinks that his friend Bassanio has hit the jackpot in Belmont. This specifically reiterates the image with which Bassanio started out on his expedition; Portia's

> sunny locks
> Hang on her temples like a golden fleece,
> Which makes her seat of Belmont Colchos' strond,
> And many Jasons come in quest of her. (1.1.169–72)

Colchos's strond is the shore east of the Black Sea where the legendary Jason won the Golden Fleece, and Bassanio is as much a questing Jason as any of Portia's suitors. The whole play turns on Bassanio's need to borrow a large sum from Antonio to fit out a proper expedition to Belmont to woo Portia. Bassanio is clearly a flesh and blood Venetian who depends on money, like the merchant adventurer Antonio, and quite unlike the mythological hero Jason.

Portia herself is hardly a pastoral figure. In her first conversation with Nerissa, her waiting gentlewoman, we see Portia as a charming, passionate, and even petulant young woman, who boasts of her "hot temper" and "madness" of youth (1.2.18–19), and who "can easier teach twenty what were good to be done, than to be one of the twenty to follow mine own teaching" (15–17). She begins the play not unlike Rosalind in *As You Like It* and Viola in *Twelfth Night*. Her satirical comments on her suitors are witty and lighthearted, and she goes through a predictable catalogue of ethnic types. She likes the young German, the Duke of Saxony's nephew, "Very vilely in the morning when he is sober, and most vilely in the afternoon when he is drunk" (85–86), and she begs Nerissa to set a deep glass of Rhenish wine on the wrong casket so that she may be rid of this sponge. Next to these suitors, Bassanio looks very attractive in anticipation.

We actually see the Prince of Morocco and the Prince of Aragon choosing the wrong caskets. In the scenes with the Prince of Morocco, we have some surprisingly sharp language from Portia. When he chooses the gold casket and exits, Portia closes the scene with a sentensious couplet: "A gentle riddance. Draw the curtains, go. / Let all of his complexion choose me so" (2.7.78–79). *Complexion* could be used as a general word for temperament, but in this context— despite the apologetics of most editors—it is mainly directed at the color of his skin. Morocco enters the play as *"a tawny Moor"* (2.1. s.d.), and his first lines could be spoken by Othello, another Moor: "Mislike me not for my complexion, / The shadowed livery of the burnished sun" (1–2). This use of *complexion* means specifically skin color. Remember that Cleopatra the Egyptian says that she is "with Phoebus' amorous pinches black" (*Antony and Cleopatra* 1.5.28).

Act 5 of *The Merchant of Venice* attempts to return the play to a lighthearted, lyrical love comedy after the perturbation with Shylock is over in act 4, but Shakespeare never succeeds in reestablishing the comic equilibrium. Act 5 is deliberately written up, and we have extraordinary speeches attesting to the powers of music, but it is difficult to cancel the dire effects of the trial scene in act 4, scene 1.

In this way Belmont can't really be juxtaposed with Venice as a contrary but equal setting. Shakespeare tries hard to revivify Belmont as a romantic setting seen in full moonlight. As Lorenzo and his loving Jessica await Portia and Nerissa, Lorenzo celebrates the quality of Belmont:

> How sweet the moonlight sleeps upon this bank!
> Here will we sit and let the sounds of music
> Creep in our ears; soft stillness and the night
> Become the touches of sweet harmony. (5.1.55–58)

Musicians enter and play music while Lorenzo discourses on "the sweet power of music" (79). Shakespeare remembers Ovid's description of Orpheus in the *Metamorphoses*, who, by the magical power of music, could draw to himself "trees, stones, and floods" because there is "naught so stockish, hard and full of rage / But music for the time doth change his nature" (80–82). It is as if music alone, by its Orphic powers, could have changed Shylock's nature—but it is now too late.

Elaborate arguments have been mounted to demonstrate that *The Merchant of Venice* is not anti-Semitic, but it is no good to try to discard the hate that energizes the play. Bassanio and his friends hate Shylock because he is a Jew, just as Shylock says that he hates Antonio because he is a Christian. *Othello* also depends upon a strongly antiblack racism that is both irrational and violent (as it is against Aaron the Moor in *Titus Andronicus*). Once you admit that *The Merchant of Venice* is blatantly anti-Semitic, you also have to admit that it has the most sympathetic defense of Jews in all of Shakespeare and probably in all of Renaissance literature. Shylock's "Hath not a Jew eyes?" speech (3.1.55–56) is a searing indictment not only of the values of Antonio, the Merchant of Venice, but also of the entire Christian community. Shylock insists on the essential humanity of Jews: "If you prick us, do we not bleed? If you tickle us, do we not laugh?" (61–62). It's hard to imagine anyone actually tickling Shylock, Tubal, or any Jew in the play, so that statement seems purely rhetorical. The point of this extraordinary speech is that it ends in a cry for revenge: "The villainy you teach me I will execute, and it shall go hard but I will better the instruction" (68–69). Like Barabas in Marlowe's *Jew of Malta*, Shylock will excel in ingenious villainy and put the Christians to shame as unimaginative plodders.

You can already see in this play Shakespeare's skill in controlling the sympathies of the audience. Although there is no doubt that Shylock is a villain, Shakespeare teases our feelings toward him so that we can never maintain one single, unalterable point of view. The elopement of his daughter Jessica with the Christian Lorenzo and her stealing from her father so many precious stones and ducats clearly sting Shylock and enrage him as nothing has done before. He is a grotesquely comic figure wandering about the streets of Venice with all the boys following him, "Crying his stones, his daughter, and his ducats" (2.8.24). Salerio and Solanio are much amused by this, especially by the pun on "stones" as precious jewels and as testicles.

But Shylock's grotesque passion reaches us in unpredictable ways. He learns from Tubal, who has been following Jessica and Lorenzo, that his "daughter spent in Genoa, as I heard, one night fourscore ducats" (3.1.101–2), presumably from the ducats she stole from her father. He also learns that one of Antonio's creditors "showed me a ring that he had of your daughter for a monkey" (111–12). This is the final blow for Shylock: "It was my turquoise; I had it of Leah when I was a bachelor. I would not have given it for a wilderness of monkeys" (113–16). This is the first and last we hear of Leah, Shylock's dead wife and Jessica's mother, who gave this ring to Shylock as a wooing present. The turquoise, or Turkey stone, was supposed to have the power to remove all enmity and to reconcile man and wife. The ring has powerful sentimental value for Shylock and that is why, good businessman that he is, he would not have sold it "for a wilderness of monkeys." It is a strange, savage, passionate image, and we sympathize with Shylock's suffering at this point. Like Lear, Shylock knows "How sharper than a serpent's tooth it is / To have a thankless child" (King Lear 1.4.290–91).

Shylock's style is brilliantly adapted to his dramatic function in the play. At the beginning when he is first introduced he hardly seems to speak at all. His first four speeches are: "Three thousand ducats—well" (3.1.1), "For three months—well" (3), "Antonio shall become bound—well" (6), and "Three thousand ducats for three months, and Antonio bound" (9–10). This is a kind of humming style, broken and inconsequential. Is Shylock taunting Bassanio? Suddenly he breaks into loquacious speech about whether Antonio is a good man. He indulges in legalistic specification as if he were speaking in the Torah style that Puritans used to translate Old Testament Hebrew—at least the stage Puritans we find in Ben Jonson's The Alchemist (1610) and Bartholomew Fair (1614).

Shylock warns Bassanio of contingencies: "there be land rats and water rats, water thieves and land thieves—I mean pirates—and then there is the peril of waters, winds, and rocks" (1.3.22–25). *Pirates* is Shylock's excruciating pun on *pie rats*, which continues *land rats* and *water rats*. His Old Testament example of Jacob and Laban and Jacob's ingeniously making the ewes breed parti-colored lambs that he would keep is an extended example of equivocation. The example seems to have Talmudic roots. Elsewhere in the play Shylock indulges in extended, incantatory repetition, of which "Let him look to his bond" is the refrain. Some of the more ordinary examples of this repetition are in act 3, scene 1, when he learns both that his daughter has fled with his jewels and his money and that Antonio's ships are wrecked at sea. His frenzy is expressed in a meaningless repetition: "What, what, what? Ill luck, ill luck?" (94) and "I thank God, I thank God! Is it true, is it true?" (96). We are reminded of Leontes' repetitions in *The Winter's Tale* to indicate the onset of his feverish jealousy: "Too hot, too hot!" (1.2.108).

The Merry Wives
of Windsor

The *Merry Wives of Windsor* is a cozy, domestic play, Shakespeare's only venture in the genre of citizen comedies such as Dekker's *Shoemaker's Holiday* (1599) and Middleton's *Chaste Maid in Cheapside* (1611) that were so popular with London audiences. It's possible that Shakespeare wasn't comfortable in this sort of middle-class, realistic play, as he wasn't really comfortable with the hard lines of farce in the style of Plautus. The setting of *The Merry Wives* is attractively familiar, and it is more convincingly redolent of town life in Elizabethan England than anything else that Shakespeare wrote (including the charming allusions to familiar animals and places in *Venus and Adonis*). Page in the first scene invites everyone home with an attractive graciousness: "Come, we have a hot venison pasty to dinner. Come, gentlemen, I hope we shall drink down all unkindness" (1.1.188–90). And in the last scene, Mrs. Page thoroughly forgives everyone and invites them all home with her and her husband:

> Master Fenton,
> Heaven give you many, many merry days!
> Good husband, let us every one go home,
> And laugh this sport o'er by a country fire;
> Sir John and all. (5.5.241–45)

The action of the plot is all "sport" and not to be taken too seriously. Not only is Falstaff reduced in stature (but not in girth) to accommodate him to *The Merry Wives*, but all the other characters are drawn to scale for the town of Windsor and its homely preoccupations. The insanely jealous Ford, in the guise of Master Brooke, is no Othello or even Leontes. He seems full of a cringing and masochistic pleasure in his own imagined cuckoldry. His tortured soliloquies are deliberately antiheroic, as Ford squirms in his own discomfiture. There are three soliloquies that are obviously related to the sentimental reflections about adultery in such domestic tragedies as *Arden of Feversham* (1591) and Heywood's *A Woman Killed with Kindness* (1603), but of course Ford has no reason at all for his frenzy.

In the first soliloquy, after Ford has forced money on Falstaff and obsequiously flattered him and solicited his aid, he exclaims as Master Brooke: "See the hell of having a false woman! My bed shall be abused, my coffers ransacked, my reputation gnawn at" (2.2.290–92). In typical fashion, Ford is most concerned about the "abominable terms" that shall be heaped upon him: "Terms! Names! Amaimon sounds well; Lucifer, well; Barbason, well; yet they are devils' additions, the names of fiends. But Cuckold! Wittol!—Cuckold! The devil himself hath not such a name" (295–99). This is almost a parody by anticipation of what Othello is incapable of saying.

In his second soliloquy, Ford hints at larger metaphysical issues than he is capable of either expounding or understanding, and the fact that he is so concerned about Page's foolish complacency is a sign that he feels a sense of triumph over his neighbor: "Good plots! They are laid, and our revolted wives share damnation together" (3.2.34–35). Ford imagines juicy scenes of judgment: "Well, I will take him, then torture my wife, pluck the borrowed veil of modesty from the so-seeming Mistress Page, divulge Page himself for a secure and willful Actaeon" (36–39). He is acting a grandiloquent role like Justice Overdo in Jonson's *Bartholomew Fair* (1614), and he revels in his own anticipated power.

The third soliloquy is more dire and pseudotragic than the other two, as Ford slips into a firm acknowledgment of his cuckoldry: "Hum! Ha! Is this a vision? Is this a dream? Do I sleep? Master Ford, awake; awake, Master Ford! There's a hole made in your best coat, Master Ford. This 'tis to be married; this 'tis to have linen and buck baskets!" (3.5.137–41). The buck basket in which Falstaff was conveyed out of Mistress Ford's house symbolizes the comic reduction of a seemingly tragic issue. Falstaff is specific about the unromantic contents of the buck basket: "Rammed me in with foul shirts and smocks, socks, foul stockings, greasy napkins, that, Master Brooke, there was the rankest compound of villainous smell that ever offended nostril" (88–92). As if this is not enough, the buck basket scene is replayed in act 4, scene 2, when Falstaff exits disguised as the fat woman of Brainford. Shakespeare cannot resist confronting Ford with another buck basket and have him farcically empty the dirty clothes on stage piece by piece with a kind of mad ferocity. Ford achieves an apotheosis of cuckoldry here that is as close as Shakespeare ever comes to the French farce idea of *fou rire*, or mad laughter. It is a distinct disappointment for Ford to find out that all his overheated imaginings are false.

The merry wives of Windsor are not so merry as we expect them to be; in fact, they are distinctly smug, moralistic, and self-satisfied. Their animus against Falstaff is excessive and they are constantly asserting their virtue in a priggish fashion. They don't really need all three tricks against Falstaff to prove their point, but they seem to take pleasure in the fat knight's discomfiture. Incidentally, it is almost inconceivable to imagine these solid citizen wives as anything but substantial and buxom women, not at all waiflike romantic figures. Their very materiality allies them with Falstaff.

Mistress Page's first thought when she receives Falstaff's love letter and doggerel poem is to be revenged. She cannot understand why she has miraculously escaped "love letters in the holiday time of my beauty, and am I now a subject for them" (2.1.1–3). Mistress Ford is equally inclined to revenge on "this whale, with so many tuns of oil in his belly" who has washed "ashore at Windsor" (63–64) and she devises the scheme "to entertain him with hope till the wicked fire of lust have melted him in his own grease" (66–67). It is a notably middle-class view of Falstaff's wooing to see it as "the wicked fire of lust." There was plenty of lust (albeit little action) for Doll Tearsheet in the *Henry IV* plays, and even for Mistress Quickly, but little for either Mistress Ford or Page in this play. Mrs. Ford's plan is inherently unattractive: "Nay, I will consent to act any villainy against him that may not sully the chariness of our honesty" (97–99). This is "honesty" in the technical sense of Dekker's *Honest Whore, Parts I and II* (1604–1605).

The buck basket episode with Falstaff pleases Mrs. Ford because it has confounded a "dishonest rascal" (3.3.181), Falstaff, and tried a jealous husband. Both of the Windsor wives are eager to play more tricks on Falstaff to entertain themselves in their domestic boredom and to cure Falstaff's "dissolute disease" (187). Notice how freely the wives throw around moral, ethical, and theological terms. In a remarkably didactic set of couplets, Mistress Page affirms their exemplary behavior:

> We'll leave a proof by that which we will do,
> Wives may be merry, and yet honest too.
> We do not act that often jest and laugh;
> 'Tis old but true, "Still swine eats all the draff." (4.2.99–102)

The attempted union of merriness and honesty lies at the heart of the play, which is essentially a middle-class tract like that parodied in Beaumont and Fletcher's *Knight of the Burning Pestle* (1607). The final trick against Falstaff is played jointly by the wives and their husbands, and we feel sharply that the deck is stacked against all remaining Rabelaisian vestiges of Merry England. As Mrs. Page boasts smugly: "Against such lewdsters and their lechery, / Those that betray them do no treachery" (5.3.22–23). *Lewdsters* seems to be a special comic word invented by Shakespeare for this play.

One of the most successful characters created for *The Merry Wives* is Slender, the marriageable nephew of Justice Shallow, who doesn't appear in *Henry IV, Part II*, but bears a type resemblance to Justice Silence. Right from the beginning of the first scene, Slender is seen to be at a loss for words and direction. He is a comic simpleton and innocent, like Sir Andrew Aguecheek in *Twelfth Night*, described as having "a little wee [as in Folio] face, with a little yellow beard—a Cain-colored beard" (1.4.22–23). (Cain-colored is red or reddish-yellow, like the beard traditionally assigned to Judas.) In the first scene, Slender has nothing of his own to say and he mercilessly parrots the shallow words of his uncle Shallow. The enormous quantity of meaningless repetition in this scene is meant to define Shallow and especially Slender. His servant is significantly named Simple.

From the episode of his pocket being picked by Pistol or Nym, Slender vows never to be drunk again "but in honest, civil, godly company . . . If I be drunk, I'll be drunk with those that have the fear of God, and not with drunken knaves" (1.1.175–78).

Slender, thinking, like almost everyone else in the play, of wooing Anne Page, wishes he had his "Book of Songs and Sonnets here" (1.1.192). This is Tottel's famous *Miscellany*, published in 1557. Like Sir Andrew Aguecheek, Slender is enamored of words for their own sake. In his wooing of Anne in this scene, Slender can think only in manly terms of Sackerson, the famous Elizabethan bear used for bear-baiting in Shakespeare's time, who may have appeared in *The Winter's Tale* in a celebrated stage direction: "*Exit, pursued by a bear*" (3.3.57 s.d.). Slender boasts that he has "seen Sackerson loose twenty time, and have taken him by the chain" (1.1.284–86). This is an endearing detail. When Slender is actually put to wooing Anne in act 3, scene 4, he is exceedingly modest and unassuming. Anne asks him directly, "what would you with me?" (3.4.59–60), to which Slender makes no grandiose, romantic claims: "Truly, for mine own part, I would little or nothing with you. Your father and my uncle have made motions" (61–63). This is indeed not to put oneself forward.

The Merry Wives of Windsor is unusual in the canon because it is the only play of Shakespeare using a middle-class, commercial setting in the town of Windsor, outside London near what is now Heathrow Airport. Windsor is, of course, the location of Windsor Castle, the chief residence of English rulers since William I. In St. George's Chapel, the Knights of the Garter were installed with medieval ceremony, and it has been claimed that Shakespeare's play was performed at the Garter Feast in Whitehall Palace in Westminster on St. George's Day, April 23, 1597. Aside from the fact that Falstaff is staying at the Garter Inn and the Host of the Garter Inn is an important character, there are many allusions to practices connected with the Knights of the Garter, especially in the last scene of the play. The unlikely Mistress Quickly as Queen of the Fairies has a celebratory speech addressed to Queen Elizabeth, who may have been present at a special royal performance, in praise of Windsor Castle and the Knights of the Garter:

Search Windsor Castle, elves, within and out.
Strew good luck, ouphs [= elves], on every sacred room,
That it may stand till the perpetual doom . . . (5.5.59–61)

Mistress Quickly continues with instructions to the fairies about the stalls of the Knights of the Garter in St. George's Chapel:

The several chairs of Order look you scour
With juice of balm and every precious flow'r.
Each fair instalment, coat, and several crest,
With loyal blazon, evermore be blest. (5.5.64–67)

The fairies' tasks are specifically heraldic. They are to occupy themselves with "each fair instalment," or stall (that is, the place where one is installed); coat of arms (presumably nailed to the back of each stall); heraldic crests set on the knights' helmets; and the blazon bearing the proud coat of arms. And the fairies are directed to write *"Honi soit qui mal y pense,"* the motto of the Order of the Garter,

In emerald tufts, flow'rs purple, blue, and white—
Like sapphire, pearl, and rich embroidery,
Buckled below fair knighthood's bending knee . . . (5.5.73–75)

These details, which have no relation to the action of the comedy, are extremely specific and suggest that the proper celebration of the occasion was important to Shakespeare and his dramatic company. One of the reasons may have been that among the five knights elected to the Order of the Garter in April 1597 was George Carey, Lord Hunsdon, who became patron of Shakespeare's company, the Lord Chamberlain's Men, after the death of his father Henry in July 1596 and Lord Chamberlain on April 17, 1597.

There is a strong tradition, first recorded in print in John Dennis's dedication of *The Comical Gallant* in 1702, that *The Merry Wives of Windsor* was written at the behest of Queen Elizabeth: "This Comedy was written at her Command, and by her direction, and she was so eager to see it Acted, that she commanded it be finished in fourteen days." In 1709 Nicholas Rowe added, in the biography published with his edition of Shakespeare, that Queen Elizabeth "was so well pleas'd with that admirable Character of *Falstaff*, in the two Parts of *Henry* the Fourth, that she commanded him to continue it for one Play more, and to shew him in Love." We don't know how literally Shakespeare interpreted the Queen's command, since Falstaff is not exactly shown in love in *The Merry Wives*, but rather seeking to repair his fortunes through wooing Mistress Ford and Mistress Page, the virtuous but fun-loving tradesmen's wives of Windsor.

If we date *The Merry Wives* in relation to the Garter ceremony performance on April 23, 1597, then the play was clearly written after *Henry IV, Part I*, and perhaps at the same time as *Henry IV, Part II*. In *The Merry Wives* Falstaff and his companions are already sunk in their fortunes and are more like the characters in the second part of *Henry IV* and in *Henry V* than the glorious, buoyant, larger-than-life figures in *Henry IV, Part I*. Pistol in *The Merry Wives* is continuous with the character in the second part of *Henry IV*, and Nym clearly anticipates the humors character of *Henry V*. Justice Shallow is like the falsely nostalgic figure in *Henry IV, Part II*, and Slender in *The Merry Wives* seems an offshoot of Justice Silence in this play.

It is obvious that despite the character links the farcical, domestic comedy of *The Merry Wives of Windsor* bears little relation to Shakespeare's *Henry IV* plays and *Henry V*, in which the main events of English history in the fifteenth century are recounted. But in the history plays Falstaff and his crew are not historical figures at all (although Falstaff is based remotely on Oldcastle and Fastolfe). They thread through most of the Major Tetralogy like contemporary Elizabethan characters right out of the rich underworld of the cony-catching rogue pamphlets of Robert Greene and others. We can see Shakespeare desperately trying to link *The Merry Wives* with the history plays when he says that the romantic wooer, Fenton, "kept company with the wild Prince and Poins" (3.2.68–69). This is pure decoration, since not only is Fenton never mentioned in the history plays, but in *The Merry Wives* he doesn't even know Falstaff.

One final point about *The Merry Wives of Windsor* is Shakespeare's preoccupation with national types. We have a Welsh parson / schoolmaster, Sir Hugh Evans, on the style of Holofernes in *Love's Labor's Lost*, who, in the words of Falstaff, "makes fritters of English" (5.5.147). His Latin language lesson in act 4, scene 1, opens the way for elaborate, obscene wordplay on the part of Mistress Quickly, which looks ahead to Katherine's racy English language lesson in *Henry V*, act 3, scene 4. *Henry V* is probably a year or two later than *Merry Wives*, but it picks up the ethnic types with their appropriate styles and accents. We have Fluellen, the Welsh Captain; Macmorris, the Irish Captain; and Jamy, the Scots Captain, who quarrel among themselves. Earlier, there is a considerable emphasis on Welsh in *Henry IV, Part I*, where we have Glendower, the Welsh leader and mighty believer in magic, whose daughter is married to Mortimer, and the sister of Mortimer, who is married to Hotspur. In act 3, scene 1, Glendower and his daughter speak Welsh together on stage, and she later sings a song in Welsh.

One other ethnic type in *The Merry Wives* is Doctor Caius, the choleric French physician for whom Mistress Quickly is servant. He speaks in a comic-strip imitation of English, as in his threats against Sir Hugh, who has not shown up for their duel: "By gar, de herring is no dead so as I vill kill him" (2.3.11–12). We are moving to the synthetic, protolanguage of the showing up of Parolles in *All's Well That Ends Well*: "*Manka revania dulche*" (4.1.81–82) and "*Oscorbidulchos volivorco*" (83). This is Shakespeare's ultimate Creole.

Much Ado About Nothing

𝓘t is surprising how much Beatrice in *Much Ado* is modeled on Kate in *The Taming of the Shrew*, given that the two plays are separated by about five years. Both heroines are decidedly antiromantic, even antimarriage, unless an ideal mate can be found. Both are witty and strong-minded but amenable to the powers of manly intelligence. Some of the same words are used to describe Beatrice and Kate. By her kindly uncle's account, Beatrice "wilt never get thee a husband if thou be so shrewd of thy tongue" (2.1.18–19). A "shrewd" or shrewish tongue is characteristic of a shrew, who puts men off by her acerbity. Leonato's brother, Antonio, continues the catalogue of Beatrice's shortcomings as a wife: "In faith, she's too curst" (20). "Curst" is virtually an exact synonym of "shrewd," and the two words are often used together.

In *The Taming of the Shrew*, Kate is described by Hortensio as

> intolerable curst
> And shrewd and froward, so beyond all measure
> That were my state far worser than it is,
> I would not wed her for a mine of gold.
> (1.2.88–91)

But Petruchio will have her were she "as curst and shrewd / As Socrates' Xanthippe or a worse" (1.2.70–71), and at the end of the play Hortensio praises him for having "tamed a curst shrow" (5.2.188). Curst and shrewish are qualities that inhibit marriageability. Leonato ends this sequence with a pun on *shrewd*, as he addresses his niece: "you apprehend passing shrewdly" (2.1.80).

Like Kate, Beatrice is described as a "haggard," which is the name for a wild female hawk, caught in her adult plumage before she undergoes the complex training by which she is mastered. Petruchio boasts of his taming of Kate in the specific language of falconry:

> My falcon now is sharp and passing empty,
> And till she stoop she must not be full gorged,
> For then she never looks upon her lure.
> > (*The Taming of the Shrew* 4.1.184–86)

In other words, Kate will not be fed until she "stoops," or is obedient to her master, and sleeplessness is an essential part of the training:

> Another way I have to man my haggard,
> To make her come and know her keeper's call,
> That is, to watch her as we watch these kites
> That bate and beat and will not be obedient. (4.1.187–90)

In the next scene Hortensio forswears Bianca, Kate's younger sister, as a "proud disdainful haggard" (4.2.39).

It is therefore no surprise that in the plot to trap Beatrice into marriage Hero uses the same imagery:

> No, truly, Ursula, she is too disdainful.
> I know her spirits are as coy and wild
> As haggards of the rock. (3.1.34–36)

By extension a haggard was a wild and intractable woman, as the jealous Othello thinks of Desdemona:

> If I do prove her haggard,
> Though that her jesses were my dear heartstrings,
> I'd whistle her off and let her down the wind
> To prey at fortune. (*Othello* 3.3.259–62)

The jesses were the straps that held the hawk's legs to the trainer's wrist. The imagery is very specific. But Beatrice, however wild a haggard, succumbs immediately to Hero's marriage plot and in a spirited sonnet declares that she is in love: "And, Benedick, love on; I will requite thee, / Taming my wild heart to thy loving hand" (3.1.111–12). The language continues the terms of falconry that were so specifically projected by Petruchio, and Beatrice in her merry war with Benedick concedes her attraction to him with the phrase "Taming my wild heart."

These themes culminate at the end of the play when Beatrice and Benedick vow to marry. Benedick asks: "Sweet Beatrice, wouldst thou come when I called thee?," and Beatrice replies: "Yea, signior, and depart when you bid me" (5.2.42–44). We don't need to believe in the exact literalness of this exchange to feel that it echoes the bet of the final scene of *The Taming of the Shrew*. In Petruchio's words:

> Let's each one send unto his wife,
> And he whose wife is most obedient
> To come at first when he doth send for her
> Shall win the wager which we will propose. (5.2.66–69)

We recognize that the contract in both plays is not really about obedience but about love.

Benedick is no Petruchio. He is much more closely allied with the young gallants who forswear love, as in the Academy of Navarre at the beginning of *Love's Labor's Lost* and especially with the figure of Adonis in *Venus and Adonis*. This is quintessentially a comic theme because love will assert its natural claims despite any amount of overheated exclamation. As Benedick says at the end after he has professed love for Beatrice and vowed to marry her: "Suffer love! A good epithet. I do suffer love indeed, for I love thee against my will" (5.2.66–67). Like other reluctant males in Shakespearean comedy, Benedick is carried away against his conscious will to love Beatrice, and Beatrice too loves him in spite of herself. The witty war in the play turns on the conflict between powerful impulse and equally powerful commitment to gender pursuits. Only Adonis in Shakespeare's early poem flees from love in earnest, and he ends tragically. In comedy, at least, Cupid and Venus are irresistible.

60

At the beginning, Benedick vows with some aplomb to avoid women and to "live a bachelor" (1.1.236–37). This is the outrageous proposition, like that in *Love's Labor's Lost*, which *Much Ado* will undo. No man (or woman, either) is allowed to defy love with impunity. As Don Pedro answers Benedick, "I shall see thee, ere I die, look pale with love" (238–39), and Don Pedro is the one who engineers the plot against both Benedick and Beatrice. Benedick's profane and bawdy protestations against the powers of love make him a likely target:

> Prove that ever I lose more blood with love than I will get again with drinking, pick out mine eyes with a ballad maker's pen and hang me up at the door of a brothel house for the sign of blind Cupid.
>
> (241–45)

The comedy is designed to show that neither Benedick nor Beatrice can get away with such sacrilegious protests against love. Like many Shakespearean comedies, the play itself is set up as a kind of wager meant to disprove the absurd propositions with which it begins. Benedick has to eat his words, as he does in his first love soliloquy: "When I said I would die a bachelor, I did not think I should live till I were married" (2.3.239–40).

We easily see through Benedick's protests against "my Lady Tongue" (2.1.272) because we understand that he is disturbed by the only character in the play who is his match in wit and intelligence (the way that Kate, for all her outrage, is irresistibly perturbed and attracted by Petruchio). Benedick deals with Beatrice in hyperboles; she is too much for him and he feels overwhelmed:

> huddling jest upon jest with impossible conveyance upon me that I stood like a man at a mark, with a whole army shooting at me. She speaks poniards, and every word stabs. (242–46)

If we listen closely to his speech, we see that it is full of mixed signals, as in the remarkable statement: "I would not marry her though she were endowed with all that Adam had left him before he transgressed" (248–50). Eve is one of the gifts that Adam had left him before he transgressed, and Benedick's mind is obviously running on Beatrice as a paradisal creature and therefore full of "disquiet, horror, and perturbation" (258–59), as if by anticipation of the Fall.

When Benedick, overhearing the plotting of Don Pedro, Leonato, and Claudio, is brought to declare his love for Beatrice, the inflamed soliloquy bears the marks of a confession of past sins. He resolves to be "horribly in love with her" (2.3.231), and he apologizes for his sudden alteration from one who has "railed so long against marriage" (233–34). At the heart of the matter is the wit combat with Beatrice, which Benedick seems loath to abandon: "Shall quips and sentences and these paper bullets of the brain awe a man from the career of his humor? No, the world must be peopled" (236–39). Presumably, the world cannot be peopled with paper bullets of the brain, but Benedick's humor has not abandoned him completely.

Unlike Malvolio in *Twelfth Night* reading the supposed love letter from Olivia, Benedick still retains a resilience and vivaciousness, even in love, that the puritanical steward never had. Both, however, are excessively concerned about their personal appearance and their dress. Benedick's beard "hath already stuffed tennis balls" (3.2.44–45), and he "rubs himself with civet" (48), a perfume derived from the civet cat. By the final scene, however, Benedick and Beatrice have recovered their ironic edge. Despite the fact that they love each other "no more than reason" (5.4.74), they will marry—Benedick "for pity" (93) and Beatrice "to save your life" (95–96). Benedick ends with witty advice to Don Pedro: "Prince, thou art sad; get thee a wife, get thee a wife! There is no staff more reverend than one tipped with horn" (122–24). This is the good-humored horn of the cuckold that Elizabethan writers never tired of alluding to. Benedick has no romantic illusions about the married state.

The melodramatic subplot of *Much Ado* leaves something to be desired in the way of psychological credibility, especially in a play where Beatrice and Benedick are such believable characters. Don John, the bastard brother of Don Pedro, Prince of Aragon, echoes Philip Faulconbridge, the Bastard in *King John*, although his part in *Much Ado* is radically abridged. As the villain in comedy, he is an anomalous figure, out of keeping with the dominant tone and mood of the play. We never really know what Don John has against Claudio, other than his favor with Don Pedro, and we certainly never learn why Don John calumniates Hero so mercilessly. In act 1, scene 3, Don John seems to be a much more important figure than he turns out to be, and this is his principal scene. He is inexplicably and immeasurably "sad," which meant dejected, depressed, and morose in Elizabethan usage. Conrade, his companion, asks: "What the goodyear, my lord! Why are you thus out of measure sad?" and Don John replies mysteriously: "There is no measure in the occasion that breeds; therefore the sadness is without limit" (1.3.1–4).

Readers of Shakespeare will recognize immediately the echo of the beginning of *The Merchant of Venice*, probably written a few years earlier. Antonio, the Merchant of Venice, begins the play with a declaration of sadness that is never explained in the course of the action:

> In sooth I know not why I am so sad.
> It wearies me, you say it wearies you;
> But how I caught it, found it, or came by it,
> What stuff 'tis made of, whereof it is born,
> I am to learn;
> And such a want-wit sadness makes of me
> That I have much ado to know myself. (1.1.1–7)

These lines could easily have been spoken by Don John—and the "much ado" of Antonio's speech provides an intertextual clue.

Don John goes far beyond Antonio to play the role of a malicious malcontent. He declares himself "a plain-dealing villain," who has "decreed not to sing in my cage" (1.3.30, 32). All of this is fascinating and puzzling, as if Don John were a character in a satirical comedy by John Marston. There is comic incongruity in Don John's other companion in mischief, Borachio, whose Spanish name means toper or drunkard. We never really learn why Don John wants to break up Claudio's marriage to Hero, except that Don Pedro has a hand in the match. Borachio is promised a "thousand ducats" (2.2.53) for his manipulation of a plot to blacken Hero in Claudio's eyes. As a kind of textbook villain, Don John declares his hatred against his brother Don Pedro, Claudio, Hero, and her father Leonato: "Only to despite them I will endeavor anything" (31–32). This kind of generalized malice does not make for a very convincing plot.

The Claudio-Hero action fits in with the villainy of Don John and raises questions about Claudio that are better left unanswered. Claudio does not seem deeply involved in his love for Hero, whom Don Pedro has wooed and won for him; it is as if she were merely a marriageable commodity. Shakespeare is not too well disposed to wooing by proxy, as we know from the Duke of Orsino's suit to Olivia through Cesario / Viola in *Twelfth Night*. No adequate explanation is ever offered for why Claudio does not woo for himself. In the calumniation scene (4, 1), Claudio is excessive in his condemnation, and his speeches foreshadow those of Leontes in *The Winter's Tale*: "There, Leonato, take her back again. / Give not this rotten orange to your friend" (30–31). An orange was an exotic and expensive tropical fruit in Elizabethan England, and we know that oranges were sold (and nuts, too) at the playhouses. Presumably, if you buy a rotten orange you are out a considerable sum of money.

Claudio speaks with an exaggerated knowingness about his intended wife's sexual proclivities: "She knows the heart of a luxurious bed; / Her blush is guiltiness, not modesty" (40–41). How does Claudio know all this from one glance at night, at a distance, of a scene that Borachio, Margaret, and Don John have arranged? The villainy in *Much Ado* seems to belong to another play and its intensity is only sketched out for a skeptical audience. The uncomfortable comic villainy implies something more profound. It is not difficult, therefore, for Claudio suddenly to reform, like Proteus in *The Two Gentlemen of Verona*. When he hears Borachio's confession, he says simply and astoundingly: "Sweet Hero, now thy image doth appear / In the rare semblance that I loved it first" (5.1.252–53). We expected more from Claudio, even though he has to wait for the dead Hero, like Hermione, to be revived especially for him.

Most obviously, the villainy in *Much Ado* is set in a comic context of the bumbling watch, incomparably played by Dogberry, Verges, and their officers. As Borachio confesses to Don Pedro, "What your wisdoms could not discover, these shallow fools have brought to light" (5.1.231–33). Shakespeare takes great delight in the spoonerisms of Dogberry, who is a lower-class counterpart to the educated and allusive wit of Beatrice and Benedick. His gravely uttered malapropisms must have been the basis for Mrs. Malaprop in Sheridan's play *The Rivals* (1775). Dogberry is always earnest and sincere and never overtly comic, which is the secret of his success. As he says to his fellow constable, or headborough, Verges, "Comparisons are odorous" (3.5.15), and he insists that the sexton "write me down an ass," as if an ass were the highest term of respect: "But, master, remember that I am an ass" (4.2.74–75).

Although the watch immediately uncovers great villainy, Dogberry insists in his instruction that they "offend no man, and it is an offense to stay a man against his will" (3.3.82–83). If they meet a thief they may suspect him to be no true man, but, since pitch defileth, as Falstaff and "ancient writers do report" (*1 Henry IV* 2.4.418–19), "they that touch pitch will be defiled" (3.3.58), and therefore "The most peaceable way for you, if you do take a thief, is to let him show himself what he is, and steal out of your company" (58–61). The mere benevolent presence of Dogberry, Verges, and the Watch undercuts the comic villainy of *Much Ado* and renders it harmless. It is as if Don John and his malicious companions are not allowed to appear in their true colors in a comedy. They are rendered impotent by the context.

Despite what he says, then, Don John is only peripherally related to the villains of tragedy. He is isolated in *Much Ado* and deliberately separated from the main action, except as a plot catalyst. In the good humor of the restorations at the end of the play it is quite easy to regard Don John as a mere intrusion in the plot.

As You Like It

Like *A Midsummer Night's Dream* of a few years earlier, *As You Like It* has a fullness in its romantic and pastoral action that suggests a studied equilibrium in the world of the play. The four pairs of lovers are set against each other in analogous relations, as if we needed them all to establish a view of love. Shakespeare liked to dabble in contraries that do not necessarily involve us in contradictions; the world of the play manifests a copiousness that includes opposites.

The wooing of Orlando and Rosalind is matched by the swift courtship of Orlando's older brother, Oliver, with Rosalind's bosom friend, Celia. The extravagant and overwrought relationship of Silvius and Phebe is a lesson to Rosalind about her own infatuation with Orlando, for, as Rosalind admits, "The sight of lovers feedeth those in love" (3.4.54). She needs Orlando finally to prove to Phebe that she is a woman and to put her seal on the marriage of Phebe and her lovesick shepherd. Touchstone, the Clown, and Audrey, the goatherd, are an antiromantic couple who frankly acknowledge their desires and "would be nibbling" (3.3.78–79), and their charming materiality helps to undercut the romantic pretensions of all the other couples. Everyone comes together at the end, and as Jaques wryly observes: "There is, sure, another flood toward, and these couples are coming to the ark" (5.4.35–36).

The banished Duke Senior, father of Rosalind, resembles Prospero in *The Tempest* in his comfortable reestablishment in the Forest of Arden. This may well be the Forest of Ardennes, on the border of Belgium and Luxembourg, but in the play it seems to be identified with Warwickshire. The name had a special significance for Shakespeare, whose mother's maiden name was Arden. *As You Like It* goes out of its way to establish the Forest of Arden as an ideal, golden world that can exist only in a pastoral setting. Charles, the wrestler, gives us a glowing account of Duke Senior's exile:

> They say he is already in the Forest of Arden, and a many merry men with him; and there they live like the old Robin Hood of England. They say many young gentlemen flock to him every day, and fleet the time carelessly as they did in the golden world. (1.1.111–15)

When we first see the Duke and some of his followers in the Forest of Arden, they enter *"like Foresters"* (2.1. s.d.), and the Duke delivers a long, contemplative speech contrasting the corrupt court and its "painted pomp" (3) with the honest simplicity of the woods. "Sweet are the uses of adversity" (12) serves practically as a motto for the romantic outlaws, and the Duke ends his speech with theological moralizing on the landscape:

> And this our life, exempt from public haunt,
> Finds tongues in trees, books in the running brooks,
> Sermons in stones, and good in everything. (15–17)

Nothing in the play really contradicts this sense of a paradisal green world set apart, except perhaps for "A green and gilded snake" (4.3.109) and "A lioness, with udders all drawn dry" (115), which Oliver reports in his encounter with his brother.

Rosalind falls firmly in love with Orlando in the wrestling match with Charles, a scene that has always seemed more significant to spectators than to readers. Rosalind's fears for Orlando before the match presage her solicitude, and when the match is over she immediately gives Orlando the gold chain from her neck: "Wear this for me" (1.2.236). There is nothing subtle about the convention of love at first sight. Rosalind doesn't hesitate to inform Orlando exactly how she feels: "Sir, you have wrestled well, and overthrown / More than your enemies" (244–45). After the ladies leave, Orlando immediately registers the effect of Rosalind on him: "What passion hangs these weights upon my tongue?" (247) and, repeating Rosalind's wrestling metaphor, "O poor Orlando, thou art overthrown!" (249). In the next scene, Rosalind is fully in love, as she confesses to Celia. Although some of her passion is for her exiled father, "some of it is for my child's father" (1.3.11). When Celia counsels her to wrestle with her affection, Rosalind can only reply: "O, they take the part of a better wrestler than myself!" (22–23). It is attractive to see how effortlessly love takes hold in this pastoral play.

In her wit and good spirits, Rosalind is an ideal Shakespeare heroine. With Orlando she leads the conversation in such a way that he doesn't have much else to do but write mediocre love poems and hang them on trees. Her intelligence and sprightliness dominate the relationship. Rosalind is only thinly disguised as Ganymede when she goes into exile, but she exploits the male bravado of the role: "A gallant curtle-ax upon my thigh, / A boar-spear in my hand," with "a swashing and a martial outside" (1.3.115–16, 118). Ganymede, "Jove's own page" (122), the cup-bearer of the gods, was a standard Elizabethan name for a catamite. The *OED* tells us, in fact, that *Catamitus* is a corruption of *Ganymedes* and defines the word coyly as "A boy kept for unnatural purposes." This is like the opening scene of Marlowe's *Dido Queen of Carthage* (1587), where we see "JUPITER *dandling* GANYMEDE *upon his knee.*" In his comedies Shakespeare titillates us with the idea of a boy actor playing a woman disguised as a man, with all its transvestite implications. In *As You Like It* the cross-dressing and the cross-wooing produce a flurry of gender complications that tease the audience. They are witty and sexual at the same time, with many covertly lesbian and homosexual suggestions. They also hint at a comic polymorphous perversity in which specific gender ceases to matter but is merely a role one assumes.

Rosalind disguised as Ganymede in act 4, scene 1, courts Orlando as if she were Rosalind with unashamed directness and good humor:

Come, woo me, woo me; for now I am in a holiday humor and like enough to consent. What would you say to me now, an I were your very very Rosalind? (64–67)

She is also richly satirical about the romantic love in which she is embroiled: "Men have died from time to time, and worms have eaten them, but not for love" (101–2). After her charming playacting with Orlando, she confesses to Celia "how many fathom deep I am in love! But it cannot be sounded. My affection hath an unknown bottom, like the Bay of Portugal" (197–99). Her self-assurance masks her involvement, but Rosalind never seems to doubt for one moment that she will soon be united with her Orlando.

The relation of Celia and Oliver, Orlando's older brother, comes late in the play and it mimics Rosalind and Orlando's, but it is sped up and intensified. As Rosalind reports it, "they are in the very wrath of love, and they will together; clubs cannot part them" (5.2.38–40).

Much more attention is devoted to the affair of Silvius and Phebe in all its pastoral absurdities. When Rosalind as Ganymede rebukes the disdainful Phebe for her scorn of the perfectly worthy shepherd Silvius, Phebe promptly falls in love with Rosalind, which is like Olivia's falling in love with Viola disguised as Cesario in *Twelfth Night*. This is an expected spice in Shakespeare's transvestite comedy. Rosalind's superior airs and her determined plain-speaking win the haughty Phebe, who seems more attracted to insult than to servile devotion: "Sweet youth, I pray you chide a year together; / I had rather hear you chide than this man [Silvius] woo" (3.5.64–65).

After Rosalind leaves, Phebe pays a gracious compliment to Marlowe, quoting a line from his *Hero and Leander* (1598): "Dead shepherd, now I find thy saw of might, / 'Who ever loved that loved not at first sight?' " (3.5.81–82). Both Orlando and Silvius are fairly passive in the play, but Silvius goes far beyond Orlando in out-and-out servility:

> I shall think it a most plenteous crop
> To glean the broken ears after the man
> That the main harvest reaps. (101–3)

This sounds like a foolish acceptance of cuckoldry as the natural state of the male lover. As Rosalind tells Silvius later: "love hath made thee a tame snake" (4.3.71).

By their frank acknowledgment of sensuality Touchstone and Audrey are at the opposite pole from the other lovers in the play.

Throughout the play the Fool doesn't pretend to be anything except a material being, who scoffs at romantic and pastoral twaddle. When the starry-eyed Rosalind says, "Well, this is the Forest of Arden," Touchstone replies: "Ay, now am I in Arden, the more fool I. When I was at home, I was in a better place" (2.4.14–16). Touchstone is no romantic lover, which seems to be a psychological state reserved for the upper classes (or at least for devoted players in the game of pastoral), but rather a sexual being who frankly admits the existence of desire:

> As the ox hath his bow, sir, the horse his curb, and the falcon her bells, so man hath his desires; and as pigeons bill, so wedlock would be nibbling. (3.3.76–79)

He ends the scene with an impromptu song on the same theme: "Come, sweet Audrey, / We must be married, or we must live in bawdry" (92–93). One can't imagine Orlando, or Oliver, or Silvius saying something like this, no less singing it.

Touchstone, of course, is not speaking the final wisdom of the play but is only one of the many voices that make up the world of the play. There is a self-consciousness about him, however, that must have delighted Shakespeare as he emerged as a kind of meta-poet and metaplaywright. Touchstone cannot resist the irrestible pun on Audrey's goats and Ovid's Goths (pronounced exactly the same), among whom Ovid was living in exile for writing erotic verses such as his *Ars Amatoria*: "I am here with thee and thy goats, as the most capricious poet, honest Ovid, was among the Goths" (3.3.6–8). There is an additional pun on *capricious*, which means "goatlike" in its Latin derivation, and we remember that the goat was considered by Elizabethans as one of the most lascivious of animals, as in Othello's exclamation: "Goats and monkeys!" (*Othello* 4.1.261). Touchstone speaks for the play when he wishes that "the gods had made" Audrey "poetical," because "the truest poetry is the most feigning" (3.3.15, 18–19), but Audrey is a simple country lass who thanks the gods for making her "foul" (37), or ugly. This is a different kind of wooing from that of Rosalind and Orlando.

In act 2, scene 4, we see at least a three-way reflection, or perhaps "deflection," of romantic love from Silvius to Rosalind to Touchstone. We begin with the absurd passion of Silvius in his conversation with the old shepherd, Corin, as Silvius shows himself too enamored even to engage in conversation:

> Or if thou hast not broke from company
> Abruptly, as my passion now makes me,
> Thou hast not loved.
> O Phebe, Phebe, Phebe! (38–41)

Silvius exits running, but not without completing the rhyme in Phebe, in good pastoral style.

Rosalind doesn't know what to think. At first she says: "Alas, poor shepherd! Searching of thy wound, / I have by hard adventure found mine own" (2.4.42–43). *Searching* is a medical term for probing or cleansing a wound. But Rosalind is soon caught up in Touchstone's parodic humor: "Jove, Jove! This shepherd's passion / Is much upon my fashion" (58–59). The doggerel rhyme and the very short lines do not indicate that Rosalind is deeply involved. She has been detoured by Touchstone's account of his wooing of Jane Smile, the milkmaid, to whom he gave two cods (with bawdy overtones) from a peapod and "said with weeping tears, 'Wear these for my sake' " (50–51). Touchstone's recital inspires Rosalind to make the standard comment on wise fools: "Thou speak'st wiser than thou art ware of" (55). Touchstone speaks unwitting wisdom because love is more complex than anyone can fathom, and no one really knows who is a fool.

The satirical malcontent Jaques does a good deal to undercut the holiday humor of *As You Like It* and its Golden Age tone. His name was pronounced "jakes" (either a single syllable or a light disyllable), which was the current Elizabethan word for a toilet or privy. Sir John Harington had recently published a mock-heroic discourse on the close-stool or water closet called *The Metamorphosis of Ajax* (1596), with illustrations, so that the name Jaques could well have been part of contemporary discussion. Touchstone plays on Jaques's malodorous name when he refers to him as "good Master What-ye-call't" (3.3.70).

Jaques speaks in the style of verse satirists of the 1590s, such as Marston, whose works had just been ordered to be burned by the

Bishops (1599), and he provides a model for the later railings of Timon in *Timon of Athens*. Basically, Duke Senior and his court in exile seek out Jaques as an entertainer, but he takes himself quite seriously as a moral commentator whose function it is to "Cleanse the foul body of th' infected world" (2.7.60). Jaques is the only one who believes in his reforming role as satirist, while the Duke reminds him of his unsavory past:

> For thou thyself hast been a libertine,
> As sensual as the brutish sting itself;
> And all th' embossèd sores and headed evils
> That thou with license of free foot hast caught,
> Wouldst thou disgorge into the general world. (65–69)

But this doesn't curb Jaques's liberty "To blow on whom I please" (49).

Jaques is enamored of Touchstone the Clown, whom he has met in the forest and whom he attempts to imitate. We hear the astounding news that Jaques "did laugh sans intermission / An hour by his dial" (2.7.32–33), but we never see him so much as smile during the course of the play. Jaques is a self-conscious stylist and rhetorician, who speaks in an affected style associated with courtiers like Osric in *Hamlet*. The line, "As I do live by food, I met a fool" (14), represents Jaques's poeticizing, as he tries for alliteration and assonance. There is the same kind of matching of the letter in Jaques's report of what the fool said: "And so, from hour to hour, we ripe and ripe, / And then, from hour to hour, we rot and rot" (26–27). This supposed quotation doesn't resemble Touchstone's style at all.

Elsewhere, Jaques invents words that call attention to themselves, what the Elizabethans called *inkhorn*, or affectedly learned, terms. To Amiens, who has just sung "Under the greenwood tree," Jaques says: "Come, more, another stanzo! Call you 'em stanzos?" (2.5.15–16). Presumably, Amiens has a puzzled look when he hears this strange variant of *stanza*. He says only, noncommittally: "What you will, Monsieur Jaques," to which Jaques answers: "Nay, I care not for their names; they owe me nothing" (17–19), with wordplay on *names*, representing the borrower's signature on a loan. In Jaques's parody song, the mysterious word *ducdame* (49) appears three times, and

Amiens inquires: "What's that 'ducdame' "? (52), which may be "a Greek invocation to call fools into a circle" (53–54), as Jaques says, or the Welsh for "Come hither," or any one of a dozen other possibilities discussed in learned footnotes. Jaques is cunning, and he is the undisputed master of *sans* in Shakespeare, challenged only by Rosaline's "Sans 'sans,' I pray you" in *Love's Labor's Lost* (5.2.417).

Jaques cultivates a fashionable melancholy—Orlando calls him "Monsieur Melancholy" (3.2.291)—and he revels in melancholy humors. As he tells Amiens, who thinks his song will make Jaques melancholy, "More, I prithee more! I can suck melancholy out of a song as a weasel sucks eggs" (2.5.10–11). This is a surly and unpleasant image, but Jaques likes striking postures and attitudinizing. His discourse on the deer, as reported by the First Lord for the entertainment of Duke Senior and his court, is full of a mawkish sentimentality, perhaps in the ironic style of Laurence Sterne. The wounded, sequestered stag is anthropomorphized into a weeping philosopher, like Heraclitus, who "Stood on th' extremest verge of the swift brook, / Augmenting it with tears" (2.1.42–43). The melancholy Jaques busily moralizes the spectacle "into a thousand similes" (45), beginning with:

> "Poor deer," quoth he, "thou mak'st a testament
> As wordlings do, giving thy sum of more
> To that which had too much." (47–49)

This is spoken before Jaques appears in the play, and he is clearly set out as a ridiculous figure, "weeping and commenting / Upon the sobbing deer" (65–66). That's why the Duke loves "to cope him in these sullen fits, / For then he's full of matter" (67–68).

Not surprisingly, at the end of the play Jaques chooses to stay in the Forest of Arden while Duke Senior returns to his court to take up his dukedom. Jaques will converse with Duke Frederick, who has just been conveniently converted by "an old religious man" (5.4.160), because "Out of these convertites / There is much matter to be heard and learned" (184–85). We are not surprised that Jaques really enjoys his melancholy isolation and the conversational opportunities it affords. Jaques is among that significant group of outcasts in Shakespearean comedy who do not wish to be won over and have no desire to return to civilization. He clearly anticipates the melancholy Malvolio in *Twelfth Night*, but he also resembles Shylock in *The Merchant of Venice* and Caliban in *The Tempest*. None of these are the gregarious, pleasure-loving persons celebrated in comedy. It seems important to Shakespeare to have characters who do not fit into the green world of comedy and cannot be converted to a comic view of life.

Twelfth Night

$\mathcal{T}$ welfth Night, January 6, is the last evening of the Christmas festivities, which begin on Christmas Day. Twelfth Night is the Feast of Epiphany, commemorating the baptism of Jesus, the miracle of Cana, and the visit of the three Wise Men of the East, or the Magi, to the newborn Jesus in Bethlehem. It marks the end of the Christmas revels and the return to ordinary life. There is no strong internal reason why this play is called *Twelfth Night*, although we know from John Manningham's Diary that the play was performed for the law students of the Middle Temple in February 1602, and there has been speculation about a performance of Shakespeare's play on Twelfth Night itself. The subtitle, *What You Will*, resembles *As You Like It*, *Much Ado About Nothing*, and *All's Well That Ends Well* in being an *ad libitum* title to which readers can assign whatever significance they please. The subtitle certainly undercuts the ritual and religious implications of the main title.

Some critics and directors have used the Twelfth Night occasion to argue that the play is autumnal or wintry in feeling, with more than a tinge of melancholy, and not at all unabashedly comic like *As You Like It*, *Much Ado*, and *A Midsummer Night's Dream*. This is a central point of contention because the autumnal and wintry view tends to sentimentalize Malvolio and to take him at his own word. He tells Olivia in the final scene, "Madam, you have done me wrong, / Notorious wrong" (5.1.330–31), and Olivia echoes his words: "He hath been most notoriously abused" (381). Whether Malvolio has been most notoriously abused, or whether he is the well-deserving victim of a practical joke that explodes his vanity, social-climbing, and pretentiousness is the point at issue. Fabian explains that the device against Malvolio grew out of "some stubborn and uncourteous parts / We have conceived against him" (363–64), and that the "sportful malice . . . May rather pluck on laughter than revenge" (367–68).

There is no doubt that the joke on Malvolio plays itself out. As Sir Toby says to Maria, "I would we were well rid of this knavery . . . for I am now so far in offense with my niece [Olivia] that I cannot pursue with any safety this sport to the upshot" (4.2.69–73). From the point of view of the plotters, it is "sport" or game, just like the setting-on of Sir Andrew and Viola / Cesario to fight each other. Malvolio is never put out of his humor and his final line in the play is the surly "I'll be revenged on the whole pack of you!" (5.1.380). Like Jaques, Shylock, and Caliban, Malvolio never enters the world of comedy; they are all inconvertible enemies of the comic. None of these characters is integrated into the world of comedy at the end of the play. It seems important to Shakespeare to establish the fact that there are some noncomic characters who don't share in the prevailing optimistic mood of the play. This sense of a noncomic Other helps to define comic values by contrast. After Malvolio's angry exit, there is mitigation in Olivia's "He hath been most notoriously abused" (381) and the Duke's "Pursue him and entreat him to a peace" (382), but we are convinced that Malvolio can never be recovered for comedy. In the same sense, Prospero's feeling for Caliban at the end—"this thing of darkness I / Acknowledge mine" (The Tempest 5.1.275–76)—does nothing to change Caliban's determination to resume his empery of the isle and not to return to Milan. Prospero never becomes his surrogate father.

The social status of Malvolio as steward is insisted on throughout the play. He is the chief officer of Olivia's household, but always a servant, an employee, and never a noble figure like Olivia, Sir Toby,

Sir Andrew, and the Duke Orsino (who is sometimes called "Count").
Maria is also much above Malvolio in status because she is a waiting
gentlewoman (not at all a charwoman, as she is sometimes presented
in modern productions). Both twins, Viola and Sebastian, are imagined to be of gentle birth, although their exact origins are left vague.
Malvolio, the steward, is beneath all these people, even Antonio,
the sea captain, which makes his overweening social ambition so
intolerable.

This is the emphasis of act 2, scene 5, well before Malvolio
actually picks up the letter he supposes to be from Olivia. What
offends his unseen auditors so sharply is his social climbing. He
imagines himself married to Olivia—"To be Count Malvolio" (35)—
and he searches for precedents for this misalliance: "There is example
for't. The Lady of the Strachy married the yeoman of the wardrobe"
(39–40). Some annotators are sure that the mysterious Lady of the
Strachy is an actual Elizabethan person who took up with her yeoman of the wardrobe, but no one has been able positively to identify
her. Malvolio projects a wonderful fantasy three months into his
married life. He sees himself as a grand figure in his "branched velvet
gown" (48), presumably elaborately embroidered with what are now
called "frogs," with his imperious manner expressed by "humor of
state" and "a demure travel of regard" (52–53).

He is trapped by his own automatic gesture as his imagination
wanders into the style of Count Malvolio:

> Seven of my people, with an obedient start, make out for him [now
> his kinsman Toby]. I frown the while, and perchance wind up my
> watch, or play with my—some rich jewel. (2.5.58–61)

In the stage tradition, Malvolio at this point reaches to play with his
steward's chain of office, which he wears around his neck (like our
modern wine stewards), and then suddenly realizes that he would no
longer have it were he Count Malvolio. "Some rich jewel" is a feeble
substitution for the poverty of Malvolio's imagination.

When he finally takes up the letter that is lying on the ground,
the folly of his character has already been fully revealed. There is
unintended ribald humor when he gravely observes: "These be her
very C's, her U's, and T's; and thus makes she her great P's" (2.5.87–

89). This off-color punning, in the style of Parson Evans's language lesson in *The Merry Wives* (4,1) and Kate's English lesson in *Henry V* (5,2), depends upon obvious double entendres (CUT = cunt and P = pee). Andrew can only ask bemusedly to drive home the point: "Her C's, her U's, and her T's? Why that?" (91).

Malvolio then goes on to imagine himself, "With Tarquin's ravishing strides" (*Macbeth* 2.1.55), proceeding to break up Olivia's Lucrece seal on the letter. Maria has cleverly created a strongly erotic Olivia, who seals her letter with the image of Lucrece, evoked from Shakespeare's poem *The Rape of Lucrece*. Malvolio, like Tarquin, thinks of himself as irresistibly attractive and of Olivia as some insatiable nymphomaniac who cannot help pursuing him. The letter itself has many obvious sexual phrases, like the closing line: "She that would alter services with thee" (2.5.158), "services" being a word with strong sexual connotations.

Consciously, however, Malvolio is closed off to any erotic cues, and this is what makes him so inauthentic as a potential lover. When Olivia says inadvertently and out of compassion "Wilt thou go to bed, Malvolio?," he can only answer naively and without taking account of any erotic implication: "To bed? Ay, sweetheart, and I'll come to thee" (3.4.30–32). In a play where love comes so furiously and so suddenly at first sight, Malvolio is an emasculated figure like the eunuch that Viola imagined as her first disguise (1.2.56). In his long soliloquy, Malvolio reveals the baseness of his design when he says of Olivia: "I have limed her" (3.4.78), meaning that he has caught her as birds are caught with sticky birdlime placed on branches. We could forgive Malvolio if he really lusted after Olivia and did not think of her solely as prey.

Maria describes him as "a kind of Puritan" (2.3.140), and he resembles Shylock in his gravity and flight from pleasure. Shylock the Jew is also "a kind of Puritan," who instructs his daughter Jessica to lock up his doors and "Let not the sound of shallow fopp'ry enter / My sober house" (*The Merchant of Venice* 2.5.35–36). But Maria won't permit Malvolio to be even a *kind* of Puritan: "The devil a Puritan that he is, or anything constantly but a time-pleaser; an affectioned ass" (2.3.146–47). Malvolio has no convictions but is only motivated by an exaggerated sense of his own importance.

Earlier in the scene, when Malvolio enters to upbraid Sir Toby,

Sir Andrew, Maria, and the Clown for their merrymaking, he speaks in the high moral tone that he imagines appropriate to express Olivia's will: "My masters, are you mad? Or what are you?" (2.3.87). We can easily understand that Malvolio is so alienated from Sir Toby and his cohorts that, in the practical joke, they are obliged to treat him as a madman. Sir Toby has the essential answer to Malvolio: "Art any more than a steward? Dost thou think, because thou art virtuous, there shall be no more cakes and ale?" (113–15). His pretense of virtue is the sort of thing for which the dramatists of Shakespeare's time were berating the Puritans, as in Ben Jonson's Ananias and Tribulation Wholesome in *The Alchemist* (1610) and Rabbi Zeal-of-the-Land Busy in *Bartholomew Fair* (1614). Sir Toby's parting shot to put Malvolio in his place is the contemptuous: "Go, sir, rub your chain with crumbs" (118–19). This is the steward's chain of office, which he polished with breadcrumbs.

Malvolio first appears in act 1, scene 5, and almost his first words in the play are to rebuke Olivia for taking delight in "such a barren rascal" (82–83) as the Fool, who is right on stage. Olivia objects: "O, you are sick of self-love, Malvolio, and taste with a distempered appetite" (90–91). The theme of self-love has a wide application to Olivia herself and to Orsino and the kind of mannered, self-conscious love rhetoric they engage in.

Almost all critics have pointed out that the Duke Orsino is in love with love, which makes the opening scene of the play comic because it sounds like a parody of amorous discourse. The Duke is in love not so much with love itself but with himself in love and the kinds of lyrical, musical, and melancholy speeches that lovers are supposed to make. The first words of the play are:

> If music be the food of love, play on,
> Give me excess of it, that, surfeiting,
> The appetite may sicken, and so die. (1.1.1–3)

This is excessively sonorous and is remembered in Cleopatra's juicy command: "Give me some music: music, moody food / Of us that trade in love" (*Antony and Cleopatra* 2.5.1–2). "Moody food" sounds like the name of a rock group, and the professional cast of "us that trade in love" is taken up when Mardian the Eunuch enters to become the butt of crude sexual jokes. The Duke doesn't mention Olivia at all or anything about her physical attractions, which is a bad sign, and he sends his recently engaged servant Viola / Cesario to make an exaggeratedly rhetorical love plea for him. This is as inauthentic as Malvolio's passion for Olivia.

Olivia, too, at the beginning of the play is sick with a histrionic self-love as she vows to mourn her dead brother for seven years. In the first scene, Valentine, the servant of Duke Orsino, describes her plight with excessive fullness and lyrical amplification:

> But like a cloistress she will veilèd walk,
> And water once a day her chamber round
> With eye-offending brine . . . (1.1.29–31)

Luckily, we hear no further about this dead brother, and Olivia immediately falls head-over-heels in love with Viola, the messenger from the Duke, in disguise as Cesario.

In the process, Olivia archly solicits flattery as she draws the veil from her face and shows it, as if it were a work of art (anticipating the statue scene in *The Winter's Tale* 5,3): "But we will draw the curtain and show you the picture. Look you, sir, such a one I was this present. Is't not well done?" (1.5.233–35). Viola cannot resist the obvious joke on cosmetics: "Excellently done, if God did all" (236), but Olivia insists on giving out an inventoried schedule of her beauty. The shrewd Viola immediately counters with the theme of self-love: "I see you what you are; you are too proud" (251). Love is the enemy of self-love, and Olivia is shaken out of her sterile preoccupation with herself by falling so swiftly in love with Viola / Cesario.

Love works its force against one's conscious will, and Olivia seems overwhelmed by her own spontaneous reactions:

> Methinks I feel this youth's perfections
> With an invisible and subtle stealth
> To creep in at mine eyes. Well, let it be. (1.5.297–99)

"Let it be" is a deliberate acceptance of fate and fortune like that of Hamlet's "Let be" (*Hamlet* 5.2.226). Olivia's final couplet in this scene restates the idea of letting love be: "Fate, show thy force; ourselves we do not owe. / What is decreed must be—and be this so!" (1.5.311–

12). This is one of many memorable couplets in this play. Later on, when Olivia seizes on Sebastian, the twin brother of Viola, for her husband, they enact a similar couplet between them:

> *Olivia.* Nay, come, I prithee. Would thou'dst be ruled by me!
> *Sebastian.* Madam, I will.
> *Olivia.*   O, say so, and so be. (4.1.64–65)

Olivia's final line is spoken with an energetic and optimistic wonder appropriate to comedy.

Twelfth Night is much indebted to *The Comedy of Errors*, especially in its handling of the twins, Viola and Sebastian. This was John Manningham's first observation in his diary when he saw the play at the Middle Temple in February 1602: "much like the *Comedy of Errors* or *Menechmi* in Plautus." Being male and female twins, Viola and Sebastian don't exactly resemble the Antipholuses and Dromios of *The Comedy of Errors*, but on the Elizabethan stage these parts would be played by boy actors who were chosen to look as much alike as possible. This is a problem on the modern stage, which has difficulty in making credible the Duke's wonder at seeing Viola and Sebastian together:

> One face, one voice, one habit, and two persons—
> A natural perspective that is and is not. (5.1.216–17)

Audiences usually laugh at these lines because what they see on stage is hardly like the illusion created by an optical perspective toy that distorts a single image into two. Antonio, the sea captain, confirms the Duke's impression:

> How have you made division of yourself?
> An apple cleft in two is not more twin
> Than these two creatures. (222–24)

We remember, too, that Olivia has taken Sebastian as her husband without questioning his identity as Viola / Cesario. These are all farcical assumptions about the exchangeability of twins taken from Plautus and *The Comedy of Errors*.

In act 4, scene 1, Sebastian echoes the asides of Antipholus of Syracuse as Adriana deals with him as if he were her husband:

> Am I in earth, in heaven, or in hell?
> Sleeping or waking, mad or well-advised?
> Known unto these, and to myself disguised?
> I'll say as they say, and persever so,
> And in this mist at all adventures go.
> (*The Comedy of Errors* 2.2.213–17)

Sebastian draws on the same imagery and also expresses his metaphysical problems in easy and fluent couplets:

> What relish is in this? How runs the stream?
> Or I am mad, or else this is a dream.
> Let fancy still my sense in Lethe steep;
> If it be thus to dream, still let me sleep! (4.1.60–63)

Like Antipholus, Sebastian has a wonderful commitment to comedy to be able to take the unknown Olivia immediately as his wife without any further questions. Only Viola seems to be aware of the possibility that her twin brother is alive and well and that she has been mistaken for him:

> Prove true, imagination, O, prove true,
> That I, dear brother, be now ta'en for you! (3.4.387–88)

This is an obvious surmise that occurs to no one in *The Comedy of Errors*, and it marks a stage beyond pure farce in the mistaken identities of *Twelfth Night*.

The Clown, Feste, protests that he is not the Lady Olivia's fool "but her corrupter of words" (3.1.37). He is unusually adept at puns and wordplay and a kind of double-talk that has baffled annotators. He quotes the wise saying of Quinapalus, "Better a witty fool than a foolish wit" (1.5.35–36), as if he were a real authority like the rhetorician Quintilian or the satirist Apuleius, author of *The Golden Ass*. Just before this the Clown enunciated the proverbial wisdom of "Many a good hanging prevents a bad marriage" (19), which anticipates modern arguments for capital punishment. Sir Andrew, who is just as enamored of Feste as Jaques is of Touchstone in *As You Like It*, quotes Feste's "gracious fooling last night" when he spoke portentously "of Pigrogromitus, of the Vapians passing the equinoctial of Queubus" (2.3.22–24). These sound like characters and places imitated from Marlowe's *Tamburlaine* (1587–1588). Pistol would have been just as happy with this weighty nonsense as Sir Andrew.

In the role of Sir Topas, the curate, the Clown quotes learnedly to Sir Toby what "the old hermit of Prague, that never saw pen and ink, very wittily said to a niece of King Gorboduc, 'That that is is' " (4.2.13–16). Feste is wonderfully inventive, and in his priestly interrogation of the mad Malvolio—presumably a preliminary to exorcism—the Clown parodies theological mumbo jumbo. "What is the opinion of Pythagoras concerning wild fowl?" (51–52) is a trick question, since the very un-Christian Pythagoras propounded the doctrine of the transmigration of souls. The naive Malvolio answers the question correctly, but he is doctrinally wrong.

Feste is self-conscious about words, which is part of his great appeal to Sir Andrew, who is an amateur of fine expressions. To Viola / Cesario, the Clown uses the word *welkin* for "sky" instead of the more familiar *element*, as a deliberate choice of more refined diction: "Who you are and what you would are out of my welkin; I might say 'element,' but the word is overworn" (3.1.58–60). The irony here is complex since the word *welkin* was itself an affectedly poetic expression, as in Don Armado's comment to his page Moth in *Love's Labor's Lost*: "By thy favor, sweet welkin, I must sigh in thy face" (3.1.68). *Element* is the prissy word that Malvolio uses to dismiss Sir Toby, Maria, and Fabian: "You are idle shallow things; I am not of your element" (3.4.129–30). The Clown plays similarly on the word *vent* at the beginning of act 4.

Twelfth Night has a linguistic vitality and virtuosity that pairs it with *Love's Labor's Lost*. Sir Toby's *Sneck up* (2.3.94) is meant as a crushing insult to Malvolio, and this is its only use in Shakespeare. A sneck is the tongue of a gate-latch and is still current in British dialectical speech. Matched with *sneck* is the odd word *geck* that Malvolio applies to himself; he has been made "the most notorious geck and gull / That e'er invention played on" (5.1.345–46). The word means fool, as it is used in the only other example in Shakespeare, in the masque in *Cymbeline* over the sleeping Posthumus, who has become "the geck and scorn" (5.4.50) of Iachimo's villainy. The words *geck* and *sneck* have an onomatopoeic contempt built into their sound, and they help to demonstrate the rich inventiveness of language in *Twelfth Night*, whose characters amuse themselves as well as us by their lively speech.

Troilus and Cressida

$\mathcal{E}$verything about this play is puzzling. It was originally intended to be printed in the Folio in the section of tragedies after *Romeo and Juliet*, and about three pages were printed before it was withdrawn and replaced by a much shorter play, *Timon of Athens*. Presumably there were difficulties over copyright. It was then printed, later than everything else in the Folio, without page numbers (with the exception of one page) and placed between *Henry VIII*, the last play in the Histories section, and *Coriolanus*, the first play in the Tragedies. It is called "The Tragedie of Troylus and Cressida" in the Folio, but in the Quarto version of 1609 it is called "The Famous Historie of Troylus and Cresseid," and in the strange printer's preface, "A never writer, to an ever reader. Newes," it is strenuously claimed to be "passing full of the palme comicall." In an elaborate discussion of Shakespeare's comedies, *Troilus and Cressida* is said to take precedence: "Amongst all there is none more witty then this." Although it ends with the death of Hector, *Troilus and Cressida* is hardly tragic in the sense of *Hamlet*, *Othello*, and *Macbeth*. It is more like the Roman history plays, *Julius Caesar*, *Antony and Cleopatra*, and *Coriolanus*, although its ultimate source, Homer's *Iliad*, is hardly history, unlike that of the Roman history plays, which were drawn from Plutarch's *Lives*.

We fall back on the genre of comedy for *Troilus and Cressida* without strong conviction. It has been called a comical satire, as if this were an independent late-Elizabethan and early-Jacobean category, but the play is clearly allied with Shakespeare's other problem comedies, *All's Well That Ends Well* and *Measure for Measure*, in its harshness, its unflattering and cynical representation of love and sex, and its philosophical disquisitions on large, abstract topics, such as the nature of law, time, and reputation. It has obvious affinities with *Hamlet*, which it probably just follows in composition, in its misogynistic views of women and the impossibilities of romantic love as well as its biting satire. Disease imagery runs rampant in this play as it does in *Hamlet*, and in both plays it points to a world-weariness and a painful breakdown of traditional humanistic values. The base, foulmouthed Thersites comments tirelessly on the folly of the supposedly heroic enterprise of winning back Helen and capturing Troy: "Lechery, lechery; still wars and lechery; nothing else holds fashion. A burning devil take them!" (5.2.192–94). "A burning devil" is presumably a reference to venereal disease, which runs through the play as it does *Timon of Athens*.

But Thersites' abusive harangue against Patroclus, "Achilles' male varlet," his "masculine whore" (5.1.15, 17), tops anything we can find in *Timon* or in *Hamlet*:

> Now, the rotten disease of the south, the guts-griping ruptures, catarrhs, loads o' gravel in the back, lethargies, cold palsies, raw eyes, dirt-rotten livers, wheezing lungs, bladders full of imposthume, sciaticas, lime-kilns i' the palm, incurable bone-ache, and the riveled fee-simple of the tetter, and the like, take and take again such preposterous discoveries! (17–24)

Tetter is one of the words used by the Ghost in *Hamlet* to describe its sudden transformation after the poison was poured in its ear:

> And a most instant tetter barked about
> Most lazarlike with vile and loathsome crust
> All my smooth body. (*Hamlet* 1.5.70–73)

A "tetter" is defined in the *OED* as "A general term for any pustular herpetiform eruption of the skin, as eczema, herpes, impetigo, ring-worm, etc." In context, Thersites' tirade against Patroclus doesn't have much specific point, but it proclaims, in hyperbolic form, Thersites' diseased and loathsome view of the world. He speaks not so much for himself as a character in *Troilus and Cressida*, but rather for the play and its hate-filled, antiheroic implications, as both Apemantus and Timon speak for the corruption and depravity of Athens.

Like the disease imagery, food indicates disgust and establishes a tone of grossness and materiality. In Thersites' view all romantic protestations are nonsense and express only the itch of sexual desire: "How the devil Luxury, with his fat rump and potato finger, tickles these together. Fry, lechery, fry!" (5.2.53–55). The Spanish or sweet potato *(Batatas edulis)* was thought to be an aphrodisiac in the six-teenth and seventeenth centuries. At the beginning of the play, Pandarus tantalizes Troilus with the sexual attraction of Cressida in the double entendres of food preparation: "He that will have a cake out of the wheat must tarry the grinding" (1.1.14–16), and the bolting, and the leavening, and "the kneading, the making of the cake, the heating the oven, and the baking. Nay, you must stay the cooling too, or ye may chance burn your lips" (25–28). Pandarus is openly leering in one of the most overtly sexual passages in all of Shakespeare, and, like Thersites, he does a good deal to subvert the romantic possibilities of the play and to render them ambiguous and problematical.

So Troilus picks up this gross imagery and speaks of Cressida finally as a being he no longer recognizes: "No, this is Diomed's Cressida" (5.2.134). In his dualistic "madness of discourse" (139), Troilus arrives at the point where his ideal image of Cressida is dissolved into a being that exists only in the sexual terms of discarded food:

> The bonds of heaven are slipped, dissolved, and loosed,
> And with another knot, five-finger-tied,
> The fractions of her faith, orts of her love,
> The fragments, scraps, the bits, and greasy relics
> Of her o'ereaten faith, are given to Diomed. (153–57)

87

Fractions, orts, and *fragments* are more or less synonymous words for scraps of left-over and half-chewed food. The bitter and defeated Antony seems to remember this passage when he upbraids Cleopatra:

> I found you as a morsel cold upon
> Dead Caesar's trencher: nay, you were a fragment
> Of Gneius Pompey's, besides what hotter hours,
> Unregist'red in vulgar fame, you have
> Luxuriously picked out. (*Antony and Cleopatra* 3.13.116–20)

Food is a vehicle for bodily needs, and it lends itself to the sexual discourse of disillusioned love. Cressida is clearly a model for Cleopatra.

Ulysses' cunning attack on the pride and indolence of Achilles is partly couched in terms of food. His long oration on degree, or hierarchy, ends in the vision of chaos by which "appetite, an universal wolf . . . Must make perforce an universal prey / And last eat up himself" (1.3.121–24). Here eating is the equivalent of destruction, but elsewhere eating symbolizes the decay and corruption of once-noble impulses. Thus Achilles' virtues, like those of the cold and disdainful friend in the *Sonnets*, "begin to lose their gloss," and "like fair fruit in an unwholesome dish, / Are like to rot untasted" (2.3.121–23). The image of flowers or fruit that rots unseen and unused is a powerful one in the *Sonnets* (e.g., 94).

Ulysses doesn't let go of this image of Achilles set apart from ordinary mortals, and he expresses his disgust in food images. Achilles "bastes his arrogance in his own seam" (2.3.187), nor will Ulysses by going to him "enlard his fat-already pride" (197). "Seam" is fat or grease that one uses in cooking, and we remember that Hamlet in a complex pun declares: "I know not 'seems' " (*Hamlet* 1.2.76). *Troilus and Cressida* echoes some of the cooking images in *Hamlet*, especially Hamlet's disgust with grease, fat, and lard in all their connotations, most luridly expressed in the Closet Scene by Hamlet's gross images of his mother's lovemaking:

> Nay, but to live
> In the rank sweat of an enseamèd bed,
> Stewed in corruption, honeying and making love
> Over the nasty sty— (*Hamlet* 3.4.92–95)

Ulysses is drawing on Troilus's sexualized imagery, which echoes *Hamlet*, and providing a pool of agreed-upon connotations. In this way the proud Achilles can share in the same greasiness that will be later applied to Cressida.

Students are quick to observe that there is something inauthentic in the love affair of Troilus and Cressida. It differs sharply from Romeo and Juliet's because it is not innocent, it is not young, and it cannot be believably romantic because of the role of Pandarus, Cressida's uncle, who acts as a pimp to bring Cressida to Troilus. There is an element of calculation in the whole affair that is summed up in Cressida's soliloquy at the end of act 1, scene 2. Structurally, this is like the soliloquy of the villain in Shakespeare when he confesses his intentions to the audience and forswears hypocrisy. Cressida tells us directly that she is playing a game that depends on her understanding of male desire:

> Men prize the thing ungained more than it is;
> That she was never yet, that ever knew
> Love got so sweet as when desire did sue. (1.2.301–3)

This is not Juliet speaking from the overflow of powerful feelings, but a woman who has spent her life trying to understand men, and the message she delivers is chilling.

She says the same thing in different ways to justify her histrionic wooing:

> Yet hold I off. Women are angels, wooing;
> Things won are done, joy's soul lies in the doing. (1.2.298–99)

Later, Cressida will acknowledge that she has loved Troilus "night and day / For many weary months" (3.2.116–17), but this has no bearing on the way she conducts herself as a lover. As feminist critics have pointed out, Cressida cannot be understood outside her patriarchal context, in which the best she can do is manipulate her inevitable fate.

The amorous discourse of Troilus is disturbing in its mixed quality. Despite his high rhetoric, he is always talking about sex in its most physical and sensual aspect. This is fundamentally different from anything in *Romeo and Juliet*, and it endows Troilus with a hypocrisy that seems separate from his high-flown speech. Why does he need Pandarus at all, and why is Cressida so totally inaccessible without her uncle? This doubleness is established in the first scene of the play, where Troilus's romantic speeches seem to fall flat.

His tone is oddly lacking in equilibrium when he speaks to Pandarus as if he were a confidant rather than a pimp:

> I tell thee I am mad
> In Cressid's love; thou answer'st she is fair,
> Pour'st in the open ulcer of my heart
> Her eyes, her hair, her cheek, her gait, her voice . . .
> (1.1.53–56)

The disease image of "the open ulcer of my heart" is unthinkable in Shakespeare's earlier comedies, and the picture of Cressida's physical properties (which constitute her beauty) being poured liberally and irritatingly into the open ulcer of Troilus's heart makes one of the most grotesque images in the play. How can Troilus pretend to be a convincing lover? He thinks, perplexingly, of Pandarus laying "in every gash that love hath given me / The knife that made it" (64–65). This is odd. How can the body of love be conceived as a series of gashes and the attributes of love—"Her eyes, her hair, her cheek, her gait, her voice"—be the knives that made the gashes? The erotic imagery seems contorted.

In the consummation scene (3,2) of *Troilus and Cressida*, which echoes a similar love scene in *Romeo and Juliet* (3,5), Troilus's doubleness is again disturbing. He speaks like a conventional lover of Shakespearean comedy, except that the presence of Pandarus mitigates the straightness of his proceeding, so that instead of dealing directly with Cressida, he seems to woo Pandarus:

> O, be thou my Charon,
> And give me swift transportance to those fields
> Where I may wallow in the lily beds
> Proposed for the deserver. (3.2.9–12)

Pandarus is hardly the mythological Charon, the ferryman, who transported dead souls across the river Styx into the underworld, and the word "wallow" signals sensual danger.

In what sense is Troilus a "deserver," and how can he reduce

Cressida metaphorically to "lily beds" in which he will wallow? There must be more to it than that. The scene is full of perils that are echoed in Sonnet 129, "Th' expense of spirit in a waste of shame." Troilus is giddy with "Th' imaginary relish" (3.2.18) of sexual fulfillment, but he also fears "Love's thrice-repurèd nectar" (21). The erotic imagery is excessively abstract, and we are tragically aware of Troilus's certain disillusion. It is for him "some joy too fine, / Too subtle, potent, tuned too sharp in sweetness / For the capacity of my ruder powers" (22–24). In this way act 3, scene 2 prepares us for the final breakdown of Troilus's romantic illusions in act 5, scene 2.

We don't see much of Helen in the play, although she lies behind the whole rationale of the Trojan war. In only one scene do we see her directly, at home with Paris in a domestic setting when Pandarus appears and sings a suggestive love song: "Love, love, nothing but love, still love still more!" (3.1.116). In this scene Helen appears as a beautiful and well-appointed call girl amid all the physical luxuries that Paris can provide. She is Paris's homely Nell, and she speaks in the sophisticated and sexually suggestive style that we might expect. She is the obvious model for Cressida and for what Cressida will become. Paris speaks fashionably to Pandarus about Cupid and the love god: "He eats nothing but doves, love, and that breeds hot blood, and hot blood begets hot thoughts, and hot thoughts beget hot deeds, and hot deeds is love" (127–29). Again, there must be more to love than that, and this speech, as it were, prepares us for the encounter of Troilus and Cressida in the next scene. Pandarus can only answer sourly (with reminiscences of Matt. 3:7): "Is this the generation of love—hot blood, hot thoughts, and hot deeds? Why, they are vipers. Is love a generation of vipers?" (130–32).

When Troilus argues in the Trojan council scene (2,2) for keeping Helen and continuing the war, we need to keep act 3, scene 1 in mind. Troilus's searing question, "What's aught but as 'tis valued?" (2.2.52) skews the whole debate about the war, turning it into a matter of honor and personal opinion. Helen is not valued in and for herself but as a theme of honor. Troilus's vision of her is remarkably abstract:

> Why, she is a pearl
> Whose price hath launched above a thousand ships
> And turned crowned kings to merchants. (81–83)

This comes right out of Dr. Faustus's evocation of the shade of Helen, passing over the stage between two Cupids in Marlowe's play (1592):

> Was this the face that launch'd a thousand ships
> And burnt the topless towers of Ilium?
>
> (*Doctor Faustus* 18, 99–100)

Helen's lips suck forth Faustus's soul, but Troilus is not so closely engaged with his images as Dr. Faustus. Helen to him is merely "a theme of honor and renown, / A spur to valiant and magnanimous deeds" (2.2.199–200). Both Cressida and Helen remain remarkably detached figures in such a male world of war and deeds of honor. This is a paradox that Hector with his arguments of reason and good sense cannot pierce, as he finally capitulates and resolves "to keep Helen still" (191), although it leads inevitably to the doom of Troy. She is, in the words of Menelaus, her husband, "a deadly theme" (4.5.180).

The wily Ulysses is a tricky figure in the play. He speaks most of the major orations, and, like the Duke in *Measure for Measure*, he discourses on such abstract themes as time, hierarchy, and reputation. Ulysses' latinate and polysyllabic style tends to give *Troilus and Cressida* its characteristic tone of gravity, reflection, and debate of large issues, but it is also crabbed and uncolloquial, with an emphasis on the formal oration. It is probably the oddly learned diction that has impelled critics to postulate a special audience of law students in the Temple for the play rather than the groundlings of the public theater. The strange preface to the Quarto edition of 1609 makes wild claims that the play was "never staled with the stage, never clapperclawed with the palms of the vulgar," as if *Troilus and Cressida* had been set apart from all of Shakespeare's other works. The odd word "clapperclawed" is, in fact, picked up from Thersites, who speaks disdainfully about the soldiers on the battlefield "clapperclawing one another" (5.4.1). There is something about the choice and learned diction of *Troilus and Cressida* that resembles *Hamlet* in its selectivity and in the number of words that are used for the first and last time in Shakespeare and in the English language (the *hapax legomena*). Hamlet, we remember, is something of a snob about his

Dido and Aeneas play, which he calls "caviary to the general" (*Hamlet* 2.2.443–44).

As a latinate and polysyllabic speaker, Ulysses is by no means alone. The armed Prologue that begins the play speaks of "princes orgulous" (2), "deep-drawing barks" that "disgorge / Their warlike fraughtage" (12–13), and of Priam's city that

> with massy staples
> And corresponsive and fulfilling bolts,
> Sperr up the sons of Troy. (17–19)

By the time we reach Ulysses' speech in the Greek council of war, we have already heard the ponderous orations of Agamemnon and Nestor. Ulysses is both long-winded and cunning. His elaborate discourse on degree, or hierarchy, is often quoted as the model of the Elizabethan world picture, but it is rather an ideal image of how things should work theoretically, like the Ptolemaic system, and it is not really an adequate account of why the Greek war effort against Troy is stymied. The chaos in the Greek camp cannot be adequately explained because "The specialty of rule hath been neglected" (1.3.78). When degree is shaken, "Each thing meets / In mere oppugnancy" (110–11). This is the first recorded occurrence of *oppugnancy* in the English language and its only use in Shakespeare. *Insisture* is another Shakespearean coinage in this speech. Ulysses is trying to impress his auditors with his semiotic powers.

In act 3, scene 3 Ulysses is reading a book like Hamlet (2.2.167 s.d.), which he quotes to Achilles in order to make his satirical point about the fickleness of reputation. Like Polonius, Achilles is immediately put on the defensive: "I'll interrupt his reading" (3.3.93). The doctrine of use is familiar in Shakespeare from the *Sonnets* and from *Measure for Measure*. In one of the Duke's first speeches in the play, he tells Angelo: "Heaven doth with us as we with torches do, / Not light them for themselves" (*Measure for Measure* 1.1.32–33). Ulysses gives this a different twist when he tells Achilles that his author says "That no man is the lord of anything . . . Till he communicate his parts to others" (3.3.115, 117). Like the Duke in *Measure for Measure*, Ulysses lectures Achilles about Time personified, who is pictured with "a wallet at his back, / Wherein he puts alms for oblivion" (145–46).

Ulysses is not testing Achilles, as the Duke is Angelo, but trying subtly to persuade him to return to battle against the Trojans. He is not philosophical at all—he speaks in Renaissance commonplaces— but intensely practical. The "One touch of nature" that "makes the whole world kin" (174) is not some deeply humanistic trait of the Judeo-Christian tradition, but the foolish characteristic "That all with one consent praise newborn gauds" (175).

If anything, Ulysses is a self-important, ironic scoffer at the follies of human nature. With his utter contempt for Cressida when she appears in the Greek camp he refuses to recognize any tragic dimension in her story. She is simply one of "these encounterers, so glib of tongue" (4.5.58), not unlike the wily Ulysses himself. She is one of the "sluttish spoils of opportunity / And daughters of the game" (62– 63). Ulysses, too, worships the goddess Opportunity, and he makes no allowances for Cressida, who is only trying to get by. Neither she nor Ulysses understand the realities of tragic experience, nor does Troilus either, although he certainly tries. Hector is the only even remotely tragic figure in this play.

What are we finally to make of this puzzling play, which is neither comedy, nor history, nor tragedy? It is difficult to believe in the normative values uttered so eloquently, especially by Ulysses, who is canny, cynical, and manipulative. Troilus's searching declaration: "What's aught but as 'tis valued?" (2.2.52) can be interpreted as a mindless attempt to defend the status quo of honor, which paralyzes Hector's sound moral decision to return Helen and end the war. Love is a form of entrapment, as Cressida recognizes so acutely, and all the brilliant romantic professions of Troilus amount to nothing against the hard realities of the Trojan War. Is everything reduced finally to the negativism of Thersites and Pandarus? Are heroic values a wish-thinking illusion, a mask for self-seeking aggrandizement at the expense of any ethical concept of honor? We can't help leaving the play with disturbing, unanswered questions. Almost by defini- tion, the play is irritating and unsatisfying, and this may be its modern attraction when other plays seem to yield up a more rational and more coherent response. As in the case of *Hamlet*, we cannot pluck out the heart of its mystery.

All's Well That Ends Well

Probably written just before *Measure for Measure* and around the time of *Hamlet* and *Othello*, *All's Well* is not one of the merry, high-spirited middle comedies of Shakespeare (like *Twelfth Night* and *As You Like It*), but bitter and dark. Along with *Measure for Measure* and *Troilus and Cressida*, it was classified a "problem play" by F. S. Boas in 1896, one of a group that might also include *Hamlet* and *Julius Caesar*. A problem for whom? Presumably Shakespeare had a problem in reconciling folklore materials with a realistic, moral plot. Helena, the physician's daughter, is able to cure the King and to fulfill her future husband's oracular conditions: "When thou canst get the ring upon my finger . . . and show me a child begotten of thy body that I am father to" (3.2.58–60), but at the end of the play Bertram only grudgingly accepts her as his wife: "If she, my liege, can make me know this clearly, / I'll love her dearly, ever, ever dearly" (5.3.315–16). The doggerel verse suggests that Bertram is not a wholehearted and enthusiastic husband.

The audience has a problem both with Bertram as a character and with the virtuous and wronged wife, Helena, who seems over-calculating in the pursuit of her unworthy husband. The bed-trick by which she ensnares Bertram seems a legalistic maneuver (as it also does in *Measure for Measure*). We are not comfortable with the fiction of substituting one woman for another, as if in bed all women were alike (which is a powerful male fantasy).

Helena seems fully aware of the ambiguity of the bed-trick, as she explains the paradoxes to the mother of Diana:

> Why then tonight
> Let us assay our plot, which, if it speed,
> Is wicked meaning in a lawful deed,
> And lawful meaning in a lawful act,
> Where both not sin, and yet a sinful fact. (3.7.43–47)

Since she will substitute herself for Diana in bed with her husband, Bertram, this is a "lawful deed" and a "lawful act," but Bertram thinks he is seducing Diana, which accounts for the "wicked meaning" and the "sinful fact." Is Bertram worth it, or is he just a "Proud, scornful boy" (2.3.152) as the King calls him, or a "rash and unbridled boy" (3.2.29) in the words of his mother? *Boy* is as familiar a word in this play as it is in *Coriolanus*, and in both plays it has distinctly derogatory connotations. In *Romeo and Juliet* Tybalt calls Romeo "wretched boy" (3.1.132) just before Romeo kills him.

The puzzling quality of *All's Well* is best summed up in the conversation of the two French Captains in act 4, scene 3. This begins as a choral scene in which the two lords announce the supposed death of Helena and comment on Bertram. The First Lord says:

> The web of our life is of a mingled yarn, good and ill together; our virtues would be proud if our faults whipped them not, and our crimes would despair if they were not cherished by our virtues. (4.3.74–78)

This doubleness looks ahead to such plays as *Antony and Cleopatra* and the late romances.

The folktale materials are strongly imposed on the action and their simple assertions tend to conflict with the psychological complexities of the plot. There are at least two basic themes: the healing of the King and the fulfillment of the tasks. As the daughter of the famous physician, Gerard de Narbon, Helena seems to possess magical secrets by which she can cure the King, who languishes from what is said to be a fistula, presumably *in ano* and not "upon his breast," as specified in the source story in William Painter's *The Palace of Pleasure* (1575), which translates Boccaccio's tale from *The Decameron* (the ninth novel of the third day). The healing process has strong magical and theological overtones, and Helena represents herself as God's minister: "Dear sir, to my endeavors give consent; / Of heaven, not me, make an experiment" (2.1.155–56). Like the male suitors in *The Merchant of Venice*, Helena hazards all for her cure and she is willing to die if the king die, but the King himself picks up the spiritual theme: "Methinks in thee some blessèd spirit doth speak / His powerful sound within an organ weak" (177–78).

We can pick up erotic cues in this scene, as Lafew indicates in his allusion to Pandarus from *Troilus and Cressida*: "I am Cressid's uncle, / That dare leave two together" (2.1.99–100). Underlying the idea of a fistula seems to be the assumption that the beautiful Helena cures the King of impotence. He is transformed. As Lafew reports, "Why, your dolphin is not lustier" (2.3.26), which is like Cleopatra's remembrance of Antony:

> His delights
> Were dolphinlike, they showed his back above
> The element they lived in. (*Antony and Cleopatra* 5.2.88–90)

The dolphin was a symbol of youthful love that appeared often in emblem books and the "back" is especially associated with sexual prowess. Lafew repeats his wonder that the King is "Lustig, as the Dutchman says. . . Why, he's able to lead her a coranto" (2.3.42–44). In this atmosphere, the King's choice of a husband for Helena is like choosing a surrogate for himself. His affection for Helena is unmistakable.

Bertram's insufferable snobbery is a discordant note:

> I know her well;
> She had her breeding at my father's charge:
> A poor physician's daughter my wife! (2.3.114–16)

It is as if Bertram is converting Helena into Malvolio, who dreams of famous Elizabethan examples of misalliance: "The Lady of the Strachy married the yeoman of the wardrobe" (*Twelfth Night* 2.5.37–

38). But Helena is not like the social-climbing Malvolio, and she doesn't dream of being the Countess of Rousillon. Bertram's niggardly ideas work against the generous feelings of this scene that convince us of Helena's godlike powers, her modesty, and her unalterable virtue. The King lectures Bertram on his narrow social view of a fitting marriage: " 'Tis only title thou disdain'st in her, the which / I can build up" (2.3.118–19). But Bertram is strangely recalcitrant on the question of honor, like Laertes in *Hamlet*, a play written shortly before *All's Well*, in which Laertes rejects Hamlet's open desire for reconciliation:

> But in my terms of honor
> I stand aloof, and will no reconcilement
> Till by some elder masters of known honor
> I have a voice and precedent of peace
> To keep my name ungored. (*Hamlet* 5.2.248–52)

This is disappointing, and I suppose that Laertes is as disappointing a character as Bertram. We expect more from both of them.

The King goes to great lengths to win Bertram over:

> If thou canst like this creature as a maid,
> I can create the rest. Virtue and she
> Is her own dower; honor and wealth from me. (2.3.143–45)

But Bertram is not to be persuaded except by threats and a show of force, so that when he finally agrees it is only with legalistic qualifications:

> When I consider
> What great creation and what dole of honor
> Flies where you bid it, I find that she, which late
> Was in my nobler thoughts most base, is now
> The praisèd of the King; who, so ennobled,
> Is as 'twere born so. (169–74)

This sounds more like equivocation than unconditional love, and we are not surprised when Bertram leaves suddenly for the wars in Florence without consummating his marriage.

His parting from Helena is particularly harsh and ungenerous. He calls her his "clog" (2.5.55), which was a weight tied to an animal to restrict its activity, and his explanations to her are full of a bureaucratic emptiness:

> For my respects are better than they seem,
> And my appointments have in them a need
> Greater than shows itself at the first view
> To you that know them not. (68–71)

But what is most hurtful is that he refuses to kiss her when they part, although Helena asks him timorously to make some gesture of love: "Strangers and foes do sunder and not kiss" (88). Clearly her husband identifies himself as a stranger or foe.

Helena goes about fulfilling, with a businesslike practicality, the oracular tasks that have been set her in order to win back her husband. The Mariana of *All's Well* looks ahead to Mariana of the Moated Grange in *Measure for Measure*, the betrothed of Angelo and the subject of the bed-trick. But Diana and her old widowed mother are the chief figures in *All's Well*, whom Helena, disguised as a pilgrim of Saint Jaques, offers rich rewards to participate in the bed-trick:

> Take this purse of gold,
> And let me buy your friendly help thus far,
> Which I will over-pay and pay again
> When I have found it. (3.7.14–17)

Helena insists on paying well for Diana's services, and, like the rich Portia in *The Merchant of Venice*, she always seems to be upping the ante: "To marry her I'll add three thousand crowns / To what is passed already" (35–36), so that the King's offer at the end of the play to pay Diana's dowry (5.3.228) is really unnecessary. I mention these details only to underscore the good sense of Helena, which hardly seems to be necessary to fulfill Bertram's arbitrary conditions about the ring and about pregnancy. There seems to be some conflict in the play between the folkloric narrative and the psychologically developed sense of character. If Helena does indeed have magical powers, why does she need to go to so much trouble to fulfill her tasks?

In the last scene *All's Well That Ends Well* defies our expectations for a happy ending by making Bertram revert to his narrow and prosaic legalism. He is like Angelo in *Measure for Measure* in defending himself to the last against what he knows to be the truth, but *Measure for Measure* ends with a large inflowing of mercy and grace that is lacking in *All's Well*. At first Bertram is penitent and admits to his affection for Helena, whom all believe dead: "That she whom all men praised and whom myself, / Since I have lost, have loved" (5.3.53–54). He is then offered the oddly named Maudlin, daughter of Lafew, whom he accepts. But the ring Bertram gives is Helena's, a gift from the King, that Helena swore never to part with "Unless she gave it to yourself in bed" (111). The plot thickens and Bertram is taken away under guard, since the King suspects him of having murdered Helena.

When Diana Capilet (who bears the same family name as Juliet in *Romeo and Juliet*) appears with her mother, Bertram denounces and calumniates her: "My lord, this is a fond and desp'rate creature, / Whom sometime I have laughed with" (5.3.178–79), "a common gamester to the camp" (188). But Diana produces Bertram's ring and he is caught. The King accuses him: "You boggle shrewdly" (233), which implies wavering and equivocation. Finally, the once-dead Helena appears with the Widow to claim her husband because she has fulfilled all the conditions. She asks him directly: "Will you be mine, now you are doubly won?" (314), to which he can only reply with legalistic rhetoric: "If she, my liege, can make me know this clearly, / I'll love her dearly, ever, ever dearly" (315–16). He doesn't rush to take her in his arms as Claudio does the newly revived Hero in *Much Ado*, or, more passionately, as Leontes does Hermione, a statue come to life, at the end of *The Winter's Tale*—"Oh, she's warm!" (5.3.109). Instead, Bertram seems to hope against hope that the conditions he has set cannot properly be fulfilled.

The comedy ends sourly, although the King enunciates the proverbial wisdom (see Tilley, A154) of the title: "All yet seems well, and if it end so meet, / The bitter past, more welcome is the sweet" (5.3.333–34). Perhaps the last lines of the play are ironic because all yet only *seems* well. The King repeats this theme in the Epilogue: "All is well ended" (2), and we recognize that the title of the play has occurred twice before. Helena closes act 4, scene 4, with a couplet expressing her optimism: "All's well that ends well; still the fine's the crown. / Whate'er the course, the end is the renown" (35–36). She is alluding to the Latin proverb *Finis coronat opus,* "the end crowns the work," as if the happy ending she is waiting for will justify all her previous grief. At the beginning of act 5, the ever-hopeful Helena again asserts her confidence in a happy destiny: "All's well that ends well yet, / Though time seem so adverse and means unfit" (5.1.25–26). We wish Helena well but, as Queen Gertrude says of the Player Queen in *The Mousetrap,* "The lady doth protest too much, methinks" (*Hamlet* 3.2.234).

From a theatrical point of view, the most striking character in the play is Parolles, who dominates the action as Malvolio does in *Twelfth Night.* Parolles is the classic braggart and *miles gloriosus,* descended from Falstaff and Pistol. He is "Mr. Words," in a play with many symbolic French names (Lafew, Lavatch). This is the point of Lafew's wordplay: if his name is Parolles (the plural of *parole*), then "You beg more than 'word' then" (5.2.42), since "word" is singular. Like Pistol, Parolles is a notable user of odd words and affected discourse. He serves Bertram as a combination companion, adviser, and confidant, and he is always pretending to a sophisticated, confidential tone. He speaks to the young Bertram as a man of the world, who always opts for pleasure and manly exercise and is a sworn enemy of love, marriage, and responsibility. Yet it is also possible that he is merely saying what Bertram wants to hear—Parolles is always serviceable.

As we might expect, Parolles speaks grandly of war and honor and against the stale pleasures of peace:

> To th' wars, my boy, to th' wars!
> He wears his honor in a box unseen,
> That hugs his kicky-wicky here at home,
> Spending his manly marrow in her arms,
> Which should sustain the bound and high curvet
> Of Mars's fiery steed. To other regions! (2.3.281–86)

Kicky-wicky is Parolles's magnificent coinage for the spoiled wife of a uxorious husband, probably derived from the French *quelque chose* (with obscene meaning), as is Shakespeare's related word *kickshaws* (2 *Henry IV* 5.1.29), or trifles. A bit further on, Parolles asks: "Will this

101

capriccio hold in thee, art sure?" (296), as if to impress Bertram with his courtly, Italianate diction. In the same way, Parolles ends act 2 with huffing and martial encouragement to Bertram: "Bravely, coragio!" (2.5.94). Bertram is like a country yokel easily impressed with courtly discourse, as we see in *The Winter's Tale*, when the beggar and thief Autolycus tries to impress the old Shepherd and his son, the Clown (4,4).

The unmasking of Parolles is elaborately overprepared in the play considering that Bertram alone seems to be taken in by his rodomontade. Lafew sees through Parolles almost immediately and he enjoys insulting him with impunity. His military dress is just as affected as his language: "Yet the scarves and the bannerets about thee did manifoldly dissuade me from believing thee a vessel of too great a burden" (2.3.204–6). Further on, Parolles seems to be dressed in the foppish style recommended to Malvolio by Olivia's supposed letter in *Twelfth Night*: "Why dost thou garter up thy arms o' this fashion? Dost make hose of thy sleeves? Do other servants so? Thou wert best set thy lower part where thy nose stands" (251–54). There is sexual insult in "lower part," as if Parolles were making legs out of his arms and his nose were an upward displacement of his penis. Although Parolles protests that Lafew gives him "most egregious indignity" (217) and "most insupportable vexation" (231–32), it is all words and all Parolles can do is to cry out vigorously against these assaults to his honor.

But Bertram understands nothing, so that the shallowness and perfidy of his true companion Parolles needs to be driven home to him. An elaborate ambush is staged in which the cowardly Parolles, supposedly going to recapture his lost drum from the enemy, is himself captured by his own troops and interrogated. Shakespeare develops a portentous mock-language to baffle Parolles, the man of words, who confesses ironically: "I shall lose my life for want of language" (4.1.71). Shakespeare amuses himself with his protolanguage, which has floating cognates with French, Italian, and other Indo-European languages: "*Manka revania dulche*" and "*Oscorbidulchos volivorco*" (80–82). The scene continues in 4, 3, with Bertram present to witness the baseness of his sworn brother, who will tell all, insult all, calumniate all including the "foolish idle boy" (227) Bertram, who is exceedingly "ruttish" (228), or lustful. Bertram can only exclaim weakly: "Damnable both-sides rogue!" (235). There is an excess of amusing detail in these scenes—much more than is necessary to make the simple point of Parolles's baseness.

Like Pistol, Parolles shows a remarkable resilience when he is exposed. His soliloquy at the end of act 4, scene 3 shows that he knows how to deal with adversity:

> Captain I'll be no more,
> But I will eat and drink and sleep as soft
> As captain shall. Simply the thing I am
> Shall make me live. (346–49)

He is now a creature without pretenses in a play in which pretense seems to rule. Since he knows himself a braggart, he is not surprised that he has been found out. Now his plan is, in the style of the true comic hero, to make use of the time: "There's place and means for every man alive" (354).

When Parolles next appears, he is humble but witty, and he holds his own against Lavatch, the Clown, who insists that he smells strongly, while Parolles protests: "Nay, you need not to stop your nose, sir; I spake but by a metaphor" (5.2.11–12). Lavatch stands aside and is not eager to deliver a letter "from fortune's close-stool" (17–18), or privy. He, too, is a snob, but Lafew is compassionate and will help Parolles: "though you are a fool and a knave you shall eat" (56–57). Thus, for Parolles, "all's well that ends well," and he manages to thrive by his own formula: "Simply the thing I am / Shall make me live" (4.3.348–49). This is more than we can say for the other characters of the play, especially Bertram, whose fate is full of dubiety, contention, and the problematic.

Measure for Measure

*M*easure for Measure is closely related
to *All's Well That Ends Well* and appears to
follow it in composition. We know that a
play called *Mesur for Mesur* by Shaxberd was
listed in the Revels Accounts as having been
acted in the banqueting hall of Whitehall on
December 26, 1604. *Measure for Measure* is
also considered a "problem" play for many of
the same reasons as *All's Well*. Both plays are
basically unsatisfying, and most productions
of *Measure for Measure* have difficulty combining the tragic and the comic elements into
an effective tragicomedy. They are either
primarily tragic or primarily comic, with a
strong visual emphasis on the underside of
Vienna, in the style of Brecht's *Three Penny
Opera* (1928) or Carol Reed's film *The Third
Man* (1949), which is also set in Vienna. An
abrupt shift in tone occurs in act 3, scene 1
of *Measure for Measure*, when the omniscient
and omnipotent Duke, in disguise as a Friar,
suggests to Isabella how she can solve all of
her problems by the bed-trick, which is even
more mechanical and more of a deus ex
machina plot device in this play than in *All's
Well*.

The Duke's bed-trick represents a sudden
inrush of comic beneficence in a play much

in need of alleviation of tone, and the offer is one that Isabella cannot possibly refuse:

> to the love I have in doing good a remedy presents itself. I do make myself believe that you may most uprighteously do a poor wronged lady a merited benefit; redeem your brother from the angry law; do no stain to your own gracious person; and much please the absent Duke . . . (3.1.200–206)

Isabella is brought in by the Duke to heal the rupture between Angelo and his betrothed Mariana, "and the cure of it not only saves your brother, but keeps you from dishonor in doing it" (239–41). It is a wonderfully neat arrangement. The nun Isabella, who was formerly so harsh both to Angelo and to her brother, is suddenly enamored of the Duke's plan: "The image of it gives me content already, and I trust it will grow to a most prosperous perfection" (264–66).

I think we can go further and say that the bed-trick inflames Isabella's erotic imagination. In her scene with Mariana of the moated grange, Isabella dwells lovingly on all the suggestive details of her surrogate assignation with Angelo in his "garden circummured with brick" (4.1.28). This is the old *hortus conclusus* of the medieval fabliaux. Isabella jangles the keys in her demonstrative discourse: the "planchèd gate" is opened with "this bigger key,"

> This other doth command a little door
> Which from the vineyard to the garden leads.
> There have I made my promise
> Upon the heavy middle of the night
> To call upon him. (32–36)

The discourse, like much of Isabella's speech throughout the play, is full of sexual innuendo and double entendre. She seems to turn Angelo's keys over to Mariana with a certain regret.

Measure for Measure is problematic not just because of the bed-trick and the sudden movement of the action toward comedy, but also because of the Duke's character. Surprisingly, the Duke in his guise as ghostly supervisor over the action delivers many long speeches or orations on abstract topics. At the beginning of the play, the Duke in his own person speaks, with excessive elaboration like Polonius, "Of government the properties to unfold" (1.1.3). All this is spoken to the wise and judicious Escalus, described in the dramatis personae as "an ancient Lord," whose "own science," as the Duke admits, "Exceeds, in that, the lists of all advice / My strength can give you" (5–7). Why does the Duke suddenly disappear, like the folktale hero Haroun al-Raschid, in order to observe the operations of his own dukedom? And why does he appoint in his place the young and puritanical Angelo to enforce the strict letter of the law, which has been allowed to lapse?

The whole scheme seems designed to test Angelo, as the Duke explains in a long speech to Friar Thomas:

> Lord Angelo is precise,
> Stands at a guard with envy; scarce confesses
> That his blood flows, or that his appetite
> Is more to bread than stone. Hence shall we see,
> If power change purpose, what our seemers be. (1.3.50–54)

Precise was a specific word used for Puritans in Shakespeare's time to indicate their literal, pharasaical interpretation of the Old Testament, and *precisian* was a synonym for Puritan. In this speech, the Duke is already skeptical of Angelo, who is precise, cold, not compassionate, a "seemer"—presumably the Duke already knows of Angelo's trickery in slipping out of his precontract with Mariana after the loss of her dowry.

The Duke is much given to orations, even sermons, as in his speech of supposed spiritual comfort to the condemned Claudio: "Be absolute for death" (3.1.5). This is a speech of more than thirty-five lines and we may well ask why the Duke, disguised as a friar, is preparing Claudio for death when he knows that he will eventually be saved. If that is the Duke's intention, then why is he delivering this solemn discourse, which goes far beyond Jaques's Seven Ages of Man speech in *As You Like It* (2, 7) to express the preacher's *de contemptu mundi* theme that we may find abundantly in Donne's sermons? Life is personified as a worthless enterprise, and Claudio, as a bemused mortal on his way to eternity,

> hast nor youth nor age,
> But, as it were, an after-dinner's sleep,
> Dreaming on both . . . (3.1.32–34)

Claudio is almost convinced, until his sister enters and stirs him up again to secular thoughts of life and death: "Ay, but to die, and go we know not where, / To lie in cold obstruction and to rot" (118–19). As we might expect, the young lover Claudio is not satisfied with theological metaphors alone.

The Duke plays a questionable role in all these proceedings, which he himself has initiated by withdrawing from Vienna and appointing the dubious Angelo to fill his place. His strange soliloquy at the end of act 3, scene 2 is in tetrameter couplets, whose doggerel movement is made to sum up the moral situation of the play at this midpoint. He assigns to himself a godlike role:

> He who the sword of heaven will bear
> Should be as holy as severe;
> Pattern in himself to know,
> Grace to stand, and virtue go . . . (264–67)

The Duke is an exemplar of grace and virtue, unlike the false-seeming Angelo: "O, what may man within him hide, / Though angel on the outward side!" (274–75). These oddly formal and stilted pronouncements have a distinctly homiletic purpose, and the Duke will now proceed with the bed-trick and the counteraction against Angelo. As the Duke says, enunciating a kind of motto: "Craft against vice I must apply" (280). Again, there is a feeling that the omniscient God-playwright / Duke has deliberately amplified the vice in order to have a worthy antagonist for his ingenious craft.

Only Lucio has negative comments about the Duke, and his opinions are qualified by his status in the play as a "Fantastic," as he is described in the Folio cast of characters, or a creature of fantasy, extravagant, grotesque, capricious, and undependable. But Lucio turns this word on the Duke, whom he describes as "the old fantastical Duke of dark corners" (4.3.159–60), who would certainly have been compassionate enough to spare the condemned Claudio. Lucio also describes him in the same way that Apemantus describes Timon in *Timon of Athens*, as if the Duke is playing a game that he enjoys: "It was a mad fantastical trick of him to steal from the state, and usurp the beggary he was never born to" (3.2.94–96).

Lucio has a conception of the Duke that the Duke strenuously denies, protesting that he is free from the tremors and perturbations of love—a dangerous claim for a comic protagonist to make: "Believe not that the dribbling dart of love / Can pierce a complete bosom" (1.3.2–3). The "dribbling dart of love" is contemptuous of Cupid's divine powers, and *complete* suggests that the Duke has perfect armor against the feeble shafts struck by love's bow. This Adonis-like defense doesn't suggest that the Duke will be a very powerful wooer of Isabella at the end of the play, and she doesn't even bother to answer his suit. The Duke's "What's mine is yours, and what is yours is mine" (5.1.540) sounds less like a love plea to his intended than the motto of a community property state.

But Lucio secretly flatters the Duke by representing him as amorous and even lecherous. He is, after all, the "old fantastical Duke of dark corners" (4.3.159–60), not at all like the precise and cold Angelo, despite what the Duke himself claims. It is against the image of a cold Angelo who "was begot between two stockfishes" and whose "urine is congealed ice" (3.2.111–13) that Lucio sets the figure of a warm and compassionate Duke: "He had some feeling of the sport; he knew the service, and that instructed him to mercy" (121–23). The Duke in disguise protests in a remark that is universally misunderstood by audiences: "I never heard the absent Duke much detected for women; he was not inclined that way" (124–25), which doesn't mean that the Duke is gay, although, taken literally, it certainly sounds like it. The fantastic Lucio goes on to fantasticate the Duke's sexual exploits: with "your beggar of fifty . . . his use was to put a ducat in her clack-dish" (128–29).

From this point on Lucio indulges in general calumniation in the style of Parolles in *All's Well*. Lucio is no doubt malicious, and in this same scene he denies bail to Pompey and insults him, and there is a strong implication that Mistress Overdone is sent to prison on information supplied by Lucio. Many of Shakespeare's truth-speakers are unattractive and sniveling characters, such as Apemantus in *Timon of Athens* and Thersites in *Troilus and Cressida*, but the fact that Lucio is amply detestable does not mean that he doesn't reveal a dimension of the Duke that he would rather not have us know about. At the end of the play, Lucio is hardly the one unpardonable character that the Duke makes him out to be. Even the Duke can't get away with his impatient desire to marry him to the whore Kate Keepdown, whom he got with child; to whip him; and then to hang him. The context of mercy requires the Duke, even against his spontaneous impulse, to forgive Lucio's slanders and to remit his "other forfeits" (5.1.523).

At the center of the play are Angelo and Isabella, and their similarity is one point that has been made increasingly clear in modern productions. Both are extremely rigid and uncompromising, both are excessively attached to abstract moral principles, and both are clearly virginal in their sexual attitudes. When they first appear, their opening lines are strikingly analogous. Angelo's second speech in the play requests the Duke to make some further proof of his virtue:

> Let there be some more test made of my mettle
> Before so noble and so great a figure
> Be stamped upon it. (1.1.48–50)

Does Angelo suspect that the Duke secretly wants to ferret out why he is so "precise" (1.3.50), or whether he is one of "our seemers" (54)?

Isabella first appears as a nun among other nuns at the convent; she is a votarist of Saint Clare, a notably strict order of white-habited nuns founded at Assisi in 1212. Her first words in the play are therefore puzzling: "And have you nuns no farther privileges?" (1.4.1). Francisca, a fellow nun, thinks that Isabella is chafing at restriction: "Are not these large enough?" (2), but Isabella surprises her with her desire for a more vigorous curb on natural impulses:

> Yes, truly. I speak not as desiring more,
> But rather wishing a more strict restraint
> Upon the sisterhood, the votarists of Saint Clare. (3–5)

This creates an interesting first impression of Isabella, who, like Angelo, is "precise," or excessively and fastidiously strict or rigid in her conception of herself.

109

Angelo is represented as legalistic and puritanical, in the sense that he is concerned only with the Old Testament letter of the law, as Shylock was with his bond in *The Merchant of Venice*, and not with the spirit, as Portia pleads for mercy and the law of love associated with the New Testament. Shakespeare goes to some length to establish Angelo's abstract legal position. He ignores intent and motive and concentrates instead on actual infractions: " 'Tis one thing to be tempted, Escalus, / Another thing to fall" (2.1.17–18), and "What's open made to Justice, / That Justice seizes" (21–22). The argument of the guilty judge carries no weight with Angelo: "You may not so extenuate his offense / For I have had such faults" (27–28). These are the same arguments that Angelo offers to Isabella when she comes to plead for her brother, and he is made to sound like Julius Caesar at his worst, alleging only his will for what he does: "Look what I will not, that I cannot do" (2.2.52), and, further, the contradictory statement: "It is the law, not I, condemn your brother" (80). Angelo's tyrannous nature is already manifest and soon it will be transferred to the sexual sense of "will," as in Sonnets 135 and 136, having one's will with another person.

Angelo is like Shakespeare's tragic protagonists in the clarity with which he understands his evil impulses, and the sense that he stands self-condemned. In his soliloquy at the end of his first scene with Isabella he takes full moral responsibility in an unforgettable image:

> it is I
> That, lying by the violet in the sun,
> Do as the carrion does, not as the flow'r,
> Corrupt with virtuous season. (2.2.164–67)

Angelo identifies himself and his desires with the carrion, or dead carcass, as the chaste violet is identified with Isabella. The carrion lying in the sun corrupts and stinks, while the violet flowers and becomes radiant. Angelo's tyranny and his self-loathing go hand in hand, but he thinks of himself self-righteously as a saint tempted to his fall by another saint: "O cunning enemy, that, to catch a saint, / With saints dost bait thy hook!" (179–80).

Angelo and Isabella come together in many respects, despite their fierce outward antagonism. Isabella is shocked and incredulous that Angelo is sexually attracted to her, but she herself speaks unconsciously in a language drenched in sexual innuendo. I think it is important to recognize this link, which impinges on how to play the scenes between Isabella and Angelo. We have to believe that they are both innocents who don't really understand the implications of what they are saying. The most blatantly erotic lines of Isabella are:

> were I under the terms of death,
> Th' impression of keen whips I'd wear as rubies,
> And strip myself to death as to a bed
> That longing have been sick for . . . (2. 4. 100–103)

The sadomasochistic image of keen whips and of Isabella stripping herself for bed with sick longing clearly inflames Angelo. He doesn't know how to deal with this kind of coded discourse. In his confusion, he can only tell Isabella that he loves her and to plead with her to follow her natural, feminine impulses: "Be that you are, / That is, a woman" (134–35). In terms of the acting of the scene, Angelo speaks with a desperate urgency in his appeal to Isabella to act like a woman: "If you be one, as you are well expressed / By all external warrants, show it now" (136–37).

Of course, none of this is to be, and Isabella rejects Angelo's pleas with violence. Neither one can possibly afford to understand the other, but Angelo goes further toward self-expression than Isabella. Once the refusal is sealed, Angelo threatens Isabella with cruel and unusual punishments for Claudio: "I'll prove a tyrant to him" (2. 4. 169). If Isabella's discourse is full of sexual innuendo, Angelo speaks with a rhetorical directness that is almost a parody of pornography. He gives his "sensual race the rein" (160) and threatens Isabella: "consent to my sharp appetite" and "Lay by all nicety and prolixious blushes" (161–62). Where did Angelo suddenly learn to talk in this inflamed way?

At the end of the play, Isabella's unpredictable sexual passion is quiescent, and she kneels to ask pardon for Angelo at the behest of his new wife, Mariana. There is a hint of the old Isabella still as she offers an extenuating reason for Angelo's fall:

> I partly think
> A due sincerity governèd his deeds,
> Till he did look on me. (5.1.448–50)

Isabella is still aware of her own irresistible attraction, and in the same speech she uses the legalistic language of Angelo, distinguishing between acts and intents:

> His act did not o'ertake his bad intent,
> And must be buried but as an intent
> That perished by the way. Thoughts are no subjects,
> Intents but merely thoughts. (454–57)

This is not how Isabella pleaded for her brother in act 2, scene 2! When the Duke, almost as an afterthought, asks Isabella to marry him: "for your lovely sake, / Give me your hand, and say you will be mine" (5.1.493–94), we are not surprised that Isabella never answers him. By the end of the play she has entirely spent her earlier passion.

The main action of *Measure for Measure* is played out against a background of whores and pimps, prisoners condemned to death, an overzealous executioner, and a foolish constable who seems borrowed from *Much Ado*. Vienna boils and bubbles with the everyday evils of comedy, while much greater evils are attached to those in high place. The politics of Vienna seem to make it necessary for the Duke to disappear and to be replaced by an abstract, Old Testament sense of justice that cannot be sustained in comedy. The death of Claudio goes far beyond the usual perturbations of comedy and seems to verge on tragicomic extremes. Something is rotten in the state of Vienna. The dilemmas in the play are resolved by the bedtrick, which is after all merely a plot trick without any intrinsic relation to character. The seemingly beneficent Duke seems to be the tricky, lecherous schemer described by the contumelious Lucio. The mixture of all these disparate ingredients does not make for a very satisfying play, although it is one of Shakespeare's most intriguing to see performed. We are pleased with the happy ending, even though it doesn't seem fully plausible.

HISTORIES

Henry VI, Part I

Henry VI, Part I is probably Shakespeare's earliest history play, dating from around 1590, although some critics put the second and third parts of *Henry VI* before the first in time of composition. I believe, perhaps simplemindedly, that the Minor Tetralogy was written in chronological, historical order. *Henry VI, Part I* is formal and rhetorical in style, with an abundance of classical allusions that are essentially decorative in intent. In this sense it resembles Shakespeare's early plays, especially *Titus Andronicus;* Tamora in *Titus* has more than a passing resemblance to the strongly conceived Joan of Arc in *1 Henry VI* and to Margaret of Anjou, Henry's queen in this play and in the other three plays of the series. Richard, Duke of Gloucester, who eventually becomes Richard III, is an imaginative, energetic, and bold villain, who provides a model for Aaron in *Titus.*

Henry VI, Part I is conceived as part of a sequence of four plays generally called the Minor Tetralogy, in contrast with the Major Tetralogy, written later, consisting of *Richard II,* the two parts of *Henry IV,* and *Henry V.* *Minor* is an unfortunately pejorative term in relation to *Major,* and the two groups of plays are sometimes called simply the First and

Second Tetralogies. We can see a patriotic, nationalistic motive in Shakespeare's revival of the history or chronicle play in the 1590s shortly after the great English victory over the Spanish Armada in 1588. The Minor Tetralogy is Shakespeare's first determined venture in the English theater, and there is something clearly grandiose in projecting an interrelated, four-part unit. No dramatist before the 1590s had attempted anything so large and so thematically consistent, and the Minor Tetralogy is remarkable for its careful and complex construction, its close attention to intertextual details among the four plays. Without doubt Shakespeare's Minor Tetralogy influenced Marlowe in conceiving his history play *Edward II* (1592), which departs radically from his previous treatment of history in the two parts of *Tamburlaine*.

Although each play of the Minor Tetralogy is part of a larger whole, it is necessary to insist that each play is also a separate, autonomous unit, meant to be seen and understood by itself. So far as we know, the four plays were never presented together in the Elizabethan theater, as they sometimes are on the modern stage. It is helpful but not obligatory to understand the first part of *Henry VI* as an anticipation of what will happen in the other two parts of *Henry VI* and in *Richard III:* the almost total loss of France, the internal dissensions and battles of the Wars of the Roses (Lancaster versus York, the Red Rose versus the White Rose), culminating in the ascension to the throne of Henry Tudor, Earl of Richmond, in 1485, who unites Yorkists and Lancastrians and founds the Tudor line, of which Queen Elizabeth, reigning in 1590, was a direct descendant. Right at the beginning of his career, Shakespeare is doing something very politically auspicious by writing the Minor Tetralogy: he is exploring dramatically the heroic origin of the Tudor line, so that the Minor Tetralogy may celebrate the Tudors emerging triumphant from the chaotic Wars of the Roses. Queen Elizabeth would surely have been pleased with these plays and have taken notice of the new dramatist on the London scene.

All the plays in the tetralogy look backward and forward, and each of the *Henry VI* plays in the series ends with an anticipation of the play that will follow. Despite these strong indications of sequence—Shakespeare's historical miniseries on the critical events of the fifteenth century—each play is separately conceived in relation to dominant characters and historical events. Shakespeare takes great liberties with the history of the period, which he learned from reading Raphael Holinshed's *Chronicles of England, Scotland, Ireland* (1587) and Edward Hall's *The Union of the Two Noble and Illustre Families of Lancaster and York* (1548). He shapes historical events to suit his dramatic purpose, and he is especially free with chronology. One could say that he fictionalizes—or, better, dramatizes—history, if it is clearly understood that he doesn't grossly change the historical data provided by his sources.

The first part of *Henry VI* covers the period from 1422, when Henry V dies, to 1444, when the Truce of Tours is concluded with France, and Suffolk arranges Henry's marriage to Margaret of Anjou. Shakespeare pushes back the death of Talbot and his son, which occurred in 1453, to some time well before the capture and burning of Joan of Arc, which actually happened in 1431 but in Shakespeare's play immediately precedes Suffolk's infatuation with Margaret and his intention to marry her to Henry VI. This is not an accurate account of the historical events of the fifteenth century, but Shakespeare takes great pains to present the characters and the events in a dramatically coherent form.

The conflict between the houses of Lancaster and York and their adherents is deliberately exaggerated and made to resemble the feud between Capulets and Montagues in *Romeo and Juliet*, as is the conflict between Humphrey, Duke of Gloucester, and Henry Beaufort, Bishop of Winchester, and their servingmen in blue coats and tawny coats. Shakespeare invents the Temple Garden Scene (2, 4), in which the conflict of the Wars of the Roses breaks out in its literal form— Yorkists pluck white roses, Lancastrians red—but we never find out in this scene what the issues are, legal or personal, that are the basis of the conflict. The scene is vivid but impenetrable.

The "noble-minded Talbot" is entrapped by "The fraud of England, not the force of France" (4.4.36), and we see him and his son going down to heroic defeat through the failure of Somerset and York to send their promised reinforcements. It is a theme of the play that France is lost through the bickering of the English nobles. The first part of *Henry VI* makes striking use of a related set of key words: *dissension, jarring, discord, strife, broils, faction, sedition,* and other forms of these words. If we take the word *dissension* as our example, we note from Spevack's Concordance that of the ten uses in Shakespeare, six are from this play, and *dissentious* provides another example.

Act 3, scene 1 (the quarrel between Gloucester and Winchester) has four occurrences of the word along with many other strife words. As King Henry says conclusively:

> Civil dissension is a viperous worm
> That gnaws the bowels of the commonwealth. (3.1.72–73)

At the beginning of the scene, Gloucester accuses Winchester of "lewd, pestiferous, and dissentious pranks" (15), which Winchester denies with characteristic circumspection: "And for dissention, who preferreth peace / More than I do?—except I be provoked" (33–34). As Exeter summarizes the action in his scene-ending soliloquy:

> This late dissension grown betwixt the peers
> Burns under feignèd ashes of forged love
> And will at last break out into a flame. (190–92)

The "base and envious discord" between Gloucester and Winchester will "breed" (194). Exeter provides an ominous chorus to the action.

Act 4, scene 1 is another scene with a great many strife words, as we see the quarrel between Yorkists and Lancastrians unfolding in Vernon and Basset's desire for single combat. York says, "Let this dissension first be tried by fight" (116), but the King wisely refuses, especially because they are in France:

> If they perceive dissension in our looks
> And that within ourselves we disagree,
> How will their grudging stomachs be provoked
> To wilful disobedience, and rebel! (139–42)

The King is not such a bad politician, but he cannot master his contentious nobles. At the end of the play, the "sharp dissension" that Henry feels in his own breast about his marriage to Margaret and his rejection of the Earl of Armagnac's daughter creates a pessimistic feeling about the future—all of which is realized by the King's own folly.

Henry VI, Part I is notable for its presentation of strong and decisive women, which looks ahead to the powerful women of Shakespeare's comedies of the 1590s. Most remarkable is Joan of Arc, but we also have the Countess of Auvergne and Margaret of Anjou (who appears in all the other plays of this tetralogy). Let me begin with the remarkable scene of the Countess of Auvergne, in which she tries to entrap Talbot and thereby destroy the English. She lays her plot carefully before Talbot enters, and she covets fame like an Amazonian equivalent of a male warrior (like Hippolyta, Queen of the Amazons, in *A Midsummer Night's Dream* and *Two Noble Kinsmen*):

> I shall as famous be by this exploit
> As Scythian Tomyris by Cyrus' death. (2.3.5–7)

Tomyris was a queen of Scythia who revenged herself against Cyrus's slaughter of her son. She cut his head off and threw it into a wineskin filled with human blood. We also learn that the Countess, like Joan of Arc in this play and Eleanor, Duchess of Gloucester in 2 *Henry VI*, has been practicing sorcery with Talbot's portrait: "Long time thy shadow hath been thrall to me, / For in my gallery thy picture hangs" (36–37).

What is remarkable about the Countess is her vivid and slangy contempt for Talbot, whom she has long revered as "some Hercules, / A second Hector" (2.3.19–20). Now when she confronts him in person, she finds him a disappointing, unheroic figure:

> Alas, this is a child, a silly dwarf!
> It cannot be this weak and writhled shrimp
> Should strike such terror to his enemies. (22–24)

As the principal male role of the play, Talbot the actor could hardly have been a "silly dwarf" or a "weak and writhled [=wrinkled] shrimp." *Shrimp* is the comic word that Holofernes uses for the page Moth, who represents Hercules in the Play of the Nine Worthies:

> "And when he was a babe, a child, a shrimp,
> Thus did he strangle serpents in his manus."
> (*Love's Labor's Lost* 5.2.586–87)

Love's Labor's Lost is a comedy written around the same time as *1 Henry VI*, and *shrimp* is obviously an amusing, affected word.

When Talbot laughs in her face, the Countess adopts a tragic, vaunting tone: "Laughest thou, wretch? Thy mirth shall turn to moan" (2.3.44), but she is forced to put aside her heroic pose by the sudden appearance of Talbot's soldiers. Talbot is strikingly gallant in dealing with the Countess of Auvergne as a misguided lady, and asks only for wine and cates, or dainty food, to serve his "soldiers' stomachs" (80). I think the Countess of Auvergne must be most disappointed by the fact that Talbot does not take her seriously as a woman warrior in the style of Tomyris.

Joan of Arc is the most unforgettable character in *Henry VI, Part I*, but she is not the quizzical, saintly maiden of later drama, as in Shaw's *Saint Joan* (1924). Rather, she is represented by Shakespeare as a clever, well-spoken impostor like Jack Cade in 2 *Henry VI*. In a contemptuous final scene, she refuses to recognize the Shepherd who is her own father:

> Decrepit miser! base ignoble wretch!
> I am descended of a gentler blood. (5.4.7–8)

The simple Shepherd, who at first wants to die with her, is puzzled by her grand airs and ends by calling her a "cursèd drab": "O, burn her, burn her! hanging is too good" (32–33).

Shakespeare plays on the doubleness of the word *pucelle*, meaning either a girl or maid (presumably a virgin) or a drab, a slut, a courtesan, as in Minsheu's Dictionary: a "trull, or stinking wench." Thus Joan La Pucelle is either "France's saint" (1.6.29), in the Dauphin's words, or, in the words of Talbot, "Pucelle or pussel, Dolphin or dogfish" (1.4.107). Later Talbot calls her "Pucelle, that witch, that damnèd sorceress" (3.2.38), and throughout there is implied wordplay on *pucelle* (spelled and pronounced "pussel" or "puzzel") and *pizzle*, the penis of an animal, especially a bull, with punning reference to the character Pistol (pronounced "pizzle") in 2 *Henry IV*.

Talbot delights in addressing Joan of Arc as *witch*, as if this word were a kind of talisman to ward off the evils of France. When she drives the English before her to retake Orleans, Talbot can think of her only as a fiend and not as a woman warrior:

> Devil or devil's dam, I'll conjure thee:
> Blood will I draw on thee, thou art a witch,
> And straightway give thy soul to him thou serv'st. (1.5.5–7)

120

Presumably, whoever could draw blood from a witch was free from her power. Again, Talbot cannot acknowledge Joan's power as an Amazonian warrior, but must attribute her victory to the devil: "A witch, by fear, not force, like Hannibal, / Drives back our troops and conquers as she lists" (21–22). Talbot then continues with an Homeric-like simile characteristic of Shakespeare's early, rhetorical style: "So bees with smoke and doves with noisome stench / Are from their hives and houses driven away" (23–24). Like Richard II, Talbot the military hero pauses a moment for apt poetic exclamation. Again, at Joan's victory at Rouen, Talbot offers the same explanation of her power: "Pucelle, that witch, that damnèd sorceress, / Hath wrought this hellish mischief unawares" (3.2.38–39).

It is not until act 5, scene 3 that the diabolic implications of Joan's power are literalized in the stage direction *"Enter Fiends"* (7 s.d.), which echoes the medieval miracle plays, where the fiends come out of a "hell-mouth" on stage, or Marlowe's *Doctor Faustus*, which, in its original form, must have preceded *Henry VI, Part I* by a few years. Joan's fiends are reluctant to do anything at all for her, although she offers successively her blood, a member lopped off from her body, and finally her soul. The fiends are given specific, pantomimic stage directions: *"They walk, and speak not"* (12 s.d.), *"They hang their heads"* (17 s.d.), *"They shake their heads"* (19 s.d.), and *"They depart"* (23 s.d.). Joan is forsaken and her "ancient incantations are too weak, / And hell too strong for me to buckle with" (27–28). When she is captured by York, she is transformed into a Homeric sorceress from the *Odyssey*. York exclaims:

> See, how the ugly witch doth bend her brows,
> As if, with Circe, she would change my shape. (34–35)

Joan is mythologized as a "Fell banning hag" and an "enchantress" (42) and therefore rendered impotent.

Joan is eroticized in the play in the language of courtly compliment by the French, but debased to "whore" and "strumpet" by the English. In her first meeting with the Dauphin, Joan declares that she was "black and swart before," but God's mother, "With those clear rays which she infused on me," endowed her with "beauty" (1.2.84–86). The Dauphin is impressed: "Thou hast astonished me with thy high terms" (93), which echoes the "high astounding terms" from the Prologue to Marlowe's *Tamburlaine, Part One* (1587). Later on the Dauphin wants to be her "servant" and not her "sovereign" (111)—"servant" in the sense of lover, which Joan immediately understands when she refuses, for the moment, to "yield to any rites of love" (113). At the end of the scene, the Dauphin is calling her "Bright star of Venus, fall'n down on the earth," and wondering "How may I reverently worship thee enough?" (144–45). This prepares the way for the erotic debasement of Joan.

To the English Joan is a trull, a whore, and a strumpet. In her final scene, she tries to escape burning by pleading that she is with child. The English nobles make satirical capital of this admission. York exclaims sarcastically: "Now heaven forfend! the holy maid with child!" (5.4.65), which is picked up by Warwick: "The greatest miracle that e'er ye wrought. / Is all your strict preciseness come to this?" (66–67). *Preciseness*, or overscrupulousness and excessive literalness in religion, was a word specifically applied to Puritans or those who think like Puritans, as the Duke says of Angelo in *Measure for Measure*: "Lord Angelo is precise" (1.3.50). In reference to Joan, "preciseness" indicates Catholic hypocrisy and is part of a large anti-Catholic reference in the Minor Tetralogy. The Pucelle keeps shifting the putative father of her unborn child, but she makes no impression on the moralistic English lords. York condemns her finally as a "strumpet" (5.4.84). It is interesting how strong a rhetorical effort is needed in this play to put down Joan of Arc, La Pucelle. She is an Amazonian warrior who has sold her soul to the devil, denied her own father and parentage, and strumpeted her body to a whole succession of perfidious French nobles. Shakespeare mounts a kind of overkill for Joan.

In the final scenes of the play, Margaret of Anjou is set up as a successor to Joan, and she will continue to flourish in the next three parts of the tetralogy. The scene with Suffolk is strangely courtly and unhistorical, as if it properly belonged in one of Shakespeare's romantic comedies. *"With Margaret in his hand"* (5.3.44 s.d.) as his prisoner, Suffolk falls in love at first sight and *"Gazes on her"* (45 s.d.). Love enters through the eye, and Suffolk speaks as one smitten:

> O fairest beauty, do not fear nor fly!
> For I will touch thee but with reverent hands;

I kiss these fingers for eternal peace
And lay them gently on thy tender side. (46–49)

In many amorous asides, Suffolk wonders at his own condition. He speaks as a conventional lover, and it is interesting that one of his lines is almost exactly echoed by Demetrius in *Titus Andronicus:*

Suffolk. She's beautiful and therefore to be wooed;
    She is a woman, therefore to be won. (5.3.78–79)
Demetrius. She is a woman, therefore may be wooed;
    She is a woman, therefore may be won . . . (2.1.82–83)

The married Suffolk finally arranges to woo Margaret as a wife for Henry VI, but also to keep her as his paramour.

Margaret plays a strange role in this scene. She utters the conventional platitudes of a young virgin, but she also seems to consent completely to Suffolk's arrangement. Her response to Suffolk's amorous asides is to play coy: "He talks at random; sure, the man is mad" (5.3.85). In the next round, she seems to overhear Suffolk's aside that he will win Lady Margaret for his king: "Tush, that's a wooden thing!" (89). She answers oddly: "He talks of wood: it is some carpenter" (90). Clearly she knows, from his armor alone no less than from his speech, that Suffolk is not a carpenter. When he ventures to kiss her before parting, we are reminded of Cressida being kissed all around by the officers in the Greek camp (*Troilus and Cressida* 4, 5). Suffolk says, "And this withal," and Margaret answers: "That for thyself; I will not so presume / To send such peevish tokens to a king" (183–85). There is something ominous about this scene. Margaret is not one of the "daughters of the game," as Ulysses calls Cressida, but she is definitely one of the "sluttish spoils of opportunity" (*Troilus and Cressida* 4.5.62–63) in this context of the fortunes of war. As a captured French princess she may be a spoil of war, but she knows how to make use of her opportunity.

Henry VI, Part II

The second part of *Henry VI* covers the period from Margaret of Anjou's arrival in England to marry the king in 1445 to the first open battle of the Wars of the Roses, the Duke of York's victory at St. Albans in 1455. Shakespeare does some shifting of chronology to emphasize the main lines in the tetralogy. York's son Richard, who later becomes Richard III, is seen as a fully functioning warrior at the battle of St. Albans, although he was actually only two years old at the time. Clifford is already referring to him, prophetically, as "foul indigested lump, / As crooked in thy manners as thy shape!" (5.1.157–58), and to Young Clifford he is a "Foul stigmatic" (215), a deformed person as it were branded by God. The disgrace of Gloucester's wife, Eleanor, is moved forward from 1441 so that Queen Margaret can participate in it as part of a general conspiracy against Gloucester. The ending of the play is extremely inconclusive and needs Part Three to complete it.

One feels that Part Two of *Henry VI* is deeply embedded in the tetralogy context, with one play preceding it and two to follow. The witchcraft of Gloucester's wife Eleanor definitely imitates Joan of Arc's in Part I, especially act 5, scene 3, where fiends actually appear to Joan, although they refuse to help her. Act 1, scene 4 of 2 *Henry VI* has the witch Margery Jourdain coming to Eleanor to conjure with the help of Roger Bolingbroke and two Catholic priests, John Hum and John Southwell, who are in the pay of Gloucester's enemies. After "*It thunders and lightens terribly*" (1.4.23 s.d.), a Spirit named Asnath appears and speaks oracularly about the future. Like all diabolic spirits in Shakespeare, especially those in *Macbeth*, Asnath is disappointing and there is a touch of petulant annoyance in Bolingbroke's final exclamations: "Descend to darkness and the burning lake! / False fiend, avoid!" (40–41). One wonders why Bolingbroke, the conjurer, is surprised to find him a "False fiend."

Eleanor has been tricked, and her lyrical ambitions for her husband are bitterly punished. Her first lines in the play are glowingly mythological:

> Why droops my lord, like over-ripened corn
> Hanging the head at Ceres' plenteous load? (1.2.1–2)

All that Gloucester, the Lord Protector of the King, needs to do is to "Put forth thy hand, reach at the glorious gold" (11), presumably of the royal crown. Eleanor seems rapt in a poetic vision of kingship in which everything is exceedingly easy. Her next line is: "What, is't too short? I'll lengthen it with mine" (12).

Her disgrace is the tenderest and most touching scene in the play, as she enters with an armed guard, "*barefoot, and a white sheet about her, with a wax candle in her hand, and verses written on her back and pinned on*" (2.4.16 s.d.). Her husband, who will soon be murdered (3, 2), has only pity for her as he awaits her coming with his men, all in "*mourning cloaks*" (2.4. s.d.): "Uneath [=scarcely] may she endure the flinty streets, / To tread them with her tender-feeling feet" (8–9). Although the scene is permeated with disgrace and death, the innocent Gloucester clings to the belief that his enemies cannot do him any harm "So long as I am loyal, true and crimeless" (63). This is to ignore the political lessons of the history plays.

In this scene of Eleanor's disgrace we come to appreciate the power of the mob, which is highly developed in this play and anticipates later plays, especially *Julius Caesar* and *Coriolanus*. The people are fickle in their political beliefs and can be easily swayed by unscrupulous leaders. Throughout Shakespeare the rabble are represented as crucial to political success—"Off goes his bonnet to an oyster-wench" (*Richard II* 1.4.31), says Richard contemptuously of the popular Bolingbroke who will become Henry IV—but ordinary people are often depicted as highly emotional and without any ideology or morality. The scene of Eleanor's disgrace already anticipates the cruelty of the commons, who regard politic events as if they were theater. Gloucester knows that his "Sweet Nell" with her noble mind can badly tolerate "The abject people gazing on thy face / With envious looks, laughing at thy shame" (2.4.11–12), and Eleanor notes "how the giddy multitude do point, / And nod their heads, and throw their eyes" (21–22) on her husband. The Duchess is aware that the rabble "rejoice / To see my tears and hear my deep-fet groans" (32–33), as if she were performing her grief for their benefit. But she herself feels her shame acutely and knows that it cannot be "shifted with my sheet" (107). The rabble are a kind of chorus for what is going on in Eleanor's own mind.

The second part of *Henry VI* has a surprising array of commoners, both high and low, pitted against the nobility, and the play develops a theme of class war that is not so vividly seen again until the bitter conflict of plebeians and patricians in *Coriolanus*. Shakespeare is hardly an apologist for patrician values or for the nobility, but he represents the plebeians or rabble or mob, especially in the Jack Cade scenes, with grotesque humor. Saunder Simpcox and his wife are pious frauds and Peter Thump and Thomas Horner are merely tools in the hands of the nobles. The political issues are deliberately balanced so that there is abundant absurdity and chicanery on both sides, but it is significant that Shakespeare so fully dramatizes popular discontent in this play, in *Julius Caesar*, and especially in *Coriolanus*, which seems to reflect his awareness of riots then taking place in England over the enclosure of pasture land. Political acts on both sides seem to be firmly set against moral and ethical acts, and there is already in the Minor Tetralogy a strong sense of the contamination of politics. In Elizabethan English *politic* had a sinister sense defined by the *OED* as "Scheming, crafty, cunning; diplomatic, artfully contriving or contrived." A politician practiced "policy," which already had a pejorative meaning in the late Middle Ages, well before Machiavelli's *The Prince* (1513).

Walter Whitmore and the Lieutenant who commands the pirates in act 4, scene 1 are educated and well-spoken men, hardly rabble, but their deadly animus against the Duke of Suffolk shapes the values of the play. Unlike most other commoners, the Lieutenant and Walter Whitmore speak in a noble verse, full of literary and mythological allusions. The Lieutenant, who distributes prisoners for ransom, begins the scene in a Senecan poetic style like that of early Elizabethan tragedies:

> The gaudy, blabbing and remorseful day
> Is crept into the bosom of the sea,
> And now loud-howling wolves arouse the jades
> That drag the tragic melancholy night . . . (4.1.1–4)

The pirates in *Hamlet* and in *Pericles* do not speak in this portentous, overblown way that sounds like parody. The Lieutenant advises Whitmore to take ransom for his prisoner, but Walter, who claims to be a gentleman, is intent upon revenge: "I lost mine eye in laying the prize aboard, / And therefore to revenge it shalt thou die" (25–26). Suffolk is so puffed up with his own importance that he proceeds to ensure his own death. He thinks of himself as god-like: "Jove sometime went disguised, and why not I?" (48).

Suffolk raises the specter of class war by his vile excoriation of both the Lieutenant and Whitmore:

> Obscure and lousy swain, King Henry's blood,
> The honorable blood of Lancaster,
> Must not be shed by such a jaded groom. (4.1.50–52)

The Lieutenant and Whitmore are hardly "grooms," or servants, but Suffolk is carried away by the symbols of nobility. His contumelious words only infuriate the pirates. Suffolk's "Base slave" (67) to the Lieutenant unleashes a flood of political judgments. The Lieutenant's attack on Suffolk sounds like a summary of the evils of the Wars of the Roses, including the King's shameful marriage to Margaret of Anjou:

127

And wedded be thou to the hags of hell,
For daring to affy a mighty lord
Unto the daughter of a worthless king . . . (79–81)

But the foolish Suffolk can only insist on his rank, as if it protected him magically like the divine right of kings: "It is impossible that I should die / By such a lowly vassal as thyself" (4.1.110–11). And later he exclaims: "Great men oft die by vile besonians" (134), which he backs up by historical examples including: "Brutus' bastard hand / Stabbed Julius Caesar" (136–37). By the time of *Julius Caesar*, Shakespeare has a very different conception of Brutus—there is no longer any hint that he may be the bastard son of Caesar.

Let me look at two more examples of commoners in the play before I go on to Jack Cade and his army, who dominate the fourth act. The scene with the beggar Saunder Simpcox and his wife is intended to show up the folly of the King and the shrewdness of Gloucester, who sees through Saunder's pretenses to be cured of blindness but yet to be lame. Gloucester knows him to be "A subtle knave" (2.1.104), but to the King he is an example of God's providential workings and the restoration of his sight provides an occasion to "glorify the Lord" (75). Gloucester explodes Saunder's "miracle" and he cures him of lameness by sending for a beadle with whips. Both Saunder and his wife are charlatans preying on the gullible King, and Gloucester enriches the context by quoting a line from Kyd's *The Spanish Tragedy* (1587), an enormously popular play of a few years earlier: "My masters of Saint Albans, / Have you not beadles in your town, / And things called whips?" (135–37). Gloucester, the political realist, will soon be destroyed by his enemies.

The incident where Peter Thump the apprentice accuses his master, Thomas Horner the armorer, of treason is also a grotesque rendering of the absurdity of the political positions of ordinary citizens. Peter charges his master with "saying that the Duke of York was rightful heir to the crown" (2.1.27–28), and in the single combat that they are egged on to in imitation of their betters, Horner enters egregiously drunk and Peter is drinking heavily too. The upper-class tournament is turned into a farcical, drunken brawl in which Peter kills his master. Does this trial by combat prove, as the King says, that "God in justice hath revealed to us / The truth and innocence of this poor fellow" (2.3.102–3), Peter? Or is the whole masquerade a demonstration of the political issues of the play: that the Duke of York is temporizing his own determined claim to the throne? The absurdly caricatured commoners are used to work out the machinations of the nobles. Suffolk manipulates Peter and his master for his own purposes.

Practically all of act 4 is devoted to Jack Cade and his almost successful rebellion against the throne. A stage direction in act 4, scene 2 sets the tone for our frightening sense of the rabble, or *"rabblement"* (4.8 s.d.), who support Jack Cade: *"Enter Cade, Dick [the] Butcher, Smith the Weaver, and a Sawyer, with infinite numbers"* (4.2.31 s.d.). *"Infinite numbers"* is an excellent example of an authorial rather than a practical stage direction. These scenes offer a remarkable preparation for the mob in *Julius Caesar,* including the grotesque scene where the mob murders Cinna the Poet, deliberately mistaking him for Cinna the Conspirator (3, 3). In *2 Henry VI,* Dick the Butcher announces: "The first thing we do, let's kill all the lawyers" (4.2.75), and Cade condemns to death the clerk of Chatham because he can write and read. When he confesses that he doesn't have a mark to himself, "Like an honest plain-dealing man" (100–101), but can actually sign his name, all shout out that he is a villain and a traitor and Cade orders him to be hanged "with his pen and ink-horn about his neck" (106–7). Cade and his mob are violent and murderous, but also capricious and grotesque. The Cade scenes are full of clownlike routines that end both in laughter and in arbitrary death. They are Shakespeare's contribution to black comedy.

Cade is full of utopian propositions that will aid the commoners. He *"strikes his sword on London Stone"* (4.6 s.d.) and decrees that "the pissing-conduit run nothing but claret wine this first year of our reign" (3–4). The pissing-conduit, so called, was a place near the Stokes Market where the lower classes in London fetched drinking water. Cade's next decree is that "it shall be treason for any that calls me other than Lord Mortimer" (5–6). A soldier who comes running in calling him Jack Cade is immediately killed, and Smith the Weaver says judiciously: "If this fellow be wise, he'll never call ye Jack Cade more: I think he hath a very fair warning" (9–10). Jack Cade's mob is conceived as a bunch of witty clowns, farcically remote from any sense of authentic history.

In Jack Cade's encounter with Sir Humphrey Stafford and his brother, there is the same sort of snobbery and class hatred as Suffolk shows to Walter Whitmore and the Lieutenant. Stafford lacks the political acumen of Menenius in *Coriolanus*, and he can only deal with the plebeians by insult:

> Rebellious hinds, the filth and scum of Kent,
> Marked for the gallows: lay your weapons down.
> Home to your cottages, forsake this groom! (4.2.119–21)

"Groom," or base, ignoble fellow or servant, is the word that Suffolk used more than once for the pirates, and Stafford drives home his point by insisting on Cade's genealogy: "Villain, thy father was a plasterer, / And thou thyself a shearman" (129–30). Cade answers cleverly: "And Adam was a gardener" (131).

Stafford pretends to be amazed at the ignorance of the rabble: "And will you credit this base drudge's words, / That speaks he knows not what?" (4.2.148–49). Cade knows how to speak to his followers in a way that will command instant assent, and the dialogue follows the predictable interchanges of clowns in Shakespeare's early comedies. Cade declares Lord Say a traitor because he can speak French and defends it with clown's logic: "can he that speaks with the tongue of an enemy be a good counselor?" (168–70). Soon the Staffords, for all their condescending bluster, will be killed and Cade and his rabble will seem invincible. What undoes Cade are the fickleness and giddiness of the mob, who are easily swayed and cannot keep to their convictions for very long.

One curious stylistic feature of this play is the extended wordplay on proper names. This is a primitive kind of wit, which is absent in Shakespeare's more mature style. In the first scene, the Duke of York angrily accuses Suffolk of betraying England by marrying King Henry to Margaret of Anjou:

> For Suffolk's duke, may he be suffocate
> That dims the honor of this warlike isle! (1.1.124–25)

Later, Suffolk is attacked under his family name, William de la Pole. The Lieutenant of the Pirates makes a complex pun on *Pole* pronounced Poole, meaning "poll," to strike off his head ("poll" = head) and *pool*, or cesspool, expanded as "kennel, puddle, sink, whose filth and dirt / Troubles the silver spring where England drinks" (4.1.71–72). The names are made to be emblematic of the persons.

The name Cade is played on by Dick the Butcher, who has a series of clown's asides that puncture his master's pretensions. When Cade proclaims: "We John Cade, so termed of our supposed father—," Dick comments aside: "Or rather, of stealing a cade of herrings" (4.2.32–34), a cade being a barrel of five hundred herrings. The puns continue in Cade's next statement: "For our enemies shall fall before us" (35), with wordplay on the Latin sense of the verb *cadere*, to fall.

Like a true Shakespearean villain, and certainly like Richard III, Cade is merry and sardonic throughout and is constantly engaged in extravagant wordplay. Lord Say, unfortunately, has a name that also refers to silk cloth, resembling serge, which provides an excellent opportunity for Cade's ingenuity: "Ah, thou say, thou serge, nay, thou buckram lord, now art thou within point-blank of our jurisdiction regal!" (4.7.24–28). There is a descending order of materials, starting with the silk say, going on to the coarser serge, and ending with buckram, made of coarse linen stiffened with glue and used for bags, curtains, and theatrical properties.

Henry VI, Part II ends inconclusively with a victory of the Yorkists at St. Albans, and the emergence of a savage and inhuman Richard, Duke of Gloucester (later to be Richard III). King Henry is pious and ineffective, without any real political sense of what is going on. When Alexander Iden enters with Cade's head, the King exclaims: "The head of Cade! Great God, how just art Thou!" (5.1.68), without any sense of who his real enemies are. This recalls his mistaken judgment of the fraudulent Saunder Simpcox, whom the King asks to explain the circumstance of his restored sight, "That we for thee may glorify the Lord" (2.1.75). Like Richard II, the King pleads with Salisbury to show him the respect appropriate to royalty: "For shame! In duty bend thy knee to me, / That bows unto the grave with mickle age" (5.1.173–74). But Salisbury has transferred his allegiance to the Duke of York. King Henry is not tragic at all, but merely pathetic. His power is transferred to Queen Margaret, and he is merely a spectator of the dire events around him.

Henry VI, Part III

$\mathcal{T}$he third part of *Henry VI* is undoubtedly Shakespeare's most military play. It opens
in 1455 after the Yorkist victory at St. Albans, but the early events are actually those
of 1460. It ends in 1471 after the Battle of
Tewkesbury with the banishment of Queen
Margaret, the reestablishment of Edward IV
as king, and the powerful emergence of his
brother, Richard, Duke of Gloucester, who
is to become Richard III. *Henry VI, Part III*
compresses the major battles of the Wars of
the Roses, which are not to end until the
defeat and death of Richard III in 1485 and
the emergence of Henry, Earl of Richmond,
the first of the Tudor line, as King Henry
VII in 1485. King Henry VI delivers a curious set piece about Richmond in 4.6.68–76:
"This pretty lad will prove our country's bliss"
(70). These lines are clearly designed to serve
the needs of the tetralogy, since they have
no relevance to their immediate context.

The first scene of 3 *Henry VI* sets the tone
for this murderous, savage, and chaotic play.
In the first line, Warwick wonders "how the
King escaped our hands" (1.1.1) after the
Battle of St. Albans, and the Yorkists are
intent on murdering him. York's sons demonstrate their prowess visually. Edward shows
his bloody sword from his encounter with

the Duke of Buckingham: "I cleft his beaver with a downright blow" (12), and Richard, in a startling gesture, throws down the Duke of Somerset's head. They are vying for their father's favor, who declares that "Richard hath best deserved of all my sons" (17). York then goes up to sit in the royal throne, where King Henry finds him when he enters. Henry is coerced to surrender the succession to York and to disinherit his own son. The scene ends with the rage of Queen Margaret, who calls Henry "timorous wretch" (23) and divorces herself from his bed and board. She will regain by force what her husband has so blithefully given away. The stage is now set for violent internal conflict.

Act 2, scene 5 powerfully enacts a symbolic tableau of the Son that hath killed his Father and the Father that hath killed his Son. This is a choral scene intended to represent what the savagery of the Wars of the Roses is all about. The Son and the Father enter from opposite doors at the same time in the Folio direction, as if they are characters in a medieval morality play. Both the Son and the Father are eager for spoil, and the baseness of their motives for killing each other underscores the tragic irony. The Son says:

Ill blows the wind that profits nobody.
This man, whom hand to hand I slew in fight,
May be possessèd with some store of crowns . . . (55–57)

Similarly, the Father says:

Thou that so stoutly hath resisted me,
Give me thy gold, if thou hast any gold;
For I have bought it with an hundred blows. (79–81)

The shock of recognition makes for a powerful scene.

The Son exclaims in horror: "Who's this? O God! it is my father's face, / Whom in this conflict I, unwares, have killed" (2.5.61–62), and he can only pray for forgiveness: "Pardon me, God! I knew not what I did" (69). The Father has an even more general condemnation of war and its butchery:

O, pity, God, this miserable age!
What stratagems, how fell, how butcherly,

133

> Erroneous, mutinous and unnatural,
> This deadly quarrel daily doth beget! (88–91)

In a play that is so overly personal and dynastic, this memorable scene rises above the petty vindictiveness of the quarrels of Yorkists and Lancastrians.

King Henry VI, sitting alone on his molehill as observer of the tragic spectacle, acts as a chorus to this scene. It is a "piteous spectacle," and these are "bloody times" (2.5.73), in which weeping is the only recourse: "Let our hearts and eyes, like civil war, / Be blind with tears, and break o'ercharged with grief" (77–78). Notice that Henry makes civil war a simile for intense weeping. For the Father, Henry can only exclaim:

> O, pity, pity, gentle heaven, pity!
> The red rose and the white are on his face,
> The fatal colors of our striving houses . . . (96–98)

The whole scene is set in the context of the King's pastoral soliloquy, which provides clues for speeches of King Richard II and for later speeches in *Henry V*, contrasting the cares of the king with the simple sleepfulness of ordinary men:

> Gives not the hawthorn-bush a sweeter shade
> To shepherds looking on their silly sheep,
> Than doth a rich embroidered canopy
> To kings that fear their subjects' treachery? (2.5.42–45)

Suddenly, Henry emerges as a figure of tragic stature, which we don't see much of elsewhere in the play. This quiet scene differs sharply from the intrigue, business, and violence elsewhere.

More typical of this play are the scenes immediately following the Battle of Wakefield, in which Rutland and his father, the Duke of York, are killed. Edmund, Earl of Rutland, who was born in 1443, is made a child by Shakespeare, so that his murder in 1460 will seem that much more savage. In act 1, scene 3, Rutland enters with his Tutor, who speaks two memorable lines before he is driven off the stage:

Ah, Clifford, murder not this innocent child,
Lest thou be hated both of God and man! (8–9)

This is like Herod's slaughter of the innocents, a favorite subject in medieval, pageant-wagon drama, but Clifford is so impelled by revenge for his father that he cannot listen to Rutland's pleas:

Sweet Clifford, hear me speak before I die.
I am too mean a subject for thy wrath;
Be thou revenged on men, and let me live. (18–20)

Clifford feels sorry for him and calls him "poor boy" (21), but he must pursue like a Fury his relentless revenge against the house of York. Rutland dies speaking a full line in Latin from Ovid's *Heroides*, which Shakespeare must have thought a triumph of his excellent grammar school education.

The murder of Prince Edward, the young son of King Henry VI and Queen Margaret, parallels the killing of Rutland. It continues the slaughter of the innocents theme. Among the sons of the Duke of York there is an unexampled savagery of which Richard, Duke of Gloucester, is only the leader. The young Edward voices predictable complaint when he is stabbed by all the sons of York:

Lascivious Edward, and thou perjured George,
And thou misshapen Dick, I tell ye all
I am your better, traitors as ye are:
And thou usurp'st my father's right and mine. (5.5.34–37)

The sons of York react with a wild and almost mechanical violence. Edward begins: "Take that, the likeness of this railer here" (38), then stabs him, followed by Richard: "Sprawl'st thou? Take that, to end thy agony" (39), and concluded by Clarence: "And there's for twitting me with perjury" (40). Richard is ready to go on to stab Queen Margaret, when his brother Edward restrains him: "Hold, Richard, hold; for we have done too much" (43). Richard is unconvinced: "Why should she live, to fill the world with words?" (44). It's as if Richard is predicting Margaret's role in the next play!

Queen Margaret mourns for her murdered son in powerful images of grief. The assassination of Caesar was no offense in comparison with this, because this murder is an unnatural and nonpolitical act: "men ne'er spend their fury on a child" (5.5.57). Margaret's "You have no children, butchers! If you had, / The thought of them would have stirred up remorse" (63–64) looks forward to Macduff's "He has no children" (4.3.216) in *Macbeth*. Shakespeare is powerfully attached to the theme of the murder of children, which occurs repeatedly in his history plays and tragedies. Although the theme is not fully developed in this play, its essential assumptions are laid out: the slaughter of innocent children who are caught up in political conflict emphasizes the cruelty and senselessness of that conflict. Both Rutland and Edward are swept away by events over which they have no control.

To return to the opening scenes of the play, the humiliation and murder of the Duke of York after the Battle of Wakefield continue a pattern of violence and retribution that was begun in the first part of *Henry VI* and will only end with the death of Richard III and the establishment of Richmond as Henry VII at the conclusion of *Richard III*. There is a pointlessness and futility in the Wars of the Roses that is much emphasized in Shakespeare, far beyond the warrant of actual history. When the Duke of York is captured, Queen Margaret postpones his death so that she can insult him and triumph over him with vicious glee: "Stamp, rave, and fret, that I may sing and dance. / Thou wouldst be fee'd, I see, to make me sport" (1.4.90–92). She anticipates Tamora, Queen of the Goths, in *Titus Andronicus* in her frenzied thirst for revenge.

The final line of her long speech bristles with archaic cruelty: "And whilst we breathe, take time to do him dead" (1.4.108). Her speech is full of self-conscious, revenge rhetoric, and her line, "Alas, poor York" (84) is almost exactly duplicated phonetically in Hamlet's "Alas, poor Yorick" (*Hamlet* 5.1.183–84). In this early play Margaret performs the role of revenger with histrionic amplification. She makes York stand upon a molehill (like Henry VI in act 1, scene 5), and asks him to wipe his tears with the bloody handkerchief ("napkin") "That valiant Clifford, with his rapier's point, / Made issue from the bosom" (1.4.80–81) of his son, Rutland. This is grotesquely cruel. Margaret's final gesture is to place a paper crown on York's head to complete his humiliation. Shakespeare is obviously remembering sensational revenge plays such as Kyd's *Spanish Tragedy* of a few years earlier. The murders in 3 *Henry VI* are as memorable in their aesthetic ingenuity as is the inflatedly eloquent revenge rhetoric. It is not enough merely to butcher someone—it has to be executed artistically. This histrionic glamour endows the murders with an unforgettable appropriateness. Margaret appeals to posterity, like the poet writing sonnets, to be remembered for her deeds. The Revenger provides a heroic model comparable to the Artist, the Actor, and the Playwright.

We begin to pity the oppressed York in act 1, scene 4, as we pity Margaret in the scene in which her son Edward is butchered (5,5), since the cruelty and violence of Yorkists and Lancastrians in this play are so symmetrical. York in his scene of agony curses Margaret in a memorable, bombastic line parodied by Robert Greene: "O tiger's heart wrapped in a woman's hide!" (1.4.137). In his *Groatsworth of Wit* (1592), Greene attacked the young Shakespeare, who was having an unaccountable success in the London theaters, as an "upstart Crow, beautified with our feathers, that with his *Tygers hart wrapt in a Players hide*, supposes he is as well able to bombast out a blanke verse as the best of you." Obviously, Greene envied Shakespeare's ability to make York's speeches so powerful. They are strong, perhaps overwritten, but passionate nevertheless.

York wants to deny that Margaret is a woman by the standard gender definitions of the time:

> Women are soft, mild, pitiful, and flexible;
> Thou stern, obdurate, flinty, rough, remorseless. (1.4.141–42)

His tears "are my sweet Rutland's obsequies, / And every drop cries vengeance for his death" (147–48). Even Northumberland weeps for York's "passions," "To see how inly sorrow gripes his soul" (171). But as Northumberland is "weeping-ripe" (172), in the scornful words of Margaret, she and Clifford proceed to stab York to death, and Margaret orders his head cut off and set on York gates, with a gruesome pun: "So York may overlook the town of York" (180).

Richard, Duke of Gloucester, enters significantly into the third part of *Henry VI*, and two of his long soliloquies are continuous with the opening soliloquy of *Richard III*. Richard was already a significant figure at the end of *Henry VI, Part II*, beginning in act 5, scene 1, although the historical Richard was only two years old at the time. At the beginning of *Part III*, Richard persuades his father to break his oath to support Henry as king because the oath was not taken "Before a true and lawful magistrate" (1.2.23). This is a sophistic argument that everyone knows is a mere pretext, but Richard enforces his speech with soaring lines that come almost directly out of the first part of Marlowe's *Tamburlaine* (1587):

> And, father, do but think
> How sweet a thing it is to wear a crown,
> Within whose circuit is Elysium
> And all that poets feign of bliss and joy. (28–31)

The sound and rhythm is authentically Marlovian as well as the imagery; it is interesting how much Shakespeare and Marlowe learned from each other. Richard is like Tamburlaine in his monomania and fixity of purpose, as if he were an instrument of fate.

In act 2, scene 2 Richard is already being addressed in the insulting imagery that runs throughout the Minor Tetralogy. Clifford calls him "Crookback" (96), and to Queen Margaret he is

> like a foul misshapen stigmatic,
> Marked by the Destinies to be avoided,
> As venom toads, or lizards' dreadful stings. (136–38)

Stigmatic was the word Young Clifford used for Richard at the end of *2 Henry VI* (5.1.215), and these are the only two uses in Shakespeare. The word refers to a branded criminal, hence to someone branded by God with deformity as if in punishment for his sins. The lexicon of deformity and the poisonous, baleful animal imagery fix Richard in his villain's role.

At the end of act 3, scene 2, Richard's long soliloquy (seventy-two lines) is a set piece that prepares for *Richard III*, and this speech is entirely in keeping with the tone of his opening soliloquy in the later play. He is sardonic and self-mocking, but he is also filled with the ambition of Tamburlaine for "The sweet fruition of an earthly crown." He reviews with some satisfaction his physical shortcomings, delighting to take the audience into his confidence. He is not made by Nature to be a lover because Nature was corrupted with some bribe

> To shrink mine arm up like a withered shrub;
> To make an envious mountain on my back,
> Where sits deformity to mock my body;
> To shape my legs of an unequal size;
> To disproportion me in every part,
> Like to a chaos, or an unlicked bear-whelp . . . (156–61)

The only thing left then for Richard is ambition: "I'll make my heaven to dream upon the crown" (168).

In this soliloquy Richard asserts his skill in acting and sets forth the qualities that will dominate *Richard III*: "Why, I can smile, and murder whiles I smile" (3.2.182). He can wet his cheeks "with artificial tears" (184), "Change shapes with Proteus for advantages, / And set the murderous Machiavel to school" (192–93). But if everything is so easy for Richard, why is he then so fearful, and why does he need to assert his preeminence so vociferously?

A remarkable passage in Richard's soliloquy about his fears makes him sound as if he were a tormented character in Dante's Hell:

> And I—like one lost in a thorny wood,
> That rends the thorns and is rent with the thorns,
> Seeking a way and straying from the way,
> Not knowing how to find the open air,
> But toiling desperately to find it out—
> Torment myself to catch the English crown . . . (3.2.174–79)

This is one of the few places where Richard seems to have a tragic dimension, like Macbeth, and the "thorny wood" prepares us for his confrontation with demons in act 5, scene 3 of *Richard III* in the dark night before the Battle of Bosworth Field.

Richard III

Richard III is the final play of the Minor Tetralogy and the role of Richard, Duke of Gloucester, who becomes Richard III in 1483, is carefully prepared, beginning with the second part of *Henry VI* and with much more detail in the third part. If we can date *Richard III* to 1591 or 1592, it was clearly the most powerful play that Shakespeare had written so far in his career, and it strongly influences Shakespeare's later depiction of the villain, as we may see in Aaron in *Titus Andronicus*, Iago in *Othello*, and Edmund in *King Lear*.

Shakespeare distorts history most notably in *Richard III*. Edward IV is almost entirely undeveloped, and Richard is demonized according to the Tudor myth, elaborately set forth in Sir Thomas More's *History of King Richard the Third*, written about 1513–1514 and printed in 1557. More's depiction was taken over by Holinshed in his *Chronicles*, which Shakespeare used as his main source. *Richard III* begins in 1471 with the restoration of Edward IV as king, but moves quickly to the death of Edward in 1483 and the assumption of the crown by Richard after a few months, during which Edward's infant son reigned as Edward V.

There is a strikingly elegiac tone in *Richard III* created by the play's preoccupation with death and conveyed chiefly by mourning and lamenting women, especially old Queen Margaret of Anjou, Henry VI's widow, whose exile in France and whose death in 1482 Shakespeare chooses to ignore. She is supported by Queen Elizabeth, the widow of Edward IV, and the mother of Edward, Prince of Wales, and Richard, Duke of York, whom their uncle Richard has murdered in the Tower. A third grieving woman is the Duchess of York, mother of King Edward IV, Clarence, and Gloucester, whose husband Richard and son Rutland were killed by Margaret at Wakefield.

Margaret of Anjou dominates the lamentations as if she were some kind of Nemesis brought on from the past to torment Richard and to warn all those present about the fickleness of fortune and the sureness of vengeance. The scenes in which she appears are excessively long, but her keening creates an unforgettable tone and undercuts Richard's homicidal optimism. We first see her in act 1, scene 3, where she speaks a series of bitter asides before she comes forward. She is like an old-fashioned memory chorus brought in to comment on the action without participating in it—a voice from the past tying together the four plays in the Minor Tetralogy. She speaks both against Richard and Queen Elizabeth, whom she considers a usurper on her prerogatives as queen, but her words are spoken as asides, and function as declarations never to be answered.

When Queen Margaret comes forward after almost fifty lines, she addresses Richard and Queen Elizabeth as "wrangling pirates, that fall out / In sharing that which you have pilled from me!" (1.3.157–58). Richard calls her "Foul wrinkled witch" (163) and wonders how she can return from being "banishèd on pain of death" (166), but although he turns away he remains fascinated by her hypnotic discourse, which seems to memorialize his baleful accomplishments. Margaret proceeds to curse all those present with elaborate fullness, especially Richard:

> Thou elvish-marked, abortive, rooting hog!
> Thou that was sealed in thy nativity
> The slave of nature and the son of hell! (227–29)

Richard doesn't leave immediately but enjoys his wit combat with Margaret. He says only "Ha?" (1.3.233) quizzically, and speculates: "I did think / That thou hadst called me all these bitter names" (234–

35). He is a playful, sardonic villain. Margaret's warning to Buck-ingham is prophetic:

> O Buckingham, take heed of yonder dog!
> Look when he fawns he bites; and when he bites,
> His venom tooth will rankle to the death. (288–90)

When Buckingham is being led to execution, he remembers Margaret's curse, which

> falls heavy on my neck:
> "When he," quoth she, "shall split thy heart with sorrow,
> Remember Margaret was a prophetess." (5.1.25–27)

Buckingham's death speech quotes the next to the last lines of Margaret's curse (1.3.299–300) before she exits.

The most concentrated scene of lamentation is act 4, scene 4, where Queen Margaret shares the stage with Queen Elizabeth and the Duchess of York. She begins alone, gloating over her growing vengeance:

> Here in these confines slily have I lurked
> To watch the waning of mine enemies. (3–4)

She hopes for a "consequence" that is "bitter, black, and tragical" (7), as if the joy of revenge provided her only reason for living. Margaret speaks aside when the Duchess of York and Queen Elizabeth enter, both mourning for the murder of Elizabeth's sons by Richard in the Tower. This is a "mother's lamentation" (14), but the Duchess of York has equally a mother's and a grandmother's lamentation backed with curses for the heartless and psychopathic Richard.

They both sit down and Queen Margaret comes forward to be with them, as in the staging of act 1, scene 3 of *Coriolanus: "They set them down on two low stools, and sew."* It is a communal, choral scene of sorrow as Margaret invites the other ladies to join her: "Tell o'er your woes again by viewing mine" (4.4.39). The action of the play seems to pause for a display of lamentation and cursing. Margaret's indictment of Richard has the ritualistic, simplified quality of a threnody:

I had an Edward [her son], till a Richard killed him;
I had a husband [Henry VI], till a Richard killed him.
Thou [Queen Elizabeth and the Duchess of York] hadst an
    Edward [son and grandson], till a Richard killed him;
Thou [Queen Elizabeth and the Duchess of York] hadst a
    Richard [son and grandson], till a Richard killed him. (40–43)

The Duchess of York reminds Margaret that she had a Richard, too—her husband—before Margaret killed him and a son Rutland that Margaret helped to kill. The Wars of the Roses are summarized in this baleful account.

Queen Margaret is a ghostlike figure, extremely old and tired, and from a past that has ceased to exist. She can only plead with the Duchess of York to bear with her: "I am hungry for revenge, / And I cloy me with beholding it" (4.4.61–62). Cloying comes from excess, especially of food and drink which at first makes one queasy. Queen Margaret is fascinated by an excess of revenge that also cloys her in the sense that it is far more than she needs to satisfy herself. She is satiated with grief and revenge. Her *ubi sunt* questions to Queen Elizabeth define the tragic atmosphere of this play:

Where is thy husband now? Where be thy brothers?
Where be thy two sons? Wherein dost thou joy?
Who sues and kneels and says, "God save the Queen"? (92–94)

Elizabeth wants Margaret to stay awhile and "teach me how to curse mine enemies" (117), but Margaret exits never to reappear. The Duchess of York's question underscores the nature of this scene: "Why should calamity be full of words?" (126). It is because a sharp distinction exists in this play between those who can bring calamity by killing and those who can lament calamity only in words. Richard, however, mediates between the two by being such a clever and eloquent speaker.

Lady Anne is another grieving and cursing woman in the play, and although she succumbs to Richard's flattery and agrees to marry him, she begins in the same elegiac mode as Margaret, Elizabeth, and the Duchess of York. She enters with the corpse of Henry VI, her father-in-law, in the maimed rites of his funeral, and she utters freely "the lamentations of poor Anne" (1.2.9), wife to Prince Edward, stabbed by Richard, and daughter-in-law of King Henry, also murdered by Richard. She curses Richard in artful rhetoric:

> O, cursèd be the hand that made these holes!
> Cursèd the heart that had the heart to do it! (14–15)

When Richard suddenly appears, Anne is at a loss about what to do. She calls him "devil" and "dreadful minister of hell" (45–46), but she has no power to resist his bold actions.

When the dead Henry's wounds "Open their congealed mouths and bleed afresh" (1.2.56), like the corpse of Caesar in *Julius Caesar*, Anne can only lash out against Richard in conventional rhetoric:

> Blush, blush, thou lump of foul deformity,
> For 'tis thy presence that exhales this blood
> From cold and empty veins where no blood dwells. (57–59)

If Richard is indeed a "lump of foul deformity," he is unlikely to blush at his misdeeds, and Anne seems to be entirely on the wrong track. Richard is easy and spontaneous and pursues his fulsome, Petrarchan flattery without the slightest hesitation. It is clear from the beginning that Anne is lost. When she says at the end, "I would I knew thy heart" (192), she is egregiously self-deceived.

Later in the play when Anne is going to Westminster to be crowned queen, she speaks more forcefully than she did in act 1, scene 2. She curses Richard and herself and foresees her inevitable murder by her husband. Again, the grieving and cursing women in the play contribute an elegiac and tragic dimension to *Richard III*. Anne wishes that "the inclusive verge / Of golden metal that must round my brow / Were red-hot steel to sear me to the brains!" (4.1.58–60) and that she were anointed with a "deadly venom" (61) that will kill her. She remembers vividly Richard's imperious wooing in 1, 2 and how her "woman's heart / Grossly grew captive to his honey words" (78–79).

Her report on her life as queen looks forward to the anxiety and sleeplessness of *Macbeth*, as do many other details in this play:

For never yet one hour in his bed
Did I enjoy the golden dew of sleep,
But with his timorous dreams was still awaked. (4.1.82–84)

We don't actually see anything of Richard's "timorous dreams" until act 5, scene 3 on the night before the Battle of Bosworth Field, but this adds to many hints of a fateful, restless, anxious doom that hangs over Richard's head. If, after the third part of *Henry VI*, he enters *Richard III* as the scourge of God, we are at once put on notice of his impending destruction.

Despite Richard's sardonic humor in his opening soliloquy and his astonishing success, *Richard III* is laved in death, lamentations, curses, and dreams of death. The dream of Clarence just before he is murdered is an essential part of this morbid atmosphere, and the dream itself is one of the most powerful speeches Shakespeare had written up to this point in his career. It is a dream of drowning in which he and his brother Gloucester are washed overboard "Into the tumbling billows of the main" (1.4.20). Clarence's terror is mixed with a strange vision of the treasures of the deep, like Ariel's "Full fathom five" song in *The Tempest* (1.2.399ff.). Clarence sees

Wedges of gold, great anchors, heaps of pearl,
Inestimable stones, unvaluèd jewels,
All scatt'red in the bottom of the sea. (1.4.26–28)

But soon Clarence passes into the "kingdom of perpetual night" (47), and in his guilt meets ghosts like those Richard sees before the Battle of Bosworth Field. Warwick and Prince Edward both confront Clarence with his wrongdoing, and Furies and foul fiends pursue him and howl in his ears to convince him that he is in hell. The horror of his own death, both in his proleptic dream and his drowning in a butt of sweet malmsey wine, anticipates the inevitable doom that hangs over his brother Richard, who will share his fate.

I have not yet spoken directly about Richard, Duke of Gloucester, because I believe that he is caught up in a tragedy in which he is only partially an active, vital force. In defiance of actual history, he is represented by Shakespeare, like Tamburlaine, as a scourge of

God. He is bold and unreflective, witty, sardonic, frank, and a wonderful actor. He has no self-pity about his own deformity, and, in fact, boasts of his ugliness as if it were a God-given mark of distinction that sets him apart from ordinary men.

His opening soliloquy continues the mood of the soliloquy in 3 *Henry VI*, in which he merrily takes inventory of his physical defects: his arm shrunk up "like a withered shrub" (3.2.156), an "envious mountain" (157) on his back, his legs of "unequal size" (159). In *Richard III* he speaks of himself objectively as

> Cheated of feature by dissembling Nature,
> Deformed, unfinished, sent before my time
> Into this breathing world scarce half made up . . . (1.1.19–21)

After he has proved to his own satisfaction that he cannot be a lover, he proceeds to woo Lady Anne against all odds and to win her, thereby disproving his own assumption. This is a typical game that delights Richard.

One of the essential points of Richard's wooing of Anne is the utter contempt he has for her acceding to his patently histrionic, insincere, and grossly flattering courtship. Richard thereby sets the pattern for all Shakespeare's villains, even Cassius in *Julius Caesar*, who so easily persuades Brutus to the conspiracy—"If I were Brutus now, and he were Cassius, / He should not humor me" (1.2.312–13). Richard has only withering disdain for the foolish and sentimental Anne, whom he is already thinking of doing away with: "I'll have her, but I will not keep her long" (1.2.229).

Richard himself sentimentalizes Anne's husband Edward, whom, three months ago, he stabbed in his "angry mood at Tewkesbury" (1.2.241):

> A sweeter and a lovelier gentleman,
> Framed in the prodigality of nature,
> Young, valiant, wise, and, no doubt, right royal,
> The spacious world cannot again afford. (242–45)

The trouble is that Richard doesn't believe a word he is saying. It is all histrionic display, and if it is true that his all does not equal "Edward's moi'ty" (249), then the conquest of Anne is a proof of charms so irresistible that even he didn't recognize them before. His conclusion is flashy and shallow, and clearly even the sardonic Richard cannot persuade himself of its truth. "Upon my life, she finds, although I cannot, / Myself to be a marv'lous proper man" (253–54) is pure sarcasm. Richard delights in toying with his own infinite possibilities, which is the mark of the true villain.

Richard's subsequent wooing of Elizabeth, the daughter of Queen Elizabeth and his brother Edward (act 4, scene 4), is strangely tentative and unfocused compared to his dashing courtship of Anne, daughter of Warwick, in act 1, scene 2. Richard is full of amorous platitudes, but he seems to lack the bravado of the earlier wooing. Is he becoming unsure of himself? He has the same utter contempt of Queen Elizabeth as he does of Anne: "Relenting fool, and shallow, changing woman!" (4.4.431), which seems to express his absolute misogyny. But Elizabeth outwits him, and her daughter marries Richmond, Richard's archenemy, who brings together the houses of York (white rose) and Lancaster (red rose).

"Conscience" is a surprisingly important word in *Richard III*. Only *Henry VIII* has more examples (twenty-four), and *Richard III* has the same number (thirteen) as *Henry V*. In descending order, *The Merchant of Venice* has ten occurrences, *Cymbeline* nine, and *Hamlet* eight. It's obvious that we think of "conscience" in *Hamlet* as more important than in any of these other plays, yet we need to pay attention to the way the word is bandied about in *Richard III*. The Second Murderer, who comes at Richard's behest to murder Clarence, has an attack of conscience, which the First Murderer cannot successfully talk him out of. At the end of the scene (1, 4) the Second Murderer refuses his fee and repents. In 4, 3 Tyrrel reports that the murderers of Edward's children "are gone with conscience and remorse / They could not speak" (20–21). It is surprising that conscience should vex professional murderers in this play.

With the wooing of Anne, Richard is proud of the fact that he could succeed with her when she has "God, her conscience, and these bars against me" (1.2.234). In the next scene, the old Queen Margaret hopes that "The worm of conscience still begnaw" (1.3.221) Richard's soul, but this is said as a curse planted in Richard's mind. Margaret doesn't believe that Richard has any conscience at all. Act 3, Scene 7 is elaborately staged between Buckingham and Richard so that it will look as if the reluctant Richard is finally persuaded to assume the kingship. Buckingham argues against Richard's overscrupulous "conscience" (173) in the matter of Edward's sons, and Richard finally agrees to accept the kingship "Albeit against my conscience and my soul" (225). *Conscience* is an important word in this scene of pretended morality and religion.

Richard's conscience really comes into play only in the scene before the Battle of Bosworth Field, where a series of ghosts appear to him and tell him to despair and die. Obviously, these apparitions are associated with his own despair as he sees his fate closing in on him. After the Ghost of Buckingham appears, *"Richard starteth up out of a dream"* (5.3.177 s.d.) and exclaims: "O coward conscience, how dost thou afflict me!" (180). It is dead midnight and the lights burn blue, as they do when the Ghost of Caesar appears to Brutus (*Julius Caesar* 4.3.272). Richard is in a cold sweat: "Cold fearful drops stand on my trembling flesh" (5.3.182). He argues with himself in a simplistic and polarized way:

> My conscience hath a thousand several tongues,
> And every tongue brings in a several tale,
> And every tale condemns me for a villain. (195–97)

Richard concludes with a spiritual aridity like that of Macbeth: "I shall despair. There is no creature loves me" (5.3.201). But at the very end, Richard decides like Macbeth to tough it out, and he resoundingly rejects conscience: "Conscience is but a word that cowards use" (310) and "Our strong arms be our conscience, swords our law!" (312). Richard's moral hesitation is over and he is resolved to face his inevitable end with determination. The manly demands of action overcome those inner and feminine needs of conscience, what was called in the Middle Ages, the "ayenbite (or agenbite) of inwit," an idea that fascinated James Joyce.

The Minor Tetralogy ends with the providential triumph of Richmond, the first of the Tudor line, who becomes Henry VII, and the utter confutation of Richard III and the Yorkist usurpation. This is the definitive end of the Wars of the Roses. It is surprising to learn that the Yorkists had a better claim to the throne than the Lancastrians, who stand in direct descendance from Henry IV, who seized the crown from Richard II and afterward had him murdered. Richmond marries the same Elizabeth of York whom Richard III wooed through her mother, Queen Elizabeth, the wife of his brother Edward. Richmond is not a developed character in the play, but he is brought in to execute the happy ending of the Minor Tetralogy. *Henry VIII*, a very late history play, follows *Richard III* in chronological sequence, but it has nothing at all to do with the Minor Tetralogy, although we might expect it to expand on the Tudor myth begun with Richmond, who becomes Henry VII. The undoing of the Wars of the Roses brings with it a sense of triumph and optimism for England. We look forward to the reign of Elizabeth, whose birth is in fact celebrated at the end of *Henry VIII*.

King John

King John reigned from 1199 to 1216, and Shakespeare's play covers more or less those years (without, of course, mentioning the Magna Carta in 1215). Unlike the events of the Major and the Minor Tetralogies, which lead up to the accession of the Tudors in 1485, King John's reign is isolated and remote from contemporary concerns. There are 161 years between the death of King John and the coming of Richard II to the throne in 1377. What happens in *King John* is not close to history as we know it. For example, Shakespeare represents the struggle between John and his nephew Arthur for legitimacy as a real conflict that opens the play, whereas historically John was the undisputed successor of his brother, Richard the Lion-Hearted (Richard I). Arthur is deliberately infantilized, and great weight is given to his grieving and querulous mother, Constance of Brittany, who is modeled on Queen Margaret, especially as she is represented in 3 *Henry VI*.

There is a certain confusion and inchoate quality in the historical narrative of *King John*. At one moment John, like Henry VIII, is defying the Pope in a way that could only please Shakespeare's Protestant audience. He refuses the orders of Pope Innocent III to appoint Stephen Langton as Archbishop of Canterbury, and speaks in a high patriotic style:

> What earthy name to interrogatories [= legal questions]
> Can task the free breath of a sacred king? (3.1.73–74)

John speaks of the Pope as having "usurped authority" (86) and vows that "no Italian priest / Shall tithe or toll in our dominions" (79–80). Unlike Richard II, King John doesn't speak further about the divine right of kings, and this passage seems to be John's only moment of asserting that he is a "sacred king" (74) and that "we, under God, are supreme head" (81).

Later in the play, John is basely yielding up his crown to Pandulph, the Papal legate, in order to be crowned again by him:

> Take again
> From this my hand, as holding of the Pope,
> Your sovereign greatness and authority. (5.1.2–4)

Pandulph asserts his power to end the war with Lewis, the French Dauphin, which he himself has stirred up because of John's "stubborn usage of the Pope" (18): "But since you are a gentle convertite, / My tongue shall hush again this storm of war" (19–20).

John is baffled in this scene and turns over the rule of England to the Bastard: "Have thou the ordering of this present time" (5.1.77). His virtual abdication at this point increases the shapelessness of the play, and he is soon dead, having been poisoned by a monk. Suddenly, John's son, whom we have never heard of before in the play, emerges to become Henry III. In the dramatic logic of the action, we expected the heroic Philip Faulconbridge, the bastard son of Richard I who dominates the play, to assume the kingship. He makes the final vaunting speech of the play:

> This England never did, nor never shall,
> Lie at the proud foot of a conqueror
> But when it first did help to wound itself. (5.7.112–14)

The tone of this speech is echoed in the dying Gaunt's exclamations in *Richard II*.

The affinities of *King John* with *Richard II* suggest that both plays were written close to each other, around 1595. My intuition is that *John* precedes *Richard*, because once Shakespeare started on the Major Tetralogy he probably wasn't distracted to write another unrelated history play. There are apparently no allusions in *King John* that might be helpful in dating. I doubt very strongly whether *King John* can be dated to 1590, as the Arden editor, E. A. J. Honigmann, and others propose. It is quite different in style from the plays of this period, such as the three parts of *Henry VI*. Its relation to *The Troublesome Raigne of Iohn King of England*, published in two parts in 1591, which used to be thought the source of Shakespeare's play, is problematical, since *The Troublesome Raigne* may echo *King John*.

The Bastard is unlike any of the early protagonists of Shakespeare, although he has some of the witty bravado of Richard III. Despite his addiction to "policy" (2.1.396), he is not by any stretch of the imagination a villain. He is, in fact, the savior of England, whose patriotic, bluff, but heroic style looks forward to Henry V. But he is much more stylistically self-conscious than Henry V. After Hubert's extremely rhetorical speech about the merits of a match between Lady Blanch and Lewis the Dauphin, the Bastard launches a satirical attack on the terms of art he has just been bombarded with: "Zounds! I was never so bethumped with words / Since I first called my brother's father dad" (466–67). It is expected of a bastard to be blunt and forthright in speech, as Edmund is in *King Lear*, but the Bastard goes beyond this to a mockery of rodomontade like Hamlet's of Laertes' rant in the graveyard scene.

Hubert launches a swollen period to exaggerate the merits of the proposed match:

> But without this match,
> The sea enragèd is not half so deaf,
> Lions more confident, mountains and rocks
> More free from motion, no, not death himself
> In mortal fury half so peremptory,
> As we to keep this city [= Angiers]. (2.1.450–55)

The Bastard makes fun of Hubert's hyperboles:

> Here's a large mouth, indeed,
> That spits forth death and mountains, rocks and seas,

Talks as familiarly of roaring lions
As maids of thirteen do of puppy-dogs. (457–60)

Hubert "gives the bastinado with his tongue: / Our ears are cudgeled" (463–64). The Bastard is wittily aware of rhetorical amplification, and the much-trumpeted match hardly outlasts act 3, scene 1.

The Bastard is an almost wholly unhistorical figure, drawn from Shakespeare's general acquaintance with bastards in the medieval period. This is another problem with *King John* as a history play, because it takes as its leading figure the Bastard, who has as tenuous a connection with historical accuracy as Falstaff. Both the Bastard and Henry V embody mythic characteristics of the great leader. On his first appearance in the play, the Bastard is accepted by King John as "A good blunt fellow" (1.1.71) and a "madcap" (84), and John's mother Elinor confirms that the Bastard "hath a trick of Cordelion's [= Richard I's] face" (85). She seems eager to acknowledge that she is his grandmother.

Philip Faulconbridge rejects his inheritance from his supposed father to pursue honor and glory as King John's nephew. He asserts his noble ambition in the style of Chapman's Bussy D'Ambois and other powerful figures from early Jacobean tragedy: "And I am I, how'er I was begot" (1.1.175). In the first of his many long soliloquies, he claims that he is a "mounting spirit" (206), a close observer of the times, who, like a successful, flattering courtier, will know how to deliver "Sweet, sweet, sweet poison for the age's tooth" (213). The Bastard's determination for his own "rising" (216) depends upon a cynical understanding of the corruption of the times. In this sense the Bastard is a much more sophisticated and complex character than Henry V.

The Bastard's first political triumph is his suggestion to the Kings of England and France to attack the city of Angiers and end its politic equivocation. It is a brilliant stratagem, which breaks the standstill in negotiations. Interestingly, the Bastard thinks in terms of histrionic imagery:

By heaven, these scroyles [= scoundrels] of Angiers flout you, kings,
And stand securely on their battlements
As in a theater, whence they gape and point
At your industrious scenes and acts of death. (2.1.373–76)

It is the theatrical mockery that the Bastard objects to, and he calls Angiers "this contemptuous city" (384) and "this peevish town" (402). Angiers manages to slide out of certain destruction by proposing a marriage between Blanch and Lewis, but the Bastard is skeptical of their good intentions: "Mad world! Mad kings! Mad composition [= compromise]!" (561).

In his most famous soliloquy in the play, the Bastard inveighs against Commodity in all of its many derogatory senses:

> That smooth-faced gentleman, tickling commodity,
> Commodity, the bias of the world . . . (2.1.573–74)

This is the business ethic Antonio speaks of in *The Merchant of Venice* that supports Shylock's bond and that the Duke cannot possibly refuse:

> For the commodity that strangers have
> With us in Venice, if it be denied,
> Will much impeach the justice of the state,
> Since that the trade and profit of the city
> Consisteth of all nations. (*The Merchant of Venice* 3.3.27–31)

Commodity, or essentially convenience and expediency for business-men, rules Venice rather than equity or natural law; without com-modity Venice as a center of trade between East and West will disappear.

This commercial sense is not exactly what the Bastard means by *commodity*, but his political meaning follows directly from the connec-tion of the word's root with wares, goods, and merchandise. It is "tickling commodity," like Thersites' invocation of "the devil Luxury," who, "with his fat rump and potato finger, tickles" Diomedes and Cressida together (*Troilus and Cressida* 5.2.54–55). The Bastard calls the personified Commodity "This bawd, this broker" (2.1.582) and "That daily break-vow" (569). Cynically, he vows allegiance to the political expediency of Commodity, who hasn't wooed him yet. He ends his soliloquy with a ringing, ironic declaration:

> Since kings break faith upon commodity,
> Gain, be my lord, for I will worship thee! (597–98)

This is the way of the world, to which disinherited bastards are especially sensitive.

Similarly, the Bastard opposes the "mad composition" that Pandulph, the papal legate, tries to impose on the wars between England and France. When John has basely yielded his crown to the Pope, the Bastard tries to stir him up to fight off the Dauphin's invasion of England: "glister like the god of war" (5.1.54). As he takes over "the ordering of this present time" (77) from John, the Bastard is at his most patriotic and his most glorious in defying the Pope and making war against Lewis the Dauphin:

> Shall a beardless boy,
> A cockered silken wanton, brave our fields
> And flesh his spirit in a warlike soil,
> Mocking the air with colors idly spread,
> And find no check? (69–73)

This is the heroic defiance of France that we shall hear later from Henry V. In the next scene the Bastard speaks, in the voice of the King, his utter contempt for the French invaders: "This harnessed masque and unadvisèd revel, / This unhaired sauciness and boyish troops" (5.2.132–33). At this point in the play, the Bastard is effectively the King of England.

Only at the end of the play, when he is poisoned, does King John seem memorable. He speaks distractedly from the effect of the poison and he has a passion now that he never had before, especially in the early scenes when he was directed by his mother Elinor (as Arthur was ruled by his mother Constance). John is burning up: "There is so hot a summer in my bosom / That all my bowels crumble up to dust!" (5.7.30–31), but no one will help him: "And none of you will bid the winter come / To thrust his icy fingers in my maw" (36–37). Shakespeare excels at metaphors of madness, but we have no previous development of John to support his present passion. John's suffering and guilt are powerful:

> Within me is a hell, and there the poison
> Is as a fiend confined to tyrannize
> On unreprievable condemnèd blood. (46–48)

These are strong speeches but the play doesn't make any effort to dramatize why there is a hell within King John.

Shakespeare is much more successful in evoking passion at the attempted blinding and killing of little Arthur by the King's loyal servant Hubert (the same Hubert who so skillfully defends the city of Angiers). Arthur, the son of John's older brother, Geoffrey, is an active claimant of the English throne who makes John seem a usurper. Although Arthur was in fact twelve when John came to the throne, Shakespeare keeps him a child in order to increase the sense of outrage and pathos at his death, which occurs when Arthur is already sixteen in 1203. His mother, Constance, shames him by speaking in baby talk about his grandmother Elinor, who supports her son John: "Give grandam kingdom, and it grandam will / Give it a plum, a cherry, and a fig" (2.1.161–62). The bitterness of Constance overwhelms her maternal feelings for her son.

The scene between Arthur and Hubert, who comes to murder him, is the most effective in the play, and it strongly anticipates the blinding of Gloucester in *King Lear* (3, 7). Hubert is responding to John's express comment that Arthur "is a very serpent in my way" (3.2.71), and, like all Shakespeare's murderers, he wants to be serviceable to his king: "I'll keep him so / That he shall not offend your Majesty" (74–75). In act 4, scene 1 Hubert provides executioners who hide in the room where he plans to murder Arthur. They are to heat irons for Hubert and to bind Arthur fast to his chair at Hubert's command—this is the way Gloucester is dealt with in *King Lear*. Unknowingly, the innocent Arthur treats Hubert as his friend, but his loving comments have a bitter irony: "I would to heaven / I were your son, so you would love me, Hubert" (4.1.23–24). Hubert's wavering is specifically indicated in his asides: "If I talk to him, with his innocent prate / He will awake my mercy, which lies dead" (25–26). Unable to speak directly, he gives Arthur a paper that informs him of his fate: Hubert must burn out both his eyes with hot irons.

Arthur indulges in elaborate conceits like those in *Richard II* to counter Hubert's determination:

> Ah, none but in this iron age would do it!
> The iron of itself, though heat red-hot,

Approaching near these eyes, would drink my tears
And quench this fiery indignation
Even in the matter of mine innocence! (4.1.60–64)

The point of the conceits is that they cannot stop, and Arthur continues with an excess of rhetorical ingenuity:

Nay, after that, consume away in rust,
But for containing fire to harm mine eye!
Are you more stubborn-hard than hammered iron? (65–67)

Arthur persuades Hubert to send away the executioners: "O save me, Hubert, save me! My eyes are out / Even with the fierce looks of these bloody men" (72–73).

Hubert finally relents after an extraordinary long scene of pleading, in which Arthur as a young Metaphysical poet works endless changes on the emblematic theme of eyes. He even offers his tongue for his eyes in a grotesque piece of pleading:

Or, Hubert, if you will, cut out my tongue,
So I may keep mine eyes. O, spare mine eyes,
Though to no use but still to look on you! (4.1.100–102)

Hubert cannot resist this eloquence "For all the treasure that thine uncle owes" (122). Ironically, Arthur afterward kills himself by jumping off the walls of the castle in his ship-boy's disguise:

O me! my uncle's spirit is in these stones!
Heaven take my soul, and England keep my bones! (4.3.9–10)

It is an affecting, childlike, animistic end, which seems to presage John's own evil fate.

The Bastard defends Hubert against Salisbury's accusation of murder in words that are echoed by Othello: "Your sword is bright, sir; put it up again" (4.3.79); Othello tells Brabantio and his followers: "Keep up your bright swords, for the dew will rust them" (*Othello* 1.2.58). The Bastard's sense of mastery and command is similar to Othello's and in this scene he underscores the pathos of Arthur's death. He tells Hubert that he is damned "Beyond the infinite and boundless reach / Of mercy" (4.3.117–18) if he did this murder. In his deep passion, the Bastard invokes extravagant hyperboles of despair for Hubert:

> A rush will be a beam
> To hang thee on. Or wouldst thou drown thyself,
> Put but a little water in a spoon
> And it shall be as all the ocean,
> Enough to stifle such a villain up. (4.3.129–33)

Although the Bastard finally comes to believe Hubert, he sees the fate of England compromised by Arthur's death:

> England now is left
> To tug and scamble and to part by th' teeth
> The unowed interest of proud swelling state. (4.3.145–47)

Henry V opens with the Archbishop of Canterbury talking about a bill against the Church "that the scambling and unquiet time / Did push . . . out of farther question" (1.1.4–5), and Henry will win Kate "with scambling" (5.2.207), or scrambling and scrimmaging like a soldier. "To tug and scamble" is to fight for something that one would assume to be inviolable and not to be disputed. These are the evil fruits of Commodity, by which even good political intentions come to grief. In his soaring imagery, the Bastard uncovers the truth of what is happening to the realm of England, which prepares us for his heroic final speech: "Naught shall make us rue / If England to itself do rest but true!" (5.7.117–18).

King John does seem an odd history play in relation to the tumultuous events of the Minor and Major Tetralogies. It has some connection with the anti-Catholic, antipapal issues of *Henry VIII*, and the defiance of the French is familiar from Shakespeare's other histories, especially *Henry V*, but *King John* still seems anomalous. Why would Shakespeare want to go back to the early thirteenth century and completely overlook the Magna Carta, which seems so important to us? The Bastard provides an outspoken, witty, and heroic model for such later figures as Henry V, and his bluffness and honesty stand as a bulwark against the political chicanery of the rest of the play. But the Bastard is suddenly at the end deprived of the kingship he so richly deserves. The conclusion is strikingly indeterminate, as if there must be some other play or plays to wind up the historical action. We expect a miniseries that never comes.

Richard II

K*ichard II* is the first play of the Major
Tetralogy, followed by the two parts of *Henry
IV* and *Henry V*. Shakespeare learned a great
deal from writing the four plays of the Minor
Tetralogy (the three parts of *Henry VI* and
Richard III), which were probably completed
in 1592 or 1593. *King John*, which was probably written just before *Richard II*, has many
stylistic affinities with it; both plays make
important use of the divine right of kings.
We can date *Richard II* fairly confidently to
1595, and the other three plays of the Major
Tetralogy follow in the next three or four
years.

It is curious that the events of the Major
Tetralogy exactly precede those of the Minor Tetralogy, which begins with the death
of Henry V in 1422 and covers the Wars of
the Roses to its conclusion at Bosworth Field
in 1485. It looks as if Shakespeare wanted
first to establish the origins of the Tudor line
and the way that Henry, Duke of Richmond
(later Henry VII), providentially ends the
Wars of the Roses and unites the houses of
York and Lancaster. The Major Tetralogy is
much more concentrated historically, beginning with the quarrel of Bolingbroke and
Mowbray in 1398 and ending with the
triumph of Henry V over France and his
marriage to Katherine, daughter of the French

king and queen, in 1420. The Major Tetralogy is more self-consciously a four-part unit than the Minor Tetralogy, with many more interconnections, echoes, and anticipations.

The events in *Richard II* are compressed into only two years, from 1398 to 1400, which helps give the play a feeling of tragedy, by concentrating so strongly on Richard's fall and creating the sense of a quick-moving and almost fateful action. Richard's hubris, insolence, presumption, and perhaps just foolishness make his fall inevitable, but once it is clear that he can no longer remain king, the play unleashes a tremendous flood of feeling for Richard in adversity. This is Shakespeare's first history play to invoke so powerfully the analogy between the fallen king and Christ in extremis. This sense of sorrow for Richard evokes tragic feelings of sympathy and compassion. We forget whatever Richard has done to bring his fate upon himself and think only of his torment and his sufferings.

More than any other Shakespeare history play, *Richard II* goes to great lengths to invoke the doctrine of the divine right of kings, which was popular in the Tudor program of homilies to be read aloud in churches. The heinous sin of Richard's deposition and murder and the ascent of Bolingbroke to the throne as Henry IV are not really resolved until the Wars of the Roses end in the victory of the Earl of Richmond in 1485, who comes to the throne as Henry VII, the first Tudor. This endows Shakespeare's two tetralogies with the large sense of Aeschylus's *Oresteia* trilogy, which finally works out the curse on the house of Atreus.

It is necessary to insist so strongly on the divine right of kings in *Richard II* in order to appreciate the magnitude of Henry IV's transgression. The Bishop of Carlisle's prophetic speech right before Richard's deposition looks forward to the bloody events of both tetralogies and is a forecast of English history in the fifteenth century:

> And if you crown him [Bolingbroke], let me prophesy—
> The blood of English shall manure the ground,
> And future ages groan for this foul act . . . (4.1.136–38)

Bolingbroke as "subject" cannot "give sentence on his king" (121), since the king is the anointed of God. As God's scourge, Bolingbroke is sure to bring an evil doom on himself and on England, which will "be called / The field of Golgotha and dead men's skulls" (143–44). The argument of divine right is all that Richard can offer to defend himself, and the conflict is lost before it ever begins. When Richard returns from Ireland to safeguard his kingdom against Bolingbroke, who has landed at Ravenspurgh, he speaks largely in "divine right" rhetoric, which his followers see as a counsel of despair:

> Not all the water in the rough rude sea
> Can wash the balm off from an anointed king;
> The breath of wordly men cannot depose
> The deputy elected by the Lord. (3.2.54–57)

Richard's sense of the forces of Nature being marshaled against the enemy of God seems ludicrous to his troops. He protests: "Mock not my senseless conjuration, lords" (23), but the King's approach to impending danger is entirely wrong.

Richard's invocation to "my gentle earth" (3.2.12) is unmilitary in the extreme: "But let thy spiders, that suck up thy venom, / And heavy-gaited toads lie in their way" (14–15). To this Richard continues to add supposedly baleful images: "Yield stinging nettles to mine enemies" (18). It is this "conjuration" of senseless things that his lords are mocking, and Carlisle tells him gently: "The means that heavens yield must be embraced / And not neglected" (29–30). The army of Bolingbroke is unlikely to be defeated by venomous spiders, heavy-gaited toads, and stinging nettles.

According to the Renaissance doctrine of the King's two bodies, the king as a public figure has a sacred body identified with the body politic, but as a private man his body is fragile and vulnerable. Richard argues on both sides of the divine right paradox. When he considers himself as a person, he is subject to all the weaknesses of mortal man, and he is far from having the invulnerable image of a king:

> I live with bread like you, feel want,
> Taste grief, need friends—subjected thus,
> How can you say to me, I am a king? (3.2.175–77)

In the pun on *subjected*—"made a subject" and "subjected to," or "liable"—lies the heart of the paradox. Richard is moving to an acute awareness of his loss of identity; by giving up the kingship he surrenders the essence of his being and he declines to anonymity and nothingness. The issue of identity becomes of crucial importance in Shakespeare's later tragedies, such as *Othello*, when Othello declares that his "occupation's gone" (3.3.354) or *Antony and Cleopatra*, when Antony "cannot hold this visible shape" (4.14.14).

The important theme of Richard's identity reaches its climax in the deposition scene, when he understands that by giving up his kingship he is giving up everything, including his sense of self:

> I have no name, no title,
> No, not that name was given me at the font
> But 'tis usurped. (4.1.254–56)

He seeks total annihilation in his wish-fulfillment imagery:

> O, that I were a mockery king of snow,
> Standing before the sun of Bolingbroke,
> To melt myself away in water drops! (259–61)

This scene anticipates Hamlet in many places, especially Hamlet's first soliloquy:

> O that this too too solid [as in Folio] flesh would melt,
> Thaw, and resolve itself into a dew . . . (*Hamlet* 1.2.129–30)

Some lines later, after Richard sends for a mirror and throws it down in disgust, he exclaims:

> My grief lies all within,
> And these external manners of laments
> Are merely shadows to the unseen grief
> That swells with silence in the tortured soul. (4.1.294–97)

These lines clearly anticipate Hamlet's sense of isolation in the Danish court in the same context I quoted before: "But I have that within which passes show; / These but the trappings and the suits of woe" (*Hamlet* 1.2.85–86). Both Richard and Hamlet feel a painful contrast between outward seeming and inward reality. They are both courting the annihilation of self.

Richard's contemplating his face in the mirror is like Hamlet's contemplating mortality in the skull of Yorick, the king's jester. It is interesting that Richard parodies Doctor Faustus's famous invocation of Helen of Troy in Marlowe's play (1592):

> Was this face the face
> That every day under his household roof
> Did keep ten thousand men? Was this the face
> That, like the sun, did make beholders wink? (4.1.280–83)

He rejects the image of his face by shattering the looking glass, thus seeking the anonymity he has been flirting with from the beginning of his griefs.

At the end of the play before he is murdered at Pomfret Castle, Richard has a long soliloquy meditating on themes of time, life and death, and his own identity. He takes up again the "nothing" theme that echoes throughout the play, as it does in *King Lear*, and that here signifies the king's awareness of his own impending death. He imagines himself as an actor, coping with a difficult reality by moving quickly between different identities: "Thus play I in one person many people, / And none contented" (5.5.31–32). Shifting between king and beggar, Richard is finally "unkinged by Bolingbroke, / And straight am nothing" (37–38). From here it is only a quick move to the final step of the reasoning: that no man "With nothing shall be pleased, till he be eased / With being nothing" (40–41). Despite the urgency of death, Richard cannot resist the pleasing cadence of the internal rhyme ("pleased-eased"); he also manages to kill two of his executioners.

The critical question whether Richard is a poet manqué or an actor manqué is a deceptive one because Richard is poetical and histrionic in playing his part as a king, especially a deposed king. Hamlet seems actually to be a friend of the traveling players, which Richard is not. Nor has Richard written at least a dozen or sixteen lines to be inserted into the *Mousetrap* play, nor does he declaim with bravado the Dido and Aeneas play as Hamlet does. But Richard poetizes actively throughout his play and indulges in elaborately ingenious poetic figures called "conceits."

Something grotesque in these excessively worked out images mingles with Richard's grief to create a sense of hysteria, as in the following:

> Or shall we play the wantons with our woes,
> And make some pretty match with shedding tears,
> As thus, to drop them still upon one place,
> Till they have fretted us a pair of graves
> Within the earth; and, therein laid, "there lies
> Two kinsmen digged their graves with weeping eyes";
> Would not this ill do well? (3.3.163–69)

The image is extremely literal in its visual requirements, which are uncomfortably specific. That is why, once again, the imagery misfires and the onlookers think it ridiculous: "Well, well, I see / I talk but idly, and you laugh at me" (169–70). In Elizabethan parlance, *idly* means both lazily and foolishly. Richard is mocking his own poetical style in the manner of Touchstone in *As You Like It*, who lays it down as gospel that "the truest poetry is the most feigning" (3.3.18–19).

Henry Bolingbroke, the son of John of Gaunt, becomes the model for Shakespeare's political figures: the unheroic, practical man who manages to survive, while more committed and more ideological persons all are doomed to an early death. Bolingbroke is neither poetical nor histrionic, but Richard envies him his ability to win political favor easily and spontaneously. Even before his return to England, Richard fears "his courtship to the common people" (1.4.24). Bolingbroke is essentially a political creature with no natural eloquence like Richard, but with an uncanny sense of the right gesture:

> Off goes his bonnet to an oyster-wench;
> A brace of draymen bid God speed him well,
> And had the tribute of his supple knee . . . (31–33)

Unlike Tamburlaine or Richard III, Bolingbroke has no grandiose visions of kingship, and he proceeds step by step without revealing, even to himself, his ultimate objective. We have to believe that when he returns to England from exile he comes only to claim his rightful inheritance from his dead father, Gaunt, and not to depose Richard and be king himself. Yet events move with incredible swiftness and inevitability, and when Bolingbroke condemns Bushy and Green, two of "The caterpillars of the commonwealth" (2.3.166), in act 3, scene 1, he is already acting like the king, who doesn't need any specific legal warrant. Bolingbroke prepares us remarkably for Claudius in *Hamlet* and perhaps also for Macbeth.

In the final scene of the play Bolingbroke resembles Macbeth remarkably in the equivocation he practices with himself. To Exton, who murders Richard II at Pomfret, Bolingbroke speaks only the ambiguous words of guilt:

> They love not poison that do poison need,
> Nor do I thee; though I did wish him dead,
> I hate the murderer, love him murderèd. (5.6.38–40)

This is essentially the Henry IV of the next two plays in the tetralogy: crafty, ineloquent, guilty, and well meaning. If Henry weren't so troubled in spirit, we would think him a gross hypocrite for making pronouncements like the following: "Lords, I protest, my soul is full of woe, / That blood should sprinkle me to make me grow" (45–46).

But Henry does nothing to prevent blood from sprinkling him and he does nothing to conceal his open complicity. He vows here what he vows time and again in the two later plays: to "make a voyage to the Holy Land, / To wash this blood off from my guilty hand" (5.6.49–50), but we are sure that he has not the slightest intention to make this voyage of contrition and expiation. This is not part of his style. He mourns over the "untimely bier" (52) of Richard II, even though it was he himself who had him murdered. Unlike Richard III Bolingbroke is not sardonic, but his sincerity is suspect as a public pronouncement, not a personal commitment.

His avalanche of couplets in his final scene reminds us that *Richard II* was written right around the time of *Romeo and Juliet* and *A Midsummer Night's Dream*, both of which it resembles in its lyric extravagance and its use of set pieces of eloquence. The dying Gaunt's vision of England is presented as an antithesis to the corruption and decay of England under Richard's misrule. Gaunt, expiring, speaks like a "prophet new inspired" (2.1.31) of "This blessed plot, this earth, this realm, this England" (50). It is an extraordinary patriotic effusion, but England is "now leased out . . . / Like to a tenement or pelting farm" (59–60). *Farm* is a derogatory word used three times in this play to indicate Richard's outrageous financial exactions. To "farm" the realm is to sell for cash the right to collect royal taxes, such as on crown lands and on customs. This is combined with "blank charters" (1.4.48), in which favorites of the king could write in whatever sum they pleased as an exaction on the nobles, and "benevolences" (2.1.250), or forced loans, to create Richard's "rash fierce blaze of riot" (33). Like a tragic protagonist, Richard is preparing his own fall.

The Garden Scene (3, 4) has often been discussed as an internal, choral commentary on the play, but its literal, allegorical quality allies it with early Shakespeare. Later, Shakespeare will embody his meanings much more intrinsically in the dramatic action rather than in symbolic set pieces. The Gardener lectures his servants pedantically about the analogy between the garden commonwealth and the body politic. With the Queen and her Ladies as audience, the Gardener expatiates on the political implications of gardening:

> O, what pity is it
> That he had not so trimmed and dressed his land
> As we this garden! (3.4.55–57)

This scene is easy to teach but it doesn't represent Shakespeare at his best.

At the end of the scene, however, the Gardener speaks a touching soliloquy in couplets:

> Here did she fall a tear; here in this place
> I'll set a bank of rue, sour herb of grace;
> Rue even for ruth here shortly shall be seen,
> In the remembrance of a weeping queen. (3.4.104–7)

We are reminded inevitably, as by so much else in this play, of *Hamlet*, particularly the mad Ophelia's distribution of flowers: "There's rue for you, here's some for me. We may call it herb of grace o' Sundays. O, you must wear your rue with a difference" (*Hamlet* 4.5.181–83).

One incident that hangs over *Richard II* and is mentioned repeatedly in the play is the murder of Thomas of Woodstock, Duke of

Gloucester and Richard's uncle, in 1397. These events are treated in the anonymous play *Woodstock* (sometimes called the first part of *Richard II* since it deals with the period 1382 to 1397, before Shakespeare's play opens), which was probably written before Shakespeare's play. *Richard II* begins in 1398 with the quarrel between Bolingbroke and Thomas Mowbray, the Duke of Norfolk, who was clearly implicated in Gloucester's death at Calais, probably under orders from Richard. The scene between Bolingbroke and Mowbray is confusing, since the men trade accusations that seem equally powerful. Bolingbroke claims that Mowbray sluiced out Gloucester's

> innocent soul through streams of blood;
> Which blood, like sacrificing Abel's, cries
> Even from the tongueless caverns of the earth
> To me for justice and rough chastisement . . . (1.1.103–6)

We never learn for sure about Mowbray's role in this murder, but we are never allowed to forget Richard's complicity.

In the next scene, the Duchess of Gloucester asks Gaunt to take revenge for his brother's murder, but Gaunt refuses. This is the first we hear of the doctrine of the divine right of kings, which is so important in the play. Gaunt says directly that the King,

> God's substitute,
> His deputy anointed in His sight,
> Hath caused his [Gloucester's] death . . . (1.2.37–39)

He adds that "God's is the quarrel" (37), for Gaunt as a subject "may never lift / An angry arm against His minister" (40–41). This makes the issue of Gloucester's murder explicit in the play. Before his death Gaunt accuses Richard directly of murdering his uncle:

> That blood already like the pelican
> Hast thou tapped out and drunkenly caroused:
> My brother Gloucester, plain well-meaning soul . . . (126–28)

This is almost at the end of Gaunt's long and prophetic death speech, in which he seems to curse Richard: "Live in thy shame" (135).

The issue of Gloucester's death comes up again in act 4, scene 1, when Bagot specifically accuses Aumerle, the son of the Duke of York (Gaunt's brother), of having killed Gloucester on orders from Richard. Bagot is joined in his accusations by Fitzwater, Percy, and others, but what is important is that this is the beginning of the deposition scene and the accusations of murder provide a context for the judgment of Richard by Bolingbroke. Richard is not such an innocent as he makes himself out to be. In his grief he makes no effort at all to defend himself, but merely expatiates on his tragic and alienated condition. The fallen king appears powerfully as a suffering individual, lyric, meditative, and philosophical in adversity.

Richard II is one of the most politically explosive of Shakespeare's plays. The Deposition Scene (most of act 4, scene 1), in which Richard abdicates the throne, was never printed during Queen Elizabeth's lifetime and first appeared in the Fourth Quarto of 1608. This is potentially seditious material for which one could be summoned before the Star Chamber. We know that the Essex conspirators got Shakespeare's company to put on a special performance of *Richard II* on the eve of their totally disastrous rebellion on February 8, 1601. Presumably, they thought that the Deposition Scene would be good propaganda for the overthrow of Elizabeth, who thought of herself as Richard II: "I am Richard II. Know ye not that?" (E. K. Chambers, *William Shakespeare*, vol. 2, p. 326). Bolingbroke is clearly labeled as a dangerous usurper in this play and in both parts of *Henry IV*, constantly anxious about his cloudy title to the throne. His son, Prince Hal, who becomes Henry V, continues these perturbations, and the issue is settled definitively only at the end of *Richard III*, when the Earl of Richmond defeats Richard at Bosworth Field and becomes Henry VII. As part of the royal myth, the Tudors take the stain off the English throne.

Henry IV, Part I

The first part of *Henry IV* continues the plot of *Richard II*, and there are many references to Richard in the play, the most striking being those in which the disappointed King compares his son, Prince Hal, to the "skipping King," who "ambled up and down / With shallow jesters and rash bavin [= kindling, brushwood] wits" (3.2.60–61). King Henry contributes to the dichotomy between his own son and Hotspur, the son of the Earl of Northumberland, by affirming: "even as I was then is Percy now" in contrast with the idle Prince Hal: "As thou art to this hour was Richard then / When I from France set foot at Ravenspurgh" (94–96). That was in 1399, and now we are approaching the Battle of Shrewsbury in 1403.

Like *Richard II*, the first part of *Henry IV* is extremely limited in historical scope. It begins in 1402 with the capture of Edmund Mortimer, fifth earl of March, by Glendower. Shakespeare merges the Earl of March's character, as do his sources, with Sir Edmund Mortimer, his uncle, who married the daughter of Glendower. The Earl of March was the rightful heir to the throne after Richard II. The year 1402 was also the year of Hotspur's victory at Homildon, and in an early scene Hotspur explains why he did not turn over his prisoners to the King for ransom (1, 3).

Henry IV, Part I ends with the Battle of Shrewsbury in 1403, in which Hotspur is killed and the coalition of the Percies is defeated. Thus, both *Richard II* and *1 Henry IV* cover a period of only two years. All the plays of the Minor Tetralogy cover a much more substantial chunk of English history and are much more firmly rooted in the conflicts of nobles with one another and with the king. In this sense, the first part of *Henry IV* neglects the actual history of the period even more conspicuously than does *Richard II*. We don't see much of King Henry IV in the *Henry IV* plays, which concentrate on Prince Hal and, in the first part, on Hal and Hotspur and their legendary and mostly fictional conflict. Shakespeare tilts *1 Henry IV* spectacularly toward fiction by making Prince Hal and Hotspur more or less the same age. Actually, Hotspur was born in 1366, a year before both Henry IV and Richard II and twenty-one years before Prince Hal. The two parts of *Henry IV* seem much more devoted to the prodigal transformation of the roistering Prince Hal into the heroic King Henry V than to the untheatrical deeds of King Henry IV in putting down the conspiracies against him.

Prince Hal, who figures in four plays that culminate in *Henry V*, may be the most extensively developed character in all of Shakespeare, but he is definitely not Shakespeare's greatest success. He remains ambiguous; as a dramatic character, he is trapped somewhere between the King's two mythical bodies, the public figure representing the body politic and the private figure representing himself as an individual person. The needs of these two bodies conflict so deeply that as much as Prince Hal and Henry V try to reconcile their demands, the issue of what they should think and what they should do is never successfully resolved.

Prince Hal is forcefully inserted into *Richard II*, although he was only three years old at the time, in terms of the scapegrace, or incorrigible rascal, Prodigal Son myth on which his character is founded. The unhappy King wonders if anyone can inform him of his "unthrifty son" (*Richard II* 5.3.1). Prince Hal is part of the prophecies of the Bishop of Carlisle and Richard and a punishment for Bolingbroke's sins of usurpation: "If any plague hang over us, 'tis he"

(*Richard II* 5.3.3). These passages exactly anticipate the next play in the sequence, and Bolingbroke even announces the theme of transformation and redemption that takes powerful shape in *1 Henry IV*:

> As dissolute as desperate; but yet
> Through both I see some sparks of better hope,
> Which elder years may happily bring forth. (*Richard II* 5.3.20–22)

King Henry needs to be reminded of these "sparks of better hope" time and time again in the next play, but this statement functions as an official anticipation of what will happen in the first part of *Henry IV*, and King Henry speaks, as it were, for the needs of the tetralogy rather than for himself as a frustrated father.

Shakespeare draws on legendary, folklore material in presenting Hal as the Prodigal Son in the *Henry IV* plays. Hal's reformation is never in any doubt because he has to wind up as the heroic King Henry V, who conquers France and who seems to remove the curse of his father's usurpation. This presents a problem in Hal's dealings with Falstaff and his merry crew because Shakespeare does not want to fault Hal with time-serving and hypocrisy. Instead, Hal pursues a carefully delimited scapegrace role. He participates in a robbery with Falstaff and his companions that is not really a robbery but rather a practical joke on Falstaff himself—the booty will be paid back in full "with advantage" (2.4.549–50), or interest. There is no harm done and no moral stain, and Hal is technically justified in his desires: "Well then, once in my days I'll be a madcap" (1.2.146). If we consider the play as the education of a prince, then Hal sees a greater variety of life than any other heir-apparent before him, and certainly more than the narrowly heroic but testy and tragic Hotspur, with whom he is always compared. As the eminently political man, like his father but much broader in his understanding, Hal learns how to survive. We are assured from the beginning that he will defeat Hotspur and go on to become the glorious King Henry V.

Still, Hal is troubling as a dramatic figure and Shakespeare never manages to overcome the deep rifts in his character. Hal's soliloquy at the end of act 1, scene 2 comes very early in the action, as if Shakespeare is anxious to assure us about Hal and to quiet our misgivings. This soliloquy strongly resembles the soliloquies of the villain, especially Richard III, who appeals to the audience and tries to win them over to his cause. Hal reassures us that we needn't worry about him, that he knows what he is doing. The deliberateness and the moralistic tone of the soliloquy are exactly what trouble us, as if Prince Hal's character is already laid out for us right up to the rejection of Falstaff at the end of Part Two and the glorious military conquest of *Henry V*. The first words that Hal speaks, "I know you all" (1.2.199), are troubling because they suggest the powerful moral ambiguity that dogs the Prince. If he knows them all for what they are, then why does he consort with Falstaff and his crew and revel in the low-life amusements at the Boar's Head tavern in Eastcheap?

Hal already speaks with confidence about the future:

> So when this loose behavior I throw off
> And pay the debt I never promisèd,
> By how much better than my word I am,
> By so much shall I falsify men's hopes . . . (1.2.212–15)

This introduces an improper note of deliberation into the Prodigal Son story, as if the spiritual transformation is already laid out from the beginning. Hal speaks of his scapegrace adventures as providing a necessary "foil" (219) for his reformation. His ringing final couplet is a declaration of purpose intended to reassure the audience (and by implication his father, if he only knew what Hal was thinking):

> I'll so offend to make offense a skill,
> Redeeming time when men think least I will. (220–21)

"Redeeming time," or making amends for wasted time, has biblical connotations, as in Eph. 5:16.

Redemption words are of special importance in this play, which has at least six examples. In the crucial interview with his father in the middle of the play, Hal promises: "I will redeem all this on Percy's head" (3.2.132), and he goes on to describe a battle redemption in blood that looks forward to the Battle of Shrewsbury:

> When I will wear a garment all of blood,
> And stain my favors in a bloody mask,
> Which, washed away, shall scour my shame with it. (135–37)

In the battle itself, Hal rescues his father from the formidable Douglas, and Henry says appropriately:

> Thou hast redeemed thy lost opinion,
> And showed thou mak'st some tender of my life,
> In this fair rescue thou hast brought to me. (5.4.47–49)

Redeem is an honor word also associated with Hotspur, who assures his father and his uncle Worcester that "yet time serves wherein you may redeem / Your banished honors and restore yourselves" (1.3.178–79). A few lines later, when Hotspur is speaking about plucking "bright honor from the pale-faced moon" (200), he sees this grand gesture as having a practical purpose: "So he that doth redeem her thence might wear / Without corrival all her dignities" (204–5). Redemption is a form of recovery, of restoration, and of making all whole again. Hal's reformation is a calculated attempt to reassert his honor and to redeem his unthrifty time—but not immediately. I think we find disturbing the fact that Hal seems to schedule the resumption of his chivalric honor.

Hal's own awareness that he is playing the role of the Prodigal Son for a limited time colors the play, but we have continual assertions of Hal's manliness, sense of honor and duty, and natural feeling of authority. One of the most striking examples—and chilling, too—is in the tavern scene in act 2, scene 4. Falstaff is histrionically elaborating on his fatness and generosity, and, already anticipating his inevitable banishment, insists that Hal agree to protect him: "old Jack Falstaff, banish not him thy Harry's company, banish not him thy Harry's company, banish plump Jack, and banish all the world!" (2.4.478–80). Falstaff's unusual repetitiveness indicates anxiety, but Hal says only: "I do, I will" (481). These are remarkable lines in their starkness and commanding threat. Hal seems to be saying in no uncertain terms: "I do banish you, I will banish you." The harsh tone is like that of the soliloquy at the end of act 1, scene 2.

Once the Battle of Shrewsbury is in preparation, Hal moves quickly into his heroic, military role. At the end of act 3, scene 3, Hal speaks a ringing, patriotic couplet:

> The land is burning, Percy stands on high,
> And either we or they must lower lie. (209–10)

This is the grand public style of *Henry V*. In a way, Hal is merely echoing the chivalric sentiments of Hotspur, which prepare him to take a commanding role at the Battle of Shrewsbury. Hal looks, acts, and speaks like a warrior, and is not very different here from his role at the Battle of Agincourt in *Henry V*.

When Hal is bleeding at the Battle of Shrewsbury and Westmoreland offers to lead him to his tent, he defies him with heroic rhetoric:

> Lead me, my lord? I do not need your help;
> And God forbid a shallow scratch should drive
> The Prince of Wales from such a field as this,
> Where stained nobility lies trodden on,
> And rebels' arms triumph in massacres! (5.4.9–13)

He sounds like Coriolanus the relentless warrior, and it is interesting that he refers to himself now as "The Prince of Wales." The name *Hal* is for another time and another place. He threatens the formidable Earl of Douglas with heroic defiance: "Hold up thy head, vile Scot, or thou art like / Never to hold it up again" (38–39) and *"Douglas flieth"* (42 s.d.). He kills Hotspur as expected and speaks a noble eulogy for him. It is clear that Hal more than fulfills his promise in the soliloquy of act 1, scene 2: "Redeeming time when men think least I will" (221).

Hotspur has all the potentialities for tragedy that Hal lacks. He is noble, chivalric, eloquent, but entirely nonpolitical. This is important in Shakespearean characterization, and in *Julius Caesar*, a tragedy presented a few years after *1 Henry IV*, Brutus, too, is nonpolitical, and he makes the erroneous decisions that lead inevitably to his doom. Hotspur and Brutus—and Othello, too—are all innocents in a world of shrewd manipulators whose practical counsels are irresistible and fatal. Act 1, Scene 3 is characteristic of Hotspur. He makes a brilliant, personal, petulant speech about why he didn't send his prisoners at the Battle of Homildon to King Henry. He begins by saying: "My liege, I did deny no prisoners" (28), which is grossly incorrect. It's obvious that he doesn't understand, except in personal terms, the political issues involved in the prisoners.

Hotspur's father, Northumberland, and his uncle Worcester understand these political issues only too well as they launch their conspiracy against the King. Worcester and Northumberland have to explain laboriously to him the significance of Mortimer, whom Richard II proclaimed as heir to his throne. Hotspur finally acknowledges: "Nay, then I cannot blame his cousin king, / That wished him on the barren mountains starve" (1.3.156–57). When Worcester "will unclasp a secret book" (186) of the conspiracy of the Percys against King Henry, he cannot engage Hotspur's attention, who keeps ranting on about plucking "bright honor from the pale-faced moon" (200). Worcester responds with impatient irony to the inappropriateness of his nephew's grand speeches:

> He apprehends a world of figures here,
> But not the form of what he should attend.
> Good cousin, give me audience for a while. (207–9)

It takes another fifty lines for Worcester to begin his explanations, which Hotspur still frequently interrupts.

Hotspur speaks in an entirely different style from his uncle and his father. Where they are sober, rational, and explanatory, Hotspur exclaims grandly about the enterprise: "Why, it cannot choose but be a noble plot" (1.3.276). He seems hardly aware of the dangers he is being led into as he concludes the scene with a ringing couplet:

> Uncle, adieu. O, let the hours be short
> Till fields and blows and groans applaud our sport! (298–99)

We are not surprised later when the villainous Worcester refuses to tell his nephew of "The liberal and kind offer of the King" (5.2.2) that would have avoided the bloodshed of the Battle of Shrewsbury. In a practical sense, Hotspur is a naive warrior who is manipulated both by his uncle Worcester and by his father, Northumberland, who doesn't show up with his forces at the Battle of Shrewsbury but, instead, as we learn later, "Lies crafty-sick" (2 Henry IV, ind., 37).

Hotspur and his wife, Kate, present a pairing that is entirely different from any that Hal has in this play, and his alliance with Falstaff stands at an opposite remove from Hotspur and Kate. Hotspur is obviously warm, domestic, and loving, although he separates sharply his life as a warrior from his life as a husband. His big scene with Kate (2, 3) anticipates the scene of Brutus and his wife, Portia, in *Julius Caesar* (2, 1), but Hotspur reveals no secrets of state. He replies to Kate with wit and charm and affection:

> *Lady.* What is it carries you away?
> *Hotspur.* Why, my horse, my love—my horse! (2.3.77–78)

Kate speaks in an intimate, colloquial prose that is both joking and desperate:

> Come, come, you paraquito [= parrot], answer me directly unto this question that I ask. In faith, I'll break thy little finger, Harry, and if thou wilt not tell me all things true. (86–89)

Presumably Kate makes a gesture to seize Hotspur's little finger. Her husband answers with bravado:

> Away, away, you trifler! Love? I love thee not;
> I care not for thee, Kate. This is no world
> To play with mammets and to tilt with lips.
> We must have bloody noses and cracked crowns,
> And pass them current too. (90–94)

These are heroic sentiments to which Hal would not literally subscribe, particularly the statement that "This is no world / To play with mammets." *Mammet* is a variant form of *maumet*, derived from *Mahomet*, whom Saracens supposedly worshiped as their God in the form of an idol. Hal has plenty of toys to play with before he takes up the business of state, but Hotspur is tragically committed, against his own impetuous and pleasure-loving nature, to "pluck up drownèd honor by the locks" (1.3.203) and to have "bloody noses and cracked crowns." He leaves his Kate with chivalrous swagger: "when I am a-horseback, I will swear / I love thee infinitely" (2.3.101–2). His Kate is very different from Henry V's Kate, who is a perfect political prize for the conqueror of France.

The first part of *Henry IV* is radically different from any history play that Shakespeare wrote before in its departure from affairs of state that concern only kings, nobles, and great lords. This play is intimately concerned with the ordinary life of England that lies

177

behind the great events and perhaps explains them. Falstaff and his companions resemble Jack Cade and his followers in *Henry VI, Part II,* but they have no significant role in what happens in the kingdom. This play, and even more so the second part of *Henry IV,* are Shakespeare's unique contributions to English social history as a way of understanding the problems facing King Henry IV at the beginning of the fifteenth century. This puts it too directly and too portentously, but the doings of Falstaff and his men and the Boar's Head tavern in Eastcheap affect our understanding of King Henry, Prince Hal, and the powerful conspiracies against the newly usurped throne.

Act 2, Scene 1, for example, is a little genre scene that takes place in an inn yard in Rochester just before the famous robbery at Gad's Hill. It is early morning, and two carriers of merchandise are getting ready to depart. The First Carrier is concerned about the comfort of his horse and speaks to Tom the Ostler within:

> I prithee, Tom, beat Cut's saddle, put a few flocks in the point [i.e., put a little wool or cotton padding in the pommel]; poor jade is wrung in the withers [i.e., badly galled in the shoulder ridge] out of all cess [i.e., excessively]. (2.1.5–7)

The Second Carrier complains about the dankness and the fleas in the inn, but remembers a better time: "This house is turned upside down since Robin Ostler died" (10–11). We never learn anything further about Robin the Ostler, but the First Carrier has a memorable line about the cause of his death: "Poor fellow never joyed since the price of oats rose; it was the death of him" (12–13). The prevalence of fleas in the inn comes about because "they will allow us ne'er a jordan [=chamberpot], and then we leak in your chimney [=fireplace], and your chamber-lye breeds fleas like a loach [=a good-eating fish that breeds often]" (20–22).

What has all this to do with the state of the nation? Gaunt speaks abstractly in *Richard II* about "This blessed plot, this earth, this realm, this England" (2.1.50), but the carriers speak less abstractly about the England they know and where they earn their living. The action soon moves to Gadshill (the person, not the place) and the Chamberlain of the inn, who prepare for the robbery (the Chamberlain furnishes useful information to the thieves). Gadshill's declaration of invincibility—"We steal as in a castle, cocksure. We have the receipt of fernseed, we walk invisible" (89–90)—is also a statement about the condition of the realm. None of this is meant allegorically, but it does provide us with a context for the other side of the social spectrum about which kings and nobles know nothing.

Falstaff himself is Shakespeare's most magnificent comic creation, and he is doubly significant, given that he features so importantly in a history play. He is a figure developed from the Vice in old morality plays and close to Sir Toby Belch in *Twelfth Night*, a play written a year or two after *1 Henry IV*. A somewhat different Falstaff is also the comic protagonist (and butt) of *The Merry Wives of Windsor*, in which, presumably, he was revived at Queen Elizabeth's command. He is corpulent and has all the eloquent and vivacious cowardice of the braggart soldier (the *miles gloriosus* of Plautus). What is Falstaff doing in a history play? For one thing, like the fool or clown in comedy, he undercuts the heroic rhetoric of his betters. Falstaff is in the play almost specifically to parody what Hotspur says about honor and presumably what Hal, in his more statesmanlike self, thinks about it, too. This parody of chivalric, military values occurs right in the midst of the Battle of Shrewsbury, as if it is a necessary comment on the pretensions on which the battle is fought.

Falstaff's long soliloquy on Honor concludes the great events of act 5, scene 1. In the form of a dialogue with himself that Falstaff recites like a catechism, he asks himself questions that he answers pithily: "Can honor set to a leg? No. Or an arm? No. Or take away the grief of a wound? No. Honor hath no skill in surgery then? No" (5.1.131–34). Then *honor* is merely an honorific word, mere "air." Therefore Falstaff rejects "honor," which is a "mere scutcheon" (140–41), or shield painted with one's coat of arms such as a noble warrior bore. Falstaff will have none of it. The soliloquy is concluded when Falstaff sees the body of the dead Sir Walter Blunt: "There's honor for you!" (5.3.32–33). In another memorable soliloquy at the end of this scene, Falstaff makes his own private declaration about honor: "I like not such grinning honor as Sir Walter hath. Give me life; which if I can save, so; if not, honor comes unlooked for, and there's an end" (58–61). This goes against everything that Hotspur most cherishes, and Hal, too, when he is playing the heroic warrior, although Hal equivocates and we could easily imagine him saying, "Give me life."

Among the many things that could be said about Falstaff, I would like to mention only two: his interest in hyperbole and his histrionic, self-dramatizing style. Falstaff is drunk with language, as if words were entities in themselves, so that his wit is a form of imaginative exercise by which he controls reality. He speaks with plenitude and copiousness, matching the physical excess of his body. Euphemism is a form of verbal magic by which painful and tawdry things are glorified. Falstaff is naturally given to poetic overstatement, and he is eager to have Prince Hal's warrant that, when he is king, he will promise to convert literal statement into poetic metaphor:

> When thou art king, let not us that are squires of the night's body be called thieves of the day's beauty. Let us be Diana's foresters, gentle-men of the shade, minions of the moon; and let men say we be men of good government, being governed, as the sea is, by our noble and chaste mistress the moon, under whose countenance we steal. (1.2.23–30)

In other words, Hal's ideal commonwealth shall depend principally on euphemism, puns, and wordplay.

In act 2, scene 4, we have the comic exaggeration of the "Four rogues in buckram" (195) who set upon Falstaff, but in his wit combats with the Prince, Falstaff always asserts his superiority. To the Prince's offering of words for obesity, Falstaff thunders in quite spontaneously with a hyperbolical catalogue of thinness:

> 'Sblood, you starveling, you eel-skin, you dried neat's tongue, you bull's pizzle, you stockfish—O for breath to utter what is like thee!—you tailor's yard, you sheath, you bowcase, you vile standing tuck [=rapier]! (2.4.244–48)

This is an extravagant display of Falstaff's stylistic virtuosity, as if the only reality were the reality of words.

Falstaff's histrionic ability seems to be professional, or at least semiprofessional, like that of Hamlet. Dame Quickly is overcome with admiration for Falstaff's "play extempore" (2.4.281): "O Jesu, he doth it as like one of these harlotry players as ever I see!" (395–96). The secret lies in Falstaff's skill in parody, and he seems to move among various antiquated styles with great facility:

> For God's sake, lords, convey my tristful queen!
> For tears do stop the floodgates of her eyes. (393–94)

In all his plays-within-a-play, both in whole and in fragments, Shakespeare had a genius for imitating an obsolete and archaic style. Like Bottom the Weaver in *A Midsummer Night's Dream*, who "could play Ercles [Hercules] rarely, or a part to tear a cat in, to make all split" (1.2.30–31), Falstaff wants a cup of sack to make his eyes look red, "for I must speak in passion, and I will do it in King Cambyses' vein" (2.4.386–87). Cambyses is the ranting tyrant in Thomas Preston's *Lamentable Tragedie, mixed full of plesant mirth* (1569).

When Falstaff plays the part of King Henry, he offers an elaborate parody of John Lyly's *Euphues* (1578), with its absurd animal and plant analogies and its intricate matching of vowels and consonants. It is entertaining in its astonishing comparisons: "For though the camomile, the more it is trodden on, the faster it grows, so youth, the more it is wasted, the sooner it wears" (2.4.399–402). Falstaff energizes Prince Hal in a way that enables him to enjoy himself, to kill Hotspur, and to emerge as the heroic Henry V. Hal is not tragic but a survivor. From Falstaff's unbounded histrionic skill, Hal learns how to play the part of the king with an authenticity that can only come from deep and various experience.

Henry IV, Part II

The second part of *Henry IV* is the least historical of Shakespeare's history plays. It begins sometime after the Battle of Shrewsbury in 1403 and climaxes with the surrender of the rebels at the Battle of Gaultree Forest in 1405 under the false pretenses of Prince John's truce. There is some allusion to the Battle of Bramham Moor in 1408, in which Northumberland perished. Shakespeare skips five years (1408–1413) and takes up the account in 1413, when Henry IV dies and Prince Hal assumes the throne as King Henry V. Little about these public events appears in the second part of *Henry IV*, which again concentrates on the doings of Prince Hal rather than the King. *Henry IV, Part II* is firmly rooted in English social history, even more fully than Part I. There is a richness in the depiction of English life, including rural scenes in Gloucestershire with Justice Shallow and Justice Silence, that is extraordinary in Shakespeare.

The second part of *Henry IV* does not continue the first part as if it were its chronological sequel, the way plays in the Minor Tetralogy do. The three parts of *Henry VI* and *Richard III* are sequential in a literal and predictable sense. Since the second part of *Henry IV* is much more steeped in myths and legends about Prince Hal than in history, it offers something like a recapitulation of the first part. Although the reformation of Prince Hal is clearly established by the time of the Battle of Shrewsbury in the first part, the wastrel Hal is once more in evidence in the second part, so that he needs to redeem himself once again as if the events in Part I never occurred. This second redemption is not exactly true, although Hal in the second part is much chastened from the prince of the first part, and he is deliberately separated from Falstaff. Yet the second part looks suspiciously as if it is replaying the first. Hal's final and indisputable redemption comes only when he becomes King Henry V and publicly repudiates Falstaff. It looks as if Shakespeare wants to have it both ways in *Henry IV, Part II*, with Hal once again a wild card to his father, to his brothers, and to the nobility, but clearly not so wild as in the first part.

The ambiguity of Hal's role is central to the *Henry IV* plays and undoubtedly to *Henry V*. As perhaps the most fully developed character in all of Shakespeare, with a large role extending over four plays, Hal is nevertheless a problem. There is no reasonable way to reconcile the contradictions in the Prodigal Son myth, and the assumption that the Prodigal Son is a richer and more developed human being for his varied experiences is true only in a limited sense. We can see Hal in the second part of *Henry IV* clearly moving toward *Henry V*, but the steps are excessively deliberate and even histrionic.

In act 2, scene 2, for example, when the Prince and Poins resolve to disguise themselves as drawers and appear before Falstaff and his companions at the Boar's Head tavern in Eastcheap, their exploit doesn't have the same scapegrace flavor as the robbery at Gad's Hill in Part I, but it is extenuated with a moralistic tone that is disturbing. Hal no longer seems comfortable with his low-life companion Poins. The Prince answers his own question, "Must I marry your sister?" (137–38), with a Sophoclean chorus: "Well, thus we play the fools with the time, and the spirits of the wise sit in the clouds and mock us" (141–43). He speaks of Falstaff somewhat remotely as the "old boar" who feeds "in the old frank" (143–46), and he compares his metamorphosis into a drawer to Jupiter's becoming a bull to seduce Europa:

> From a God to a bull? A heavy descension! It was Jove's case. From a
> prince to a prentice? A low transformation! That shall be mine, for in
> everything the purpose must weigh with the folly. (173–76)

The justification is so overwrought that the escapade no longer
sounds like fun. At the end Hal apologizes formally to Poins: "By
heaven, Poins, I feel me much to blame, / So idly to profane the
precious time" (370–71). This is not the carefree tone of the old
Hal, who now seems to be self-consciously bent on "Redeeming time
when men think least I will" (*1 Henry IV* 1.2.221).

The two contiguous scenes, 4 and 5 of act 4, bring us much closer
to the time when Prince Hal becomes the new king. Henry IV is
sick, as he is for much of the second part, and he contemplates with
alarm the succession of his son Hal to the throne. But he tempers his
fear of Hal's "headstrong riot" (4.4.62) with traditional images of
generosity and graciousness: "Most subject is the fattest soil to weeds"
(54). Warwick reassures him that the Prince is only studying his
companions "to gain the language" (69), and "in the perfectness of
time," he will certainly "Cast off his followers" (74–75).

Act 4, scene 5 is central to the play in clarifying the relation of
Prince Hal to his father. Hal's soliloquy when he comes upon his
sick father sleeping, with the crown lying on a pillow beside him,
curiously echoes the earlier soliloquy of the King, unable to sleep "in
the calmest and most stillest night, / With all appliances and means
to boot" (3.1.28–29). The King's concluding line, "Uneasy lies the
head that wears a crown" (31), provides the theme for the later
scene, when Prince Hal, supposing his father dead, puts on the
crown and invests himself as king.

Prince Hal's concerns focus much more on the crown itself than
on his dying father. He speaks like Tamburlaine in apostrophes of
hypnotic fascination:

> O polished perturbation! Golden care!
> That keep'st the ports of slumber open wide
> To many a watchful night! (4.5.22–24)

The formal rhetoric of exclamation reduces any sense of personal
grief or even involvement. This troubles the King when he awakes,

but father and son have many similarities. The Prince vows "The noble change that I have purposèd" (154), and King Henry is impressed with his son's kingly ardor, although his personal argument might be shaky. They are both equivocators, and Henry dies remembering the "indirect crooked ways / I met this crown" (184–85) and that he has finally accomplished his religious vow by dying if not in Jerusalem on a holy crusade then at least in the royal chamber called "Jerusalem."

The rejection of Falstaff follows this scene directly, and King Henry V's eloquent speech confirms the expectations of his early soliloquy in *Henry IV, Part I* about his "reformation, glitt'ring o'er my fault" (1.2.217). What is surprising about the speech is its homiletic quality. Henry speaks in religious and theological terms that he has never used before and will not use again. Falstaff is advised to "Fall to thy prayers" (5.5.48). He is "So surfeit-swelled, so old, and so profane" (51) that "the grave doth gape / For thee thrice wider than for other men" (54–55). The theme of the King's discourse is memento mori, remember that you will die, and he speaks like a preacher about abandoning carnality and awakening to thoughts of salvation: "Make less thy body hence, and more thy grace" (53).

King Henry speaks with all the fervent conviction of a reformed sinner:

> For God doth know, so shall the world perceive,
> That I have turned away my former self.
> So will I those that kept me company. (5.5.58–60)

Hal uses the language of his worst critics in order to emphasize his reformation: Falstaff was not his boon companion but "The tutor and the feeder of my riots" (63). All this sermonizing means nothing to Falstaff, who is genuinely baffled by Hal's conduct now that he has become king. He can only believe, vainly, that "I shall be sent for in private to him" (78–79).

The temporizing and political expediency that are so strong in Prince Hal and his father are also expressed in the unforgettable figure of Northumberland, the father of Hotspur. He is an important personage in *Richard II*, a strong and immediate ally of Bolingbroke against King Richard. The aging King Henry IV remembers Northumberland in a brooding, meditative scene in which he tries to understand "the revolution of the times" (3.1.46). By the unpredictable turnings of history, less than ten years ago Richard and Northumberland, "great friends, / Did feast together, and in two years after / Were they at wars" (58–60). And only eight years ago

> This Percy was the man nearest my soul,
> Who like a brother toiled in my affairs
> And laid his love and life under my foot . . . (61–63)

Henry goes so far as to quote, almost exactly, the words that Richard spoke to Northumberland in *Richard II* (5.1.55ff.):

> "Northumberland, thou ladder by the which
> My cousin Bolingbroke ascends my throne"—. . . (3.1.70–71)

Quotation from another play is rare in Shakespeare, but it serves here to bind together the plays of the Major Tetralogy. Richard's prophecy about Northumberland is now proved true. This is the burden of Warwick's speech about "the hatch and brood of time" (86), which demonstrates that "There is a history in all men's lives" (80). By this insight,

> King Richard might create a perfect guess
> That great Northumberland, then false to him,
> Would of that seed grow to a greater falseness,
> Which should not find a ground to root upon,
> Unless on you. (88–92)

This is the most philosophical and reflective scene in all of Shakespeare's histories. It has a distinct historiographical edge.

Northumberland is the great no-show of Shakespeare's histories, and the second part of *Henry IV* opens with the devious induction of "*Rumor, painted full of tongues*," who sets the political tone of the play. Rumor is an odd, allegorical figure more appropriate to a masque than a history play, but he sows an initial confusion and chaos that are never fully dissipated. We learn clearly that Hotspur's father has deserted him by never appearing at the Battle of Shrewsbury, where Hotspur was killed by Prince Hal. Northumberland "Lies crafty-sick" in his "worm-eaten hole of ragged stone" (ind., 35–37). In the confusing first scene of the play, he makes some grotesque and unfeeling puns about his son's death: "Said he young Harry Percy's spur was cold? / Of Hotspur Coldspur?" (1.1.49–40).

Later in the play, Hotspur's widow, Kate, accuses Northumberland directly of abandoning his son on the field of Shrewsbury:

> Him did you leave,
> Second to none, unseconded by you,
> To look upon the hideous god of war
> In disadvantage . . . (2.3.33–36)

Ironically, both his daughter-in-law and his wife now advise Northumberland to abandon Archbishop Scroop and the other conspirators and to flee to Scotland. Northumberland has already broken his word to Hotspur and lost his honor at the Battle of Shrewsbury; he has no more honor to lose by fleeing to Scotland. Kate tragically calls up the figure of her husband, who, like Hamlet, was "The glass of fashion, and the mold of form, / Th' observed of all observers" (*Hamlet* 3.1.154–55). So Hotspur "was the mark and glass, copy and book, / That fashioned others" (2.3.31–32), even in "speaking thick" (24), or impetuously and quickly.

Falstaff in the second part of *Henry IV* is somewhat different from the figure in the first part, but not radically changed. Part II puts a strong emphasis on his age and mortality. In act 1, scene 2 with the Lord Chief Justice, Falstaff's insistence on his youth is a sure sign of his sense of decay. The Lord Chief Justice lays it out with physiological details:

> Do you set down your name in the scroll of youth, that are written down old with all the characters of age? Have you not a moist eye, a dry hand, a yellow cheek, a white beard, a decreasing leg, an increasing belly? Is not your voice broken, your wind short, your chin double, your wit single, and every part about you blasted with antiquity, and will you yet call yourself young? Fie, fie, fie, Sir John! (185–93)

Falstaff engages the Lord Chief Justice in a combat of repartee and riposte that he maintains for almost two hundred lines, speaking in the style of the clown or fool in Shakespeare's earlier comedies.

187

To the Lord Chief Justice's charges, he says only:

My lord, I was born about three of the clock in the afternoon, with a
white head and something a round belly. For my voice, I have lost it
with hallowing and singing of anthems. To approve my youth further,
I will not. The truth is, I am only old in judgment and understanding
. . . (194–99)

Throughout the scene, the Lord Chief Justice is the straight man for
Falstaff's merciless wordplay, as in the following exchange:

Chief Justice. There is not a white hair in your face but should have his
effect of gravity.
Falstaff. His effect of gravy, gravy, gravy. (166–68)

The mad Hamlet plays a similar role with Polonius of infinite re-
sourcefulness and unstoppable punning. Both Falstaff and Hamlet
insist on having the last word.

Falstaff's scenes with Justice Shallow and Justice Silence in Gloucestershire are different from anything in the first part of *Henry IV*
because they are so buoyantly rustic. Justice Shallow exalts his heroic
youth as a law student at Clement's Inn, where he knew "Jack Falstaff,
now Sir John, a boy, and page to Thomas Mowbray, Duke of
Norfolk" (3.2.25–27). Shallow reminisces nostalgically, and perhaps
drunkenly, of the mad days of his youth: "O, Sir John, do you
remember since we lay all night in the Windmill in Saint George's
Field?" (199–200). Falstaff remembers Jane Nightwork, but she is
"Old, old, Master Shallow" (211). As Silence informs us, that was
fifty-five years ago. Falstaff admits that "We have heard the chimes
at midnight" (220), but later, in a soliloquy, he discourses on "how
subject we old men are to this vice of lying" (312–13). He recalls
Shallow as a forlorn figure: "When 'a was naked, he was, for all the
world, like a forked radish, with a head fantastically carved upon it
with a knife" (319–21). Now that Shallow has "land and beeves"
(338) he will be Falstaff's prey; using an image from alchemy, Falstaff
calls him "a philosopher's two stones [testicles] to me" (3.2.340). All
this is enacted when Falstaff returns to Gloucestershire in act 5.

Again, Falstaff's scenes with Dame Quickly and Doll Tearsheet
emphasize his age and physical decrepitude. Prince Hal as observer
of the maudlin scene in the Boar's Head tavern says: "Look, whe'r

the withered elder hath not his poll clawed like a parrot" (2.4.265–66), presumably by Doll herself, who is scratching his head in the style of Titania scratching the ass's head of Bottom in *A Midsummer Night's Dream*. Poins is even more cruelly direct: "Is it not strange that desire should so many years outlive performance?" (267–68). But Falstaff holds his own in this scene. He is not only witty and gracious but he also sings various scraps of old ballads to indicate his high spirits. In the same way Doll Tearsheet is not only drunk but also excessively affectionate as she toys with Falstaff's old body: "Thou whoreson little tidy Bartholomew boar-pig, when wilt thou leave fighting o' days and foining o' nights, and begin to patch up thine old body for heaven?" (235–38). Falstaff can only answer her as if she were in herself a memento mori: "Peace, good Doll! Do not speak like a death's-head. Do not bid me remember mine end" (239–40). The scene concludes with a sentimental acknowledgment of Falstaff's power to inspire affection. The Hostess says: "I have known thee these twenty-nine years, come peascod-time, but an honester and truer-hearted man—well, fare thee well" (391–94). And Doll Tearsheet comes running to say goodbye to Falstaff, who is off to the wars. In the Hostess's report, "She comes blubbered" (400), with a tear-stained face.

Perhaps the most remarkable character in the play is Falstaff's "ancient," or ensign or standard-bearer, Pistol (in *Othello* Iago is "his Moorship's ancient" [1.1.30]). There are endless puns on Pistol's name, which was pronounced "pizzle," the word for an animal's penis, especially a bull's. Thus Pistol threatens to "discharge" upon Dame Quickly "with two bullets," but Falstaff claims that "She is pistol-proof" (2.4.116–18). The Hostess in fact calls him "Good Captain Pizzle" (165). Pistol's great specialty is parody, and he speaks grandiloquently in scraps and tags from the playhouse. His speech is like a garbled anthology of contemporary heroic literature.

His great love, however, is Marlowe, especially the mighty lines of Marlowe's *Tamburlaine*. While the Hostess is trying to calm his ferocious but entirely histrionic anger, Pistol emotes with furious rodomontade:

> These be good humors, indeed! Shall pack-horses
> And hollow pampered jades of Asia,

> Which cannot go but thirty mile a day,
> Compare with Caesars, and with Cannibals,
> And Trojan Greeks? Nay, rather damn them with
> King Cerberus, and let the welkin roar. (2.4.167–72)

This is more than a little mixed up. By *Cannibals* Pistol obviously means *Hannibals*, and Marlowe's famous lines from the beginning of act 4, scene 3 of the second part of *Tamburlaine* are:

> Holla, ye pamper'd jades of Asia!
> What, can ye draw but twenty miles a day?

King Cerberus is the three-headed dog that stood guard over the underworld, and *welkin* is a fancy, affected word for "sky," as in the Clown's speech in *Twelfth Night*: "Who you are and what you would are out of my welkin" (3.1.58–59). Pistol's exuberance and comic invention are an essential part of Shakespeare's imagination for the second part of *Henry IV*. Its official history is steeped in a sense of England as it is, in all its wildness and adventurous possibilities, both in people and in language.

Henry V

Henry V came to the throne in 1413, an event that occurred in the last act of *Henry IV, Part II. Henry V* begins with preparations for Henry's expedition against France, which seems to follow the dying advice of his father, Henry IV: "to busy giddy minds / With foreign quarrels" (2 *Henry IV* 4.5.213–14). The English embark for France from Southampton in 1415, where Henry executes the conspirators Scroop, Cambridge, and Grey. This is the last we hear about plotters against the throne. The great English victories at Harfleur and Agincourt both take place in 1415. Shakespeare skips the Normandy campaign of 1417–1420, but he uses the peace treaty of Troyes in 1420 in act 5. Henry V dies in 1422, but that is beyond the scope of this play. Thus the history in *Henry V* concentrates chiefly on events from the year 1415, but its attention to historical matters is fairly minimal.

The emphasis in this final play of the Major Tetralogy is on the heroic celebration of Henry as the ideal English king, who seems to take the stain off the house of Lancaster for usurping the throne and killing Richard II. Henry remembers Richard and prays to God to overlook his father's crime:

Not today, O Lord,
O, not today, think not upon the fault
My father made in compassing the crown! (4.1.297–99)

This is the only mention of Richard in the play, and like the language in the rest of the play, it is formal and public, although it occurs in a soliloquy. We never have much sense of Henry as a personal figure, and this is a problem in the two plays that precede this one in the Major Tetralogy. Henry's soliloquies tend to be formal orations, much like his battle speeches.

The soliloquy that precedes the one from which I have been quoting takes up the familiar topic of the King's two bodies, but it is disappointing on the private side of the equation: "What infinite heart's-ease / Must kings neglect that private men enjoy!" (4.1.241– 42). All that we hear of private men is that they sleep soundly, like the "wretched slave, / Who, with a body filled, and vacant mind" (273–74) manages to sleep all night in Elysium.

But Henry speaks grandly of the "thrice-gorgeous ceremony" (4.1.271) of kingship in the elevated, divine right style of Richard II and Marlowe's Tamburlaine:

the balm, the scepter, and the ball,
The sword, the mace, the crown imperial,
The intertissued robe of gold and pearl,
The farcèd title running fore the king,
The throne he sits on, nor the tide of pomp
That beats upon the high shore of this world . . . (265–70)

There is no speech on kingship in Shakespeare more glorious than this one, and it is interesting that such resounding rhetorical display occurs in a soliloquy. Just before this Henry spoke with adoration of "thou idol Ceremony" (245): "Art thou aught else but place, degree, and form, / Creating awe and fear in other men?" (251–52). In all of Shakespeare's histories, Henry is the figure most fitting to be king, and the play, with minor exceptions, celebrates his kingship.

The self-indulgent Prince Hal is remembered only to be soundly refuted. How wrong the Dauphin is to send Henry a tun of tennis balls, which he mocks with patriotic fervor:

> When we have matched our rackets to these balls,
> We will in France (by God's grace) play a set
> Shall strike his father's crown into the hazard. (1.2.261–63)

This begins a speech of excessive length full of puns and inflamed exhortation. Later the Dauphin makes the same mistake when he speaks with the French Lords of Henry as "a vain, giddy, shallow, humorous youth" (2.4.28). Henry is none of those things, nor ever was, and the Constable of France tries to correct the Dauphin.

Prince Hal's vanities "Were but the outside of the Roman Brutus, / Covering discretion with a coat of folly" (2.4.37–38). This refers not to Marcus Brutus of *Julius Caesar* but rather to Lucius Junius Brutus of *The Rape of Lucrece*, who "throws that shallow habit by / Wherein deep policy did him disguise" (1814–1815) and rouses the Romans to expel the Tarquins. The Chorus to act 5 speaks of Henry's return to England after the Battle of Agincourt as if he were a Roman hero in a triumphal procession:

> The mayor and all his brethren in best sort—
> Like to the senators of th' antique Rome,
> With the plebeians swarming at their heels—
> Go forth and fetch their conqu'ring Caesar in . . . (5.25–28)

Shakespeare is already preparing in *Henry V* to write his next play, *Julius Caesar*.

The choruses in *Henry V* that precede each act are unusual in Shakespeare, occurring again only in *Pericles*, in which Gower is given an important narrative function. But in *Henry V* the role of the Chorus is more epic than narrative, in the sense that the Chorus attempts to exploit the largeness of scope of the play and its nationalistic fervor. In *Henry V* the Chorus is constantly apologizing to the audience for the limitations of the theater and appealing to them to "Piece out our imperfections with your thoughts" (1.23). This shouldn't be taken to mean that Shakespeare was chafing at the bit about his pitiful theatrical resources, but rather that he wanted to claim some grandeur in his theme that the theater was inadequate to deliver.

The prologue to act 1 begins with an invocation of the Muse that imitates epic:

> O for a Muse of fire, that would ascend
> The brightest heaven of invention:
> A kingdom for a stage, princes to act,
> And monarchs to behold the swelling scene! (1–4)

The Muse is to inspire the poet to rise to "The brightest heaven of invention," *invention* being a strictly rhetorical term for finding topics to write about and also a metonymy for imaginative creation. The royal scene, and especially "princes to act," suggests the occasion of masques, which were expensive and allegorical exhibitions presented at court and at great houses. But *Henry V*, a public theater play, is none of these grand things that it aspires to. The Prologue asks pardon for trying to "bring forth / So great an object" "On this unworthy scaffold" (10–11).

The formal choruses preceding each act endow *Henry V* (and *Pericles*, too) with a five-act structure unusual in Shakespeare, but in this play the choruses also serve to present each act as if it were a separate demonstration of King Henry's greatness. The warlike Harry should function like an allegorical figure from the masques. He should "Assume the port of Mars" (1.6) and at his heels, Famine, Sword, and Fire should "Crouch for employment" (8). This is what the Chorus would like to present but cannot, yet we feel throughout the play that the Chorus's pretensions are not entirely unrealized. The excessive fullness of Henry's speeches often comes close to epic vaunting rather than ordinary dramatic conversation. There is a tremendous appeal in the choruses to the audience's thoughts, which are supposed to make up for any deficiences in the author's, or actors', or theater's execution.

The choruses to acts 2 and 3 begin with the kind of "flourish" or trumpet fanfare that precedes the entrance of royalty. In the preparation at Southampton for embarkation to France, the English soldiers are mythologized as "Following the mirror of all Christian kings / With winged heels, as English Mercuries" (2.6–7). The personified figure of Expectation sits in the air with a heraldic sword filled "With crowns imperial, crowns and coronets / Promised to Harry and his followers" (10–11). The expedition clearly has an allegorical cast. In the Chorus to act 3, "chambers," or small cannons, are shot off to illustrate the action of the "nimble gunner" (32), and, we are told, for effect: "And down goes all before them" (34). Some thirty-five lines later, *"chambers go off"* again to celebrate Henry V's "Once more unto the breach" oration before Harfleur. Throughout, the Chorus appeals to the audience to "Play with your fancies" (7) and "eke out our performance with your mind" (35).

The Chorus before act 4 is on the night before the Battle of Agincourt, and it prepares us for the tremendous odds against the English. This Chorus is like a narrative set piece describing the theatrical scenes we are about to see. Most prominently, we perceive a larger-than-life figure of the King, circulating among his troops and offering them encouragement and good cheer: "A little touch of Harry in the night" (47). Again, the Chorus exalts Henry into a mythological figure: "A largess universal, like the sun, / His liberal eye doth give to everyone" (43–44).

The Chorus before act 5 is the most narrative in its function, asking the audience to "brook abridgment" (44) as the King and his troops are carried to Calais, to London, and back to France again. There is even an allusion to the Earl of Essex's expedition to Ireland in March 1599 to suppress the rebellion of Tyrone. The Chorus "prompts" those in the audience "that have not read the story" (1) of Henry V in Holinshed and in other sources that Shakespeare used. This is an unusually self-conscious act, and it fits in well with the Chorus's appeal to the audience's "quick forge and working house of thought" (23). The image of the forge recalls Falstaff's soliloquy on the operation of "sherris-sack," which makes the brain "apprehensive, quick, forgetive, full of nimble, fiery, and delectable shapes" (2 *Henry IV* 4.3.102–3). This is the only adjectival use of *forgetive* in Shakespeare.

Even in Henry's admirable wooing of Kate, the French princess, there is something impersonal and larger than life. Henry is adopting the impetuous bravado of Hotspur in his relations with his wife, Kate, but the personal dimension is almost entirely factitious. Although the wooing is enacted privately between Henry and Katherine, accompanied by her gentlewoman and interpreter, Alice, it is nevertheless a dynastic event crucial to the agreed-upon terms of the Treaty of Troyes with the King of France. It is a foregone conclusion that Kate doesn't have the prerogative of refusal, yet the scene is acted with wit and verve on both parts.

Kate is charming and seductive and Henry represents himself as a "plain king" (5.2.127) and a "plain soldier" (153) with a "good heart" (167) who will win his woman like a warrior "with scambling" (212), a word remembered from *King John* (4.3.146). *Scamble* is defined by the *OED* as "to struggle indecorously or rapaciously to obtain something, scramble." It occurs in the first sentence of the play when the Archbishop of Canterbury explains that the bill against the temporal possessions of the clergy was almost passed in the eleventh hour of Henry IV's reign, "But that the scambling and unquiet time / Did push it out of farther question" (1.1.4–5). An element of scambling can be found in the Archbishop's endless, genealogical discourse about how the Law Salique (barring inheritance of the French throne through the female line) is invalid. Henry's invasion of France is sanctioned by the clergy in exchange for his opposition to the bill cutting off the temporal possessions of the clergy. The opening of *Henry V* is thus endowed with a sophistic, even cynical argument.

It is odd but characteristic of Henry that he should use such a pejorative word as *scambling* for his wooing of Kate, as if she were a conquest of war (which she indeed is). Henry's impetuous desire for a kiss may be echoed from the ending of *The Taming of the Shrew*— "Come on and kiss me, Kate" (5.2.182)—although Henry never uses the exact phrase of Petruchio. In the translation of Alice, *kiss* is ambiguous, but it already suggested the vulgar meaning of *baiser* in modern French: "Dat it is not be de fashon pour le ladies of France— I cannot tell wat is 'baiser' en Anglish" (273–74). This is not exactly a love scene but a wonderful demonstration of the irresistible attractions of Henry as a man and as a king. The English language scene (3, 4) certainly plays on all the bawdy implications of perfectly innocent English words for "le pied et la robe" (49). *Foot* and *count* are clearly "gros, et impudique, et non pour les dames d'honneur d'user" (52–53), but Katherine nevertheless has a good time speaking ribald words and making macaronic puns.

Henry V has the most developed French scenes of any play of Shakespeare and throughout demonstrates an interest in presenting ethnic characteristics. The English army has an Irish captain, Macmorris, and a Scots captain, Jamy, with their appropriate mannerisms and accents, but great emphasis falls on the Welsh, as it does in the first part of *Henry IV*, with Owen Glendower, Hotspur's wife, Kate (who is Mortimer's sister), and Mortimer's wife, who speaks no English and who sings a song in Welsh. In *Henry V* Henry is emphatically Welsh, as he protests to Pistol that Harry le Roy is not a Cornish name: "No, I am a Welshman" (4.1.51). With Fluellen Henry celebrates Saint Davy's Day by wearing a leek in his cap: "I wear it for a memorable honor; / For I am Welsh, you know, good countryman" (4.7.107–8). Fluellen exclaims with patriotic fervor: "All the water in Wye cannot wash your Majesty's Welsh plood out of your pody" (109–10) and "By Jeshu, I am your Majesty's countryman, I care not who know it!" (114–15).

Fluellen is one of the most attractive figures in the play. He is learned in the disciplines of the wars (especially the Roman wars), eccentric, kindly, but also bluff and hearty as a soldier should be. He speaks with a broad Welsh accent like the comic Parson Evans in *The Merry Wives of Windsor*. It is interesting that Fluellen should deliver a moving eulogy for Falstaff that matches the elegiac comments of Falstaff's boon companions, especially Mistress Quickly's: "The King has killed his heart" (2.1.91).

Fluellen expatiates on the comparison of Henry with Alexander the Great that seems to come right out of Plutarch's parallel lives of Greeks and Romans, with the comparisons that ended each pairing. Fluellen is a little off on the details of the comparison, but Macedon, where Alexander was born, is like Monmouth, where Henry was born. Both places have rivers "and there is salmons in both" (4.7.32), and Alexander

> in his rages, and his furies, and his wraths, and his cholers, and his moods, and his displeasures, and his indignations, and also being a little intoxicates in his prains, did, in his ales and his angers, look you, kill his best friend, Cleitus. (36–41)

So Harry Monmouth,

> being in his right wits and his good judgments, turned away the fat knight with the great-belly doublet—he was full of jests, and gipes, and knaveries, and mocks; I have forgot his name. (49–52)

So Falstaff is memorialized by the compassionate Fluellen, who before this time had no demonstrable relation at all to him.

Fluellen doesn't appear until the middle of the play, but he serves the important function of making King Henry seem more human. He forces Pistol, Nym, and Bardolph into the breach at Harfleur according to the high rhetoric of the King's oration: "Up to the breach, you dogs! Avaunt, you cullions!" (3.2.20). Fluellen objects amusingly but furiously to the digging of the mines ordered by the irascible Irishman, Captain Macmorris. It is "not according to the disciplines of war" and "The concavities of it is not sufficient" (61–62), so there are both theoretical and practical reasons against it. Fluellen is loquacious and polite, but "the disciplines of the pristine wars of the Romans" (83–84), which he has read about only in books, take precedence. Macmorris is the stereotypical Irish wild man, who protests that there is not enough time to discourse: "And there is throats to be cut, and works to be done, and there ish nothing done, so Chrish sa' me, law!" (113–15). But Fluellen persists in his rational and historical investigations, while Macmorris threatens: "I will cut off your head" (135).

One of the most brilliant creations in *Henry V* is Corporal Nym, who appears only briefly; we learn later that both he and Bardolph have been hanged (4.4.75–76). It is surprising that Nym should first appear in *Henry V* and not in the earlier *Henry IV* plays among Falstaff's companions. Perhaps Shakespeare invented Nym as an answer to Ben Jonson's comedy of humors, since Nym is clearly a humorous man who refers to his humors, or whims and caprices, as the cause and root of his conduct. The noun *nym* or *nim* is a canting term for thief, and the verb *nim* is a familiar word for pilfer or steal (from Teutonic *nehmen*, to take). The Boy who follows Bardolph, Pistol, and Nym (presumably Falstaff's Boy) knows that they are all three "swashers" (3.2.29), or swaggerers, and that "They will steal anything, and call it purchase" (42–43). Nym affects taciturnity because "he hath heard that men of few words are the best men, and therefore he scorns to say his prayers, lest 'a should be thought a coward" (37–39). Like the others, he is a braggart soldier who affects brave words but " 'a never broke any man's head but his own, and that was against a post when he was drunk" (41–42). The Boy's commentary is in the witty style of seventeenth-century "characters," on the model of Theophrastus.

Nym's way of speaking is inimitable in its portentous but meaningless gravity. He utters a sphinxlike and threatening discourse, with deep roots in proverbs and clichés. When Bardolph says that Nell Quickly, who is now married to Pistol, did Nym wrong because he was "troth-plight" (2.1.21) to her, Nym answers vatically:

> I cannot tell. Things must be as they may; men may sleep, and they may have their throats about them at that time, and some say knives have edges. It must be as it may; though patience be a tired mare, yet she will plod; there must be conclusions. Well, I cannot tell.
>
> (22–27)

This is supremely indeterminate and fatalistic but also vaguely threatening. Is "some say knives have edges" a warning? It really doesn't matter because the bitter quarrel between Pistol and Nym is purely a matter of words and not of bloody deeds. Although Nym threatens Pistol—"If you would walk off, I would prick your guts a little in good terms, as I may, and that's the humor of it" (60–62)—we know that nothing can possibly happen.

Nym is a parody of Henry's blustering, heroic rhetoric. In response to the King's ringing oration before Harfleur, "Once more unto the breach, dear friends, once more" (3.1.1), Corporal Nym is not antiheroic but merely self-protective when he says: "The humor of it is too hot; that is the very plain-song of it" (3.2.5–6). Nym doesn't refuse to fight; it is merely inconceivable to him. And in the death of Falstaff, he is not so presumptuous to accuse the King of killing his heart, as Dame Quickly does, but says only: "The King hath run bad humors on the knight; that's the even of it" (2.1.124–25). Nym is so attractive because his speech is so profoundly incomprehensible. In a play as purposive and epic as *Henry V* it is a distinct pleasure to hear Nym grumble in the meaningless jargon of humors.

Henry V ends with an epilogue spoken by the Chorus that sums up in brief the Major and the Minor Tetralogies. Henry V is the great hero of the Major Tetralogy, "This star of England" (6), who conquered France, "the world's best garden" (7). It is interesting that the epilogue calls attention so critically to the Minor Tetralogy, written so many years ago and played so often—"oft our stage hath shown" (13). Henry VI, Henry's son, makes a mess of things because he is no true leader: "Whose state so many had the managing, / That they lost France, and made his England bleed" (11–12). This is a very pithy summary of the action of the Minor Tetralogy, but the epilogue seems anxious to free the heroic Henry V from the taints of his unheroic son. The epilogue's neat little Shakespearean sonnet is the only place that the two tetralogies are compared, to the glory of Henry V and to the shame of his son.

Henry VIII

Henry VIII is the last of Shakespeare's history plays, and it can be confidently dated to 1613 (or late 1612) because the first Globe theater burned down on June 20, 1613, during a performance of this play by Shakespeare's company, the King's Men. It was probably written right after *The Tempest* and just before *The Two Noble Kinsmen*, the latter of which is generally taken to be the product of a collaboration between Shakespeare and John Fletcher. Shakespeare's sole authorship of *Henry VIII* was not questioned until the middle of the nineteenth century by James Spedding, who claimed that more than half the play was written by Fletcher. But there is nothing Fletcherian about the style of *Henry VIII*, as there is palpably in *The Two Noble Kinsmen*, except perhaps for the prologue and epilogue.

The vogue of the history or chronicle play had run its course in the 1590s, so that *Henry VIII* is something of an anachronism in 1613. In comparison with the plays of Shakespeare's Minor and Major Tetralogies, *Henry VIII* is not much of a history play. It doesn't emphasize any particular political point, like the winning of France or the losing of France, and it seems a nostalgic celebration of Tudor power under Henry VIII, the breakaway from

Catholic domination, and the grand birth and christening of Henry's daughter, Elizabeth. It could possibly have been a continuation of *Richard III*, with Henry following the Earl of Richmond, the first Tudor king, who became Henry VII by defeating Richard at Bosworth Field. But *Henry VIII* is an entirely different kind of play from *Richard III*. Henry came to the throne in 1509 and died in 1547, but the play concerns itself only with the period between the peace treaty with France celebrated on the Field of the Cloth of Gold in 1520 and the birth of Elizabeth in 1533. It puts strong emphasis on pageantry and ceremony, and the King is represented as a mythical, omniscient, and beneficent figure, as if he were the secret power behind the throne. This has little to do with what we know of the period, and King Henry VIII is highly fictionalized.

One way to explain the anomalous character of *Henry VIII* as a history play is to set it in its context in Shakespeare's career. It was probably written right after the romances—*Pericles, Cymbeline, The Winter's Tale,* and *The Tempest*—and it is strongly colored by the assumptions of those plays. There are obvious continuities with the romances in the trial of Queen Katherine, which resembles the trial of Hermione in *The Winter's Tale,* in the use of masque elements in the King's much abbreviated pastoral masque at York Palace (1, 4), and in Queen Katherine's vision of "*six personages, clad in white robes, wearing on their heads garlands of bays, and golden vizards on their faces*" (4.2.83 s.d.). Despite these similarities, however, I still think that *Henry VIII* is primarily a history play rather than a romance and that this generic distinction affects our understanding of the play. There is a teasing comparison of Henry with Prospero, and one might even compare him with Duke Vincentio, the "old fantastical duke of dark corners" in *Measure for Measure* (4.3.158–59), but he is actually much closer in spirit to Henry IV.

The atmosphere of regeneration, recuperation, and recovery in the romances doesn't work well for *Henry VIII,* which puts so much emphasis on the fall of princes. The birth and christening of Elizabeth at the end of the play is hardly like the reunion of Perdita, Imogen, and Marina with their families. For all its mythic qualities, *Henry VIII* is still a history play, which tries to show us, as the prologue explains, "The very persons of our noble story / As they were living" (26–27). The romances are purely fictional and don't aspire to any historical quality at all. Admittedly, *Henry VIII* is not a history play like the plays of the Minor and Major Tetralogies, but it is the only play of Shakespeare that deals with Tudor history of the recent past and events that lie immediately behind the Elizabethan period. As the play emphasizes so strongly, Henry was Elizabeth's father and James I's grandfather (through his daughter Mary, born to his first wife Katherine).

There is also a strongly anti-Catholic and antipapal tone that recalls some aspects of *King John*. The King in an aside indicates that he is aware of papal duplicity about his divorce from Katherine:

> These cardinals trifle with me. I abhor
> This dilatory sloth and tricks of Rome. (2.4.236–37)

Cranmer is elevated early in the play as a counterweight to papal influence, and, with the King's help, he withstands Gardiner's accusations that he is a "sectary" (5.3.70) and heretic, "filling / The whole realm . . . with new opinions" (15–17). Cardinal Wolsey early on opposes the King's marriage to Anne Bullen because she is "A spleeny Lutheran" (3.2.99), but these are the "new" Protestant opinions that will prevail in England.

Henry VIII was not written directly for the marriage of Princess Elizabeth, King James's daughter, with Prince Frederick, the Elector Palatine on February 14, 1613, but it is associated with the elaborate public celebrations of that great event. Frederick was a leader of the Protestant union in Germany, and a play about the fall of Wolsey and the rise of Cranmer would have been understood as an appropriate political gesture.

The christening of Henry VIII's new daughter, Elizabeth, born to Anne Bullen, in the last scene of the play is a spectacular compliment to Queen Elizabeth and to James I, too. Archbishop Cranmer delivers an extraordinarily soaring speech about Elizabeth's prospects:

> This royal infant—heaven still move about her!—
> Though in her cradle, yet now promises
> Upon this land a thousand thousand blessings,
> Which time shall bring to ripeness. (5.5.17–20)

And when she dies, Elizabeth will pass on her miraculous virtues, like the phoenix, to James I:

> Who from the sacred ashes of her honor
> Shall star-like rise, as great in fame as she was,
> And so stand fixed. (45–47)

This kind of rapturous celebration is typical of the play.

Henry VIII is an odd kind of history play, devoted almost exclusively not to the events of the King's reign but rather to the fall of great persons—Buckingham, Queen Katherine, and Wolsey—along with the inevitable rise of Cranmer and the triumph of Protestantism. Cardinal Wolsey dominates the first three acts of the play, in which the King plays almost a minor role. Wolsey is seen unfavorably right from the beginning, when he is instrumental in bringing about the disgrace of the Duke of Buckingham and his execution. Wolsey is always the archpolitician, who relies on professions of honesty and candor combined with hints and innuendos of the wrongdoing of others. He is a convenient instrument for an indolent king.

In the first scene Buckingham reminds his friends of Wolsey's reputedly base origin as a butcher's son:

> I wonder
> That such a keech can with his very bulk
> Take up the rays o' th' beneficial sun,
> And keep it from the earth. (1.1.54–57)

A "keech" is the fat of a slaughtered animal rolled up into a lump; the suggestion is that Wolsey is a portly man who blocks the light of the sun, or king. Dame Quickly refers to "goodwife Keech, the butcher's wife" in *Henry IV, Part II* (2.1.92–93), and Buckingham later in this scene speaks of Wolsey contemptuously as "This butcher's cur" (1.1.120). "As surly as a butcher's dog" is a proverbial expression (Tilley, B764). Buckingham's hatred of Wolsey is partly founded on snobbery, as in his last statement in this speech: "A beggar's book / Outworths a noble's blood" (122–23). In other words, learning in a beggar like Wolsey is of more value nowadays than aristocratic lineage. Buckingham's protest is mere exclamation because he doesn't have the power "to muzzle him" (121). Again, the subtle Wolsey is associated with an untamable animal.

Wolsey is presented as a prime mover in the King's divorce from Katherine, the widow of his brother Arthur, whom he married with a papal dispensation. Now Henry claims that his conscience troubles him to marry within the forbidden degrees of consanguinity mentioned in Leviticus. The King's conscience is politicized, as Suffolk shrewdly interprets it: "No, his conscience / Has crept too near another lady" (2.2.17–18). In all this affair, Wolsey manipulates theological argument and public opinion, so that Norfolk calls him

> the king-cardinal,
> That blind priest, like the eldest son of Fortune,
> Turns what he list. (19–21)

Wolsey promotes the feeling of sanctimoniousness in this sordid divorce from a queen that "like a jewel has hung twenty years / About his neck, yet never lost her luster" (2.2.31–32). As Norfolk comments ironically: "How holily he works in all his business, / And with what zeal!" (23–24). The play projects the acceptable illusion of a naive king being misled by his counselors. As the Chamberlain puts it:

> Heaven will one day open
> The King's eyes, that so long have slept upon
> This bold bad man. (41–43)

But we know in retrospect that Henry was using Wolsey as a convenient instrument to execute his will and to take the blame for unpopular decisions of the King.

In Queen Katherine's trial, she knows Wolsey for her bitter enemy and utterly refuses that he should also be her judge. She doesn't trust him. She sees through his hypocrisy and false seeming more acutely than any other character in the play:

> Y'are meek and humble-mouthed.
> You sign your place and calling, in full seeming,
> With meekness and humility, but your heart
> Is crammed with arrogancy, spleen, and pride. (2.4.107–10)

Wolsey has exalted his "person's honor" over his "high profession spiritual" (116–17), which is exactly what he says of himself after his fall:

> Had I but served my God with half the zeal
> I served my King, he would not in mine age
> Have left me naked to mine enemies. (3.2.455–57)

In the play Wolsey's spiritual function virtually disappears and he is seen only as a ruthless political intriguer.

Wolsey's fall is made inevitable from the beginning of the play. It is brought about through a mistake whereby he sends the King his letter to the Pope containing the shocking inventory of his personal possessions. But the letter is only a pretext because Henry has deeper reasons for wanting to get rid of the cardinal. Wolsey mistakes the King's affections completely when he opposes Anne Bullen and insists that the King marry the Duchess of Alençon. In fact, the King has already married Anne. Wolsey speaks with haughty insolence, as if the King were merely his creature:

> Anne Bullen? No. I'll no Anne Bullens for him;
> There's more in't than fair visage. Bullen?
> No, we'll no Bullens. (3.2.87–89)

The contemptuous tone is completely wrong, as is Wolsey's use of the "royal we."

This is a wonderful actor's speech but entirely unmetaphorical, which is characteristic of the style of this play. It is strikingly unpoetic in its language but remarkably apt for performance. In Wolsey's farewell soliloquy to all his greatness, there is only one remarkable image, which may be the most memorable figure of speech in the entire play:

> I have ventured
> Like little wanton boys that swim on bladders,
> This many summers in a sea of glory,
> But far beyond my depth. (3.2.358–61)

The figure is original, but it is hardly appropriate to identify Wolsey with little wanton boys swimming with water wings beyond their depth. There is something grotesquely self-pitying in this image of helplessness in the "rude stream" (364). Wolsey knew exactly what he was doing and took greater and greater risks as his power increased.

Anne Bullen emerges as probably the most vivid character in the play. She first appears in the reception that Wolsey gives in York Place, a charming scene of social grace and witty sexual banter. Lord Sands, talking "a little wild" (1.4.26), and perhaps a little drunk too, kisses Anne and offers her elaborate compliments. When the King arrives with other masquers, he chooses Anne Bullen as his partner for the dance and immediately speaks impassioned words: "The fairest hand I ever touched! O beauty, / Till now I never knew thee!" (75–76). This sounds like love at first sight in all its impassioned commitment. Like Romeo at the Capulet's ball, the King inquires his partner's name, exclaims on her beauty—"By heaven, she is a dainty one" (94)—and then kisses her. This is the only scene in the play where we see the King lighthearted and a lover: "Let the music knock it" (108).

The charming act 2, scene 3 is almost entirely devoted to Anne, whom we see conversing with an Old Lady who is also one of the Queen's waiting gentlewomen. Modest and unassuming, Anne is troubled by the Queen's cruel divorce from Henry, and has no desire at all to be queen herself. This the Old Lady finds almost impossible to understand:

> You that have so fair parts of woman on you,
> Have too a woman's heart, which ever yet
> Affected eminence, wealth, sovereignty . . . (27–29)

The Old Lady thinks it only natural that every woman wants to be queen, but Anne foresees only disaster:

> I swear, 'tis better to be lowly born
> And range with humble livers in content
> Than to be perked up in a glis'tring grief
> And wear a golden sorrow. (19–22)

When the Lord Chamberlain comes to announce that the King has made Anne Marchioness of Pembroke, Anne is dismayed by her future prospects, which she has no power to refuse: "It faints me / To think what follows" (2.3.103–4). She cannot comprehend what the

ambitious Old Lady means about having "your mouth filled up /
Before you open it" (87–88). In the Coronation Scene (4, 1) Anne
has no lines but is presented as an ornamental object of the King,
with her hair hanging loosely, *"richly adorned with pearl, crowned"* (36
s. d.). As the Second Gentleman explains:

> Our King has all the Indies in his arms,
> And more and richer, when he strains [= clasps] that lady.
> I cannot blame his conscience. (45–47)

Anne's earlier fears of royalty are more than justified.

Cranmer is spoken of throughout the play as the antithesis of
Wolsey. He is humble, devout, a true Christian without any interest
in secular power. When the King is annoyed by the trifling of Rome,
he prays for the return of "My learned and well-belovèd servant,
Cranmer" (2.4.238). When he is accused by Bishop Gardiner and
cited to come before the Council, he kneels to the King and instead
of pleading for his royal favor, he says only that he is

> right glad to catch this good occasion
> Most throughly to be winnowèd, where my chaff
> And corn shall fly asunder . . . (5.1.109–11)

He speaks like a Christian saint, impressing the King with his humility.

Cranmer understands that he is being insulted by being made to
wait before the entrance to the council chamber " 'Mong boys,
grooms, and lackeys" (5.2.18), but he is resolved to "attend with
patience" (19). To the King this is a dishonor to the throne, like the
putting of Kent in the stocks in *King Lear*, a piece of knavery:

> A man of his place and so near our favor
> To dance attendance on their lordships' pleasures,
> And at the door too, like a post with packets. (30–32)

The King extricates Cranmer from his enemies, "This good man,"
"This honest man," who has been made to "wait like a lousy footboy /
At chamber door" (5.3.138–40). From here it is an easy step to the
triumphant ending of Elizabeth's christening and Cranmer's rapturous
speech on the future of England under Elizabeth and James I. The
King produces the happy ending practically by fiat of his royal will.

TRAGEDIES

Titus Andronicus

*T*itus Andronicus, Shakespeare's first tragedy, has fared so badly with critics that it is
necessary to remind ourselves how strong,
passionate, and eloquent the play is and how
clearly it prepares for later tragedies, especially *King Lear*. The most intemperate judgment is from T. S. Eliot, who called *Titus*
"one of the stupidest and most uninspired
plays ever written, a play in which it is incredible that Shakespeare had any hand at
all, a play in which the best passages would
be too highly honored by the signature of
Peele." This judgment is parodied in Woody
Allen's *Side Effects*: "Even the works of the
great Shakespeare will disappear when the
universe burns out—not such a terrible
thought, of course, when it comes to a play
like *Titus Andronicus*." Eliot here echoes the
sentiments of nineteenth-century disintegra-
tors of Shakespeare, who wanted to attribute
anything unworthy of the Master to a lesser
dramatist, but *Titus* is included in Shakespeare's First Folio and it is spoken of, confidently, as Shakespeare's own by Francis Meres
in 1598. The argument about non-Shake-
spearean authorship is now rare, and we have
had some memorable productions, most notably Peter Brook's with the Royal Shakespeare Company in 1955, Gerald Freedman's

New York Shakespeare Festival's production in 1967, and Deborah Warner's recent exciting version at the New Swan in Stratford, England (1987).

It is interesting that *Titus Andronicus* should be so much more successful with audiences than with readers. This alerts us to something powerfully nonverbal and presentational in the play that eludes readers too concerned with the heightened, even flamboyant, tragic style steeped in classical allusion. The role of Lavinia, Titus's daughter, is a case in point. At the beginning of act 2, scene 4, she appears as a mute emblem of horror and despair: *"her hands cut off, and her tongue cut out, and ravished."* Her speaking part ends at this scene and, for readers, she more or less disappears from the play. But for audiences her pantomimic role is crucial for the tragedy from this point on. She is a "Speechless complainer" (3.2.39), and her father vows to learn her thoughts: "In thy dumb action will I be as perfect / As begging hermits in their holy prayers" (40–41). From all of her mute signs, Titus "will wrest an alphabet, / And by still practice learn to know thy meaning" (44–45). Lavinia's alphabet is vital to the play.

She is on stage for most of Titus's big scenes, and her reactions guide the audience in its tragic apprehension. At one point, in an important stage ritual, she kisses her father (3.1.249) and presumably vows him to revenge. Titus's next line is one of the most moving in the play and marks his affinity with Lear: "When will this fearful slumber have an end?" (252). This is followed by the grotesque, mock-military procession of the Andronici off the stage, bearing the heads of Titus's executed sons, Quintus and Martius, and Titus's hand. As Titus says with mad urgency: "Bear thou my hand, sweet wench, between thy teeth" (282). Lavinia the hand-bearer is matched grotesquely with Lavinia the basin-bearer, who carefully catches the blood of Tamora's sons, Chiron and Demetrius, as Titus kills them (5.2.166 s.d.).

Lavinia is strongly indebted to the story of Philomela, Procne, and Tereus in Ovid's *Metamorphoses*, which enters metadramatically into the action of *Titus* in 4,1, when Lavinia reveals the identity of her attackers. It is not surprising that Francis Meres declared in 1598 that "the sweete wittie soule of *Ouid* liues in mellifluous & honytongued *Shakespeare.*" The young Shakespeare is eager to display his indebtedness to Ovid in *Titus Andronicus* by frequent allusions and by a highly wrought, decorative style. Many quotations in Latin both from Ovid and from others are meant to give weight and dignity to Shakespeare's first attempt at tragedy, but these quotations are usually sententious commonplaces (like Horace's *"Integer vitae"* 4.2.20) and slightly misquoted. Sometimes the quotation is inappropriate for the speaker, as when Demetrius ends the first scene of act 2 with lines derived from Seneca's *Hippolytus: "Sit fas aut nefas, . . . Per Stygia, per manes vehor"* (2.1.133, 135): Be it right or wrong to pursue Lavinia, he will press on, carried through the regions of Styx, through the shades of the underworld. The cloddish Demetrius is an odd speaker of lines that are so classically grandiloquent about the brutal rape and dismemberment of Lavinia.

The influence of Ovid on this play is felt in an erotic nostalgia and indeterminacy that color the action, or at least in Shakespeare's sense of Ovid's lyrical intensity and strangeness. Marcus's reaction when he first comes upon his brutalized niece in the forest is typically Ovidian. His long and eloquent oration has been much criticized for its lack of attention to the actual situation, but I think this criticism fails to take account of the dramatic context. Marcus speaks a gravely mellifluous and elegiac lament for Lavinia:

> Alas, a crimson river of warm blood,
> Like to a bubbling fountain stirred with wind,
> Doth rise and fall between thy rosèd lips,
> Coming and going with thy honey breath. (2.4.22–25)

To ask the practical question why Marcus, like a medical corpsman, doesn't go to the aid of his niece who is bleeding at the mouth is to misunderstand the Ovidian quality of this scene.

We not only see the pitiful figure of Lavinia before us but also her powerful reaction to her uncle's discourse. In the stage picture we cannot legitimately separate Marcus's words from Lavinia's highly emotional reactions: "Ah, now thou turn'st away thy face for shame!" (2.4.28). The scene is constructed like a reversed pietà. Marcus is memorializing Lavinia as she once was, and his words introduce an aspect of comfort and of celebration:

> O, had the monster seen those lily hands
> Tremble like aspen leaves upon a lute,

And make the silken strings delight to kiss them,
He would not then have touched them for his life! (44–47)

As in Ovid, Marcus's oration is lyric, nostalgic, evocative, and supremely ambiguous about the mystery of things. The image of broken music dominates Marcus's lament.

We can see the closeness of *Titus Andronicus* to Shakespeare's long narrative poem, *The Rape of Lucrece,* which must have been written right after the play (or right before it). In some ways the mute Lavinia has advantages over Lucrece, who discourses endlessly about her condition. Lucrece, unfortunately, is deprived of a dramatic context so that nothing can be represented or enacted without words. Both works use the Trojan War significantly as a background of chaos and disruption. The play and the poem show a similar conception of rape as destroying the value and personal identity of the woman, even though she had no complicity in her undoing. Family honor can only be retrieved by death, and Lavinia at the end of the play is as eager for death as is Lucrece. In terms of Renaissance values, no other solution exists.

Like Lear, Titus is a man "More sinned against than sinning" (*King Lear* 3.2.60). He is overwhelmed and driven mad by an endless torrent of grief that makes us sympathize with his sufferings. As a tragedy, *Titus* is powerful in performance. It doesn't follow Aristotelian criteria for the tragic hero (nor does any play of Shakespeare except perhaps *King Lear*), but it is full of mystery and astonishment at the fall of princes and the capriciousness of fortune. In the first act Shakespeare is at pains to show us the worst side of Titus. His hubris (tragic insolence) is developed at great length. He agrees to the ritual slaughter of Alarbus, the oldest son of Tamora, the Queen of the Goths, who is his prisoner. To the great surprise of his brother Marcus, he refuses the Roman empery that is offered to him as a great military hero. He supports the foolish Saturninus as Roman emperor instead of his much better brother, Bassianus, and he even slays his own son Mutius while he is supporting the wrongful cause of Saturninus. By the end of act 1 Tamora's revenge has already begun with the aid of Aaron and Saturninus.

Titus is the great man cast down. Before act 1 is over he has alienated the audience almost completely by the savage murders of

Alarbus and Mutius. Like Lear, Titus recovers his stature through suffering. His sons, Quintus and Martius, are trapped by Aaron and soon executed. His daughter Lavinia is raped and dismembered. In another sardonic plot by Aaron, Titus offers up his hand to free his sons, but it is returned with mocking scorn. The griefs accumulate with inevitable and shocking pressure, and Titus is soon distracted, if not actually mad. In this early revenge tragedy, Shakespeare uses madness cleverly as an outlet for violent and uncontainable emotions in Titus. He is mad and not mad as the situation seems to warrant, and in this respect the presentation of Titus looks forward to Hamlet. Lear also follows Titus's course closely, and there is an additional analogy between Lavinia and Cordelia.

Like Horatio in *Hamlet,* Marcus is the reasonable, moderate, unheroic man who tries to rein in his brother and keep him from violating the restraints of reason. But the unmitigated evil of Aaron, Tamora, and Saturninus cannot be comprehended by reason, morality, and justice. The assault on reason is at the heart of the tragedy. These issues are prominent in act 3, scene 1, although the justice theme also runs throughout the play (as it does in *King Lear*). Marcus pleads with his brother to "speak with possibility, / And do not break into these deep extremes" (214–15), but Titus argues from the magnitude of his griefs:

> Is not my sorrow deep, having no bottom?
> Then be my passions bottomless with them. (216–17)

When Marcus still insists that reason should "govern thy lament" (218), Titus attacks reason as irrelevant:

> If there were reason for these miseries,
> Then into limits could I bind my woes:
> When heaven doth weep, doth not the earth o'erflow? (219–21)

From this point Titus goes on to exclaim "I am the sea" (225) and to vent his fury like a force of nature.

When Marcus finally realizes the futility of reason, Titus is already far gone in distraction and fixed in a kind of exaltation of grief. Speaking in the lyric high style of Shakespeare's tragic protagonists, he seems to be touching on the metaphysical underpinnings of tragedy. Marcus is literal while his brother is prophetic, so that there is an unbridgeable gap between their discourses. Marcus forswears any further attempt to "control thy griefs" (3.1.259), and he is surprised by the silence of his once voluble brother: "Now is a time to storm; why art thou still?" (263). At this point, in a surprising reversal of our expectations, Titus laughs: "Ha, ha, ha!" (264). Marcus objects: "Why dost thou laugh? It fits not with this hour" (265), but Titus replies with tragic appropriateness: "Why, I have not another tear to shed" (266). This is like Cleopatra's scene-closing advice to Charmian: "Pity me, Charmian, / But do not speak to me" (*Antony and Cleopatra* 2.5.118–19). Heroic and nonheroic persons are mysteriously separated from each other in a division that cannot be explored. Titus's laughter seems to move the tragedy one step further to revenge and resolution.

The Fly Scene (3,2), which was added to *Titus Andronicus* sometime after its original composition (and appears for the first time in the Folio), contains the same spirit of madness and lyric intensity, and a frenzy and hysteria bordering on the farcical. We may consider it, stylistically, either a crucial scene to set a certain tone and mood or, from the point of view of the narrative, completely unnecessary for the movement of the action. During a frugal family meal (or "banket"), we see the Andronici indulging their mutual grief. Titus puns wildly and grotesquely on "hands": "O, handle not the theme, to talk of hands, / Lest we remember still that we have none" (29–30). Suddenly, Marcus strikes the wooden dish (or "trencher") he is eating from with his knife and impales a black fly.

This sets the unstable Titus off on a tragic speech in the high style that is more than faintly ridiculous in its context: "Out on thee, murderer! Thou kill'st my heart; / Mine eyes are cloyed with view of tyranny" (3.2.54–55). Marcus protests: "I have but killed a fly" (59), but Titus is inexorable in his flight of fancy:

> "But!" How, if that fly had a father and mother?
> How would he hang his slender gilded wings,
> And buzz lamenting doings in the air! (60–62)

The young Shakespeare lets himself go to "buzz lamenting doings in the air," and Titus's madness continues on to the real object of his lamentation, as he strikes wildly at the fly "That comes in likeness of a coal-black Moor" (78). This scene foreshadows the violence, both real and metaphorical, of the grieving Titus. The madness mediates between high-flown imaginings and shocking deeds.

The most brilliant and fully developed character in *Titus Andronicus* is the Moor Aaron, a free-floating mercenary like the Moor Othello, who is brought captive to Rome in Titus's triumph. Aaron is also the lover of Tamora, Queen of the Goths, and in his first speech in the play, a vaunting soliloquy imitating Marlowe's "mighty line," Aaron boasts that he holds Tamora prisoner,

> fettered in amorous chains,
> And faster bound to Aaron's charming eyes
> Than is Prometheus tied to Caucasus. (2.1.15–17)

The classical allusion is altogether typical of the heightened style of the play. Aaron is a grand adventurer like Tamburlaine, the Scythian shepherd, who expects to make his fortune now that Tamora is Empress of Rome:

> Away with slavish weeds and servile thoughts!
> I will be bright and shine in pearl and gold
> To wait upon this new-made empress. (18–20)

The style is buoyant, and it includes a specifically sexual component that is foreign to Marlowe.

Aaron will "mount" Tamora's "pitch" (2.1.14)—a term from falconry, but with a double entendre here encouraged by the word *mount*. Later Aaron encourages Demetrius and Chiron in their plan to rape Lavinia: "Why then, it seems, some certain snatch or so / Would serve your turns" (95–96). Later, when we hear about Tamora's black baby, Aaron shocks even the sons of Tamora: "I have done thy mother" (4.2.76). This sounds like the sexual boasting associated with the game of the dozens.

An extraordinary drawing from 1595, attributed to Henry Peacham, of a composite scene from *Titus Andronicus* may represent the way the characters looked on stage. Titus is dressed in a Roman toga, and other characters are attired in a mixture of Roman and Elizabethan military costumes, but Aaron is the most striking figure of all. He is coal-black, Negroid, with thick lips, and wears an imitation of light Roman body armor. The black Aaron looks for-

217

ward, ironically, to the white Iago. Both are wonderfully improvisatory, cheerful, frank, and eager to remain on good terms with the audience. In this sense Aaron is the prototype for all Shakespeare's later villains. He establishes the need for the villain to be sardonic. When he tricks Titus into letting him cut off his hand, Aaron remembers that when he had it, he drew himself apart "And almost broke my heart with extreme laughter" (5.1.113). And in the upshot, "When for his hand he had his two sons' heads" (115), Aaron the onlooker, "pried me through the crevice of a wall . . . / Beheld his tears and laughed so heartily / That both mine eyes were rainy like to his" (5.2.114, 116–17). This merry device resembles the mischievous and deadly pranks of Barrabas and Ithamore in Marlowe's *Jew of Malta* (1589). Aaron is unrepentant and diabolic, and in his rabid atheism he scorns the Christian god of the Andronici. It comes as a surprise, then, that Aaron is so devoted to his black baby, who is a kind of heroic Caliban in miniature. In later plays the villain is not endowed with such an endearing, redeeming trait.

The savagery and violence of *Titus Andronicus* are connected with the historical period in which the play is imagined to take place: in the late Roman Empire around the fourth or fifth century A.D., when Rome was seriously threatened by the barbarian hordes. In the first scene, Marcus has to remind his brother: "Thou art a Roman, be not barbarous" (1.1.379), and there is a definite feeling of barbarity in the ritual slaughter of Alarbus, a prisoner of war and the eldest son of Tamora, Titus's impetuous killing of his own son Mutius, and the carrying off of Lavinia once she is betrothed to Saturninus. "*Suum cuique*" (280), says Marcus, which is later echoed by Bassianus: "Rape, call you it, my lord, to seize my own?" (406). This is not the high moral Rome of *Julius Caesar, Antony and Cleopatra*, or even *Coriolanus*, all of which are based on Plutarch's *Lives*. It is more the Rome of Tarquin in *The Rape of Lucrece*. Both the play and the poem have an archaic, primitive quality that Shakespeare never repeated. Rape in both works is a political act in which the innocent victim is punished with death—family honor takes precedence over individual life. In *Titus Andronicus* Rome is already in decline, perhaps decadent, and the Andronici are striving to preserve, imperfectly and nostalgically, older Roman values that are already out of date.

Romeo and Juliet

Romeo and Juliet is an early tragedy from around 1595, but its affinities are much more with the romantic comedies written at this time, especially A Midsummer Night's Dream. Mercutio's Queen Mab speech, which is a lyrical set piece on the fairy world, seems directly lifted out of that play. Mercutio confesses that he talks "of dreams, / Which are the children of an idle brain, / Begot of nothing but vain fantasy" (1.4.96–98), which allies him with "The lunatic, the lover, and the poet" of A Midsummer Night's Dream (5.1.7).

Shakespeare has trouble endowing Romeo and Juliet with tragic stature, in some ways they are not tragic at all. They definitely don't bring the tragedy on themselves, despite their haste to get married, and they have no identifiable tragic flaw or weakness of character. They don't qualify as tragic protagonists under the criteria of Aristotle's Poetics, and only the ancient feud between the Montagues and the Capulets separates them from each other. Romeo and Juliet are "A pair of star-crossed lovers," as the prologue informs us (6), and in some sense they are scapegoats for the feud, which cannot end without their deaths. This is what the prologue means when he says that the lovers' "misadventured piteous overthrows / Doth with their death bury their parents' strife" (7–8), and at the end of the play old Capulet speaks of Romeo and Juliet as "Poor sacrifices of our enmity" (5.3.304). If the lovers are only "Poor sacrifices" of the family feud, then their tragic role is reduced to victimization.

This is a problem, it seems to me, that Shakespeare had to grapple with in writing the play. He chose to fill the earlier parts of the play with forebodings and portents that aren't always relevant to the dramatic context. At the end of Mercutio's Queen Mab speech and before Romeo even meets Juliet, he is worried without any cause about "Some consequence yet hanging in the stars" (1.4.107). This is puzzling, but Romeo, with tragic omniscience, anticipates exactly what will happen. Some ill-starred consequence

> Shall bitterly begin his fearful date
> With this night's revels and expire the term
> Of a despisèd life, closed in my breast,
> By some vile forfeit of untimely death. (108–11)

Does this add dimension to Romeo or do these lines appear merely to assert a larger and more painful tragic consequence?

Juliet, too, has a foreboding of disaster, and in the midst of the ecstatic orchard scene, she introduces metaphysical fears that seem in context to be without foundation:

> I have no joy of this contract tonight.
> It is too rash, too unadvised, too sudden;
> Too like the lightning, which doth cease to be
> Ere one can say it lightens. (2.2.117–20)

But the audience seems to see Juliet taking great joy in her "contract" with Romeo, and apart from this statement she is light, lyrical, and committed. She doesn't seem to believe that what she is doing is "too rash, too unadvised, too sudden; / Too like the lightning." In what Juliet says here, she seems to be speaking not for herself but for the play, and tragic implications are cooked up in an artificial way.

Juliet begins the play like a heroine of comedy, not unlike Helena and Hermia in A Midsummer Night's Dream, but she becomes a tragic heroine through circumstance, specifically Tybalt's death, the banishment of Romeo, and her arranged marriage to Paris. All these events come together to produce disastrous results. Before that, however, Juliet is witty, intelligent, lyrical, sexual—as perfect a heroine of comedy as the later Rosalind in *As You Like It* (there is, in fact, a nonappearing Rosalind in *Romeo and Juliet*, who is Romeo's first love).

Romeo and Juliet woo each other in a sonnet, in which she not only holds her own but manages to top Romeo. This dramatic, enacted sonnet is interesting in relation to Shakespeare's nondramatic sonnets that he was writing at this time. Romeo speaks the first quatrain (abab), offering an erotic proposition:

> If I profane with my unworthiest hand
>> This holy shrine, the gentle sin is this:
> My lips, two blushing pilgrims, ready stand
>> To smooth that rough touch with a tender kiss. (1.5.95–98)

Juliet's answering quatrain (cdcd) raises teasing objections to Romeo's argument:

> Good pilgrim, you do wrong your hand too much,
>> Which mannerly devotion shows in this;
> For saints have hands that pilgrims' hands do touch,
>> And palm to palm is holy palmers' kiss. (99–102)

The religious imagery is very witty, especially the arch pun on *palmer.*

The third quatrain is divided between the lovers, and they share the concluding couplet:

> *Juliet.* Saints do not move, though grant for prayer's sake.
> *Romeo.* Then move not while my prayer's effect I take. (1.5.107–8)

Unlike the nondramatic sonnets, this sonnet ends in a kiss. It is lovely but artificial, and the wooing proceeds by deeper stages of involvement—the more personal it gets the less rhetorical it seems—until the lovers agree on marriage. Except for the feud between their families, nothing that Romeo and Juliet say or do has tragic implications. Even Tybalt at this point seems to be an affected fop like Osric in *Hamlet.*

Friar Lawrence is a puzzling and ambiguous figure, like the meddlesome Duke Vincentio in *Measure for Measure*. He is at once a raisonneur, a plot manipulator, a natural philosopher, and a scheming old man. He also speaks with unusual fullness, perhaps even platitudinousness, in a fast-moving play. Friar Lawrence is the *senex* who spouts traditional wisdom mixed with tedious ceremoniousness, like Nestor in *Troilus and Cressida* and Polonius in *Hamlet*. We first see him in a long soliloquy in act 2, scene 3, gathering herbs and speaking in extremely formal couplets. He espouses a riddling sort of animism about the two-fold character of Nature:

> I must upfill this osier cage of ours
> With baleful weeds and precious-juicèd flowers.
> The earth that's nature's mother is her tomb.
> What is her burying grave, that is her womb . . . (7–10)

As in the Garden Scene in *Richard II* (3, 4), the meaning of the play is formulated in choral platitudes.

It all seems too neatly balanced and antithetical, and the Apothecary who sells Romeo poison is a more vibrant character than Friar Lawrence—he is certainly not so long-winded. I think it no accident in the play that the Friar means well but brings disaster. Why does his vital letter to Romeo never arrive? Why doesn't he stay with Juliet in the tomb? Why is he so enmeshed in secrecy and ingenious devices that tragically misfire? The tragedy is compromised by the Friar's blundering finickiness.

Old Capulet is also a puzzling and contradictory figure in the play, but his role is more vital and developed than that of the Friar. In many ways he is like Prospero in *The Tempest*, but he goes beyond him in the variousness of his part. We first see him in the opening quarrel, when he enters suddenly *"in his gown"* (1.1.77 s.d.), or dressing gown, with Lady Capulet, as if disturbed in his domestic tranquillity. He calls for his "long sword" (78), an old-fashioned weapon too massive to be effective against rapiers. He is irascible and a bit farcical in this scene. Lady Capulet properly puts him down by saying satirically: "A crutch, a crutch! Why call you for a sword?" (79).

In the next scene, with Paris, who wants Juliet for his wife, Capulet puts him off for at least two more years:

My child is yet a stranger in the world,
She hath not seen the change of fourteen years;
Let two more summers wither in their pride
Ere we may think her ripe to be a bride. (1.2.8–11)

He is concerned that early marriage may mar his only daughter, who is "the hopeful lady of my earth" (15). He advises gentle Paris to woo her and "get her heart" (16), because his consent is dependent on his daughter's: "And she agreed, within her scope of choice / Lies my consent and fair according voice" (18–19). I quote Capulet's words exactly because they so radically contradict his assertions of a savage patriarchal authority in act 3, scene 5.

During the masked ball in act 1, scene 5, Capulet plays the gracious host. He welcomes Romeo and forbids Tybalt to bluster and swagger. It seems clear that he is not at all intent on furthering the feud between the Capulets and Montagues and would just as soon see it lapse. He is an enthusiastic and whimsical host, who welcomes "Ladies that have their toes / Unplagued with corns" (1.5.18–19) to dance and celebrate the evening. He not only chides Tybalt for his foolish fierceness but also praises Romeo:

'A bears him like a portly gentleman,
And, to say truth, Verona brags of him
To be a virtuous and well-governed youth. (68–70)

Capulet addresses Tybalt affectionately but firmly as if he were a child who needed to be scolded: "Go to, go to! / You are a saucy boy. Is't so, indeed?" (84–85). The colloquial, avuncula. tone is remarkably well controlled.

Aside from a few brief lines in act 3, scene 2, we don't see Capulet again until act 3, scene 4, where he is in earnest conversation with Paris. After the sudden death of Tybalt, for whom Juliet grieves, he now suggests that Paris marry her immediately—"A Thursday let it be" (3.4.20)—to ease her sadness. This is all compassionate and fatherly, yet there is also a certain sense of tyrannical, patriarchal authority like that of Egeus, the father of Hermia in *A Midsummer Night's Dream*: "I beg the ancient privilege of Athens: / As she is mine, I may dispose of her" (1.1.41–42). Capulet makes a "desperate tender" of Juliet's love: "I think she will be ruled / In all respects by me; nay more, I doubt it not" (3.4.13–14). This is a dangerous assertion, and when his daughter flouts him in the next scene, he rages with vivid, colloquial scorn. He is touched to the quick by what he sees not only as his daughter's disobedience but also as the withdrawal of her love. His unrestrained petulance anticipates King Lear's disappointment with Cordelia. In the preparations for the dutiful Juliet's wedding to Paris, Capulet is once more genial, whimsical, and officious, as he was in the scene of the ball (1, 5), so that it seems as if his rage in act 3, scene 5 was merely a passing emotional storm without any real conviction.

At Juliet's supposed death, Capulet mourns with an intensity to match his earlier anger:

> O child, O child! My soul, and not my child!
> Dead art thou—alack my child is dead,
> And with my child my joys are burièd! (4.5.62–64)

At the end of the play, he mourns for the unnecessary deaths of his daughter and Romeo, who are "Poor sacrifices of our enmity!" (5.3.304). Capulet is not the leading part of *Romeo and Juliet*, but its range of emotion demands great acting skill. Unlike Egeus in *A Midsummer Night's Dream*, he goes far beyond the comic blocking father in Plautine comedy and touches on tragic themes and tones. If he is like Polonius in some ways, he surpasses him in his grief and approaches King Lear in his earnest attempt at reparation.

Everything changes with the death of Mercutio; it is odd that the play should take such a sudden and determined turn to tragedy. There seems to be a rush now to realize the implications of all the forebodings. Why should Mercutio be such a crucial character? He is Romeo's devoted friend, but a scoffer at love and full of boisterous, bawdy humor. He attributes an exaggerated sexuality to Romeo, whom he imagines wishing that "his mistress were that kind of fruit / As maids call medlars when they laugh alone" (2.1.35–36). A medlar is a fruit like the persimmon, which, when rotten-ripe, was popularly thought to resemble the female genitals. Mercutio is carried away with his own image of sexual fruit to his emphatic, obscene conclusion: "O, Romeo, that she were, O that she were / An open-arse, thou a pop'rin pear!" An "open-arse," from the Arden edition, is a dialectal name for the medlar, and a pear from Poperinghe, near Ypres, is also, punningly, a "pop-her-in" pear resembling the male organ. Why does the merry Mercutio precipitate the tragedy? He is not a tragic figure at all, but when he has been mortally wounded by Tybalt, he puts an excessive thematic emphasis on the feud: "A plague a both houses! I am sped" (3.1.93), which is repeated four times in seventeen lines.

The death of Mercutio seals the tragedy in *Romeo and Juliet*, but the tragic movement is felt most strongly in Juliet. She develops over the course of the play much more strikingly than Romeo. Act 3, scene 5 begins with the beautiful leave-taking of the lovers. Juliet is bemused by the departure of her new-found husband: "Art thou gone so, love-lord, ay husband-friend?" (43). This is touching, but we move immediately to her parents' plan to marry her, "early next Thursday morn" (113) to Paris. Her father is savage in his insistence on parental prerogative, but when he exits, Juliet appeals to her mother in heartfelt, foreboding terms:

> O sweet my mother, cast me not away!
> Delay this marriage for a month, a week;
> Or if you do not, make the bridal bed
> In that dim monument where Tybalt lies. (200–203)

But her mother answers coldly and unfeelingly: "Talk not to me, for I'll not speak a word. / Do as thou wilt, for I have done with thee" (204–5).

Abandoned by her mother, Juliet then turns to the Nurse: "Comfort me, counsel me. . . / What say'st thou? Hast thou not a word of joy? / Some comfort, nurse" (3.5.210, 213–14). Juliet is a fourteen-year old girl appealing for emotional support, but the Nurse responds with irrelevant practical counsel about secrecy and bigamy. It is at this point that Juliet realizes that she is alone, and she separates herself decisively from the Nurse: "Go, counselor! / Thou and my bosom henceforth shall be twain" (241–42). In the concluding couplet of her soliloquy, she is moving to a different reality: "I'll to the friar to know his remedy. / If all else fail, myself have power to die" (243–44). Juliet is now ready for the Friar's ingenious device of the sleeping potion and the mock death.

Juliet's long soliloquy in act 4, scene 3, when she drinks the Friar's vial, is full of ominous forebodings. Like Hamlet in the Graveyard Scene (5,1), she anticipates death and tries vividly to imagine what it will be like. She rejects the momentary impulse to call back the Nurse: "Nurse!—What should she do here? / My dismal scene I needs must act alone" (18–19). The acting imagery underscores Juliet's sense of spectacle—her "dismal scene" is also her big scene that will prove her ability to act in her own behalf. And she has a dagger ready in case the potion does not work. Juliet raises the possibility that this is a poison that the Friar has given her to get her out of the way, but she rejects this malicious thought because "he hath still been tried a holy man" (4.3.29).

Notice how seriously Juliet asks herself a series of questions and tries to imagine all the possibilities. She is far from the coy and flirtatious Juliet we saw at her father's ball in act 1, scene 5. Here Juliet grapples with "The horrible conceit of death and night, / Together with the terror of the place" (4.3.37–38), the family burial vault in which the "bloody Tybalt, yet but green in earth, / Lies fest'ring in his shroud" (42–43). If she awakes suddenly in this desperate place, shall she not run mad and in her rage dash her brains out "with some great kinsman's bone" (53)? She takes the potion at the moment when she seems to see Tybalt's ghost seeking out Romeo in revenge, and she ends by pledging Romeo in a toast: "Romeo, Romeo, Romeo, I drink to thee" (58).

The representation of love is magical in this play, yet this is also Shakespeare's bawdiest play. (A bowdlerized version of *Romeo and Juliet* is regularly foisted on high-school students, which may explain why they were so enamored with Zeffirelli's erotic film version in 1968, with adolescent protagonists.) The bawdiness is obviously related to the intense and celebratory innocence; one depends upon the other. Romeo needs Mercutio, and Juliet needs the Nurse so that they can insist on their separate worlds of erotic discourse. Romeo, and especially Juliet, are both very sexual, but their committed sexuality is different from the leering suggestiveness of Mercutio and the Nurse, both of whom mock at love.

The endless joke about Juliet that the Nurse tells over and over again at her first appearance is good-hearted but coarse, and it sets the tone for Juliet's eventual separation from her. When the child Juliet falls and gets a bump on her brow "as big as a young cock'rel's stone" (1.3.53), or young rooster's testicle, the Nurse's late husband makes his immortal wisecrack, which the Nurse cannot help repeating with glee:

> "Yea," quoth he, "dost thou fall upon thy face?
> Thou wilt fall backward when thou hast more wit;
> Wilt thou not, Jule?" (41–43)

In the Nurse's homely wisdom, women are the weaker vessel and were meant, by nature, to fall backward and to prove their sex upon their backs. We can see why Juliet and the Nurse have to part company.

There is a curious concern with gender issues in act 3, scene 3. The banished Romeo, who has just slain Tybalt, is with Friar Lawrence, and he grows increasingly frantic about his separation from Juliet. He seizes on the grotesque image of carrion flies, who have more opportunity to court his love than he does:

> More validity,
> More honorable state, more courtship lives
> In carrion flies than Romeo. They may seize
> On the white wonder of dear Juliet's hand
> And steal immortal blessing from her lips . . . (3.3.33–36)

Romeo's emotional instability at this point is expressed in his over-wrought, conceited image, which culminates in an absurd pun: "Flies may do this but I from this must fly" (41). Romeo is near the distraction of despair—"Thou fond mad man" (52), as Friar Lawrence calls him—because he feels his grief so overwhelmingly. He answers the Friar with adolescent passion: "Thou canst not speak of that thou dost not feel" (64). The Friar's function then, with the help of the Nurse, is to banish Romeo's histrionic, and therefore womanish, disposition and to recall him to being a man.

The gender line, based on Renaissance commonplaces, is consistent in Shakespeare and nowhere more fully developed than in *Mac-*

beth, where Lady Macbeth defines for us specifically what it means to be a man. In *Romeo and Juliet* the Friar is offended by Romeo's lying on the ground "with his own tears made drunk" (3.3.83). The Nurse confirms that he is mimicking Juliet: "Even so lies she, / Blubb'ring and weeping, weeping and blubb'ring" (86–87). She orders Romeo to "Stand, and [-if] you be a man" (88). The Friar concurs: "Art thou a man? Thy form cries out thou art; / Thy tears are womanish" (109–10). As Laertes says when he weeps for the dead Ophelia, when his tears are gone, "The woman will be out" (*Hamlet* 4.7.189). So the weeping Romeo digresses "from the valor of a man" (3.3.127). To be a man is understood to be the opposite of what it means to be a woman, and Romeo's deep feeling needs to be disguised and tempered in order that he should not seem "like a misbehaved and sullen wench" (143). One of the charms of *Romeo and Juliet* is that the protagonists exchange their prescribed gender roles; while Romeo blubbers, Juliet has manlike resolution.

Even though the love affair of Romeo and Juliet ends in death, love tragedy is often ambiguous, and we are made to question whether death is not the fitting consummation of love, as in the Tristan and Isolde story. It is clear in the play that Romeo and Juliet are young adolescent lovers who are caught in the deadly feud between their families. Their lyrical and committed love is set apart from the currents of enmity and hate in Verona, so the love story offers a way to resolve the feud, but there is a fatality in the play right from the opening prologue, which insists that this is a "death-marked love" (9). The Prince offers an explicit moral commentary at the end for the grieving Capulets and Montagues: "See what a scourge is laid upon your hate, / That heaven finds means to kill your joys with love" (5.3.292–93). Despite the sense of tragic foreboding created in the play, Romeo and Juliet bear no culpability in their fates. Unlike Antony and Cleopatra, they do not violate any large moral and political imperatives. But *Antony and Cleopatra*, too, as a love tragedy is not fully tragic. It is exceedingly difficult to make an emotion as complex and ambivalent as love seem an adequate motivating cause for tragedy.

Julius Caesar

The politics of *Julius Caesar* are acutely
imagined and resemble, in their seriousness
and intensity, the politics of the English history plays, especially *Richard II* and the two
parts of *Henry IV*, which precede *Julius Caesar*
by a few years. Politics means not just ideology, and, in fact, ideology is of lesser
importance than character. It is not what
characters say that matters but what they do.
Brutus makes elaborate professions of republican ideology, but we know that he was
won to the conspiracy against Caesar by
Cassius's machinations, especially his flattery. Brutus acutely wants to be a certain
kind of political hero, and what actually
happens in the play matters less to him than
the image of peace, freedom, and enfranchisement that the conspiracy represents.

"Let's be sacrificers, but not butchers"
(2.1.166), he says to Cassius, as if he could
deliberately choose to be an unwilling sacrificer, forced to kill his dear friend Caesar
against his personal judgment by the spirit
of the times, as he resoundingly rejected the
role of butcher that he indeed was. It is
ironic that Brutus, the sacrificer and not the
butcher, calls for his fellow conspirators to
"bathe our hands in Caesar's blood / Up to
the elbows, and besmear our swords"

(3.1.106–7). Antony, who is politically astute almost to the point of cynicism, echoes this language in his apologetic soliloquy to Caesar's corpse: "O pardon me, thou bleeding piece of earth, / That I am meek and gentle with these butchers!" (254–55).

We may approach the politics of *Julius Caesar* in many different ways but I think most effectively through the middle of the play by looking at an important block of action extending from act 3, scene 1 through act 4, scene 1. The assassination of Caesar takes place in act 3, scene 1, and it is significant that Caesar the man is so strikingly undercut. We have already learned about Caesar's epileptic fits ("falling sickness") in the marketplace when a crown was offered him, as well as about his deafness in the left ear and his possible sterility. In 3, 1 Caesar is given several absurdly grandiose speeches that seem to deny that he is a man like other mortals. In reply to Metellus Cimber's petition for his banished brother, Caesar denies that he can be moved like other men: "But I am constant as the Northern Star" (3.1.60), and in the world of men

> I do know but one
> That unassailable holds on his rank,
> Unshaked of motion. (69–71)

Ironically, the petition of Metellus Cimber is the signal for Caesar's assassination. We suddenly hear many political slogans: "Liberty! Freedom! Tyranny is dead!" (78), " 'Liberty, freedom, and enfranchisement!' " (81), "ambition's debt is paid" (83), but these shibboleths have very little reality and almost no bearing on the outcome of the revolution.

The powerful metadramatic references show that the conspirators are merely playacting, or at least that they conceive of the heroic events in which they are engaged as theatrical actions for posterity. Cassius exclaims:

> How many ages hence
> Shall this our lofty scene be acted over
> In states unborn and accents yet unknown? (3.1.111–13)

Brutus matches him exactly in enthusiastic assertions:

How many times shall Caesar bleed in sport,
That now on Pompey's basis lies along
No worthier than the dust! (114–16)

The conspirators seem altogether too eager for applause to be sin-
cerely believed—it is an assassination that is strangely lacking in
ideology. If we conceive of the conspiracy this way, it seems doomed
almost from the beginning. Brutus does everything wrong—not con-
senting to Antony's death and letting him deliver a funeral oration
for Caesar—but it really doesn't matter since it is difficult to imagine
Cassius as a winner.

Brutus's funeral oration in prose is no match for Antony's verse
oration in act 3, scene 2. The point really is that Brutus's speech is a
formal oration like that of Claudius in the second scene of *Hamlet* and
cannot fully appeal to his auditors' emotions. Yet the plebeians are
acclaiming Brutus in ways that undo whatever political ideas the
conspiracy was based on: "Let him be Caesar" and "Caesar's better
parts / Shall be crowned in Brutus" (3.2.52–53). Isn't Brutus aware
that the mob has completely misunderstood the purpose of the
assassination? We have no onstage reaction to these exclamations,
but the audience registers that the conspiracy has done nothing for
the popular imagination except murder Caesar.

Antony's oration is slippery and, like Othello, he disclaims any
eloquence:

I am no orator, as Brutus is;
But (as you know me all) a plain blunt man
That loves my friend. (3.2.219–21)

Antony only speaks "right on" and lacks "the power of speech / To
stir men's blood" (224–25). These disclaimers are dangerously artful.
Antony teases the mob along with his speech, which doesn't seem
like a speech at all, and he deliberately suspends expectations. The
will of Caesar is mentioned but is then dropped for more than a
hundred lines, and Antony does everything in his power to dramatize
Caesar's murder. Holding up the mantle of the dead Caesar, he
attempts to identify the deadly slashes in Caesar's body—all thirty-
three of them. There is no way that Antony can know any of this,

which makes him supremely histrionic at this point. Once the angry mob has been stirred up to unmitigated violence, Antony stands back cynically and separates himself from the emotional upshot of his oration: "Now let it work: Mischief, thou art afoot, / Take thou what course thou wilt" (263–64). This is chilling. Politics, it seems, is a dirty and impersonal business that depends upon an unholy zeal and fervor.

The real conclusion of Antony's oration is in the next brief scene, which brilliantly demonstrates the political reality of the mob at work. The plebeians in Jack Cade's rebellion in *Henry VI, Part II* were similarly comic and terrifying. This is the essence of Shakespeare's grotesque, what we would call black, comedy. Cinna the Poet just happens to be on the street after a night of bad dreams, and he just happens to meet up with the mob. In response to a whole series of questions like those in Harold Pinter's *Birthday Party*, he can only answer "directly and briefly, wisely and truly" that "I am a bachelor" (3.3.15–16). But language is pointless in this scene and serves only a supremely histrionic purpose: no matter what Cinna says the mob is determined to stomp him to death for his name only. When he protests that he is Cinna the poet and not Cinna the conspirator, the Fourth Plebeian insists: "Tear him for his bad verses! Tear him for his bad verses!" (30–31). The Fourth Plebeian knows nothing about the quality of Cinna's verses (nor do we), but, as we hear later in the Quarrel Scene: "What should the wars do with these jigging fools?" (4.3.136). We would naturally expect Brutus to be a friend of poetry, but he isn't. With Cinna the Poet names become the reality in true metadramatic fashion. As the Fourth Plebeian says, summing up the mood of the mob: "pluck but his name out of his heart, and turn him going" (3.3.34–35).

Act 4, scene 1 functions as an anticlimax to the excitement of the Cinna the Poet Scene. Here we see the three triumvirs—Antony, Octavius, and Lepidus—with the proscription list of those who are marked to die in their hands. Everything is so cool and matter-of-fact in this scene that it intensifies the grotesque horror of the immediately preceding scene of Cinna the Poet. As Antony says right at the beginning, "These many then shall die" (4.1.1), by committee decision as it seems, but there is eager horse trading. Lepidus will consent to Octavius's suggestion that his brother's name must be pricked down (or "checked off,") as we would say) if Antony's sister's son will also be marked for death. Antony consents without a murmur: "He shall not live; look, with a spot I damn him" (6). We are not surprised when Antony then proceeds to "cut off some charge in legacies" (9) in Caesar's will, which figured so importantly in Antony's oration. When Lepidus leaves, Antony tries to persuade Octavius to get rid of him for good, a matter that will be taken up again in *Antony and Cleopatra*. Act 4, scene 1 concludes this sequence about Caesar's assassination and its political consequences. It is an intensely political scene in the sense that it shows us the cynical operation of power in the state. Human lives are involved in what seems to us casual bickering.

Brutus is clearly an unpolitical character, and it is surprising in Shakespeare how closely unpolitical figures and tragic protagonists correlate. Being political is a way of surviving, just as Prince Hal is certain to defeat Hotspur, and Octavius in *Antony and Cleopatra* puts down Antony without great effort. It all seems inevitable. Hotspur, Antony, Brutus, Othello, and others are self-defeating in their idealism, or love, or commitment to honor; they don't need a powerful antagonist to destroy them. *Julius Caesar* is almost ingenuous in making Brutus wrong in every political decision. It even has unfortunate consequences for him to share his secrets with his wife. In Brutus we feel that tragedy is a complex matter of a noble figure who lacks any practical sense of what is actually going on. In this sense, Cassius functions as the all-knowing villain who wins Brutus over easily by unfair means.

Brutus's important soliloquy in his "orchard," or garden, where he debates with himself whether to kill his friend Caesar, is so overtly illogical as almost to be a parody of authentic reasoning. Brutus begins with the conclusion—"It must be by his death" (2.1.10)— then figures out how speciously to arrive at the place where he began. Unlike Cassius, Brutus knows "no personal cause to spurn" (11) at Caesar, so that he is forced to deal with hypothetical generalities: "He would be crowned. / How that might change his nature, there's the question" (12–13). His whole movement to murder is based on a conditional assumption: "So Caesar may; / Then lest he may, prevent" (27–28)—in other words, the murder will be a preventive strike. No other killing in Shakespeare is based on such a flimsy argument. It is as if Brutus is imagining himself impersonally in a heroic mold. He is especially prone to be distant and impersonal, as

233

if he were dramatizing political roles for himself that he is personally incapable of fulfilling. In this respect he looks forward to Hamlet in his elaborate fictionalizing and "dream of passion."

Brutus comes alive in the Quarrel Scene (4, 3) under the prodding of Cassius and the revelation of Portia's death. This is one of the great theatrical scenes in Shakespeare because it does so much to break through the facade of reasonableness in Brutus. At first, he is extremely priggish and self-righteous. He accuses Cassius of having

> an itching palm,
> To sell and mart your offices for gold
> To undeservers. (4.3.10–12)

But it is Brutus himself who speaks so disdainfully about money, as if it were a base thing to which he felt infinitely superior:

> shall we now
> Contaminate our fingers with base bribes,
> And sell the mighty space of our large honors
> For so much trash as may be graspèd thus? (23–26)

The last line is accompanied by a contemptuous gesture, yet Brutus and Cassius both need money to fight the war.

Brutus places himself ethically so much above Cassius that we can sympathize with Cassius's exasperation in this scene. Instead of a peer, Cassius is reduced to an errant schoolboy chided for his carelessness and irresponsibility. Brutus says, unfeelingly:

> There is no terror, Cassius, in your threats;
> For I am armed so strong in honesty
> That they pass by me as the idle wind,
> Which I respect not. (4.3.66–69)

We can see how the actor playing Cassius cannot really respond to Brutus but must keep firm control over his silence or speak only in a noncommittal and indirect way. Cassius is in danger of exploding.

Brutus begins to break down around line 106, when he has more than fully expressed his righteous indignation. He "carries anger" only

as the flint bears fire,
Who, much enforcèd, shows a hasty spark,
And straight is cold again. (4.3.110–12)

It is surprising to learn, after what we have just heard, that Cassius is "yokèd with a lamb" (109) in gentleness and that Brutus is only making a fierce show in the cause of righteousness. We soon find out that Brutus is troubled by news that he has only recently heard: "No man bears sorrow better. Portia is dead" (146). This revelation comes as a bomb, and we are now fully sympathetic to the sorrowing Brutus. Portia's death seems to reiterate the fact that Brutus is a tragic figure. He now speaks with a sweetness and lyric simplicity we haven't much heard before: "Speak no more of her. Give me a bowl of wine. / In this I bury all unkindness, Cassius" (157–58). We know from the elegiac tone that the cause of the conspirators is doomed. We need no Ghost of Caesar, who appears at the end of the scene, to tell us this, but he seals Brutus's fate.

Portia is a remarkable woman, a peer of Brutus and unlike Hotspur's Kate in *Henry IV, Part I,* who does not share at all in her husband's secrets. Portia is a Roman matron who defines marriage very differently from Katherine in *The Taming of the Shrew* (especially in her oration in 5, 2): marriage is a union between equals. Anything else is whoredom and subjection. Portia speaks to her husband with an unusual intimacy and frankness:

> Within the bond of marriage, tell me, Brutus,
> Is it excepted I should know no secrets
> That appertain to you? (2.1.280–82)

She defines the role of the ordinary wife with special acuity: "To keep with you at meals, comfort your bed, / And talk to you sometimes" (284–85). This is to be an entertainer, not a true wife, and we are surprised by Portia's boldness: "If it be no more, / Portia is Brutus' harlot, not his wife" (286–87). In terms of the stage action, Portia has a striking gesture when she shows her husband the "strong proof" (299) of her constancy, "Giving myself a voluntary wound / Here in the thigh" (300–301). Even with the boy actors playing women's roles, this is a significant bit of stage business when Portia shows her husband the wound she has inflicted as proof of her martial spirit. It combines the sexual and the ethical in a noteworthy way.

Apparently, Shakespeare went to a lot of trouble to develop a special Roman style for *Julius Caesar*. Coming between *Henry V* and *Hamlet*, this play has almost the smallest vocabulary in Shakespeare, and it makes little use of figures of speech. Shakespeare seems to be restraining his verbal resources at a moment of high creativity in his career around 1599. At its best the Roman style is simple, lyric, often monosyllabic, grave, deliberate, and ethical. Romans avoid flamboyant speeches, and their eloquence is, at its best, direct, moderate, and conversational. The Roman style does not accommodate bursts of emotional expression.

Brutus's reply to Portia's appeal—"Portia is Brutus' harlot, not his wife" (2.1.287)—is moving because it sounds so deeply felt:

> You are my true and honorable wife,
> As dear to me as are the ruddy drops
> That visit my sad heart. (288–90)

We can't imagine Brutus saying anything more personal to express his love. The image of the "ruddy drops" is homely, and the personification implied in "visit" is not felt as artful but rather as old-fashioned and formal. Brutus cannot speak with the emotional and rhetorical freedom of Romeo. In the line quoted from the Quarrel Scene—"No man bears sorrow better. Portia is dead" (4.3.146)—we feel the effect of the caesura as an intense, elegiac pause. This is the hidden factor that explains why Brutus is so testy and so superior in this scene.

After the Quarrel Scene, we are so certain that the conspirators are moving to their doom, that we are sure beforehand that the Battle of Philippi must go against them. When Brutus and Cassius have their formal leave-taking, it is as if they must acknowledge that they are both going to die. The Roman style emphasizes the elegiac and the sad, as if this occasion were a farewell to life. Brutus says:

> Forever, and forever, farewell, Cassius!
> If we do meet again, why, we shall smile;
> If not, why then this parting was well made. (5.1.116–18)

Cassius almost exactly echoes Brutus's words:

> Forever, and forever, farewell, Brutus!
> If we do meet again, we'll smile indeed;
> If not, 'tis true this parting was well made. (119–21)

This is not conversation, but in its lyrical, poetical assertion it is a preparation for what is to come. Only Romans speak this way in Shakespeare. If the Roman style limits a character's range, it is also an intensely formal, somewhat wistful mode of expression.

Julius Caesar has been described as a problem play. Although it is so simple and straightforward in its style that it is a great favorite in high schools, it is nevertheless deeply ambiguous. We grow increasingly certain after the middle of the play that the conspirators will lose, but we feel a strange balancing of values between the party of Brutus and the party of Caesar. It is not at all certain that Shakespeare was a great partisan of republican values, but he is certainly not a spokesman for the imperial. The conspiracy against Caesar is wrongheaded but noble.

Caesar himself is deliberately undercut and given infirmities that don't exist in the classical sources. Antony is both deeply moved to avenge Caesar and detached from the violence that inevitably follows. Octavius coldly and soberly looks ahead to *Antony and Cleopatra;* he is an unsympathetic winner in both plays. Cassius is a passionate man, and he strangely mixes peevish, personal motives for the assassination of Caesar with broader, political verities. It is hard to choose between the conspirators and the party of Caesar. Shakespeare seems to have picked a dramatic subject that energizes opposing points of view. I think he would have taken it as a mark of theatrical success that *Julius Caesar* seems so problematical. Virtues and defects are skillfully balanced against each other, and the tragic protagonist who made it all happen is finally praised by his enemy for his personal integrity. Antony says of Brutus:

> His life was gentle, and the elements
> So mixed in him that Nature might stand up
> And say to all the world, "This was a man!" (5.5.48–50)

Hamlet

At a crucial moment in his soliloquy at the end of act 2, Hamlet is disturbed that the Player in the Dido and Aeneas play that he has just heard should break down in speaking about Hecuba: "What's Hecuba to him, or he to Hecuba, / That he should weep for her?" (2.2.569–70). It is "monstrous"—and this is a strong word—that the Player should react so powerfully: "But in a fiction, in a dream of passion" (562). In other words, the old play about the fall of Troy and the murder of Priam that the Player recites is only a fiction, literature, a mimesis of feeling, whereas Hamlet's own situation is not a fiction, not a dream of passion, but the real thing. It is Hamlet's real father who was so horribly murdered and his real mother who so quickly married the murderer, with whom she may have been having an adulterous relationship. Gertrude is a more passionate figure than the fictional and mythical Hecuba, the "mobled queen" (513), about whose "lank and all o'erteemèd loins, / A blanket in the alarm of fear caught up" (519–20).

Hamlet is full of self-reproach—"O, what a rogue and peasant slave am I" (2.2.560)—because his reactions are so inferior to those of the Player. If the Player weeps for Hecuba,

What would he do
Had he the motive and the cue for passion
That I have? (570–72)

But Hamlet can think only of rant and bad acting as appropriate reactions: "He would drown the stage with tears / And cleave the general ear with horrid speech" (572–73). This is the kind of over-wrought effect that Hamlet condemns himself for later: "Why, what an ass am I! This is most brave" (594).

In his advice to the Players, Hamlet specifically condemns this kind of emotional acting: "O, it offends me to the soul to hear a robustious periwig-pated fellow tear a passion to tatters, to very rags, to split the ears of the groundlings" (3.2.8–11). This is like Bottom's claim in *A Midsummer Night's Dream* that he "could play Ercles [Hercules] rarely, or a part to tear a cat in, to make all split" (1.2.30–31). Hamlet desires that the Player's "very torrent, tempest, and (as I may say) whirlwind" of passion be controlled by "a temperance that may give it smoothness" (3.2.6–8). So if we apply Hamlet's advice to the Players to his own self-accusing soliloquy at the end of act 2, we are left in a quandary about what "passion" might mean and what is Hamlet's fiction and dream of passion.

Tom Stoppard understood very well the crucial role of the Players in his own version of *Hamlet* in *Rosencrantz and Guildenstern Are Dead*. As in Shakespeare, his Players present their own reality: they never need to get into costume, they are always "on," and they can never really die (because they are actors). If we see *Rosencrantz and Guildenstern Are Dead* as a critique of Shakespeare's play, then we are aware of its enormous histrionic vitality. Acting, playing, self-dramatizing, and trying out roles are all of overwhelming significance in *Hamlet*. The plays-within-the-play are not merely an entertainment, as they are in *A Midsummer Night's Dream* (the Pyramus and Thisby play, close to the plot of *Romeo and Juliet*), and *Love's Labor's Lost* (the play of the Nine Worthies). The fall of Troy in the Dido and Aeneas play provides as crucial a tragic background in *Hamlet* as it does in *The Rape of Lucrece*, and the events of *The Murder of Gonzago*, or *The Mousetrap* are intended to test the truth of the Ghost's accusation. Hamlet's soliloquy in 2,2 ends triumphantly: "The play's the thing / Wherein I'll catch the conscience of the King" (616–17). This is the upshot of his speculations about why he is a rogue and peasant slave.

The blank verse of the Dido and Aeneas play is very different from the blank verse of *Hamlet* itself. It is orotund, rhetorical, declamatory, with many old-fashioned words like "mobled," or muffled, and "bisson rheum," or blinding tears, and pictorial hyperbole, like the hellish Pyrrhus "o'ersizèd [or smeared over with size, a glue-like substance] with coagulate gore, / With eyes like carbuncles" (2.2.473–74). This has none of the passionate and conversational speech characteristics of the main play, but the Dido and Aeneas play is set apart as something that was "caviary to the general" (447), an acquired and special taste like caviar for the general playgoing public. The Dido and Aeneas play recapitulates and projects in a different mode the issues of *Hamlet*: the murder of Old Priam is analogous to the murder of Hamlet's father, the grieving Hecuba is what Gertrude should be, and Pyrrhus the revenger provides a model for Hamlet, Laertes, Claudius, and Fortinbras. In act 4, scene 7, Laertes speaks in the inflated rhetoric of Pyrrhus when he answers Claudius's catechistic question about what he would undertake to show himself his father's son in deed more than in words: "To cut his throat i' th' church!" (126). Even Claudius seems shocked by such a formulaic, revenger's answer.

The Mousetrap play or *The Murder of Gonzago* is even more deliberately archaic or archaistic than the Dido and Aeneas piece. It is written in formal, end-stopped couplets, with a kind of singsong effect, and its characters, especially the Player King and the Player Queen, are wooden caricatures of the full-blooded figures in *Hamlet*. Like the play of the Nine Worthies in *Love's Labor's Lost* and the Pyramus and Thisby play in *A Midsummer Night's Dream*, this is a crude, old-fashioned play to which the aristocratic audience can feel superior, but *The Mousetrap* is very pointed. As Hamlet says with satirical bravado, "Marry, this is miching mallecho," an odd phrase that means something like "sneaking skulduggery," or, as Hamlet translates it right afterward: "it means mischief" (3.2.144).

In the long, preliminary dumb show, the action of the play is shown in pantomime, including the vivid description: *"The Queen returns, finds the King dead, makes passionate action"* (3.2.140 s.d.). This disappears in the acted play and serves as a kind of stage direction for the player of the Queen. It is by its artificiality and distance that *The Mousetrap* manages to catch the conscience of the King—he is caught unaware, "frighted with false fire" (272), or blanks, like "guilty creatures sitting at a play" (2.2.601), who have been struck to the soul "by the very cunning of the scene" (602). Lucianus, nephew to the King, pours poison in the Player King's ears and thus reenacts Claudius's murder, but he poisons "in jest; no offense i' th' world" (3.2.240–41). By purposely suspending the reality of the murder between the play world and the real world, Hamlet makes a deadly histrionic point.

One of the qualities of Shakespearean tragedy hardest for modern readers and audiences to accept is the vividness of evil. Shakespeare's villains are among his most compelling characters, and the villain is generally practical, intelligent, resourceful, and without illusions. Starting with Aaron in *Titus Andronicus* and continuing with Richard III, Edmund, Iago, and others, the villains appeal to the audience for their understanding and sympathy. Claudius is clearly conceived in this mode, and he has remarkable resemblances to Bolingbroke in *Richard II* and the *Henry IV* plays and to Macbeth. It is pointless to argue what an effective king Claudius is—much more efficient an administrator than Hamlet might have been—and how well he guides the ship of state. All the optimistic and benevolent appearances are based on Claudius's secret murder of his brother. Like Cain's murder of Abel, "It hath the primal eldest curse upon't, / A brother's murder" (3.3.37–38).

Later in the play we see Claudius, like Macbeth, prepared to kill again: his nephew / stepson Hamlet is sent to instant death in England, and he allows his Queen to drink the poisoned cup without a word, except the tepid: "Gertrude, do not drink" (5.2.291). His aside at this point is in the cold style of the true Machiavel: "It is the poisoned cup; it is too late" (293). He does nothing to save the woman who is

> so conjunctive to my life and soul,
> That, as the star moves not but in his sphere,
> I could not but by her. (4.7.14–16)

The plot takes priority over his intensely possessive love.

The real Claudius, as opposed to the smiling public man, is a frightening figure, who has a frenzy to dispose of his enemies. Hamlet is represented as a dire disease: "like the hectic [-fever] in my blood he rages" (4.3.66), and the King of England must cure Claudius by Hamlet's instant death. As we learn later from Hamlet's amused account: "No, not to stay the grinding of the ax, / My head should be struck off" (5.2.24–25). In his soliloquy at the end of 4,3, Claudius anticipates Macbeth in the inevitable sequencing of murder: "Till I know 'tis done, / Howe'er my haps, my joys were ne'er begun" (68–69). At this point late in the play, Claudius is still nowhere without the death of Hamlet, and tranquillity permanently eludes him. As the proverbial saying has it, blood will have blood (Tilley, B458), and no single murder is enough.

Claudius's conscience is much in evidence in the play, but there is a certain self-indulgence and sentimentality in his pangs of self-reproach. Just before the "To be, or not to be" soliloquy in Act 3, Scene 1, Polonius will "loose" (2.2.162) his daughter to Hamlet, and he stage-manages her role as a bait for Hamlet to reveal his secrets:

> Read on this book,
> That show of such an exercise may color
> Your loneliness. (3.1.44–46)

But the old father has misgivings about his duplicity:

> We are oft to blame in this,
> 'Tis too much proved, that with devotion's visage
> And pious action we do sugar o'er
> The devil himself. (46–49)

At this point the King has an aside of conscience that looks forward to the Prayer Scene (3,3):

> O, 'tis too true.
> How smart a lash that speech doth give my conscience!
> The harlot's cheek, beautied with plast'ring art,
> Is not more ugly to the thing that helps it
> Than is my deed to my most painted word.
> O heavy burden! (3.1.49–54)

This conveniently acknowledges the King's guilt *before* the *Mousetrap* play and Hamlet's "To be, or not to be" soliloquy, but Claudius's moral professions have nothing to do with his actions in the rest of the play. His powerful confession has no consequences. It is interesting that Hamlet takes up the familiar hypocrisy theme in cosmetics almost a hundred lines later in his attack on Ophelia: "I have heard of your paintings, well enough. God hath given you one face and you make yourselves another" (144–46). It is as if Hamlet had overheard Claudius's aside.

The Prayer Scene after the *Mousetrap* play is devoted to the King's long confessional soliloquy in which he tries to pray. Here again we see Shakespeare developing sympathy for the villain as he takes stock of his spiritual condition, but the whole scene is a mockery because the King cannot pray for very specific moral and religious reasons. Claudius has no illusions about the magnitude of his own guilt, and his questions to God are searing in their passionate intensity:

> What if this cursèd hand
> Were thicker than itself with brother's blood,
> Is there not rain enough in the sweet heavens
> To wash it white as snow? (3.3.43–46)

Of course there is, or else God's mercy would be a mockery, and these issues are clearly foreshadowed in the damnation of Doctor Faustus in Marlowe's play.

Claudius speaks of his spiritual state with extraordinary lucidity, but he has no penitence. He knows that he cannot be forgiven

> since I am still possessed
> Of those effects for which I did the murder,
> My crown, mine own ambition, and my queen. (3.3.53–55)

One cannot be pardoned and "retain th' offense" (56). Maybe it is possible "In the corrupted currents of this world" (57), but in heaven "There is no shuffling" (61). It is as if Claudius had overheard Hamlet's "To be, or not to be" soliloquy, because he echoes Hamlet's word "shuffling":

> For in that sleep of death what dreams may come
> When we have shuffled off this mortal coil,
> Must give us pause. (3.1.66–68)

Shuffling refers to the moral obliquity of mortals in the corrupted currents of this world.

Claudius's guilty aside just before Hamlet's "To be, or not to be" soliloquy has such a clear moral function in the play that it seems excessively planned—perhaps even planted. The King is speaking directly to the audience and circumventing dialogue and character interplay. Two other asides in the play, by Gertrude and by Laertes, also seem to serve the needs of the narrative rather than those of the immediate context. Just before the mad Ophelia enters, Gertrude sums up the fears of her sick and guilty soul in two neat couplets that function as a kind of prologue for Ophelia:

> To my sick soul (as sin's true nature is)
> Each toy [-trifle] seems prologue to some great amiss;
> So full of artless jealousy is guilt
> It spills [-destroys] itself in fearing to be spilt. (4.5.17–20)

This sounds like a pronouncement rather than a statement, and its formality emphasizes its deliberateness. Why does Gertrude have a pang of conscience right at this point? We hear nothing further about her sick soul.

In the case of Laertes, Shakespeare is evidently moving to reconcile Laertes and Hamlet. Just before the third and fatal bout of the fencing match, Laertes vows to the King that he will hit his opponent with the poisoned rapier he is holding in his hand: "My lord, I'll hit him now" (5.2.296). When the King replies "I do not think't" (296), Laertes launches his highly significant aside of conscience: "And yet it is almost against my conscience" (297). We have already heard Hamlet's apology to Laertes: "Give me your pardon, sir. I have done you wrong" (227), which Laertes rejects for technical, legalistic reasons: "But in my terms of honor / I stand aloof" (247–48).

But as his inevitable death approaches, Laertes has a change of heart, and he touches Hamlet with the poisoned rapier almost against his conscience. Why the lingering hesitation in Laertes' "almost"? It would seem to be an ethical matter that either is or is not against Laertes' conscience—there are no middle possibilities. At the end Laertes confesses his guilt: "I am justly killed with mine own treachery" (5.2.308) and puts all the responsibility on Claudius: "The King, the King's to blame" (321). Laertes' aside is the turning point of his change of heart, and, although it seems crucial for the rehabilitation of Laertes and his moral status in the play, it also seems in its context too deliberate an effect. Laertes is not the type of character whom we would expect to have any asides of conscience.

Another aspect of *Hamlet* difficult for modern audiences and readers to accept is Hamlet's role as revenger. Revenge is morally ambiguous. Private revenge is specifically forbidden by Christian doctrine— "Vengeance is mine saith the Lord"—and the revenger in Elizabethan and Jacobean plays almost always perishes in his own revenge. "Taint not thy mind" (1.3.85), says the Ghost to his son, thinking specifically of protecting Gertrude, but there is no way that a revenger can preserve his innocence, ward off complicity, keep clean hands or an untainted mind. As in Sonnet 111 about acting, Hamlet's "nature is subdued / To what it works in, like the dyer's hand." In the familiar Elizabethan proverb, pitch defileth (Tilley, P358), or, as Falstaff mockingly tells Hal: "This pitch (as ancient writers do report) doth defile" (*1 Henry IV* 2.4.418–19). These insoluble problems face Hamlet from the beginning, so to be a revenger means that one is certain to die. The play is full of revengers, most notably Pyrrhus in the Dido and Aeneas play, but also Fortinbras and Laertes. Fortinbras is out to revenge his old father, who lost his single combat with old Hamlet, but at the end of the play it is essential that he be there to take over the Danish kingdom. Hamlet's last words express his concern for Fortinbras, his successor in Denmark: "But I do prophesy th' election lights / On Fortinbras. He has my dying voice" (5.2.356–57).

A revenger's rhetoric comes naturally to Hamlet in some parts of the play, but he laughs it to scorn elsewhere. This divided mind about the swelling, ranting style is best seen in the "rogue and peasant slave" soliloquy. Hamlet is accusing himself of being a coward, and in the process of posing damaging questions, he cheers himself up with vaunting:

> or ere this
> I should ha' fatted all the region kites
> With this slave's [i.e., the King's] offal. Bloody, bawdy villain!
> Remorseless, treacherous, lecherous, kindless villain!
> O, vengeance! (2.2.589–93)

At this moment occurs one of those marvelous Shakespearean transformations that make Hamlet different from all other Elizabethan revengers; he scorns himself for speaking so grandiloquently: "Why, what an ass am I! This is most brave" (2.2.594). He is aware that he is making a grand but empty speech and that he

> Must, like a whore, unpack my heart with words
> And fall a-cursing like a very drab,
> A scullion! (597–99)

Again, the image of the whore and the scullion (as in Folio), or kitchen maid, is used to indicate hypocrisy and a false expression (as in Claudius's aside about "The harlot's cheek, beautied with plast'ring art" [3.1.51]). Hamlet is indulging in mere rant, and he moves quickly to the play, which will catch the conscience of the King.

Hamlet is an accomplished parodist, as in the scene with Osric (5,2), but his mocking of the revenger's style is most explicit in the wit combat with Laertes over the grave of Ophelia. Laertes speaks in the amplified, numerical rhetoric that is a mark of his shallowness throughout the play:

> O, treble woe
> Fall ten times treble on that cursèd head
> Whose wicked deed thy [i.e., Ophelia's] most ingenious sense
> Deprived thee of! (5.1.248–51)

Hamlet is most offended by Laertes' style, which he thinks inappropriate to mourn the dead Ophelia:

> What is he whose grief
> Bears such an emphasis, whose phrase of sorrow
> Conjures the wand'ring stars? (256–58)

Laertes' grief bears a false emphasis, to which Hamlet replies in a wildly exaggerated and extravagant style:

> And if thou prate of mountains, let them throw
> Millions of acres on us, till our ground
> Singeing his pate against the burning zone,
> Make Ossa like a wart! (282–85)

Laertes prates like his father Polonius, "Who was in life a foolish prating knave" (3.4.216), and Hamlet is answering him in kind: "Nay, an thou'lt mouth, / I'll rant as well as thou" (285–86). Hamlet is self-consciously parodying an inflated and ranting style.

Yet Hamlet as a revenger speaks with a bravado that is quite different from his more sober moments. When he stabs Polonius through the arras in the Closet Scene, he does it unthinkingly and with a gambler's oath: "How now? A rat? Dead for a ducat, dead!" (3.4.25). This is not exactly the sensitive, thoughtful Hamlet of Romantic criticism, nor is the image of Hamlet that we have from the Prayer Scene, which immediately precedes this one. Dr. Johnson was right in thinking it too horrible to be read or to be uttered, since Hamlet wants to damn Claudius in body and soul.

To kill the King while he is praying is not a good enough revenge for Hamlet. He wants something more flamboyant and more ironically appropriate. He therefore puts up his sword to wait for "a more horrid hent" (3.3.88), or occasion for seizing it again:

> When he is drunk asleep, or in his rage,
> Or in th' incestuous pleasure of his bed,
> At game a-swearing, or about some act
> That has no relish of salvation in't—
> Then trip him, that his heels may kick at heaven,
> And that his soul may be as damned and black
> As hell, whereto it goes. (89–95)

The scene is brilliantly arranged so that the murderer Claudius draws our sympathy by his confessional desire to pray while Hamlet the revenger offends us by his overblown revenger's rhetoric.

All this is made explicit in Hamlet's least quoted soliloquy at the end of act 3, scene 2 after the *Mousetrap* play. Here Hamlet is seen in

247

a posture most like Pyrrhus, who, we remember, is "total gules, horridly tricked / With blood of fathers, mothers, daughters, sons" (2.2.468–69). *Gules* is the heraldic word for "red." Like the Norse warrior of the sources, Hamlet in his soliloquy takes a heroic posture: "Now could I drink hot blood" (3.2.398). This is not exactly the meditative, philosophical Hamlet of the "To be, or not to be" soliloquy, and he is preoccupied in this speech with steeling himself from matricide: "let not ever / The soul of Nero [who put his mother Agrippina to death] enter this firm bosom" (401–2). Hamlet literally follows the Ghost's injunction, "Taint not thy mind" (1.5.85), but his resolve, "Let me be cruel, not unnatural" (3.2.403) comes awfully close to matricide. We need to be reminded that in the Closet Scene, Gertrude has good reason to think that her son might kill her when she cries out for help: "What wilt thou do? Thou wilt not murder me? Help, ho!" (3.4.22). It is at this moment that Hamlet stabs Polonius through the arras. The homicidal mood and tone of Hamlet at least comes to some sort of misdirected culmination.

Madness is often misunderstood in *Hamlet* and in Shakespearean tragedy. A crucial difference exists between the heightened emotion of Hamlet's "wild and whirling words" (1.5.133) after he has seen the Ghost and the madness of Ophelia after her father's murder, "Divided from herself and her fair judgment, / Without the which we are pictures or mere beasts" (4.5.85–86). As in the source story, Hamlet feigns madness in order to protect himself from his enemies; like poetic license, madness allows for a certain margin of imaginative freedom. Hamlet tells Horatio of his plan: "As I perchance hereafter shall think meet / To put an antic disposition on" (1.5.171–72) and swears him to secrecy. *Antic* meant both grotesque and antique, and Hamlet deliberately "puts on" an antic disposition as an actor might put on a costume. An antic disposition means playing the fool as if one were mad.

Polonius is the first to believe in Hamlet's madness, "the very ecstasy of love" (2.1.102), caused by Ophelia's rejecting him. This provides a convenient pretext for Hamlet. But Polonius is puzzled by Hamlet's wit: "How pregnant sometimes his replies are! A happiness that often madness hits on, which reason and sanity could not so prosperously be delivered of" (2.2.210–13). Like many tragic protagonists (such as Titus Andronicus, for example), Hamlet is both mad and not mad, and the illusion of madness is a wonderful stalking-horse for satire and wit. Hamlet can attack his enemies with seeming impunity. Thus in the interplay with the King about the body of Polonius, the prisoner Hamlet can exercise a biting, imaginative freedom because of his antic disposition. Hamlet's sermon on mortality is a witty diatribe against vanity that anticipates the Graveyard Scene. Polonius is at supper "Not where he eats, but where 'a is eaten. A certain convocation of politic worms are e'en at him" (4.3.19–21). The Diet of Worms pronounced its ban on Luther in 1521.

Ophelia's madness is entirely different from Hamlet's. As the First Quarto graphically describes it, she enters in act 4, scene 5 *"playing on a Lute, and her haire downe singing."* A lady with her hair unpinned, or "down," is assumed to be distracted, as in our weaker expression "to let your hair down." Ophelia sings snatches of popular Elizabethan ballads, some of them bawdy, and she speaks in the free associational style typical of mad people:

> I hope all will be well. We must be patient, but I cannot choose but weep to think they would lay him i' th' cold ground. My brother shall know of it; and so I thank you for your good counsel. Come, my coach! Good night, ladies, good night. Sweet ladies, good night, good night. (68–73)

This lyrical and poignant style was much imitated in later mad ladies on the stage, including the Jailer's Daughter in Shakespeare's late play, *The Two Noble Kinsmen.*

The intuitive, highly emotional Ophelia is very different from the dutiful daughter of act 1, scene 3, who said to her father: "I do not know, my lord, what I should think" (104). In her madness Ophelia suddenly comes alive as a character and forces us to reckon with her innuendoes. Claudius fears her power and counsels surveillance (as he does for Hamlet in act 1, scene 2): "Follow her close; give her good watch, I pray you" (4.5.74). In less than twenty-five lines her brother Laertes is breaking through the palace guard and threatening to take over the kingdom. Shakespeare divides Ophelia's part into two in act 4, scene 5 and has her enter twice. The second time she distributes flowers (a sentimental connection continued in the mad King Lear) and sings a moving elegy for her father.

Ophelia's death is reported by the Queen in act 4, scene 7 in what seems like a pastoral eclogue. The mad Ophelia is "one incapable of her own distress" (178) as "she chanted snatches of old lauds" (177). In an animistic image,

> her garments, heavy with their drink,
> Pulled the poor wretch from her melodious lay
> To muddy death. (181–83)

Ophelia's madness is not satirical and biting like Hamlet's but sets her apart as a beautiful, unworldly creature who, like a fool, speaks strange, illogical, and hieratic sentiments. She is a fragile creature destroyed by the very grief in which Hamlet triumphs over his enemies.

Unlike the madness of the dynamic heroines of the comedies, her madness reveals the silent woman who is suffering acutely from her passive acceptance of things. In her only soliloquy in the play, she speaks proleptically of Hamlet's madness as if it were her own: "Now see that noble and most sovereign reason / Like sweet bells jangled, out of time and harsh" (3.1.160–61). And she ends her meditation with a mysterious line that looks to a clouded and sorrowful future: "O, woe is me, / T' have seen what I have seen, see what I see!" (163–64). She is the almost silent witness, who attests to the tragedy.

Othello

Othello is the most limited in scope of all Shakespeare's tragedies. It does not deal with kings and princes, nor does it have strong metaphysical overtones. Nothing in the play matches Macbeth's dealing with the Witches, or King Lear on the heath probing the relation of man to Nature, or Hamlet's feverish exploration of being and not being and the moral obligations of revenge. No one is philosophical in Othello, and the theme of male cuckoldry is usually associated with comedy. Othello is a domestic tragedy, but the genre of domestic comedy is much more familiar. Domestic is in itself a devaluing word, as if to warn us of the restriction in imaginative vision. Othello brings everything down to earth, yet it is the most concentrated and most intense of Shakespeare's tragedies. It arouses pity and sympathy and compassion for Iago's victims: Othello, Desdemona, Cassio, Roderigo, and Emilia. Like Claudius and Macbeth, Iago is a murderer who is not touched by the milk of human kindness. Othello's anguished cry resounds in our ears: "But yet the pity of it" (4.1.197). This is something Iago cannot understand.

In this scene Othello seems to intuitively understand his own tragedy yet cannot bring this awareness to the level of consciousness.

This is a characteristic Shakespearean touch, as if the tragic protagonist could instinctively foresee his own doom. Othello is convinced by Iago's crafty persuasion: "Ay, let her rot, and perish, and be damned tonight; for she shall not live. No, my heart is turned to stone; I strike it, and it hurts my hand" (4.1.183–85). But Othello's gesture of striking his heart unconsciously turns him against himself. His heart, which should be the seat of all tender feeling, especially love, has turned to stone, and the pain of striking his own stony heart precipitates him into an entirely different discourse: "O, the world hath not a sweeter creature! She might lie by an emperor's side and command him tasks" (185–87). Othello is not an emperor, and he is filled with awe for the stature of Desdemona as a commanding creature. Iago is more at a loss here than anywhere else in the play. His feeble reply is not what we expected: "Nay, that's not your way" (188). But Othello's passionate remembrance is not to be stopped: "So delicate with her needle. An admirable musician. O, she will sing the savageness out of a bear! Of so high and plenteous wit and invention—" (189–92). Wit and invention are the qualities of the artist, like Shakespeare's own gifts in writing this play. Othello evokes Desdemona as she really is, a precious and gifted being infinitely superior to him in every way. She is a paragon of women, endowed with the highest of feminine qualities.

Again, Iago's blocking rejoinder is ineffectual: "She's the worse for all this" (4.1.193). Why worse except that Iago despises all grace and beauty, as in his strange remark about Cassio: "He hath a daily beauty in his life / That makes me ugly" (5.1.19–20). That the beauty is "daily" emphasizes the absolute separation between Iago and Cassio. This all leads to Othello's wrenching declaration: "But yet the pity of it, Iago. O Iago, the pity of it, Iago" (4.1.197–98). Iago is the last person in the world to be able to understand Othello's anguish, so that he can only answer with a narrow petulance, as if offended by his general's simplemindedness. Othello seems to have an uncanny ability to formulate his tragedy without being able to do anything about it. It is as if he is as much Iago's passive victim as Desdemona is his. It is as if he has been hypnotized by Iago to murder his wife, whom he knows instinctively to be the sweetest creature in the world. Othello seems to be enveloped in a bad dream, and, once Iago has gotten to him, he acts like a sleepwalker. He has been mysteriously paralyzed and poisoned (a frequent word in the play). Yet Othello in the midst of his crisis also seems to draw on an alternative set of ecstatic images.

This may explain the extraordinary ambivalence of the scene in which he comes to murder his wife. Surely Desdemona is right when she says: "That death's unnatural that kills for loving" (5.2.42). There is no doubt that Othello comes as a lover, and the death scene is charged with powerful erotic imagery. He gazes on her and speaks in an intensely voyeuristic style:

> Yet I'll not shed her blood,
> Nor scar that whiter skin of hers than snow,
> And smooth as monumental alabaster. (3–5)

This is the language of the *Sonnets* and of *Romeo and Juliet.* In a strongly sensuous gesture, Othello smells the sleeping Desdemona, as if she were a rose:

> I'll smell thee on the tree.
> O balmy breath, that dost almost persuade
> Justice to break her sword. (5.2.15–17)

He smells her and he kisses her and then he weeps. Like Brutus in *Julius Caesar,* who tells Cassius: "Let's be sacrificers, but not butchers" (2.1.166), Othello wants to kill Desdemona in a priestly ritual, but he is forced to smother her with his bare hands. She comes alive thirty lines later, and he has to strangle her again. Desdemona's physical presence in the scene forces Othello to "call what I intend to do / A murder, which I thought a sacrifice" (5.2.64–65).

Why is Othello so vulnerable to Iago? This question has been posed so many times and with such seriousness that it looks as if *Othello* is not a work of fiction at all but a case study of actual people. Yet the question has remarkable persistence. We want to know what remarkable attraction in Iago makes him so believable and so persuasive. First of all, Othello shares with all of Shakespeare's tragic protagonists a straightforwardness and a lack of suspicion that make him easily duped. As Iago says in one of his many self-explaining soliloquies:

> The Moor is of a free and open nature
> That thinks men honest that but seem to be so;
> And will as tenderly be led by th' nose
> As asses are. (1.3.390–93)

Free is a word of wide implication in Shakespeare's language, with strong association with the medieval sense of noble, honorable, generous, and frank; Othello acts like a person of noble birth or breeding.

He is "open" in the sense of being accessible, available, impressionable, and unobstructed, so that the word functions as a synonym of *free;* meaning generous, candid, or unconcealed. A free and open nature is terribly vulnerable to someone as cunning and duplicitous as Iago. Thus Hamlet, in the words of Claudius,

> being remiss,
> Most generous, and free from all contriving,
> Will not peruse the foils. (*Hamlet* 4.7.134–36)

Likewise Brutus's "honorable mettle may be wrought / From that it is disposed" (*Julius Caesar* 1.2.307–8). In the contemptuous view of Cassius: "who so firm that cannot be seduced?" (310). Othello is therefore an easy mark for Iago.

But the question of why Othello falls so easily is more complicated than that. In some radical sense, Iago represents the night side of Othello's mind, the unconscious, the id, the forbidden world of dreams. Othello needs Iago desperately to complete his being, and Dr. Iago is his mentor to answer questions about what the world is really like. Although Othello confesses repeatedly and excessively that he is old—"the young affects / In me defunct" (1.3.258–59)—, he is particularly eager to hear about sex from Iago. Iago's discourse is prurient, if not actually pornographic, and he encourages Othello in his own intense voyeurism.

Not surprisingly, Othello demands "ocular proof" (3.3.357), "Make me to see't" (361). Nothing is easier for Iago, who teases Othello with visions of an excruciating lasciviousness: "Would you, the supervisor, grossly gape on? / Behold her topped?" (392–93). This both horrifies and fascinates Othello, as if it were the primal scene.

Othello is egging Iago on to provide him with lewd examples, and Iago's account of being abed with Cassio and Cassio's talking in his sleep is feeble but effective:

> Then kiss me hard,
> As if he plucked up kisses by the roots
> That grew upon my lips; laid his leg o'er my thigh . . . (419–21)

This thinly disguised homoerotic imagery leads immediately to the handkerchief, which becomes a palpable symbol of Desdemona's chastity. Othello is inflamed.

Othello picks up Iago's language, his syntax, his insidious questions, his broken discourse, his imagery of animals, poison, and hate. It all happens so quickly that we need to imagine an aptness in Othello to be transformed utterly, to be plunged into the diabolic world of Iago, and to experiment so alarmingly with being the Other. One telling example is Iago's word "Ha," which functions as an interjectional grunt. As soon as Cassio leaves Desdemona in act 3, scene 3, Iago says tentatively: "Ha! I like not that" (35). Iago is characteristically trying out words and attitudes, not all of which work as well as his opening "Ha." He is a supreme improviser, who watches Othello's reactions in order to know how to proceed. *Ha* is extremely successful phonetically as a cacophonous exclamation implying doubt and contempt, an innuendo, since Iago works "by wit, and not by witchcraft" (2.3.372).

Othello is soon appropriating Iago's word *Ha*. When he enters at line 326, the first thing he says is in a new, harsh style: "Ha! ha! False to me?" (3.3.330). He can only deal with Desdemona's betrayal in rage. In the next scene there is another Iago-like "Ha" when Othello is quizzing Desdemona about the loss of the handkerchief. Suddenly it takes on a wild importance, and Desdemona exclaims: "Then would to God that I had never seen't!" (3.4.77), to which Othello answers only: "Ha! Wherefore?" (78). Like the visual sign of the handkerchief, "Ha" becomes the spoken sign of betrayal. There is a last enigmatic "Hah" (5.2.155) in the final scene when Othello learns the truth about Iago from Emilia.

Like the black villain Aaron in *Titus Andronicus*, Iago's style shows a vividness of colloquial and slangy diction. In his second speech in the play, Iago is already complaining about Othello's pompous, official style, full of "bombast circumstance, / Horribly stuffed with epithets of war" (1.1.12–13). "Bombast" was cotton material used to line or stuff Elizabethan garments, and it was applied metaphorically to a turgid and inflated style. Iago speaks directly and without circumstance; he never ventures into an inappropriate high style. His colloquial mastery makes him so believable, so "honest"—an ironic word taken up from Antony's oration in *Julius Caesar*. Like Richard III and all Shakespeare's villains, Iago is a wonderful actor, who, as he tells Roderigo in the first scene, "will wear my heart upon my sleeve / For daws to peck at; I am not what I am" (61–62).

But Iago is also master of a withering and dismissive contempt. In the first scene Iago and Roderigo awake Brabantio, Desdemona's father, with news of her elopement with Othello. Iago uses a gross, sexual vocabulary for Othello that sets the tone for the play: "Even now, now, very now, an old black ram / Is tupping your white ewe" (1.1.85–86). The insidious repetition of "Even now, now, very now" is pure pornography. Iago is sure to emphasize the theme of miscegenation and the image of Othello as an old black lecher. Desdemona is white, spotless, and above all a passive maiden, being tupped forcibly by an old black ram (whose prominent horns already look forward to cuckoldry). Iago, who remains anonymous in this scene and eventually slips away, delights in the most vulgar animal imagery: "your daughter and the Moor are making the beast with two backs" (113–14); "you'll have your daughter covered with a Barbary horse" (108–9)—"cover" is a standard word for animal intercourse. Surely Iago is projecting himself as an intensely male, animallike ravisher.

It's interesting that in his long soliloquy at the end of act 2, scene 1, Iago confesses that he loves Desdemona, "Not out of absolute lust, though peradventure / I stand accountant for as great a sin" (292–93). This is curious, but it occurs in a context of random sexual jealousy in which Iago mentions casually: "I do suspect the lusty Moor / Hath leaped into my seat" (295–96). Further on in this speech, Iago fears "Cassio with my nightcap too" (307). The Moor is lusty only in Iago's inflamed imagination, and it looks as if Iago is sexually preoccupied—as if all that all men think about all the time is making the beast with two backs. But Iago himself, like Aaron in *Titus*

Andronicus, has displaced sex onto revenge, and he satisfies his lust in vaunting and macho discourse.

Iago's contemptuousness is nowhere more violent than when he is setting Roderigo up to kill Cassio: "I have rubbed this young quat almost to the sense, / And he grows angry" (5.1.11–12). To rub "to the sense" is to rub raw, a cruel and painful image. This is the only use of *quat*—a pustule, small boil, or pimple—in Shakespeare, and it sums up Iago's feelings about Roderigo. Iago is at pains to tell us that he expends time "with such a snipe / But for my sport and profit" (1.3.376–77). In *Twelfth Night*, Sir Toby Belch uses Sir Andrew Ague-cheek as Iago uses Roderigo—"Thus do I ever make my fool my purse" (*Othello* 1.3.374)—but there is a good fellowship in *Twelfth Night* that is lacking in *Othello*.

Roderigo is not only a snipe (a proverbially stupid game bird, such as a woodcock) and a quat, but Iago would be pleased to have him disposed of. There is real indifference in Iago's calculating comment:

> Now, whether he kill Cassio,
> Or Cassio him, or each do kill the other,
> Every way makes my gain. (5.1.12–14)

This goes far beyond the dehumanizing word *quat* (like *twit* or *twat*) to what the courts call a depraved indifference to human life. Later it is Iago who stabs Roderigo and utters feigned exclamations of concern: "O murd'rous slave! O villain!" (61). Roderigo's last line is one of the most telling in the play: "O damned Iago! O inhuman dog!" (62). Later, Iago will kill his wife, Emilia, on stage (at 5.2.232), and he is instrumental in the deaths of Desdemona and Othello. Like all murderers in Shakespeare, he is "inhuman," an "inhuman dog" (and we know that Shakespeare did not have a soft spot in his heart for dogs). He is a cold-blooded, calculating murderer, damned, inhuman, and diabolical.

There is a great deal of devil imagery in the play for Iago, which continues a theme strongly presented in Aaron and Richard III. At the end, Othello says significantly:

> I look down towards his feet—but that's a fable.
> If that thou be'st a devil, I cannot kill thee. (5.2.282–83)

Iago doesn't have cloven hooves like a devil, but Othello cannot kill him with his sword. It is an unnecessarily facile explanation to claim that Iago is the devil, but he shares in the diabolic fascination of evil. Unlike other Shakespearean villains, he is given no redeeming qualities such as Aaron's love of his black baby or Edmund's "some good I mean to do / Despite of mine own nature" (*King Lear* 5.3.245–46).

When Othello asks him his searing question about motive, Iago chooses to remain silent forever:

> *Othello.* Will you, I pray, demand that demi-devil
> Why he hath thus ensnared my soul and body?
> *Iago.* Demand me nothing. What you know, you know.
> From this time forth I never will speak word. (5.2.297–300)

Unlike other villains, Iago forgoes any vaunting speech at the end, and he denies Othello any comforting reasons for his damnation except his own credulity and stupidity. No one has ensnared Othello except himself. Iago forswears speech and thus prepares stoically for his torture and death. He is not a tragic figure at all but rather a comic vice figure who knows how to keep his own counsel. Iago has a great many soliloquies in the play. He wants earnestly to share his thoughts with the audience, which is taken into his confidence and which is expected to applaud his wit, ingenuity, and invention. Iago is not a hypocrite—at least not with the audience. He has no self-questionings, unlike Othello, nor doubts about himself. He never needs to apologize.

Othello (and *The Merchant of Venice*) are not taught in most public schools because they are considered racist and inflammatory. Perhaps this is just why they should be taught, if great dramatic poetry and the tough exploration of ethnic issues has any meaning. Othello is black, and Shylock is a Jew, but beyond that both are aliens and strangers in the commercial society of Venice. Both perform an essential service for the state, but it is inconceivable that either could be citizens. Iago is a Venetian, and he takes great pleasure in casting ethnic slurs on Othello. He is "an old black ram" tupping Brabantio's "white ewe" (1.1.85–86). In the same scene Roderigo speaks disparagingly of "the thick-lips" (63), and in the next scene Brabantio conceives his daughter's ill-starred marriage entirely in ethnic terms.

Why, except through the use of charms and magic, should Desdemona shun "The wealthy, curlèd darlings of our nation" and run "to the sooty bosom" (1.2.67, 69) of the Moor?

The Duke of Venice, who is friendly to Othello, nevertheless sees the issue in terms of color. As he graciously tells Brabantio: "If virtue no delighted beauty lack, / Your son-in-law is far more fair than black" (1.3.284–85). Even Desdemona unconsciously testifies to her husband's blackness: "I saw Othello's visage in his mind" (247), which must be called to attention and apologized for, since black is the color of the devil. Othello himself is acutely conscious of his blackness that sets him apart from polite Venetian society:

> Haply for I am black
> And have not those soft parts of conversation
> That chamberers have . . . (3.3.262–64).

This is another aspect of his vulnerability to Iago, whom Othello imagines to be completely at home in a bed chamber and an expert on sex. In *Titus Andronicus*, Aaron, the villainous Moor, is even more directly conscious of being black than Othello, but in that play the black man plays a part analogous to Iago's. There are many echoes of *Titus Andronicus* in *Othello*.

From Shakespeare's comedies we know that something is radically wrong with Othello's wooing of Desdemona and their subsequent love and marriage. Desdemona may be young, innocent, intelligent, and wittily sensual like Juliet in *Romeo and Juliet* and Rosalind in *As You Like It*, but Othello has no resemblance to Romeo or to Orlando. He represents himself as mature if not middle-aged, and he specifically denies any interest in sex, as if that might be appropriate to a Venetian but not to a black man who is an alien in Venice. He doesn't support Desdemona's request to accompany him to Cyprus

> To please the palate of my appetite,
> Nor to comply with heat—the young affects
> In me defunct . . . (1.3.257–59)

It sounds as if he thinks of himself as impotent, like the old Pantalone figure of the commedia dell'arte. He assures the Duke and the Venetian Senate that the "light-winged toys / Of feathered Cupid" (263–

64) shall not interfere with his military command. This devaluation of love and sex bodes badly for his marriage.

Othello's wooing speech is remarkable for its recitation of grand, romantic adventures in all parts of the globe:

And of the Cannibals that each other eat,
The Anthropophagi, and men whose heads
Grew beneath their shoulders. (1.3.142–44)

The young Desdemona is entranced with a hero-worshiping response: "My story being done, / She gave me for my pains a world of kisses" (157–58). There is a remoteness about the old Othello wooing the adolescent Desdemona with the story of his life. It is unlike any love relationship in Shakespeare's comedies, which depend upon mutuality and a burning desire to unite immediately with a paramour in the marriage bed. The upshot of Othello's wooing speech is disappointing: "She loved me for the dangers I had passed, / And I loved her that she did pity them" (166–67). Not to put too fine a psychological interpretation on this statement, it doesn't suggest anything personal in the relationship, any common awareness, or any agreements and disagreements in conversation. Beyond their immediate attraction, the wooing suggests that neither Othello nor Desdemona understand each other—or themselves. Both are extremely vulnerable to the tragedy that overtakes them.

We should beware of our own dangerous tendency to be influenced by Iago's view of Desdemona. To him she is like all Venetian women, a whore by nature, subtle and sexual, as he explains to Roderigo:

When the blood is made dull with the act of sport, there should be a game to inflame it and to give satiety a fresh appetite, loveliness in favor, sympathy in years, manners, and beauties; all which the Moor is defective in. (2.1.225–29)

Does Iago really believe this? There is no way of knowing except that he is cynical about all women and powerfully misogynistic.

But it is absolutely clear that there is no basis for thinking this in relation to Desdemona, who is innocent in an almost folkloric way. In her conversation with Emilia in act 4, scene 3, Desdemona cannot even conceive "That there be women do abuse their husbands / In such gross kind" (63–64). Despite Emilia's amusing banter that the whole world "is a great price for a small vice" (70–71), and that "who would not make her husband a cuckold to make him a monarch" (77–79), Desdemona insists with wonderful credulity: "I do not think there is any such woman" (86). She is in an entirely different world of discourse from Emilia, and we feel that the scene recapitulates a conversation of Juliet and her Nurse in *Romeo and Juliet.*

It is almost impossible to protect oneself entirely from Iago's calumniation of Desdemona, and we find ourselves wanting to know what Desdemona means when she says suddenly: "This Lodovico is a proper [-handsome] man" (4.3.36). Her mind seems to be wandering on alternatives to her fate. Desdemona's relation to Cassio, on which Iago's innuendos build so cleverly, is represented in the play as completely innocent politeness. It is exactly paralleled in *The Winter's Tale* by the pregnant Hermione's relation to her husband's friend Polixenes, which sparks off Leontes' jealousy—he is his own Iago. Desdemona is genuinely disturbed by the plight of Cassio, and she tries with all her charm and goodwill to bring him back into favor. She seems surprised by Othello's hesitation and takes it as a sign that she herself has mysteriously fallen out of favor. She cannot anticipate Iago's machinations because she cannot see anything wrong in what she does.

This goes to the irrational heart of jealousy in the play. As Iago correctly observes:

> Trifles light as air
> Are to the jealous confirmations strong
> As proofs of Holy Writ. (3.3.319–21)

Therefore Iago doesn't need Cassio, or Desdemona's earnest solicitation of her husband, or even the handkerchief to work his mischief. He can improvise on anything. In the next scene Emilia enunciates the same view of jealousy. Jealous souls "are not ever jealous for the cause, / But jealous for they're jealous" (3.4.159–60). But the childlike Desdemona has no way of understanding the implications of what Emilia says.

The most acutely painful scene in the play is act 4, scene 2, called the Brothel Scene because Othello feigns to visit Desdemona as a prostitute and treats Emilia as her bawd. The pity arises because Desdemona and Othello are so profoundly mistaken about what is actually happening; they are both caught in Iago's web of lies and deceit. But Othello seems to be unconsciously aware of some other reality, and his double consciousness lies behind his nostalgia and sense of grief. He accuses his wife harshly: "Heaven truly knows that thou art false as hell" (4.2.38), but his next speech is in an entirely different tone: "Ah, Desdemon! Away! Away! Away!" (40). He too would like to flee, and his murderous impulses break over into tears, as Desdemona observes: "Alas the heavy day! Why do you weep? / Am I the motive of these tears, my lord?" (41–42). She is confused by these contradictory signals, but she seems to be able to do nothing except protest her innocence.

Most notable in the scene is a sense of thwarted purposes and motives that have gone astray. The puzzled Othello can only speak of a beauty that has been lost:

> O thou weed,
> Who art so lovely fair, and smell'st so sweet,
> That the sense aches at thee, would thou hadst never been born!
> (4.2.66–68)

Again, the only surcease is in disappearance or annihilation, according to the Sophoclean tragic dictum: not to be born is best. In terms of sensuous values, it is interesting that the smell of Desdemona is so much emphasized. When he comes to murder her, we remember that Othello smells her like a rose on a tree (5.2.15).

Finally, it is worth noting how much Emilia is developed in the last scene. From a complacent, practical character (like the Nurse in *Romeo and Juliet*) who steals the handkerchief to give to Iago and who banteringly denies any possibility of pure innocence, Emilia suddenly develops tragic stature. She confronts Othello with the folly and the magnitude of his murder: "Thou dost belie her [i.e., Desdemona], and thou art a devil" (5.2.132). There is a sticking-place when Othello implicates Iago, and Emilia at first recoils in incredulity: she repeats "My husband?" four times. Once she is convinced of Iago's guilt, Emilia becomes reckless with her new insight.

She is not intimidated by Othello: "I care not for thy sword; I'll make thee known, / Though I lost twenty lives" (5.2.162–63). And she interrogates her husband with energetic firmness. The subtle Iago cannot frighten her: "I will not charm my tongue; I am bound to speak" (181). Emilia is no longer the obedient housewife who will do her husband's bidding. Suddenly everything is overturned and she says daringly: "Perchance, Iago, I will ne'er go home" (194). It is almost anticlimactic when Iago stabs her on stage. Ironically, she is the last person he suspected to reveal his ingenious plot. Undone by speech, Iago's final act is to take a vow of silence: "From this time forth I never will speak word" (300).

King Lear

*I*t is important for tragedy to define the limits of its world, and, especially in Shakespearean tragedy, we touch on an unfathomable evil. It comes as a surprise to the protagonist to discover the depths of villainy into which he has been plunged. It is certainly true that Othello is particularly vulnerable, because he could not even imagine an Iago, and Hamlet, "Th' expectancy and rose of the fair state, / The glass of fashion, and the mold of form" (*Hamlet* 3.1.153–54), is suddenly thrust into something rotten in the state of Denmark. Macbeth acts as his own worst villain, and his way of life "Is fall'n into the sear, the yellow leaf" (5.3.23), so that "Direness, familiar to my slaughterous thoughts, / Cannot once start me" (*Macbeth* 5.5.14–15). Lear, too, undergoes an enormous transformation from the presumptuous and petulant King, who "hath ever but slenderly known himself" (1.1.295–96). This is the most savage and unredeemed of Shakespeare's tragedies, and at the very end "all's cheerless, dark and deadly" (5.3.292).

The viciousness of Gloucester's blinding in act 3, scene 7, defines the nature of the tragedy. It is perhaps the cruelest scene in Shakespeare, yet it is all done in such a practical and specific way. This is one of the reasons why the cruelty is so unimaginable.

It serves to define the world of the play, especially the world of Cornwall and Regan and her sister Goneril, and also by implication Edmund, who betrays his old father to Cornwall. This scene proves Gloucester's frightening line: "His daughters seek his death" (3.4.166). And the scene also illustrates Albany's high-minded attack on moral chaos: "Humanity must perforce prey on itself, / Like monsters of the deep" (4.2.49–50). In this sense the blinding of Gloucester is an enabling moment because through it we can understand how the characters can perform the acts that they do in other parts of the play. Like the murder of Macduff's wife and children in *Macbeth*, gratuitous cruelty is the sign of the breakdown of all human values because of the perverse pleasure that the mere exercise of arbitrary power brings.

The scene is built on random suggestions that enter casually into the action rather than on a fixed plan. Like Iago, Cornwall improvises his revenge against Gloucester from bits and pieces he picks up as the scene unfolds. Everything stems from the suggestion of Goneril: "Pluck out his eyes" (3.7.6). But later in the scene Gloucester himself explains why he helped the old King to Dover: "Because I would not see thy cruel nails / Pluck out his poor old eyes" (57–58). All these images are seeding Cornwall's mind, but he acts in sardonic response to Gloucester's imprecation: "But I shall see / The wingèd vengeance overtake such children" (66–67), that is, Goneril and Regan. Cornwall chooses to seize on the word "see": "See't shalt thou never. Fellows, hold the chair. / Upon these eyes of thine I'll set my foot" (68–69).

But Cornwall only stamps out one eye with his boot, and Regan cheers him on to complete the deed: "One side will mock another. Th' other too" (3.7.72), so that there will be no offense to symmetry. But it takes at least another fifteen lines for the other eye. Meanwhile, Cornwall has been mortally stabbed by a servant, whose last words precipitate Gloucester's total blindness: "O, I am slain! my lord, you have one eye left / To see some mischief on him" (82–83). At this point Cornwall seizes on the words of the dying Servant to gouge out with his fingers Gloucester's remaining eye: "Lest it see more, prevent it. Out, vile jelly. / Where is thy luster now?" (84–85). Gouging out an eye on stage in full view of the audience is an act of unimaginable cruelty, yet Cornwall maintains a tone of sardonic glee.

How are we to understand this scene? Cornwall's cruelty is matched by Regan's. When Cornwall orders Gloucester to be bound, Regan adds with anger: "Hard, hard! O filthy traitor" (3.7.33), and when he is tied to a chair, Regan plucks hairs out of his white beard. Gloucester protests as a gentleman, but he understands nothing of the savagery of his antagonists: "By the kind gods, 'tis most ignobly done / To pluck me by the beard" (36–37). There is a profound incongruity when Gloucester asserts: "I am your host" (40), as if Cornwall and Regan need only to be reminded of the laws of hospitality. It is Regan who insists on the other eye of Gloucester, and it is she who runs the First Servant through with Cornwall's sword. Her final line resounds with sadistic cruelty: "Go thrust him out at gates, and let him smell / His way to Dover" (94–95). The blind Gloucester haunts the play until the end.

It is an extraordinary confrontation when he meets the mad Lear near Dover. He immediately recognizes the King: "I know that voice" (4.6.96) and is deferential throughout, as if to acknowledge that madness is a greater grief than mere blindness. To Lear, Gloucester is "Goneril with a white beard" (97), and he unlocks a tremendous diatribe against women. But Gloucester plays the loyal subject: "O, let me kiss that hand!" Lear must wipe it first because "it smells of mortality" (134–35). Gloucester is a kind of straight man for Lear in this scene, who identifies him as blind Cupid: "Dost thou squiny at me? No, do thy worst, blind Cupid; I'll not love" (138–40). Gloucester's blindness is the cue for Lear's attack on hypocrisy and injustice: "A man may see how this world goes with no eyes" (152–53). Gloucester sees it "feelingly" (151), and, like Poor Tom, his mere presence on stage stimulates the mad Lear to heights of bitter eloquence. Lear refuses to pity him, but uses his blindness as an occasion to lash out against the social and political evils of the world. As Edgar comments in his choral and didactic function: "I would not take this from report: it is, / And my heart breaks at it" (143–44). "It is" is the indication of the existential reality.

In the love action of the play, one of the strangest lines expresses Edmund's satisfaction that both Goneril and Regan have died for his sake:

> Yet Edmund was beloved:
> The one the other poisoned for my sake,
> And after slew herself. (5.3.241–43).

He seems pleased that he should have been the love object of two such powerful women, and the self-satisfied mood continues in his soliloquy at the end of act 5, scene 1: "Which of them shall I take? / Both? One? Or neither?" (57–58). Like Iago at the beginning of the fifth act of *Othello*, who cares little whether Roderigo kill Cassio or Cassio kill him—"Every way makes my gain" (5.1.14)—so Edmund is incapable of love, which may be one of the sure signs of the villain in Shakespeare. Edmund's narcissism overwhelms any feeling toward Goneril and Regan, except that he is flattered by their infatuation and their love sacrifice.

All of this is very sexual, and in Goneril's eyes Edmund is a macho prince compared with her rational and bland husband, Albany:

> O, the difference of man and man!
> To thee a woman's services are due:
> My fool usurps my body. (4.2.26–28)

Edmund the Bastard inherits some of his father's salaciousness: "there was good sport at his [i.e., Edmund's] making" (1.1.23–24), and he is vain about his physical attraction. Even though the bodies of Goneril and Regan are brought on stage in what should be a tragic exhibition, Edmund is gratified by the proof that he was "beloved" (5.3.241). Apparently he needs this proof to realize his manhood, and it is at this point that he relents and tries to save Lear and Cordelia: "some good I mean to do, / Despite of mine own nature" (245–46). This is a curiously moralistic line, as if Edmund had been influenced by his didactic brother.

Along the lines of Aristotle's *Poetics*, Lear is the most fully developed of Shakespeare's tragic protagonists. He moves from tragic blindness and hubris through a suffering and madness in which he experiences tragic recognition. He is entirely different at the end of the play when he is recuperated from his madness and reconciled with his daughter Cordelia. But he cannot escape his tragic fate, and the innocent Cordelia shares this fate: "For thee, oppressèd King, I am cast down" (5.3.5). This helps to define the kind of tragedy that powerfully evokes pity and fear, in Aristotle's terms. There is no justice in the death of Cordelia, yet she is indissolubly linked with Lear: "We are not the first / Who with best meaning have incurred the worst" (3–4). This is the paradox of tragedy, that the worst comes inevitably even to those who proceed with best meaning. Both Lear and Cordelia "take upon's the mystery of things, / As if we were God's spies" (16–17). Spies on God or spies in the service of God? It all comes down to the same unfathomable mystery.

The first of Lear's phases from which all else flows is the foolish love contest of act 1, scene 1. This is developed in a highly ritualistic way resembling folktale, especially the story of Cinderella. We know from the way the scene is arranged that Lear intends to give the largest portion to his youngest daughter, Cordelia, and he enters with "*one bearing a coronet*" (34 s.d.) for her. It is no wonder that Goneril and Regan have prepared speeches that they seem to know by heart. They are just responding to Lear's set question: "Which of you shall say doth love us most" (53). It is like a bad retirement party, but Cordelia disrupts the proceedings by refusing to play by the rules and by insisting on her own speechless honesty. It will hardly do to examine the deeper motives of these folklore characters, who speak with a sort of Brechtian self-consciousness of role. Lear's rage, despite its fury, is merely petulant, as Kent recognizes so well: "What wouldst thou do, old man?" (147–48)—not king nor your majesty nor even liege, but merely "old man." This is a wonderfully deflationary line, but Lear is not to be stopped in his rhetorical display.

The scene is defined not so much in terms of its heightened rhetoric or its emphatic contrasting of "nothing" and "all"—"nothing will come of nothing" (1.1.92) and "They love you all" (102)—but in relation to the chilling speeches of Goneril and Regan afterward. Lear's conduct is proof of his foolishness: "He always loved our sister most, and with what poor judgment he hath now cast her off appears too grossly" (292–94). Goneril and Regan acknowledge no involvement in all this; they merely played their parts as expected. Their old father "hath ever but slenderly known himself" (295–96) and is now showing all the signs of second childhood.

In an extraordinary colloquial phrase, Goneril proposes to her sister: "let's hit together" (1.1.306), meaning agree on a plan or plot against the foolish Lear, but also carrying some of its modern connotations of hitting on someone. I think it is important to recognize the sisters' malevolence right from the beginning so that Gloucester's later statement does not surprise us: "His daughters seek his death"

(3.4.166). At the end of the first scene, Goneril is already actively plotting against her father: "We must do something, and i' th' heat" (1.1.311). One of the qualities of villainy in Shakespeare is that it is so lucidly announced and that it occurs so early in the action, but it is axiomatic that the villainy is incomprehensible to its victims until it is too late to prevent it.

Lear moves quickly into suffering and adversity as his daughters conspire against him. In act 1, scene 4, Lear curses Goneril with sterility, and there is already a sense of incipient madness. Lear's manhood is shaken, and he weeps "hot tears" (305) to think "How sharper than a serpent's tooth it is / To have a thankless child" (295–96). Part of the elemental power of *King Lear* lies in its focus on family relations and the violation of the natural bond between parents and children (a point which Arthur Miller took up in *All My Sons* and *Death of a Salesman*). By act 2, scene 4, the conspiracy against Lear and his hundred knights has deepened, and Lear has left the household of Goneril to seek out his other daughter, Regan, but she has deliberately vacated her premises and gone to stay with Gloucester.

The old King, who has been infantilized and marginalized by his daughters, cannot accommodate himself to the new reality of Goneril, Regan, and Cornwall. He cannot understand the cold calculation of his daughters, and he insists on speaking in the passionate family discourse that is totally irrelevant to the present situation. To Goneril he says:

I prithee, daughter, do not make me mad.
I will not trouble thee, my child; farewell.
We'll no more meet, no more see one another.
But yet thou art my flesh, my blood, my daughter . . .   (2.4.217–20)

There is an outraged tenderness here, but there is no appropriate response from either Goneril or Regan. They deal with their old father as if he were a refractory child.

Lear's "I gave you all" (2.4.249) echoes the "nothings" and "alls" of the first scene, but Regan's response cuts off the metaphysical overtones: "And in good time you gave it" (249). The argument over the hundred knights is merely a bargaining chip, by which the daughters undo the original agreement. Regan's bold sally, "What need one?"

(262), cuts through the pretense of politeness and occasions Lear's passionate defense of his dignity:

> O reason not the need! Our basest beggars
> Are in the poorest thing superfluous.
> Allow not nature more than nature needs,
> Man's life is cheap as beast's. (263–66)

These assertions are answered in act 3, scene 4 on the heath when Lear meets Poor Tom and throws off his clothes. At this point his life is as cheap as a beast's. The storm and tempest begin at the end of Lear's "reason not the need" speech in 2,4. He forcibly prevents himself from weeping, but instead his reason is slipping, and he exits with a resounding exclamation: "O Fool, I shall go mad!" (285).

Shut out on the heath during a wild storm, the mad Lear is preoccupied with justice:

> Tremble, thou wretch,
> That hast within thee undivulgèd crimes
> Unwhipped of justice. (3.2.51–53)

He is exploring one of the fundamental themes of Shakespearean tragedy. In the moral audit, he is "a man / More sinned against than sinning" (59–60). Fundamental to his vision of a more just society is his invocation of "poor naked wretches, wheresoe'er you are, / That bide the pelting of this pitiless storm" (3.4.28–29). This is what he has taken "Too little care of" (33) when he was King, and we seem to see a transformation of Lear on the heath. He is now exposed to "feel what wretches feel" (34), and the pomp of majesty (so brilliantly displayed, for example, in *Henry V*) must now "Take physic" (33), or a cathartic purge, in order to cure itself.

It is only a short step from this point to Lear's overwhelming attraction to Poor Tom, who is "the thing itself; unaccommodated man" (3.4.109–10), and Lear tears off his clothes and tries to imitate the Bedlam beggar: "Off, off, you lendings! Come, unbutton here" (111). But Poor Tom is actually Edgar in disguise, who is playing the role of Bedlam beggar with consummate skill. In a sense, Lear is still deceived by false appearances as he always was. It is interesting how completely Edgar as Poor Tom displaces the Fool, who disappears from the play with the line: "And I'll go to bed at noon" (3.6.84).

Another sighting of King Lear occurs in act 4, scene 6, where he enters, *"fantastically dressed with wild flowers"* (80 s.d.), in the field near Dover. He is completely mad, but he speaks the trenchant "Reason in madness" (177). In the scene with the blind Gloucester (and his son Edgar, as a kind of chorus), he launches a wildly misogynistic attack on women and sexuality that is much repeated in Shakespeare (for example, in *Othello, Hamlet, Titus Andronicus,* and *Troilus and Cressida*). There is a strong sex nausea in Lear's exclamation, "Let copulation thrive" (116). Fine clothes and courtly manners provide another false appearance by which women in society conceal their lustful nature:

> Down from the waist they are Centaurs,
> Though women all above:
> But to the girdle do the gods inherit,
> Beneath is all the fiend's. (126–29)

Sexuality is seen in animalistic, diabolic terms: "There's hell, there's darkness, there is the sulphurous pit, / Burning, scalding, stench, consumption" (130–31). As in many of Shakespeare's tragedies, no maternal figure moderates the antifeminine ardor. There is no Mrs. Lear or Mrs. Polonius or a mother for Cressida, and in both *Macbeth* and *Coriolanus* the women have deliberately unsexed and masculinized themselves.

King Lear's preoccupation with justice is the leading theme of his madness, and by justice is meant the inner truth that will be revealed by stripping off false appearances. Thus, "Robes and furred gowns hide all" (4.6.167), whereas Truth in its emblematic representation is naked. The "rascal beadle" is lashing the whore that he "hotly lusts to use . . . in that kind / For which thou whip'st her" (164–65). The image of the world in this scene, with the blind Gloucester as an almost mute witness to Lear's imaginings, is very bleak. This is a low point for Lear in the play, and his homicidal frenzy mixes with more general images. There is wild energy in his "delicate stratagem, to shoe / A troop of horse with felt" and steal "upon these son-in-laws, / Then, kill, kill, kill, kill, kill, kill!" (188–89). The frenzy of these six repetitions of *kill* look forward to the five repetitions of *never* at the end of the play (5.3.310).

The redemption of Lear, his recovery from madness, and his reconciliation with Cordelia take place in the next scene (4,7), which may be the most tender and moving in the play. The old King believes that he is a soul in hell, and he needs to be convinced that he is alive and that his daughter Cordelia is speaking to him:

> You do me wrong to take me out o' th' grave:
> Thou art a soul in bliss; but I am bound
> Upon a wheel of fire, that mine own tears
> Do scald like molten lead. (45–48)

This scene comes closest in Shakespeare to fulfilling the criteria of Aristotelian tragedy because Lear's return from madness brings with it an intense recognition of his fallible humanity: "I am a very foolish fond old man, / Fourscore and upward, not an hour more nor less" (60–61).

His acknowledgment of Cordelia is done with extraordinary simplicity; Shakespeare seems to avoid any sense of writing up this powerful scene in which the dramatic pressures are so acute. Lear says modestly:

> Do not laugh at me,
> For, as I am a man, I think this lady
> To be my child Cordelia. (4.7.68–70)

Cordelia replies with a triumphant gush of emotion that echoes her father's "as I am a man": "And so I am, I am" (70). This could all seem simplistic if the dramatic action were not so keyed up and highly wrought. Lear and Cordelia exit with a line that seems deeply religious: "You must bear with me. Pray you now, forget and forgive. I am old and foolish" (84–85). This is so different from anything in the first scene of the play that it marks the radical transformation of Lear.

Our final image of the King at the end of the play is "cheerless, dark and deadly" (5.3.292), in the words of Kent. He enters with the dead Cordelia in his arms, and there is a brief and heartbreaking illusion that she may still be alive. But Lear at this point is beyond tragedy. His death is foreordained to accompany Cordelia's, but there is a flickering hallucination that she may still be breathing: "Do you see this? Look on her. Look, her lips, / Look there, look there" (312–13). The questions Lear asks remain unanswerable:

> Why should a dog, a horse, a rat, have life,
> And thou no breath at all? Thou'lt come no more,
> Never, never, never, never, never. (308–10)

The *never*'s are a final voice of doom, which teases the ingenuity of the actor to convey a sense of parting and otherworldliness. The appropriate eulogy is spoken by Kent: "The wonder is he hath endured so long: / He but usurped his life" (318–19). We have the sense of Lear as preternaturally old and drifting off from a life that he has long since given up.

There is a remarkable symmetry in the two actions of *Lear*, with the Gloucester plot following the main plot and matching sons against daughters. At times Shakespeare draws the obvious link between them, as when Edgar observes that Lear is "childed as I fathered" (3.6.109)—this is before Edgar learns the truth about Gloucester. Although the actions share many parallels, they are quite different in tone, and it is interesting to observe how explicit, even moralistic, the Gloucester unit is, whereas the Lear part insists on mystery and astonishment. Much depends on Edgar, especially in his role as Poor Tom, the Bedlam beggar, in his relation both to Lear and to Gloucester. Edgar takes on this disguise as a way of escaping from the murderous ambitions of his bastard brother, Edmund. He deliberately chooses

> the basest and most poorest shape
> That ever penury, in contempt of man,
> Brought near to beast. (2.3.7–9)

Why this shape rather than another? Edgar seems perversely to reach for extremes, as if he could fulfill himself only by being one of the "Poor naked wretches" (3.4.28) and by this means finding an imagined martyrdom.

Edgar also seems to be too good at his role of Poor Tom and to want to prolong it to the last possible moment. On the heath, he answers Lear with a fullness about his past history that is too appropriate for the situation in hand, as if Edgar is inventing the kind of story that he senses Lear most wants to hear. The history that he makes up for Lear's benefit is strongly sexual and fits admirably well with the mad King's sex nausea: "served the lust of 'my mistress' heart, and did the act of darkness with her" (3.4.86–88), and "One that slept in the contriving of lust, and waked to do it" (90–91), and "in woman out-paramoured the Turk" (92). Lear seizes upon Poor Tom as the paragon of "unaccommodated man" (109), a "poor, bare, forked animal" who owes "the worm no silk, the beast no hide, the sheep no wool, the cat no perfume" (110, 106–8). Poor Tom is too perfect in his role, and it is no surprise that he displaces the Fool at this point. During Lear's mad arraignment of Goneril, Edgar speaks a significant aside that breaks his histrionic role as Poor Tom: "My tears begin to take his part so much / They mar my counterfeiting" (3.6.59). This admission is close to sentimentality, and I think the audience feels somewhat ambiguously about Edgar in his excessive warmheartedness.

With his blind father, Edgar functions as a spiritual companion and teacher. Most notably, he acts to cure his father of despair when he is cast out to smell his way to Dover. Gloucester believes that "As flies to wanton boys, are we to th' gods, / They kill us for their sport" (4.1.36–37), and he wants to commit suicide by jumping off Dover Cliffs. Edgar devises an elaborate scenario in which he will lead his father to the edge of the cliff, let him seem to jump off, then appear to him again and claim that he has been miraculously delivered from death. All this is very histrionic and extremely didactic. Edgar tells us, in a significant aside: "Why I do trifle thus with his despair / Is done to cure it" (4.6.33–34)—as if it were imperative that the audience share in his moral lesson.

The outcome of Gloucester's simulated suicide is a proof that "Thy life's a miracle" (4.6.55). The demonstration seems to work and Edgar drives home the moral: "Think that the clearest gods, who make them honors / Of men's impossibilities, have preserved thee" (73–74). Gloucester is convinced: "henceforth I'll bear / Affliction" (75–76). Later on, Edgar cheers his father up again when he has ill thoughts with one of the most quoted lines in the play:

> Men must endure
> Their going hence, even as their coming hither:
> Ripeness is all. (5.2.9–11)

But in their immediate context the lines have a certain preachy and sermonistic flavor.

Edgar's mortal combat with his brother is oddly formal, like the prepared tournament between Mowbray and Bolingbroke at the beginning of *Richard II*. It is not surprising that he wins, because it is morally necessary that truth triumph over deceit, but his final speech to the dying Edmund is the most painfully didactic sermon in the play:

> The gods are just, and of our pleasant vices
> Make instruments to plague us:
> The dark and vicious place where thee he got
> Cost him his eyes. (5.3.172–75)

It is hard to believe that the gods are just in this play, and Lear's "Howl, howl, howl, howl!" (259) less than a hundred lines later drowns out Edgar's pieties.

It is also impossible to believe Edgar's account of rewards and punishments for his father, Gloucester: that his lustfulness in begetting Edmund (described with amusement at the beginning of the play) "Cost him his eyes." This literalism makes a mockery of the blinding of Gloucester in act 3, scene 7. It is odd that when Edgar speaks the final couplets of the play in the Folio version, he of all people should so much insist on feeling and sincerity: "The weight of this sad time we must obey, / Speak what we feel, not what we ought to say" (5.3.325–26). More than any other character in *King Lear*, Edgar seems to be following a prescribed part and not just spontaneously expressing his inner truth. Maybe now for the first time he will be free to speak what he feels and not what he ought to say.

Macbeth

*M*acbeth is full of splendid psychological insights expressed in a dramatic form.
Lady Macbeth understands her husband with
remarkable clarity, and she reveals truths that
Macbeth would prefer to conceal—even from
himself. All this is apparent in act 1, scene
5, when Lady Macbeth is alone on stage
reading her husband's letter and speaking the
first important soliloquy in a play notable for
its intense and passionate soliloquies. Macbeth speaks in his letter about meeting the
Witches and their more than "mortal knowledge" (3–4). The Weird Sisters saluted Macbeth as Thane of Cawdor, which King Duncan then bestowed on him, and they then
greeted him with: " 'Hail, King that shalt
be!' " (10–11). Macbeth writes to his wife as
"my dearest partner of greatness" (12), so
that she might not "lose the dues of rejoic-
ing, by being ignorant of what greatness is
promised thee" (13–14). He asks her to "Lay
it to thy heart" (14). "Greatness," repeated
twice, can only mean being King and Queen
(although the Witches say nothing about the
queen). The letter seems abundantly clear in
its implications.

Lady Macbeth's commentary on the letter
shows her keen intuition into her husband's
nature. She is not specifically ambitious here,

although that motive has been given an exaggerated importance. Rather, she will be the catalyst to help her husband realize his secret thoughts, which are not so secretly expressed in his letter. She fears Macbeth's nature not because he is a coward, but because he is full of blatant contradictions between desiring and acting. As Brutus says in his orchard soliloquy when he is pondering whether to join the conspiracy against Caesar:

> Between the acting of a dreadful thing
> And the first motion, all the interim is
> Like a phantasma, or a hideous dream. (*Julius Caesar* 2.1.63–65)

Macbeth shares some of Brutus's shaky reasoning, as his wife understands so acutely:

> Thou wouldst be great,
> Art not without ambition, but without
> The illness should attend it. (1.5.19–21)

Again, *great* is a code word for being king, but Macbeth wants to avoid any ill-doing that might empower his ambition. In Sartre's terms, he wants to have "clean hands."

Lady Macbeth puts the matter pithily and aphoristically in the comment that follows:

> What thou wouldst highly,
> That wouldst thou holily; wouldst not play false,
> And yet wouldst wrongly win. (1.5.21–23)

There is no doubt in her mind that Macbeth consents to the deed, yet she is sharply aware of his hypocrisy. This gets to the heart of the tragedy because these paradoxes cannot be resolved. You can only wrongly win by playing false, and to wish something to appear "holily" is itself a commitment to false appearances. Macbeth's unquiet mind is already apparent in this soliloquy before he enters the scene. He is not a natural murderer like Richard III, Claudius, Iago, and Edmund. When Lady Macbeth says that his nature "is too full o' th' milk of human kindness / To catch the nearest way" (18–19), she already understands the impediment that the milk of human kindness imposes, which is associated elsewhere with the milk of a nursing mother. But this is mere sentimentality and pretense because Lady Macbeth assumes that Macbeth "shalt be / What thou art promised" (16–17).

Her task, then, is not so much to persuade her husband to an act that he objects to, but to show him the web of illogicalities in his thinking: "Thou'dst have, great Glamis, / That which cries 'Thus thou must do' if thou have it" (1.5.24–25). Lady Macbeth reasons in binary opposites: "And that which rather thou dost fear to do / Than wishest should be undone" (25–26). The problem is that Macbeth has already consented to the murder but is merely revolted by the physical details of its execution. That is why Lady Macbeth wants her husband to come, "That I may pour my spirits in thine ear" (27). She will chastise him with the valor of her tongue, as if the persuasion were a routine matter in their married life. Macbeth needs his wife to provide a context for what he intends to do anyway. We begin the play with an elaborate network of pretense and rationalization.

Lady Macbeth's second soliloquy comes after a messenger has announced that "The King comes here tonight" (1.5.32) and before Macbeth enters. King Duncan is already dead in Lady Macbeth's thoughts—"The raven himself is hoarse / That croaks the fatal entrance of Duncan" (39–40)—but she goes on in her thoughts to "unsex" herself and become what she imagines to be a man. Manliness is a crucial issue in the play, and it is closely connected with the idea of tragedy. By being unsexed, Lady Macbeth can abandon her female sense of compassion, sympathy, pity, and tender feeling for her fellow creatures to adopt "direst cruelty" (44), a "fell" or savage "purpose" (47), and the "keen"—both sharp and eager—"knife" (53), as if she herself were going to murder Duncan. It is interesting that later she says: "Had he not resembled / My father as he slept, I had done't" (2.2.12–13).

By unsexing herself she becomes a surrogate man, and she acts out the role that she expects Macbeth to play. She defines manliness for him. If her husband "is too full o' th' milk of human kindness / To catch the nearest way" (1.5.18–19), she herself prays to the spirits that tend on mortal thoughts to "take my milk for gall" (49), and later she forswears the tenderness of the nursing mother:

I have given suck, and know
How tender 'tis to love the babe that milks me:
I would, while it was smiling in my face,
Have plucked my nipple from his boneless gums,
And dashed the brains out, had I so sworn as you
Have done to this. (1.7.54–59)

The unsexing is imagined with a vividness and a brutality that is echoed in Coriolanus's heroic mother, Volumnia:

The breasts of Hecuba,
When she did suckle Hector, looked not lovelier
Than Hector's forehead when it spit forth blood
At Grecian sword . . . (*Coriolanus* 1.3.43–46)

The mixture of mother's milk and warrior's blood pervades the imagery of Lady Macbeth and Volumnia. When Macbeth finally enters this scene, he is noncommittal: "We will speak further" (1.5.72). But Lady Macbeth will direct "This night's great business" (69), forcing her husband to reconcile what he wants "highly" with what he longs should appear "holily."

Assumptions about gender are especially prominent in this play, possibly because Macbeth and his wife are joint rulers and linked protagonists. The conventional beliefs that action is male and feeling female come into question in these early scenes, where they are not only enacted but also reversed. In act 1, scene 7, before the murder of King Duncan, Macbeth makes moral objections: "We will proceed no further in this business" (31), but Lady Macbeth insists on a consistent relation to act and desire, as she did earlier:

Art thou afeard
To be the same in thine own act and valor
As thou art in desire? (39–41)

From this point on Macbeth cannot retreat into sentimental declarations of moral principle: "I dare do all that may become a man; / Who dares do more is none" (1.7.46–47). What does it mean to do all that may become a man? Lady Macbeth simplifies the complex definition of a man into the willingness to do manly deeds, namely, to commit murder, and sex and murder mingle curiously in her emphatic discourse: "When you durst do it, then you were a man" (49). This is immediately followed by her declaration of unsexing— how she would dash the brains out of her milking babe. It is not surprising that Macbeth should acknowledge his wife as a phallic, female warrior:

> Bring forth men-children only;
> For thy undaunted mettle should compose
> Nothing but males. (72–74)

Gender assumptions are again evident in the scene of Banquo's Ghost. Macbeth's absolute terror of the Ghost—which gives some indication of how to play the Ghost scenes in *Hamlet*—immediately arouses questions about his manliness. "Are you a man?" (3.4.59), says his wife accusingly, and she continues on the manliness theme. Macbeth is "unmanned in folly" (74) and his flaws and starts "would well become / A woman's story at a winter fire" (65–66). He protests that he cannot deal with supernatural beings: "What man dare, I dare" (100), and once the Ghost exits he declares: "I am a man again" (109). This suggests a shifting definition of what it means to be a man.

Elsewhere in the play, when Macbeth is marshaling the murderers to kill Banquo, the First Murderer agrees unequivocally: "We are men, my liege" (3.1.91). This is like the Captain's assurance to Edmund that he will murder King Lear and Cordelia: "I cannot draw a cart, nor eat dried oats; / If it be man's work, I'll do't" (*King Lear* 5.3.39–40). It seems that murder is specifically set apart in Shakespeare as "man's work." Finally, we have Macduff's counterstatement of what it means to be a man when he first hears of the slaughter of his wife and children. Malcolm urges him to "Dispute it like a man" (4.3.220), in other words, to react stoically and unemotionally, but Macduff protests: "I shall do so; / But I must also feel it as a man" (220–21). Macduff doesn't want to be trapped into the manly Roman reaction of Brutus to the death of Portia: "No man bears sorrow better. Portia is dead" (*Julius Caesar* 4.3.144).

Macbeth is unusual in structure because it has a villain-hero— Macbeth is his own Iago—and it splits the role of protagonist between husband and wife. In terms of dramatic logic, Macbeth is set against Lady Macbeth, and they seem to move in opposite directions. Thus Macbeth declines from acute moral sensitivity to an arid feeling of callousness, desiccation, and meaninglessness, while Lady Macbeth moves from the crassness of "A little water clears us of this deed" (2.2.66) to the mad desolation of "All the perfumes of Arabia will not sweeten this little hand" (5.1.53–55). She seems to pick up the very awareness and sensitivity that Macbeth is losing.

Before the murder, Macbeth is already defending Duncan and accusing himself in a manner that resembles Claudius in the Prayer Scene of *Hamlet* (3,3). In his lucidity and self-awareness Macbeth seems to be modeled on Claudius, and particularly in the fact that none of these moral scruples prevent him from being a vicious murderer. Macbeth knows full well that his murderous blow might succeed "here, upon this bank and shoal of time" (1.7.6), but there is a real danger that "We'd jump the life to come" (7), which is exactly what troubles Claudius. In a line that echoes the last scene of *Hamlet* and the poisoned chalice that Claudius is forced to drink, Macbeth fears that

> this even-handed justice
> Commends th' ingredients of our poisoned chalice
> To our own lips. (10–12)

In a metaphoric explosion, Macbeth envisions the aftermath of the deed: there will be only "pity, like a naked newborn babe, / Striding the blast" (21). We will soon hear about Lady Macbeth's naked newborn babe: she will pluck "my nipple from his boneless gums" and dash his "brains out" (57–58). The grieving Macduff says significantly: "He has no children" (4.3.216), as if Macduff cannot even imagine Macbeth as a father. Macbeth's honesty with himself is chilling; his only motive for the murder of Duncan is "Vaulting ambition" (1.7.27).

As he is going to do the deed, Macbeth sees a terrifying vision of a dagger, "The handle toward my hand" (2.1.34), which appears suddenly like an apparition. The visionary dagger and the real dagger that Macbeth now draws are unified to marshal him "the way that I was going" (42). Now the dagger appears again proleptically: "on thy blade and dudgeon gouts of blood, / Which was not so before" (46–47). What is so frightening about this soliloquy are Macbeth's foresight and lucidity: "It is the bloody business which informs / Thus to mine eyes" (48–49). He is a fully informed and self-conscious murderer, who is horrified by his own intentions. He proceeds toward his design "With Tarquin's ravishing strides" (55), and like Tarquin in *The Rape of Lucrece*, he knows exactly what he is doing yet moves on like a sleepwalker. Macbeth realizes dramatically what is only implicit in Shakespeare's early poem. At the end of the soliloquy, Macbeth speaks like a confirmed murderer: "Whiles I threat, he lives: / Words to the heat of deeds too cold breath gives" (60–61). The couplet confirms his resolution, and his imaginative waverings for the moment are over: "I go, and it is done" (62). This has a murderous finality.

After the murders of Duncan and Banquo, we are aware of a growing imperviousness to feeling in Macbeth. The Ghost of Banquo unmans him with otherworldly terror, and at this point he resolves to kill Macduff and his family, as if to take revenge on the unquiet spirit of Banquo. Macbeth and his wife are spending sleepless nights, and in the proliferation of murder there is a false hope of security: "Things bad begun make strong themselves by ill" (3.2.55). What is so disturbing about the plot against Macduff and his family is that murder is depersonalized; it is no longer a horrible imagining but only something "tedious." The speech to Lady Macbeth at the end of act 3, scene 4 is the first sure sign of Macbeth's spiritual aridity:

> I am in blood
> Stepped in so far that, should I wade no more,
> Returning were as tedious as go o'er. (137–39)

The vision of the sea of blood has replaced the apparition of the airborne dagger. There is a strong sense of stasis and *tedium vitae*.

By the end of the play, Macbeth is cold and apathetic. His tragedy is to lose all feeling of tragedy and to move in the play like a mechanical warrior. His despair is already evident in his words to his officer, Seyton: "I have lived long enough. My way of life / Is fall'n into the sear, the yellow leaf" (5.3.22–23). This is like the opening of Sonnet 73, which could be an image of the late autumnal or wintry Macbeth:

> That time of year thou mayst in me behold
> When yellow leaves, or none, or few, do hang
> Upon those boughs which shake against the cold,
> Bare ruined choirs where late the sweet birds sang.

But Macbeth still sees his own situation with remarkable clarity. He cannot have what should humanly accompany old age, "As honor, love, obedience, troops of friends" (5.3.25)—he doesn't even mention grandchildren—but only "Curses not loud but deep, mouth-honor" (27). There is a horror in Macbeth's fate and a double horror in his own acute realization of it. We sympathize with his loss of everything that is most characteristically human, and we feel for his own clear-sighted recognition of what is happening to him. I think we also feel instinctively that his fate is something fearful, something that no human being would want at whatever cost. This amply fulfills Aristotle's criteria of pity and terror for the tragic protagonist.

Macbeth's final speeches to Seyton come after the mysterious and frightening *"cry within of women"* (5.5.8 s.d.) that marks Lady Macbeth's death. He cannot react properly to his wife's death, and he remembers, nostalgically, the time when his "senses would have cooled / To hear a night-shriek" (10–11). He has become apathetic like a war-weary, shell-shocked veteran: "I have supped full with horrors" (13). Macbeth's "Tomorrow, and tomorrow, and tomorrow" speech is a sign of despair because life has become tedious, repetitive, and meaningless. He hopes for death—"Out, out, brief candle!" (23)—and he speaks of the pointlessness of living in images of the bad actor, "That struts and frets his hour upon the stage / And then is heard no more" (25–26).

Is the "poor player" also pitiable like Macbeth himself? There is an imaginative reduction in the "tale / Told by an idiot, full of sound and fury / Signifying nothing" (5.5.26–28). Does nothing signify, have any significance or meaning? This tends to negate the meaning of everything that has happened in the play. Macbeth ends with an ironic but meaningless defiance to tough it out:

Ring the alarum bell! Blow wind, come wrack!
At least we'll die with harness on our back. (51–52)

In the light of Macbeth's despairing "Tomorrow, and tomorrow, and tomorrow" speech, this couplet can only be perceived as a simulacrum of the heroic.

Lady Macbeth begins the play with a good deal of callousness and bravado. From her early speeches on unsexing and becoming the female warrior, to her taunting her husband to be a man, she seems indifferent to Macbeth's nice qualms of conscience. She does not experience his metaphysical terrors, nor does she (nor, in fact, can she) see the Ghost of Banquo (as Gertrude cannot see the Ghost in the Closet Scene of *Hamlet*). After the murder of Duncan, she speaks like Jocasta to Oedipus in Sophocles' *Oedipus Rex*. To Macbeth's terrified admission that he could not say " 'Amen,' / When they did say 'God bless us!' " (2.2.28–29), she says only: "Consider it not so deeply" (29). When her husband insists on pursuing the question of why he could not pronounce Amen—presumably he thinks himself already damned—she can only offer practical advice: "These deeds must not be thought / After these ways; so, it will make us mad" (32–33). In the next exchange, when Macbeth is expanding parenthetically on the sleep he has murdered, she cuts him off with a telling question: "What do you mean?" (39). This identifies her as in a different world of discourse from her husband. This uneasy relation with him culminates in what seems like an astoundingly facile truism: "A little water clears us of this deed: / How easy is it then!" (66–67). Macbeth seems dismayed by his wife's imperceptiveness.

Lady Macbeth's sleepwalking and madness are therefore an amazing transformation. Suddenly, she is full of an inassuageable guilt, and the Doctor of Physic and the Waiting-Gentlewoman serve as a chorus to this "great perturbation in nature" (5.1.10). Like the mad Ophelia in *Hamlet*, Lady Macbeth freely associates in snatches of discontinuous thought. She is preoccupied with blood, and the obsessive ritual of hand-washing will never remove the "damned spot" (38). "What, will these hands ne'er be clean?" (46) echoes Macbeth's early preoccupation with guilt:

Will all great Neptune's ocean wash this blood
Clean from my hand? No; this my hand will rather

The multitudinous seas incarnadine,
Making the green one red. (2.2.59–62)

Her madness is a glimpse into hell—"Hell is murky" (5.1.39)—
because nothing will suffice to save her and to restore her to the past.
In this sense, she and Macbeth are both in despair:

Here's the smell of the blood still. All the perfumes of Arabia will not
sweeten this little hand. Oh, oh, oh! (53–55)

Like the mad Lear, who asks for "an ounce of civet" (*King Lear*
4.6.130), a musky perfume from glands in the anal pouch of the
civet cat, to sweeten his imagination, Lady Macbeth also deals with
the inescapable "smells of mortality" (*King Lear* 4.6.133). Her triple
O-groans are usually associated with death, as in Hamlet's last words
after "the rest is silence" (*Hamlet* 5.2.360), but her death is announced
later in the terrifying "*cry within of women*" (5.5.8 s.d.). By this point,
however, Macbeth is cold and unfeeling: "She should have died
hereafter" (17).

Macbeth's concern with equivocation seems to be directly related
to the Gunpowder Plot to blow up the Houses of Parliament that
was discovered on November 5, 1605. In the trial of Father Garnet
that followed in March 1606, the Jesuit defended himself by the
Catholic doctrine of equivocation, which meant essentially lying in
a good cause. In the Porter's Scene in *Macbeth*, the Porter pretends to
be keeper of hell gate, interviewing all who enter:

Knock, knock! Who's there, in th' other devil's name? Faith, here's an
equivocator, that could swear in both the scales against either scale;
who committed treason enough for God's sake, yet could not equivo-
cate to heaven. (2.3.7–11)

The Porter is preoccupied with equivocation. Drink itself is an
"equivocator with lechery: it makes him and it mars him; it sets him
on and it takes him off . . . in conclusion, equivocates him in a
sleep, and giving him the lie, leaves him" (34–38). As a rhetorical
device, equivocation is like paradox, and the whole play turns on
teasing pronouncements and oracles that mean the opposite of what
they seem to say. Macbeth's final statement is crucial:

> I pull in resolution, and begin
> To doubt th' equivocation of the fiend
> That lies like truth. (5.5.42–44)

"Lies like truth" is the essence of equivocation.

This echoes the opening scene of the play, which sets the tone of ambiguity, dark meaning, and equivocation: "Fair is foul, and foul is fair" (1.1.10) croak the Witches in unison to end their short scene, which takes place in thunder and lightning. *Foul* is both foul weather and ugliness, as Touchstone calls his Audrey "a foul slut" (*As You Like It* 3.3.35), but his own. Macbeth unconsciously echoes the Weird Sisters when he enters on the blasted heath with Banquo: "So foul and fair a day I have not seen" (1.3.38). The Witches precipitate the play into binary oppositions, so that equivocation is a sign of their power. As Macbeth says when they vanish, "This supernatural solic-iting / Cannot be ill, cannot be good" (130–31). The contradictions in the play are deliberately exploited for tragic effect. The Witches' rhetoric of equivocation undoes Macbeth.

If *Macbeth* was written in 1605–1606 and performed at Hampton Court in 1606 for James I, his Danish wife, Anne, and his brother-in-law, King Christian of Denmark, then the number of political allusions in the play is not surprising. King James was the ostensible patron of Shakespeare's company, the King's Men, and he had come to the throne just a few years before in 1603. As a Stuart, James was thought to descend from Banquo, and in the pageant of eight kings in act 4, scene 1, James follows as the ninth Stuart monarch. Shake-speare goes out of his way to make polite tributes to James, including his ability to cure the "king's evil," or scrofula, by his magical, heaven-sent touch. He has a "healing benediction" (4.3.156), as well as

> a heavenly gift of prophecy,
> And sundry blessings hang about his throne
> That speak him full of grace. (157–59)

These beneficent allusions are necessary in a play that represents Scotland so scathingly in the character of Macbeth, and for a new Scottish king the play could seem dangerously close to sedition. Incidentally, an old theatrical tradition associates *Macbeth* with all sorts of catastrophe. It is supposed to be bad luck even to call the play by its proper name rather than "the Scottish play."

External nature is important in *Macbeth*, and portents and perturbations are as deliberately set out here as they are in *Julius Caesar*. They have a universally evil signification. Particularly in act 2, scene 4, which is one among many choral scenes, Ross and a nameless Old Man are brought on to recite portents that will frame the murder of King Duncan. The method is allegorical; as Ross says:

> Ha, good father,
> Thou seest the heavens, as troubled with man's act,
> Threatens his bloody stage. (4–6)

" 'Tis unnatural," as the Old Man exclaims, "Even like the deed that's done" (10–11). This is not subtle dramaturgy, but it drives home the moral, analogical point with force and horror.

The most striking portent is about Duncan's horses, "Beauteous and swift, the minions of their race" (2.4.15), who "Turned wild in nature" (16) and ate each other. This savage act, which Ross witnessed "to th' amazement of mine eyes" (19), is a sign of a world turned awry by Macbeth's murder. In a literal sense, the order of nature and natural law has been turned upside down. Nature imagery of a wide scope pervades *Macbeth*. Macbeth's plotting to kill Banquo and Fleance is expressed in dire images of "seeling," or eye-closing, night, when "Light thickens, and the crow / Makes wing to th' rooky wood" (3.2.50–51). Light seems to thicken like blood clotting, and the crow and the rook are both birds of ill-omen and of the same genus (*Corvus*). As a harbinger of death and disaster, the crow flies to the wood that is already full of rooks. The nature images portend death.

The murder of Macduff's wife and children in act 4, scene 2 is a scene of unimaginable cruelty, like the blinding of Gloucester in *King Lear* (3,7). It is as if Shakespeare wants to give us "ocular" proof of the kind of savage world that Macbeth has created. The scene is choral in the sense that it has no crucial relation to the action, and the characters in it, including Ross and the nameless messenger, are peripheral to the play. Lady Macduff refuses to flee, while accusing her husband of deserting his family: "He loves us not; / He wants the natural touch" (4.2.8–9). This charge is never answered in the play, except in Macduff's uncontrollable grief when he hears the news. The murderers are anonymous figures like the murderers of Banquo in act 3, scene 3, but they are agents of Macbeth's blind fury, expressed in an aside at the end of act 4, scene 1. Now Macbeth, like Claudius in *Hamlet*, is a creature of pure will: "The very firstlings of my heart shall be / The firstlings of my hand" (147–48). He will surprise the castle of Macduff and "give to th' edge o' th' sword / His wife, his babes, and all unfortunate souls / That trace him in his line" (151–53). Macbeth's murders are now becoming more mechanical, more pointless, and more abstract.

We feel the full horror of the murder scene through Macduff's son, whose cockiness and bravado are tempered by his absolute innocence. His mother affectionately calls him "poor monkey" (4.2.57) and "poor prattler" (62), and the boy defends his father with unself-conscious vigor. He replies to the murderer, who calls his father a traitor, with unabashed courage: "Thou li'st, thou shag-eared villain!" (81). *Shag-eared* refers to something distinctive in the appearance of the murderer, probably his hairy ears. The scene reenacts the Slaughter of the Innocents, and the full effect of the horror is not felt until Macduff hears the news from Ross in the next scene.

His first reaction is to question the humanity of Macbeth—"He has no children" (4.3.216)—as if anyone capable of so savage a slaughter would also be incapable of parentage. Lady Macbeth claims, "I have given suck" (1.7.54), but neither she nor her husband are associated with children in the play. Macduff is devastated by the totality of the destruction: "All my pretty ones? / Did you say all? O hell-kite! All?" (4.3.216–17). He takes full responsibility for their murder: "Sinful Macduff, / They were all struck for thee!" (224–25), but the issue of his fleeing is never engaged, and he turns his rage against Macbeth, "this fiend of Scotland" (233). At this point in the play, we feel like Claudius at Laertes' rebellion in *Hamlet*, which, "Like to a murd'ring piece, in many places / Gives me superfluous death" (4.5.96–97). This sense of superfluous death makes the murder of innocent women and children all the more terrible. Macbeth seems to speak for the audience when he says at the end of the play: "I have supped full with horrors" (5.5.13).

Antony and Cleopatra

The most puzzling figure in *Antony and Cleopatra* is Cleopatra herself, Shakespeare's most complex representation of a woman. As Enobarbus explains her charms (and the reason that Antony, though newly married to Octavia, will return to Egypt), "Age cannot wither her, nor custom stale / Her infinite variety" (2.2.241–42). Cleopatra is no young ingenue like Juliet, but an experienced and artful lover, "with Phoebus' amorous pinches black / And wrinkled deep in time" (1.5.28–29). How old is that? Certainly closer to Gertrude's age in *Hamlet* than to Ophelia's. Her "infinite variety" in the play is expressed in terms of artifice and erotic games, as she explains to Charmian: "If you find him sad, / Say I am dancing; if in mirth, report / That I am sudden sick" (1.3.3–5). She plays in contraries in a way that frightens Charmian, who follows conventional women's doctrine: "In each thing give him way, cross him in nothing," which Cleopatra is certain is wrong: "Thou teachest like a fool: the way to lose him!" (9–10).

As Enobarbus attests elsewhere, Cleopatra is "a wonderful piece of work" (1.2.155–56), and he celebrates her infinite variety in a specifically sexual sense:

other women cloy
The appetites they feed, but she makes hungry
Where most she satisfies; for vilest things
Become themselves in her, that the holy priests
Bless her when she is riggish. (2.2.242–46)

Rig is a common word for strumpet, and *riggish* means wanton and licentious. In Enobarbus's account the imagery of appetites and feeding is sexual and there is a dark innuendo in "vilest things." Why should the holy priests bless Cleopatra's lasciviousness if it doesn't represent some apotheosis of sexuality? Enobarbus's paradoxes puzzle us, and his sense of wonder and admiration for Cleopatra is entirely different from Antony's, who is personally involved with her.

It is not surprising that Enobarbus should speak the heightened description of Cleopatra in her barge on the river Cydnus. He describes her mythologically as she first appeared when she went to meet Mark Antony. Unlike his commanding general, he is an objective observer of the marvels of Egypt, which he never hesitates to celebrate. In Shakespeare's play Antony could never possibly utter this hyperbolic oration because he is too aware of Cleopatra's dangers. He never speaks of her in hyperbole, or overwrought, exaggerated, even excessive rhetorical figuration. Actually, Enobarbus says almost nothing about Cleopatra herself except that, in the Marlovian fashion of invidious comparison, she is "O'erpicturing that Venus where we see / The fancy outwork nature" (2.2.206–7).

Enobarbus expends his effort in describing "The barge she sat in, like a burnished throne" (2.2.197), whose "poop was beaten gold" (198), and whose sails were purple (presumably the royal purple, or deep red). In a notable sadomasochistic image very relevant to the context, the silver oars of the barge "made / The water which they beat to follow faster, / As amorous of their strokes" (201–3). This is like the stroke of death, which, like a lover's pinch, "hurts, and is desired" (5.2.296). Cleopatra's costume and stage setting is opulent in the style of a Busby Berkeley musical. It is really overwrought, and the sense of stasis creates a feeling of puzzlement and wasted effort, as in the description of the pretty dimpled boys with divers-colored fans, "whose wind did seem / To glow the delicate cheeks which they did cool, / And what they undid did" (209–11). This sense of defeated motion may be part of a larger pattern of "discandying" in the play.

We see a very different Cleopatra in act 2, scene 5, while she is waiting for the absent Antony to return. A high degree of sexual innuendo, an impatient shifting of mood, an impetuous violence— all steeped in an impenetrable boredom—permeate this scene. Cleopatra begins by calling for music: "music, moody food / Of us that trade in love" (1–2), which recalls Duke Orsino's langourous lament at the beginning of *Twelfth Night*: "If music be the food of love, play on" (1.1.1). Cleopatra is histrionic, even faintly ridiculous, in speaking of music as "moody food" and of herself as a trader in love, like Pandarus in *Troilus and Cressida*.

But as soon as Mardian the Eunuch enters, she abandons music and wants to play billiards, a wildly anachronistic game for ancient Egypt. Charmian, her waiting woman, begs off: "My arm is sore" (2.5.4), and sets up an obvious sexual pun: "best play with Mardian" (4). Cleopatra cannot resist the unsubtle wordplay: "As well a woman with an eunuch played / As with a woman" (5–6), but she drives home the sexual point with a knowing smirk: "And when good will is showed, though't come too short, / The actor may plead pardon" (8–9). We already know from a previous encounter in act 1, scene 5, that Mardian the Eunuch has "fierce affections" and thinks "What Venus did with Mars" (17–18). So Cleopatra has already played this scene before with its set dialogue and prepared jokes.

But Cleopatra suddenly switches her interest to fishing, and her image of hooking "tawny-finned fishes" (2.5.12) is violently sexual:

> My bended hook shall pierce
> Their slimy jaws; and as I draw them up,
> I'll think them every one an Antony,
> And say, "Ah, ha! y' are caught!" (12–15)

Slimy jaws is not exactly attractive, but the image of Antony floats in a wide medium of instantaneous sexual attraction. Earlier, it was "O happy horse, to bear the weight of Antony" (1.5.21), and later Cleopatra commands the messenger with phallic impudence: "Ram thou thy fruitful tidings in mine ears, / That long time have been barren" (2.5.24–25).

291

Reporting the news of Antony's marriage to Octavia, the messenger is struck down, haled up and down, and threatened with a knife. This is the Cleopatra of the "vilest things" (2.2.244) that the holy priests bless when she is riggish. At the end of the scene, when the grieving Cleopatra has been fully informed about Antony's new wife, Octavia, she utters to Charmian a mysterious line that is one of her most characteristic flourishes: "Pity me, Charmian, / But do not speak to me" (2.5.118–19). She is infinitely above Charmian in social station and in complexity of feeling; she wants her pity but not her conversation. This teeters on the edge of magnificence and absurdity, like Mae West's "Beulah, peel me a grape."

Octavia, Caesar's sister, is set out as the opposite of Cleopatra, as hard and material Roman values are set against the luxuriance of Egypt. Enobarbus, who is an insightful observer, says that Octavia is "of a holy, cold, and still conversation" (2.6.122–23)—*conversation* is used in the larger sense of personal behavior and manner. Menas asks naively: "Who would not have his wife so?" (124), meaning that this describes an ideal Roman wife, but Enobarbus answers definitively: "Not he that himself is not so; which is Mark Antony. He will to his Egyptian dish again" (125–26).

Cleopatra is irresistibly presented in terms of food and sensual attraction, while Octavia unfortunately shares in the coldness and impersonality of Rome, expressed in building imagery: she is the "piece of virtue" who is set between Caesar and Antony "as the cement of our love / To keep it builded" (3.2.29–30). Cement is not a very romantic image, nor is the alternative military siege instrument: "the ram to batter / The fortress of it" (30–31). Cleopatra could never be presented in such alternative images: either the positive "cement" or the negative "ram." Later on Octavia herself speaks of wars between Caesar and Antony in the metal-working image of solder: "As if the world should cleave, and that slain men / Should solder up the rift" (3.4.31–32). All these images separate the Roman world of Octavia from the Egyptian world of Cleopatra and focus the alternatives on which the play turns.

Antony is caught in this bifurcated system of values. The play opens with a choral scene between the Roman soldiers, Demetrius and Philo, who comment directly on Antony's degeneration in Egypt. All the heroic, military, manly values of Rome have been destroyed by Cleopatra, and the first words of the play are about Antony's "dotage," which "O'erflows the measure" (1.1.1–2). *Dotage* is an Elizabethan word specifically connected with foolishness in love, especially on the part of an old lover for his young mistress. The warlike Antony, whose eyes "glowed like plated Mars" (4)—Mars in his resplendent armor—"now bend, now turn / The office and devotion of their view / Upon a tawny front" (4–6). There is a pun on *front*, both battlefront and Cleopatra's dark and sensual forehead or face (or her own "front" in a more general sense). This is dotage, when the doter forgets his manliness and duty and is overwhelmed by the love object. Antony's "captain's heart" (6) now "reneges all temper" (8)—and the image is one of the hardness and resiliency of metal, especially the blade of a sword—"And is become the bellows and the fan / To cool a gypsy's lust" (9–10). Then, in a very Shakespearean move to connect words with gestures, Antony and Cleopatra enter with their train and *"with Eunuchs fanning her"* (10 s.d.). This specifically identifies Antony with the Eunuchs because he has been made effeminate in Egypt.

The representation of Antony in this play oscillates between Roman and Egyptian images, and there is a sense of dichotomy that cannot be bridged. Caesar praises Antony for his fortitude and endurance (as Cassius praises himself in *Julius Caesar* for his physical superiority to Caesar). After the battle of Modena, a famine followed and Antony "didst drink / The stale of horses and the gilded puddle / Which beasts would cough at" (1.4.61–63). These are admirable qualities for a soldier but not for a lover, especially the ability to drink horse piss. One can see why Caesar admires this. He continues, with a hyperbolic enthusiasm rare for him in this play, to enumerate Antony's accomplishments: "The barks of trees thou browsed" (66), and, most climactic of all, on the Alps "It is reported thou didst eat strange flesh, / Which some did die to look on" (67–68). Caesar's admiration borders on the ridiculous. Antony is the ideal Roman soldier whom Caesar wants his sister Octavia to marry, and it is clear that Caesar understands nothing about love either for himself or for Antony.

But Antony thinks of his own tragic conflict in the dichotomized terms of Caesar and Philo and Demetrius. He always sees Cleopatra as perilous, even when he is most attracted to her—especially when he is most attracted to her. When he has lost the Battle of Actium through Cleopatra's machinations, he speaks of "My sword, made weak by my affection" (3.11.67), and there is a strongly erotic association of sword throughout the play. Cleopatra's simple apology immediately elicits the rapturous vaunting of love rhetoric: "Give me a kiss; / Even this repays me" (70–71). There is no way to reconcile Antony's contradictory impulses. He is rendered both effeminate and noble by Cleopatra, and the unresolvable paradox deepens the meaning of *Antony and Cleopatra*. Shakespeare doesn't work out the love / honor dichotomy, unlike Dryden in *All for Love, or The World Well Lost* (1678), his version of Shakespeare's play.

In the extraordinary death scenes that occupy our attention in act 4, scenes 14 and 15, and in act 5, scene 2, the play moves away from tragedy as we know it from earlier Shakespearean plays to a celebration of the lovers united finally in death. The moral formulas of Egypt versus Rome are forgotten, and we glory in the grand passions and poetic speeches of the protagonists. After his final defeat, everything becomes deliquescent for Antony, and Shakespeare has invented a *dis-* prefix set of words to carry this meaning: *disarming, dissolving, discandying, dislimning.* At the beginning of act 4, scene 14, Antony sees the masquelike cloud shapes (like those in *The Tempest*) that keep changing and that symbolize his present reality: "here I am Antony, / Yet cannot hold this visible shape" (13–14). Like Othello, Antony's "occupation's gone" (*Othello* 3.3.354); he is "No more a soldier" (4.14.42), and with his occupation his identity is gone, too. Therefore, like the cloud shapes he sees,

> That which is now a horse, even with a thought
> The rack dislimns, and makes it indistinct
> As water is in water. (9–11)

This dislimning is in the languorous Egyptian style of the barge on Cydnus passage.

It is not surprising in this symbolic setting that Antony cannot successfully run on his sword and accomplish his Roman suicide. He has to beg Diomedes to "give me / Sufficing strokes for death" (4.14.116–17). He is heaved aloft, mortally wounded, to Cleopatra in her monument, and she puns on the erotic overtones of the dying

Antony: "Here's sport indeed!" (4.15.32)—*sport* is a specifically sexual word—"How heavy weighs my lord! / Our strength is all gone into heaviness" (32–33). This echoes the earlier exclamation: "O happy horse, to bear the weight of Antony!" (1.5.21). There is no feeling of contradiction between these two different contexts. By the time we reach Cleopatra's dream of Antony, Antony has been mytholog-ized: "It's past the size of dreaming; nature wants stuff / To vie strange forms with fancy" (5.2.94–95). The Roman issue of effeminacy and unmanliness has ceased to exist and there is only room to exercise the imagination, yet even to imagine an Antony as once having really existed is "nature's piece 'gainst fancy, / Condemning shadows quite" (99–100). Shakespeare was fond of debating the properties of nature and art, as in the talk of the gillyvors (or pinks) in *The Winter's Tale* (4.4.73ff.).

Roman history enters powerfully into *Antony and Cleopatra*, espe-cially as Shakespeare encountered it, in biographical form, in Plu-tarch's *Lives*. Some things in the play are difficult to understand without reference to Plutarch. The role of Pompey, who also figured in *Julius Caesar*, is notably compressed in *Antony and Cleopatra* and depends upon some historical knowledge outside the play (or at least a diligent reading of the notes). The politics in this play are strongly presented, as they are in *Julius Caesar*, and there is a significantly chilling sense of amorality and brute force. Antony's oration, the death of Cinna the Poet, and the proscription scene right afterward in *Julius Caesar* all show us the frightening implications of revolution. In *Antony and Cleopatra*, two scenes that follow each other reveal how politics really works: the scene on board Pompey's galley (2,7) and the scene of Ventidius's victory over the Parthians (3,1).

The scene on board Pompey's galley is a wonderfully composed social unit, where the three world-sharers and their associates cele-brate the peace that Pompey has made. Everyone is tipsy or well on the way, including Octavius Caesar, whose "own tongue / Splits what it speaks" (2.7.125–26), and there is also vigorous singing and danc-ing. Lepidus is the farthest gone of all, and Antony makes merciless fun of him, for example, in his truistic description of the crocodile: "It is shaped, sir, like itself, and it is as broad as it hath breadth" (43–44).

Beneath the joviality and good fellowship, Menas takes Pompey aside and offers him the whole world:

> These three world-sharers, these competitors,
> Are in thy vessel. Let me cut the cable;
> And when we are put off, fall to their throats.
> All there is thine. (2.7.72–75)

It is wonderfully simple, but Pompey reluctantly refuses: "Ah, this thou shouldst have done, / And not have spoke on't" (75–76). Pompey's refusal of the world is disturbingly political, since it is based not on moral realities but on appearances: "Being done unknown, / I should have found it afterwards well done, / But must condemn it now" (80–82). This is Machiavellian in the sense of the manipulation of political events that we find in the history plays, such as *Richard III*. Menas thinks Pompey merely a fool and will never follow his "palled fortunes more" (84). His desertion is like that of Enobarbus.

Act 3, scene 1 immediately following repeats the same political reality in a different form; it is a companion scene to act 2, scene 7. Antony's general, Ventidius, is having a great triumph over the Parthians in Syria, but he rejects Silius's sound advice to continue the war and pursue the "fugitive Parthians" (7), which Silius thinks will please Antony, who will "Put garlands on thy head" (11). Ventidius feels, however, that he should stop and that there is a political dimension to military triumph (this is quite unlike Coriolanus's personal victory over the Volscians). There is a certain wistful melancholy in Ventidius's speech to Silius:

> O Silius, Silius,
> I have done enough: a lower place, note well,
> May make too great an act. (11–13)

This kind of compromise seals the fate of Antony, which we understand that Ventidius is forecasting: "Who does i' th' wars more than his captain can / Becomes his captain's captain" (21–22), and in paraphrase: "I could do more to do Antonius good, / But 'twould offend him" (25–26). This is unusually explicit, and it explains why Antony may be full of bravado but he is not a heroic figure. Ventidius perceives him in all his vanity and political weakness.

There is a great deal that is theatrical in *Antony and Cleopatra*, or, more properly, metatheatrical, since it is the theater conscious of itself in Brecht's sense. Cleopatra doesn't want to be staged in Caesar's triumphal procession, and she goes into detail about the kinds of scenes she wants to avoid, like the mob scenes in *Julius Caesar* for Brutus and Antony's orations: "mechanic slaves / With greasy aprons, rules, and hammers shall / Uplift us to the view" (209–11). Not only will Cleopatra and her girls be "shown" (208) in Rome in a public spectacle, but they will also be the subject of extempore plays like those put on by commedia dell'arte troupes: "The quick comedians / Extemporally will stage us, and present / Our Alexandrian revels" (16–18).

Cleopatra cannot bear the thought of the histrionic impersonation of scenes that were already quite histrionic when they took place in reality:

> Antony
> Shall be brought drunken forth, and I shall see
> Some squeaking Cleopatra boy my greatness
> I' th' posture of a whore. (5.2.218–21)

This is alarmingly specific, since the role of Cleopatra on the Elizabethan stage was played by an adolescent boy actor, whose squeaking voice was just breaking. The reference is doubly histrionic since Cleopatra's "real" part is exceedingly stagy. The passage on Caesar's triumph leads directly into the ending, where Cleopatra wants to be staged appropriately: "Show me, my women, like a queen: go fetch / My best attires" (227–28). Costume and properties are emphasized in Cleopatra's final sequence: "Give me my robe, put on my crown, I have / Immortal longings in me" (280–81).

Another staged scene is the mysterious act 4, scene 3, where a company of soldiers enter—there are only three speaking parts—and then *"place themselves in every corner of the stage"* (7 s.d.). Presumably Shakespeare is remembering the medieval staging of the world and its four corners. There are also portentous sound effects: *"Music of the hautboys is under the stage"* (11 s.d.). This is like the music of hautboys, or oboes, in *Macbeth* when the Witches' caldron sinks (4.1.106 s.d.). The scene of the anonymous soldiers in *Antony and Cleopatra* signifies that "the god Hercules, whom Antony loved, / Now leaves him" (4.3.15–16). The music in the air and under the earth, like the uncanny music of Ariel in *The Tempest*, indicates the defeat of Antony because his tutelary deity, Hercules, now departs.

This gives a mythological largeness to this strange scene. Incidentally, it is probable that this is the exact moment when Enobarbus also leaves Antony. The theatricality of act 4, scene 3 changes the dimension of the play, whose dramatic realities it translates onto another level of significance. I think Shakespeare wanted us to think that there is no way of separating the histrionic from the real: there is only a single reality in *Antony and Cleopatra* composed of many contradictory parts.

Coriolanus

Aufidius understands Coriolanus and knows how to undo him. Not that Coriolanus is so difficult to understand, but like most of Shakespeare's tragic protagonists, especially Othello, Coriolanus is not politic. As the intensely political Menenius says, with a kind of wonder:

His nature is too noble for the world:
He would not flatter Neptune for his trident,
Or Jove for's power to thunder. His heart's his
    mouth:
What his breast forges, that his tongue must
    vent . . . (3.1.254–57)

Aufidius acknowledges that he is the lesser man to Coriolanus and that he must defeat him by fair means or foul: "I'll potch at him some way, / Or wrath or craft may get him" (1.10.15–16). Aufidius is not heroic, as the mean word *potch* (like *botch*) indicates, but he studies carefully his antagonist and his weaknesses. Coriolanus, however, is simple and doesn't consider it worthy to study Aufidius at all. He has only contempt for him, a man who has no other status than as a military rival.

   In a long, reflective speech at the end of act 4, Aufidius considers why Coriolanus is sure to undo himself:

not moving
From th' casque to th' cushion, but commanding peace
Even with the same austerity and garb
As he controlled the war . . . (4.7.42–45)

This states explicitly one of the large thematic splits in the play: the casque is the symbol of military glory while the cushion represents civil life—we remember that two officers at the beginning of act 2, scene 2 enter "to lay cushions, as it were, in the Capitol." As Aufidius perceives so well, Coriolanus cannot move easily from the casque to the cushion, and, in fact, he cannot move at all in the sphere of civil life, with its restrictions on individual heroic action and its network of political compromises.

Shakespeare deliberately chooses to present a paradoxical hero, full of a harsh integrity and violently antidemocratic. But to say *antidemocratic* is not right either because Coriolanus so rigidly sets himself apart from Roman politics. He is not "political," in the sense that he is not at all politic. We can't imagine him, like Menenius, coming in to appease the angry mob with his specious and patronizing Fable of the Belly and the Members in the first scene of the play. Coriolanus, in fact, does just the opposite. He infuriates the plebeians with angry taunts and insults, but at least he is honest in expressing what he thinks. He is so exclusively committed to patrician values that he has no conception of civil society at all, and, in fact, his social views do not extend beyond his family and close friends. He not only hates the plebeians but cannot imagine that they have any role at all to play in a well-ordered society. The more politic patricians, like Menenius and Coriolanus's mother, Volumnia, pretend that they do, but the Machiavellian tribunes of the people, Brutus and Sicinius, understand very well the shallowness of patrician professions.

There is a curious rejection of poetry and the poetic in this play as being connected with peace and the pleasures of civilian life, and all the best poetic images have an inverted function. Thus, when Volumnia is speaking with heavy irony about the role her son must play in seeking the favor of the Roman mob, she instructs him specifically in gesture and stage action: "this bonnet in thy hand" (3.2.73), "Thy knee bussing the stones" (75), "waving thy head" (77), and then, most humiliating of all:

300

Now humble as the ripest mulberry
That will not hold the handling . . . (79–80)

This is a remarkable image from nature closely observed, because ripe mulberries are easily crushed as they are slipped off the white pulpy core around which they form. The poetic conceit resembles the fresh nature images of *Venus and Adonis*, except that here Coriolanus's ripest mulberry is a shameful sign of fawning and deceit. We know that he cannot do it, and we are proud of him for it. The dramatic action endows the mulberry image with a cloying sweetness, which represents the worst side of the patricians' cunning and falsehood.

In this same scene, Coriolanus shows his own shameful fawning in imagery that is dulcet both in sound and sense, but not in this context. He promises his mother and her advisers (especially Cominius and Menenius) that he will obey their histrionic instructions: "Away, my disposition, and possess me / Some harlot's spirit!" (3.2.111–12). Admittedly, *harlot* does not specifically mean prostitute as it does today, but the sense of Coriolanus's declaration is like Claudius's sudden aside in *Hamlet*:

The harlot's cheek, beautied with plast'ring art,
Is not more ugly to the thing that helps it
Than is my deed to my most painted word. (*Hamlet* 3.1.51–53)

Both Coriolanus and Claudius are involved deeply in pretense, but only the villain Claudius has the effrontery to face it out.

Coriolanus expands on what it means to have a "harlot's spirit":

My throat of war be turned,
Which quired with my drum, into a pipe
Small as an eunuch or the virgin voice
That babies lulls asleep! (3.2.112–15)

The beautiful alliterative patterning of "the virgin voice / That babies lulls asleep" and the metaphorical extravagance of "a pipe / Small as an eunuch" are meant as extremely negative images of what can happen when the "throat of war" is shamefully transformed into its civilian equivalent. Whatever is dulcet and poetic is attached to the nonwarrior and is firmly rejected.

One curious inversion in *Coriolanus* is that the values of love are strongly subordinated to the values of war. Both Lady Macbeth and Volumnia unsex themselves, and it comes as no surprise, for example, that Mrs. Siddons should be preeminent in both roles. Act 1, scene 3 in *Coriolanus* is an all ladies scene, very domestic, which opens when Volumnia and Virgilia, Marcius's mother and wife, *"set them down on two low stools, and sew."* They are later joined by the Roman matron Valeria, a friend of Volumnia's. This scene provides the ideological basis for the play. In a strikingly incestuous image, Volumnia praises honor over love: "If my son were my husband, I should freelier rejoice in that absence wherein he won honor than in the embracements of his bed where he would show most love" (1.3.2–5). Sex is a civilian quality naturally subordinated to feats of war, and Volumnia gives a new turn to the Petrarchan sonnet tradition of representing love as a kind of warfare. The "embracements" of the hero's marriage bed are a feeble substitute for honor won on the field of battle. Volumnia is not subtle, but still her imagination of her son as her husband is strange. She controls him in all aspects, even in so minor a matter (to her, at least) as the embracements of the marriage bed. We can understand why Marcius's wife, Virgilia, feels so terrorized in this scene.

In the spirit of Lady Macbeth, Volumnia sees her son proving his manhood by his heroic deeds in a "cruel war" (1.3.14–15). When Virgilia objects to her mother-in-law's image of Marcius's "bloody brow," when he goes forth, mechanically, "Like to a harvest-man that's tasked to mow / Or all or lose his hire" (39–40), Volumnia celebrates blood and its aesthetic superiority to mother's milk:

> The breasts of Hecuba,
> When she did suckle Hector, looked not lovelier
> Than Hector's forehead when it spit forth blood
> At Grecian sword . . . (43–46)

This echoes Lady Macbeth's ferocious image of the lactating mother plucking the nipple from the boneless gums of the babe that milks her and dashing his brains out (*Macbeth* 1.7.54–58). What's Hecuba to her and she to Hecuba, one may well ask, but Volumnia casts herself in the role of Hecuba, and her Hector is no other than her son Coriolanus. Symbolically, blood is a superior fluid to mother's milk, and nurturance (in the food imagery) and the nurturing mother are rejected in this play.

Aufidius plays a role similar to Volumnia's in the war over love imagery. In terms of the theme I am developing, Aufidius speaks in conventional heroic terms, which don't need to be literalized as they are in productions that present him as a strongly homoerotic character. It is not surprising that when Aufidius recognizes Coriolanus, who comes *"in mean apparel, disguised and muffled"* (4.4. s.d.) to Antium, he greets him with an enthusiasm that overpowers merely sexual interest:

> Know thou first,
> I loved the maid I married; never man
> Sighed truer breath. But that I see thee here,
> Thou noble thing, more dances my rapt heart
> Than when I first my wedded mistress saw
> Bestride my threshold. (4.5.117–22)

This is an overtly heterosexual passage, but the eroticism of male bonding between warriors clearly transcends the attractions of married love. Later on the Third Servingman testifies to what we see in the stage action: "Our general himself makes a mistress of him; sanctifies himself with's hand, and turns up the white o' th' eye to his discourse" (204–6). This is a tribute to heroic values, which are so eroticized that mere sexual love or married love is easily marginalized.

Coriolanus is strangely abstract and ideological as a play, dedicated to military honor and the heroic warrior ideal. This may explain why Coriolanus is so fixated on words, as if in themselves they represented the things that they stand for. There is a good deal of verbal magic in the play. When Coriolanus objects to the public praise of Cominius's oration, he asserts: "Yet oft, / When blows have made me stay, I fled from words" (2.2.72–73). This probably means the opposite of what it seems to say: Coriolanus is so attracted by the magical power of words that he must flee in order not to hear his "nothings monstered" (78). Certainly his enemies understand how easy it is to undo the heroic warrior with mere words.

The tribunes Sicinius and Brutus, like true villains, calculate a provocative assault on Coriolanus through words; their method is random but not unplanned. It is a scattershot technique. Sicinius doesn't exactly know what will be effective, but he is certain of success. When he says, "It is a mind / That shall remain a poison where it is, / Not poison any further" (3.1.86–88), Coriolanus becomes impaled on the word *shall*, which torments him:

> Shall remain!
> Hear you this Triton of the minnows? Mark you
> His absolute "shall"? (88–90)

Once enraged, Coriolanus cannot be quieted, and *shall* echoes through his next speech four times: "Shall!" (90)—said with wondering disbelief—"his peremptory 'shall' " (94), "who puts his 'shall,' / His popular 'shall,' against a graver bench / Than ever frowned in Greece" (105–7). It's as if Sicinius as a character is reduced to a single vexing word.

Later on, Sicinius's word *traitor* does the same trick as *shall*: "you are a traitor to the people" (3.3.66). Coriolanus cannot believe his ears: "How! Traitor!" (67), and again: "Call me their traitor, thou injurious tribune!" (69). Coriolanus's attempt to answer the charge with even more stinging invective leads directly to his banishment. He is not politic or even rational, so his piercing cry "I banish you" (123) plays directly into the tribunes' hands. Shakespeare slants the issues in the play by making the tribunes so manipulative, but the plebeians have real grievances that they have difficulty in expressing. They are badly served by their meanspirited leaders, as they are in *Julius Caesar*, but there is nevertheless a real political conflict in the play between patricians and plebeians. There is an acute feeling of class hatred, as there is in the second part of *Henry VI*. This paradoxical and unresolved quality intensifies the dramatic interest of *Coriolanus*.

There may be a "world elsewhere" (3.3.135), but Aufidius plays the same trick as Sicinius with the word *traitor* when he is determined to bring his enemy down in Corioles:

> Read it not, noble lords;
> But tell the traitor in the highest degree
> He hath abused your powers. (5.6.84–86)

Coriolanus is enraged instantaneously and is therefore extremely vulnerable: "Traitor! How now!" (87). Aufidius repeats the charge: "Ay, traitor, Marcius!" (87). Notice that Aufidius also refuses to call Marcius by "thy stol'n name / Coriolanus, in Corioles" (89–90). There is onomastic pressure in Marcius, which now becomes a name of contempt.

One further naming leads directly to Coriolanus's death. When he calls upon Mars, the god of war, to witness what is being said, Aufidius forbids this invocation: "Name not the god, thou boy of tears!" (5.6.101). *Boy* is the final, magical insult, which drives Coriolanus directly to his doom. He recoils in disbelief: "Ha!" (102), which is exactly the word with which Iago began his campaign against Othello: "Ha! I like not that" (*Othello* 3.3.35) in response to Cassio's talk with Desdemona. Again, Coriolanus cannot believe what he is hearing, and the word *boy* seems to drive him mad: "Measureless liar, thou hast made my heart / Too great for what contains it. 'Boy'! O slave!" (5.6.103–4)

Coriolanus is not exactly fleeing from words, but seems enchanted by them, and this leads him to the kind of heroic boasting among the Volscians that ensures his assassination:

> 'Boy'! False hound!
> If you have writ your annals true, 'tis there,
> That, like an eagle in a dovecote, I
> Fluttered your Volscians in Corioles.
> Alone I did it. 'Boy'? (5.6.113–17)

The final *boy* sounds plaintive as well as unbelieving. We don't expect political characters such as Aufidius or Menenius to talk with such frankness and emotional honesty. In many ways Coriolanus acts out the fact that he is indeed a boy of tears, but in the midst of his heroic vaunting we feel the terrible tragic pull of self-destruction.

Coriolanus has unusually specific references to acting and the theater, as if civil society and politics demanded the sort of role-playing that is absent from military endeavor. Coriolanus particularly bridles at soliciting the Roman mob in the gown of humility for their votes (or "voices") to be consul: "I cannot / Put on the gown, stand naked, and entreat them, / For my wounds' sake, to give their suffrage"

(2.2.137–39). As in most of Shakespeare, acting has negative connotations: it is presenting a false appearance. Coriolanus says directly that to stand for consul "is a part / That I shall blush in acting" (145–46).

The imagery comes to its natural climax in act 3, scene 2, when his mother and Menenius are trying to school him in how to play a humble role before the Roman mob. To act is to be "False to my nature"; the honest alternative is to "play / The man I am" (15–16). In what sense does Coriolanus "*play* / The man I am*," if not to undo acting entirely? Volumnia claims that her son is "too absolute" (39) and lacks "policy" (48), and she vows to instruct him in the details of his prepared role. He must "dissemble" (62) with his nature and speak "words that are but roted in / Your tongue, though but bastards and syllables / Of no allowance to your bosom's truth" (55–57). Volumnia teaches him the gesture and stage action of his part, "for in such business / Action is eloquence" (75–76), but Coriolanus is certain of disaster: "You have put me now to such a part which never / I shall discharge to th' life" (105–6). *To th' life* means in a lively and convincing manner, as a good actor would try to persuade the audience of the truth of his role. Thinking to help, Cominius even says: "We'll prompt you" (106). Coriolanus vows to win by trickery and deceit: "I'll mountebank their loves, / Cog their hearts from them" (132–33), as if he were a matinee idol.

At the end of the play, when his family intercedes with him to spare Rome, acting imagery again is used to mark the artificiality of the occasion. Coriolanus is determined to stand fast, "As if a man were author of himself / And knew no other kin" (5.3.36–37), but this declaration is already a sign of weakness. It is the rigid part that Coriolanus has prepared for himself. In a few lines he is confessing his failure: "Like a dull actor now, / I have forgot my part and I am out, / Even to a full disgrace" (40–42). He kneels to his mother much as he did when he returned from the wars (2.1.177 s.d.), but then Volumnia goes him one better by kneeling to him. "Action is eloquence" (3.2.76), and Coriolanus is being outplayed.

In his climactic gesture, Coriolanus "*Holds her by the hand, silent*" (5.3.182 s.d.), and this seems to be the only moment in the play when he displays emotions too strong for words. But it is a fatal moment, and the gods as spectators scorn this perverted, histrionic scene:

> Behold, the heavens do ope,
> The gods look down, and this unnatural scene
> They laugh at. (183–85)

It is an unnatural scene for the mother to be soliciting her son, as all histrionic scenes and role-playing are inherently false. Coriolanus seems to be acutely conscious of the histrionic embarrassment of his yielding.

Coriolanus is an intensely political play, and we know that it has a close relation to the food and enclosure riots that were taking place in England around the time of its composition. In this sense, it may be more topical and more timely than any other play of Shakespeare, even the second part of *Henry VI* with its frightening Jack Cade rebellion. The patrician-plebeian conflict is presented in an extreme form, set firmly in angry invective. The tribunes, Sicinius and Brutus, who are conceived as manipulating villains, are not more villainous in their doctrine than are the patricians in their expression of antidemocratic values. Volumnia and Menenius are as calculating as the tribunes in their desire to produce political effects. Act 3, scene 2 is, in fact, a shamelessly political scene, in which Volumnia and Menenius combine their forces to teach Coriolanus how to dissemble before the people and to combine "Honor and policy" (42).

Coriolanus, however, is not political at all, and his honesty and harsh integrity provide the basis for the tragedy. We are vividly aware of how unpolitical Coriolanus is when he appears before Aufidius's house in Antium *"in mean apparel, disguised and muffled"* (4.4. s.d.) and delivers his important soliloquy: "O world, thy slippery turns!" (12). His speech shows no awareness of the powerful events that have precipitated his banishment. Everything seems to happen not by some inexorable political necessity but for trivial reasons, "On a dissension of a doit" (17), a coin of little value. So the banished Coriolanus now stands in disguise before the house of his chief enemy "by some chance, / Some trick not worth an egg" (20–21).

This is an apolitical explanation that echoes the Captain of Fortinbras's expedition in *Hamlet*, who fights "to gain a little patch of ground / That hath in it no profit but the name" (*Hamlet* 4.4.18–19), and of which Hamlet knows "Two thousand souls and twenty thousand ducats / Will not debate the question of this straw" (25–26). The essence of Coriolanus's separation from politics is in his banishment speech, when he banishes the Roman mob that has banished him and says darkly, "There is a world elsewhere" (3.3.135). But the tragedy seems intent on demonstrating that there is not a world elsewhere and that ultimately everything Roman is involved with everything Volscian. They cannot exist as separate entities.

Timon of Athens

imon begins with a framing action that strongly influences how we should understand the play. The first characters to appear are a Poet, a Painter, a Jeweler, and a Merchant, who enter *"at several doors."* They are all waiting for Timon, their patron, to come on stage, and they pass the time by speaking about art and poetry in Athenian society. Everything that is beautiful and significant is given a specific commercial value. As the Jeweler later tells Timon about the price of his stone, "My lord, 'tis rated / As those which sell would give" (1.1.168–69), or, in other words, I will let you have it at wholesale (i.e., at what other sellers would give for it). It is interesting that these statements here (and also in act 5, scene 1, when the Poet and Painter return) are the most extensive commentary on art in all of Shakespeare, and they present it in its basest, most devalued, and most money-grubbing aspect. The Poet and the Painter appear with the Jeweler and Merchant because they all have tangible commodities for sale. *Timon* begins then by setting up a sharply satirical and mercenary context. This is what we need to know about the city before Timon of Athens appears.

The Poet and Painter are sharply observed satirical characters, vain and self-preoccupied like the prominent Athenians Timon sends to for money in the first three scenes of act 3. The Poet wonders at Timon's "Magic of bounty" (1.1.6), which has drawn all these suitors soliciting rewards. There is even a fashionable awareness in the Poet and the Painter that their own pursuit is a form of hucksterism. They are supersalesmen. The Poet and Painter are careful to praise each other's work and to speak of their art in the coy, self-deprecating, and fulsome language of professionals. The Poet's "dedication / To the great lord" (19–20) is merely "A thing slipped idly from me" (20), and in a wonderfully unctuous image, "Our poesy" is defined "as a gum, which oozes / From whence 'tis nourished" (21–22). The oozing kind of poetry only oozes when the fountain of patronage is turned on. Of Shakespeare's works only *Venus and Adonis* and *The Rape of Lucrece* are dedicated to a patron, Henry Wriothesley, Earl of Southampton. Their short, dedicatory epistles seem insincere and fulsome to us but are very modest by late Elizabethan and early Jacobean standards. In a period when publishing was not usually profitable for authors, patronage of the kind Shakespeare is satirizing in *Timon* was common, and authors depended on noble patrons for their livelihood. This might account for a lot of cloying flattery in the dedications, and even in the poetry and prose, of the period. It was very hard, almost impossible, to earn one's living solely as an author.

The Poet in a companionable way praises the Painter's painting (which he conveniently has with him for all to admire). It just so happens to be a flattering portrait of Timon:

> Admirable. How this grace
> Speaks his own standing! What a mental power
> This eye shoots forth! How big imagination
> Moves in this lip! (1.1.30–33)

This seems to be the oozing kind of painting.

The Poet goes into considerably more detail about his "rough work" (1.1.43), which he also conveniently has with him, and his poem, which emphasizes the instability of Fortune, serves as a prologue for the play. To the Poet, Timon is a man "Whom this beneath world doth embrace and hug / With amplest entertainment" (44–45). On the high and pleasant hill of Fortune are scattered all sorts of hustlers who labor "To propagate their state" (i.e., to get ahead), while at the top of all is Lord Timon, "Whom Fortune with her ivory hand wafts to her" (70). But the Poet really has only contempt for Timon, because his followers—"Some better than his value" (79)—flatter him only for the moment. When the fickle Fortune "Spurns down her late beloved" (85), then all his dependants "let him slip down" the mountain's top, "Not one accompanying his declining foot" (87–88). This is an allegory in which the Poet and the Painter, the Jeweler and the Merchant, anticipate Timon's fall from prosperity. They obviously want to get all the rewards they can from Timon while the getting is good.

When the Poet and Painter reappear in act 5, they are even more nakedly mercenary and hypocritical. Now that they have heard that Timon has gold, they think it politic to put in an appearance: "Therefore 'tis not amiss we tender our loves to him in this supposed distress of his" (5.1.12–14). Like all the other base Athenians in the play, the Poet and Painter conceive that distress can only come from want of cash. The Painter catches beautifully the cynical mood of the times when he contrasts promise and performance:

Promising is the very air o' th' time; it opens the eyes of expectation. Performance is ever the duller for his act, and but in the plainer and simpler kind of people, the deed of saying is quite out of use.

(23–27)

The "deed of saying" is actually doing what one promises.

In all these speeches there is an air of fantasy, fiction, and counterfeiting that Timon finally recognizes. He puns on *counterfeit*, a standard Elizabethan word for a portrait, as in *The Merchant of Venice* when Bassanio opens the lead casket and recognizes his beloved's picture: "What find I here? / Fair Portia's counterfeit!" (3.2.114–15). So Timon berates the Painter: "Thou draw'st a counterfeit / Best in all Athens. Th'art indeed the best; / Thou counterfeit'st most lively" (5.1.81–83). As for the Poet's "fiction," or imaginative feigning, "Why thy verse swells with stuff so fine and smooth / That thou art even natural in thine art" (86–86). As Touchstone points out, in the endless comic quibbling about poetic mimesis, "the truest poetry is the most feigning" (*As You Like It* 3.3.18–19).

311

The Poet and Painter, Jeweler and Merchant begin the play and they provide us with a context by which to understand Timon. By the time the trumpets sound at line 94 and Lord Timon appears *"addressing himself courteously to every suitor,"* we know what to expect. Timon in prosperity is a dreamlike figure, but he insists on public declamation and the active exhibition of his exceeding favors to all. The first scene of the play is therefore extremely histrionic, as if Timon is acting out the Poet's allegory of Fortune's hill.

There is an air of unreality in what the Senator says at the beginning of act 2, as if he cannot pass up such a marvelous scam: "If I want gold, steal but a beggar's dog / And give it Timon—why the dog coins gold" (2.1.5–6). *Dog* has consistently negative connotations in Shakespeare, and in this play it is associated with the Cynic philosophy of Apemantus. It is as if the Senator cannot believe how simple-minded Timon actually is. He continues with more animal images:

> If I would sell my horse and buy twenty moe
> Better than he—why give my horse to Timon,
> Ask nothing, give it him, it foals me straight,
> And able horses. (2.1.7–10)

The animal imagery conveys the unnatural baseness of the concept "it foals me straight."

Timon's protest, "Unwisely, not ignobly, have I given" (2.2.184), seems irrelevant in this wildly satirical context. In the Banquet Scene, Timon's earnest reprobation of his fellow men seems to fall on deaf ears: "Uncover, dogs, and lap" (3.6.86). In the old Timon play, probably imitated from Shakespeare rather than a source, the dishes were filled with stones painted to look like artichokes. Timon's farewell speech, like Coriolanus's "I banish you" (*Coriolanus* 3.3.124), is full of despairing, misanthropic venom: "Burn house, sink Athens, henceforth hated be / Of Timon man and all humanity" (3.6.105–6).

But the senators and other lords driven out of Timon's house care nothing for his speech. Effectively, they have not heard it, and the scene ends with a mad scramble to find the items that have been lost:

> *Third Lord.* Push, did you see my cap?
> *Fourth Lord.* I have lost my gown.

First Lord. He's but a mad lord, and naught but humors sways
him. He gave me a jewel th' other day, and now he has
beat it out of my hat. Did you see my jewel?
Third Lord. Did you see my cap? (3.6.110–16)

This is not tragic but farcical, as are the Poet and the Painter, the Jeweler and the Merchant. One of the difficulties of the play is that Timon is so out of touch with the world he operates in, both in prosperity and in adversity, that his tragic invective against mankind fails to carry any weight and seems merely rhetorical. *Timon of Athens* may be an after-vibration of *King Lear*, as Coleridge thought, but the bleakness and desolation of *Lear* is trivialized and made absurd in *Timon*.

Actors have complained about how difficult it is to do Timon convincingly, especially in the last two acts. Some of this material is grotesquely comic, as in Timon's long soliloquy outside the walls of Athens at the beginning of act 4: "Son of sixteen, / Pluck the lined crutch from thy old limping sire, / With it beat out his brains" (4.1.13–15). Timon's imperative invectives are not spoken to anyone in particular—they are addressed to the audience—and they have a certain vague generality about them, as if Timon is too new to the role of moral exhorter: "To general filths / Convert o' th' instant green virginity; / Do't in your parents' eyes" (6–8). "General filths" is not very shocking, and we are certain that Apemantus could do a better job of specifying what he means by *general filths*. Timon's "let confusion live" (21) echoes Lear's "Let copulation thrive" (*King Lear* 4.6.114), but it lacks Lear's mad context. "All's obliquy" (4.3.18) is much more memorable as a statement of Timon's disillusion, but it still needs a meaningful dramatic context. It is at this point, ironically, that Timon digs and finds gold rather than roots.

It is possible that *Timon* is Shakespeare's most Absurdist tragedy, and the very things that draw it so close to grotesque comedy make it potentially more congenial and therefore more bitter for modern audiences. Peter Brook's *Timon* at the Bouffes du Nord Theater in Paris in 1974 impressed audiences with its similarity to Samuel Beckett. Timon doesn't hope to convince any of his many visitors in the last two acts, but he exhorts them energetically, and perhaps also clownishly, to share his misanthropic vision of mankind. His visitors all take his newfound gold, but they scarcely even listen to his message. This is not unlike the farcical lack of contact between Timon and the objects of his philanthropy earlier in the play.

Phrynia and Timandra, the drunken whores of Alcibiades, the Chocolate Soldier, listen to Timon's rantings in act 4 as if they were some sort of kinky foreplay. They speak together, like musical comedy twins: "More counsel with more money, bounteous Timon" (4.3.168). Unlike Lear, Timon doesn't have the benefit of madness to endow his speeches with a special poignancy. Instead, he plods on with mounting intensity: "Hold up, you sluts, / Your aprons mountant" (135–36), as if, in the heraldic image, Phrynia and Timandra were like Danaë, who catches Zeus's shower of gold in her lap. He loads them with a long string of imperatives about the effects of venereal disease, ending with: "Plague all, / That your activity may defeat and quell / The source of all erection" (163–65). Presumably, Phrynia and Timandra's activities will render impotent and kill all their customers. This is the closest Shakespeare comes to sounding like the apocalyptic Marquis de Sade.

Whether *Timon* is a fully finished play has been actively debated. Some things definitely need work, especially the subordinate action with Alcibiades. Act 3, scene 5 is a fully developed and exciting scene, in which Alcibiades pleads eloquently and in vain for a soldier who has committed murder. Alcibiades has many resemblances to Coriolanus, and there are elaborate verbal links between the two plays, but something seems to be missing in the portrait of Alcibiades. His appearance before the cave of Timon in 4,3 with Phrynia and Timandra seems particularly unsatisfying as a sequel to the moving scene of 3,5, ending in Alcibiades' banishment.

Other loose ends in *Timon* can be explained away more easily, but there is a sense in the last two acts that Timon's fall is not fully dramatized. At the end he seems to fade away "Upon the beachèd verge of the salt flood" (5.1.217)—the epitaph is given in at least two different forms. The ending of the play is surprisingly inconsequential. There are memorable lines, such as the Second Senator's "And by the hazard of the spotted die, / Let die the spotted" (5.4.34–35), but no memorable action. One plausible theory is that *Timon* was put aside for a further revision and polishing that never took place. There is no record of its ever having been performed in the early seventeenth century.

If the play is not fully worked out, it has nevertheless some scenes that are extraordinarily good. The first three scenes of act 3, when Timon's servants visit his friends for a loan, are among the most trenchantly satirical that Shakespeare ever wrote. He is completely at home in the vivid, wheedling, colloquial style of Timon's friends, who represent the prevailing mores of Athenian society as accurately as the Poet and Painter, Jeweler and Merchant. At the house of Lucullus, the master is unctuously flattering to Flaminius, who seems to be coming with a gift from Timon: "And what hast thou there under thy cloak, pretty Flaminius?" (3.1.15–16). When it proves to be only an empty box in which to collect money for Timon, Lucullus is genuinely astounded: "La, la, la, la!" (23), and he has the gall to lecture Flaminius about his master's failings: "Every man has his fault, and honesty is his. I ha' told him on't, but I could ne'er get him from't" (29–31). Although Lucullus has profited from Timon's honesty, or generosity, he berates him for it with hearty cynicism. Throughout the scene, Lucullus treats Timon's servant as if he were in league with him and all right-thinking men: as anyone with any common sense would understand, "this is no time to lend money, especially upon bare friendship without security" (44–45). Lucullus doesn't grasp why Flaminius doesn't take a bribe of three solidares to say that he wasn't at home. He exits full of bemused contempt: "Ha? Now I see thou art a fool, and fit for thy master" (51–52).

A sureness in Lucullus and a verve in the writing of act 3, scene 1, are not manifested elsewhere in the play. Lucullus has none of the uncertainty of Alcibiades or even of Timon, about whom Shakespeare seemed to have conflicting impressions. Lucius and Sempronius in the next two scenes of act 3 are not as effective as Lucullus, but they promote the savage, mercenary quality of Athens. Timon is an innocent in this world of self-interest and intrigue. It is interesting how much of a bubble is Timon's "magic of bounty." As Flavius, his steward, makes so abundantly clear in act 2, scene 2, all Timon's lavish gifts are bought with borrowed money. It is all a fantasy of meaningless exchange. When Timon says to Flavius, "Unwisely, not ignobly, have I given" (184), one can't help interpret *not ignobly* to mean flamboyantly, in a grand manner befitting a person as noble as myself. It is all display, based upon an impossible premise: "there's none / Can truly say he gives, if he receives" (1.2.10–11). This is the myth of endless conspicuous consumption, like the self-defeating potlatch ceremony of the Kwakiutl Indians of the Pacific Northwest. It is essentially a ritual of aggressive self-assertion that has nothing whatsoever to do with beneficence to other people.

Timon has many resemblances to a dramatic fable, with type characters and archetypal situations. Flavius is the faithful steward like Kent in *King Lear* and like the King's groom of the stable at the end of *Richard II*. He understands Timon's situation almost from the beginning, and he feels compassion for his master: "I bleed inwardly for my lord" (1.2.210). There is extraordinary passion in the confrontation with Timon in 2,2 because Flavius sees what is going on and is powerless to stop it:

> When all our offices have been oppressed
> With riotous feeders, when our vaults have wept
> With drunken spilth of wine, when every room
> Hath blazed with lights and brayed with minstrelsy,
> I have retired me to a wasteful cock,
> And set mine eyes at flow. (168–73)

This suggests some tragic implications of Timon's fall that are not developed in the play. His immediate reaction to Flavius's revelations is completely wrong. Timon decides energetically to borrow money from his friends, but we are assured by Flavius that these are hollow friends: "Feast-won, fast-lost" (181).

At the end of the play Flavius is something of an embarrassment to Timon because he throws a wrench into his absolute misanthropy. Timon wants to believe that "I never had honest man about me" (4.3.486), but Flavius forces him to admit: "I do proclaim / One honest man" (505–6). Flavius weeps, but Timon refuses to take him back as his steward, and Flavius is driven off with a broken heart. There is something shallow in Timon's grudging exception:

> How fain would I have hated all mankind,
> And thou redeem'st thyself. But all save thee
> I fell with curses. (508–10)

It's as if Flavius is spoiling Timon's self-indulgent wish to hate all mankind absolutely, and in the same speech Timon is still suspecting Flavius of duplicity: "Is not thy kindness subtle, covetous, / A usuring kindness?" (517–18). Timon cannot accept Flavius's "merely love" (524), and by doing so he destroys any possibility of his own redemption.

The cynical and base Apemantus understands Timon perfectly right from the beginning, although Apemantus himself is an extremely unattractive character, like Thersites in *Troilus and Cressida*. Both Apemantus and Timon specialize in histrionic effects; they are performers of their role to a shocked and disbelieving public. At the end of the play Apemantus accuses Timon of usurping his role: "Thou dost affect my manners, and dost use them" (4.3.200), with the warning: "Do not assume my likeness" (219). Apemantus is perversely proud of his churlish, truth-speaking manner, which he has taken pains to develop over a long period of time, whereas Timon is merely a novice at misanthropy: "Thou'dst courtier be again / Wert thou not beggar" (242–43). Like Coriolanus, Timon is an absolutist, as Apemantus knows full well: "The middle of humanity thou never knewest, but the extremity of both ends" (301–2). This echoes what Volumnia says of her warrior son:

> You are too absolute;
> Though therein you can never be too noble
> But when extremities speak. (*Coriolanus* 3.2.39–41)

Apemantus is brilliantly characterized in the stage direction for Timon's first banquet: *"Then comes dropping after all, Apemantus, discontentedly, like himself"* (1.2. s.d.). We cannot imagine Timon "dropping after all" or in any form of humility either feigned or natural. He harangues his fellow men, and when that proves to be futile, he wishes only for a quiet annihilation in the "embossèd froth" of the "turbulent surge" (5.2.218–19). Part of his self-created epitaph is the forswearing of speech: "Lips, let four words go by and language end" (221), which powerfully resembles Iago's vow: "From this time forth I never will speak word" (*Othello* 5.2.300).

After *King Lear* and *Macbeth* Shakespeare seems to be moving away from tragedy firmly based on the character of the protagonist. In

Antony and Cleopatra there is definitely a feeling of romance, especially in the ending, which moves toward the fulfillment and triumph of love tragedy. *Coriolanus* is a deeply paradoxical tragedy, and the hero is narrowly conceived, without the range of sympathy and complexity of feeling we find in Hamlet, Othello, King Lear, and Macbeth. As the last of Shakespeare's tragedies, *Timon of Athens* is disappointing because it is so overwhelmingly satirical, so incomplete in its conception of its tragic protagonist. Timon is so neatly divided between excessive love and excessive hatred of mankind that he doesn't seem tragic at all. He seems to have trouble understanding his own extreme positions, as does Coriolanus, and the play develops, especially in the second part, a certain farcical, black-comedy aspect. Perhaps Shakespeare wanted to experiment in different and inherently less satisfactory and less plausible kinds of tragedy after the period of the four so-called great tragedies. It may be for just this reason that *Antony and Cleopatra, Coriolanus,* and *Timon* have gained enormously in reputation over the last fifty years. They have become much more teasing and provocative for contemporary audiences and readers, who may have metaphysical doubts about the possibility of tragedy in our time.

ROMANCES

Pericles

Four of Shakespeare's late comedies—*Pericles, Cymbeline, The Winter's Tale,* and *The Tempest*—are often put together in a group called the "romances," or the "late romances" (to distinguish them from earlier comedies of Shakespeare that have many romantic elements). To this group I have added *The Two Noble Kinsmen,* which is probably a collaboration of Shakespeare and Fletcher, and which has some strongly romantic and pastoral qualities. The editors of the First Folio did not think of romance as a separate genre, such as comedy, history, and tragedy. *The Tempest* is the first play in the book, beginning the comedies section, and *The Winter's Tale* is the last of the comedies. Strangely, *Cymbeline* is the last of the tragedies and the very last play in the book. Neither *Pericles* nor *The Two Noble Kinsmen* appear in the First Folio.

The late romances are all comedies with a strong admixture of tragicomedy. Deaths occur but the supposedly dead person is usually revived by magic tinged with religion. The endings of the romances specialize in the restoration of families, particularly of husbands and wives and fathers and daughters. There is an emphasis on the marvelous, expressed in a highly concentrated lyric poetry with an abundant use of music and masquelike stage effects. There are many romance elements in all of Shakespeare's comedies, beginning with *The Comedy of Errors*, which uses shipwreck and the reuniting of family, but the tragicomic aspect is particularly apparent in the late romances. Shakespeare was inclined to a romantic view of comedy rather than a realistic one, and, with the possible exception of *The Merry Wives of Windsor*, he wrote no comedies about London life, unlike Middleton, Dekker, Jonson, Heywood, and others.

Pericles was not included in Shakespeare's collected works until the second issue of the Third Folio in 1664. It was first published in a relatively bad Quarto edition in 1609, which is our only basis for the present text. There is, however, one other possible authority: in 1608, George Wilkins published a prose narrative called *The Painful Adventures of Pericles Prince of Tyre*, which purports on the title-page to be "the true history of the play of *Pericles*, as it was lately presented by the worthy and ancient Poet John Gower." If the play *Pericles* was presented by Shakespeare's company, the King's Men, in late 1607 or early 1608, then Wilkins could have written his prose narrative to capitalize on the popularity of the play, which we know from other sources was one of the most popular of Shakespeare's works. Wilkins also borrowed about a third of his narrative from one of Shakespeare's main sources, Laurence Twine's *The Pattern of Painful Adventures*, printed at least three times between 1576 and 1607.

I agree with the prevailing opinion that acts 1 and 2 of the Quarto version of *Pericles* are not by Shakespeare and that acts 3, 4, and 5 are, and my discussion of the play emphasizes the last three acts and minimizes the first two. Acts 1 and 2 have been variously attributed, without any certainty, to Thomas Heywood, George Wilkins, John Day, and others.

The romance of Apollonius of Tyre, which lies behind Shakespeare's *Pericles*, was one of the frequently told stories of the Middle Ages and Renaissance, which may account for the enormous popularity of Shakespeare's play. John Gower used the Apollonius story from the *Gesta Romanorum* in his own poem, *Confessio Amantis*, Book VIII, printed in 1532 and 1554, but written in the late fourteenth century. It is therefore no surprise that Shakespeare makes Gower the chorus or presenter of *Pericles*, who speaks seven introductory and expository prologues, with three interpolated dumb shows, and an epilogue.

Gower plays a considerable role in shaping our attitude to *Pericles*, and his appeal to the audience echoes the exhortations of the Chorus in *Henry V* to let us "On your imaginary forces work" (prologue 18) and to "Piece out our imperfections with your thoughts" (23).

In the prologue to act 3, Gower asks the audience to "Be attent, / And time that is so briefly spent / With your fine fancies quaintly eche" (11–13). *Eche* is an old spelling of *eke*, meaning to eke out or augment, which is the same message as the Chorus delivers in *Henry V*. Gower makes a similar appeal in the prologue to act 4:

> Only I carry wingèd time
> Post on the lame feet of my rhyme;
> Which never could I so convey
> Unless your thoughts went on my way. (47–50)

He is on familiar and confidential terms with the audience, whom he addresses as "you." In the prologue to act 5, he again calls for the active imagination of the spectators to support the play: "In your supposing once more put your sight" (21), and in the next prologue, he acknowledges the audience's magical powers, which have made the king and all his company appear at Ephesus: "That he can hither come so soon / Is by your fancies' thankful doom" (5.2.19–20).

Pericles is mediated through Gower, who acts as a presenter of the action, as if it were his story from *Confessio Amantis*. Shakespeare is nowhere else so literally indebted to the author himself of his chief source—we can't imagine him invoking the figure of Plutarch in the Roman plays or Raphael Holinshed in the English histories. Shakespeare goes to great trouble to create an archaic fourteenth-century atmosphere in Gower's part, and he imitates the tetrameter couplets in which *Confessio Amantis* is written. This adds to the already remote romantic action of the play, which is like a marine version of the picaresque novel, with adventures not on the road but in various harbors and port towns of the Eastern Mediterranean and Asia Minor.

The archaic is chiefly conveyed by medieval or pseudomedieval diction (as in Edmund Spenser's *Shepheards Calender*, 1579). Gower's report of the marriage feast of Pericles and Thaisa is homely and rustic: "Now sleep y-slackèd hath the rout" (prol. 3, 1), and various domestic animals indicate the ordinariness of the occasion: "The cat, with eyne of burning coal, / Now couches 'fore the mouse's hole" (5– 6). The tone of this is cute and the singsong quality of the tetrameter couplets assures us that, for the moment, all is well. After the plain pantomime of the dumb show, Gower indicates that Pericles and his new wife must depart from their newfound happiness at Pentapolis:

> By many a dern [= drear] and painful perch [= measure of land]
> Of Pericles the careful search
> By the four opposing coigns
> Which the world together joins . . . (15–18)

Shakespeare manipulates the tetrameter, with its frequent rhymes and excessive regularity, to make it sound archaic and to displace the action of *Pericles* onto the fairyland of romance. We remember Shakespeare as a master of stylistic displacement from the plays-within-a-play in *Love's Labor's Lost*, *A Midsummer Night's Dream*, and *Hamlet*, but in *Pericles* there is a much closer relation in tone between Gower's antiquated language and the romantic adventures of Pericles and his family.

Pericles looks ahead to the other romantic comedies that follow, especially *The Winter's Tale*, but it also has affinities with *Cymbeline* and *The Tempest*. All these plays stress wonder, awe, and admiration. Specifically, one experiences a magical rebirth, revival, and restoration. In both *The Winter's Tale* and *Pericles*, the once-dead wives, Hermione and Thaisa, are brought to life again after a long period. There are strong links between Thaisa's daughter, Marina, and Hermione's daughter, Perdita, who are reunited with their mothers and fathers at the end of the play. There is a powerful insistence on magic in the revivals of Thaisa and Hermione, and we remember that in *The Tempest* Prospero is a thaumaturge, or natural magician, who practices a white magic that he has learned from deep study, like Doctor Faustus in Marlowe's play before he makes his pact with the devil.

Cerimon in *Pericles* is endowed with religious power associated with the Temple of Diana at Ephesus. During the mighty storm at sea in act 3, scene 1 in which Marina is born and Thaisa dies in childbirth, Thaisa's corpse is thrown overboard in its "satin coffin," well "Caulked and bitumèd" (68, 72). This womblike receptacle then washes up on the shores of Ephesus, where it is brought to Cerimon. He is a learned magus who has always believed that "Virtue and cunning were endowments greater / Than nobleness and riches" (3.2.27–28), and who, like Friar Lawrence in *Romeo and Juliet*, has studied "the disturbances / That nature works, and of her cures" (37–38), the "secret art" of physic "Making a man a god" (31). Like a priest, he opens Thaisa's coffin and smells its delicate odors "Balmed and entreasured with full bags of spices!" (65).

Thaisa looks remarkably "fresh," and Cerimon knows that

> Death may usurp on nature many hours,
> And yet the fire of life kindle again
> The o'erpressed spirits. (3.2.82–84)

He brings Thaisa back to life with "fire and cloths" (88), music, and boxes of natural medicaments. It is a miracle of homeopathy. Thaisa awakes to life slowly and lyrically. A "warmth / Breathes out of her" and "she 'gins to blow / Into life's flower again!" (94, 97). With great dramatic appropriateness, the simple stage direction reads *"She moves"* (106 s.d.), which is like the statue of Hermione coming down from its pedestal in *The Winter's Tale* (5,3). Thaisa already intuits that she owes her life to the goddess Diana: "O dear Diana, / Where am I? Where's my lord? What world is this?" (106–7), like Miranda's exclamation of wonder in *The Tempest*: "O brave new world / That has such people in't!" (5.1.183–84).

In the final scene of *Pericles*, husband and wife are reunited, and mother and daughter, too, in a transcendent climax that provides the model for the final scene of *The Winter's Tale*. Cerimon is the man "Through whom the gods have shown their power" (5.3.59), and Pericles praises him by affirming that "The gods can have no mortal officer / More like a god than you" (61–62). The whole scene takes place in the Temple of Diana, in which Thaisa is a vestal votaress— Pericles, in fact, calls her a "nun" (15).

Thaisa is filled with wonder at the awesome quality of the events, and she enumerates the primary tokens of romance in her question to her husband: "Did you not name a tempest, / A birth and death?" (5.3.33–34). Like Leontes in *The Winter's Tale*, Pericles insists on kissing her to seal their new union:

> You shall do well
> That on the touching of her lips I may
> Melt and no more be seen. O come, be buried
> A second time within these arms. (40–43)

We are given to believe that death can be redeemed in resurrection. We also have the amusing graphic detail that the wild-looking Pericles will now cut his hair and beard and "clip to form . . . what this fourteen years no razor touched" (73–74).

Pericles' reunion with his daughter, Marina, is even fuller and more lyrical than his encounter with Thaisa, and it is written with strong awareness of King Lear's ecstatic recognition scene with Cordelia of a few years earlier (which probably relies on Titus Andronicus's relation with his maimed daughter, Lavinia). Pericles' touching scene with Marina in act 5 undoes the frightening incest of Antiochus and his daughter in the opening scene of act 1. Pericles moralizes on the hideous atrocity: "And both like serpents are, who though they feed / On sweetest flowers, yet they poison breed" (1.1.133–34). Pericles' wanderings at sea begin with his flight from the loathsome Antiochus and his daughter.

In act 5, the distraught Pericles is still wandering at sea. His ship docks off the coast of Mytilene, and he is within, in a deep depression, unkempt, and clad in sackcloth. He has spoken to no one for three months after he has learned of the supposed death of his daughter, Marina, and he has eaten only to prolong his grief. Lysimachus, the governor of Mytilene, sends Marina to cure him, as Helena goes to cure the King's fistula in *All's Well That Ends Well*:

> She questionless, with her sweet harmony,
> And other chosen attractions, would allure,
> And make a batt'ry through his deafened ports . . . (5.1.44–46)

Marina's narration is touching, particularly when she challenges her father that she "hath endured a grief / Might equal yours" (5.1.89–90). From wildly inarticulate beginnings—"Hum, ha!" (85)—Pericles begins to speak in perfectly formed iambic pentameter about the resemblance of Marina to his dead wife: she has "my queen's square brows" (110). This is an odd detail and Pericles goes on to echo a line from *Antony and Cleopatra*: "Who starves the ears she feeds, and makes them hungry / The more she gives them speech" (114–15). In Enobarbus's report, Cleopatra "makes hungry / Where most she satisfies" (*Antony and Cleopatra* 2.2.239–40).

Pericles is full of admiration at the wonderful turns of Fortune, and he can hardly believe the miracle that his dead daughter has been restored to him: "But are you flesh and blood? / Have you a working pulse, and are no fairy? / Motion as well?" (5.1.155–57). It is "the rarest dream that e'er dulled sleep / Did mock sad fools withal" (164–65). The purpose of the scene, then, and of Pericles' endless questions, is to establish that Marina is a living, breathing human being. He moves toward an ecstasy that he fears will cost him his life, which is why he asks Helicanus to strike him:

> Give me a gash, put me to present pain;
> Lest this great sea of joys rushing upon me
> O'erbear the shores of my mortality,
> And drown me with their sweetness. (194–97)

The sea, which has played such a baleful role in the romance, is now "this great sea of joys," and Pericles is being restored to the very life he rejected. The essence of the romance is in the line "Thou that beget'st him that did thee beget" (5.1.198), which insists on the perfect continuity and circularity of family life. Like Lear, at the end of the scene Pericles calls for "fresh garments" (217), and he falls asleep to what he takes to be the music of the spheres. It is at this point that the goddess Diana appears to him in a vision and bids him go to her temple at Ephesus, where he will encounter his supposedly dead wife, Thaisa. Gods and goddesses appear freely in Shakespeare's late romances, and scenes seem to come directly out of masques and courtly entertainments.

The brothel scenes in Mytilene are among the bawdiest—or at least the most professionally sexual—in Shakespeare and go far beyond what we are offered in *Measure for Measure* of Mistress Overdone, Pompey, and the promiscuity of Vienna. These scenes are strangely different from the remote and romantic atmosphere of the rest of *Pericles*. The Pander and his wife, the Bawd, are very specific about their economic situation and speak matter-of-factly about sexual matters without any erotic overtones. Like good businesspeople, they send their servant Boult to market to buy women: "We lost too much money this mart by being too wenchless" (4.2.4–5). This is the only occurrence of the word *wenchless* in Shakespeare, if not in the English language (the OED lists only this example).

We learn some alarming details about the brothel in Mytilene: "The poor Transylvanian is dead that lay with the little baggage" (4.2.22–23). We never hear anything further about the poor deceased Transylvanian, who is the only Transylvanian mentioned in Shakespeare. This is also the last we hear about the little baggage, who, we are told, "quickly pooped him; she made him roast meat for worms" (24–25). Despite what lexicographers say, *pooped* is surprisingly like the contemporary American slang word for *exhausted*.

Marina is purchased as a virgin from the Pirates who have abducted her from Tharsus (and thus saved her from being murdered by Leonine), and buoys up the hopes of the brothel. Boult expresses his enthusiasm in an odd image: "I warrant you, mistress, thunder shall not so awake the beds of eels as my giving out her beauty stirs up the lewdly inclined" (4.2.149–51). That eels were disturbed by thunder seems to have been proverbial, but the reasons are difficult to trace. Perhaps eels are sensitive to the electrical and auditory stimulation of thunder and lightning. At the end of this scene, Marina prays to Diana, the goddess of chastity, to keep "Untied" her "virgin knot" (155). One would expect, at least in terms of imagery, that she would pray to keep her virgin knot tied.

Marina's function in the brothel is, to say the least, disappointing to the Pander and his Bawd, who are remarkably tolerant of her marring their business. She plays a homiletic role in converting her prospective clients. The First Gentleman who exits from the brothel is amazed "to have divinity preached there" (4.5.4) and affirms that he is "out of the road of rutting forever" (9). The Bawd sees, rightly, that Marina "would make a puritan of the devil, if he should cheapen a kiss of her" (4.6.9–10), and she begs her to abandon her "virginal fencing" (60). To the Bawd, Marina hardly seems a heavenly inspired creature, but is rather a cunning girl who is playing the angles.

These brothel scenes are filled with amusing commercial details—for example, when Boult places a comparative value on chastity: "your peevish chastity, which is not worth a breakfast in the cheapest country under the cope" (4.6.128–30). From here it is just a quick step to figure out the value of chastity in 1607 measured against the cost of breakfast in the cheapest country in the world. Marina's conversion of Lysimachus through her oratory is fully conceivable, but her conversion of Boult himself is well nigh miraculous: "For what thou professest a baboon, could he speak, / Would own a name too dear" (183–84). Throughout these brothel scenes, the language and the imagery are unusually pungent. They are hardly romantic at all.

Music plays an unusually large role in *Pericles* and in all Shakespeare's late romances. When Pericles is at the court of Simonides in Pentapolis and wooing his daughter, he is represented to be "music's master" (2.5.30). Simonides is much beholden to him "For your sweet music this last night" (26). Among Marina's accomplishments is singing to the lute, which, Gower reports, "made the night-bird [=nightingale] mute" (prol. 4,26), and in the reunion with her father, Marina begins by singing a song (5.1.81 s.d.). Music is an important aspect of the ceremony by which Cerimon revives Thaisa: "The still and woeful music that we have, / Cause it to sound" (3.2.89–90). The music has therapeutic value—"The viol once more! How thou stirr'st, thou block!" (91)—as if the musical instrument, which is only a block of wood, is itself coming alive and setting an example for Thaisa. In a few lines Cerimon announces that "a warmth / Breathes out of her" (94–95). In the same way music is used to recall the old King Lear from madness (4.7.25) and to bring the statue of Hermione to life in *The Winter's Tale*: "Music, awake her: strike" (5.3.98).

Most significantly, music is used in the reunion of Pericles and Marina. He seems to hear the music of the spheres that only angelic beings are aware of, that is, the music made, according to the Ptolemaic system, by the heavenly bodies in their circular revolution around the earth. Pericles is definitely tuned in to this heavenly music when he says: "But hark, what music?" (5.1.226) and again: "But what music?" (229), and we in the audience are, too. Presumably, no other character on stage hears these "Rarest sounds" (234), which are taken as a sign of Pericles' total exhaustion. He moves easily from music into sleep:

> I hear most heavenly music.
> It nips me unto list'ning, and thick slumber
> Hangs upon mine eyes. Let me rest. (235–37)

This is the only use of *nips* in this sense in Shakespeare, and it suggests that one doesn't choose voluntarily to listen to the music of the spheres, but that one is drawn into the experience by a kind of magical adherence.

Cymbeline

Cymbeline has the most complex plot in Shakespeare. In the final scene no less than twenty-five knots in the plot are untied. Is this something intrinsically good, or do we have a sense of overloading and excess? It does seem too much to ask of a reader or a spectator that Imogen should mistake the headless corpse of Cloten for her beloved husband Posthumus and address him with tender distraction: "O Posthumus, alas, / Where is thy head? Where's that? Ay me, where's that?" (4.2.320–21). And, in the last scene, we are expected to believe that Posthumus, grieving for Imogen, should strike down Fidele, the page of Lucius, who is actually Imogen in disguise. As Pisanio, the faithful servant of Posthumus, exclaims: "O my lord Posthumus, / You ne'er killed Imogen till now" (5.5.230–31).

These details are extravagant but not uncharacteristic of the play as an endless romance, weaving its complications without much regard for probability and psychological truth. We are strongly aware of the fictionality of Cymbeline, as this might impinge on an understanding of its characters and situations. The action in ancient Britain at about the time of Christ is exceedingly remote, more so even than the comparable action in *King Lear*. *Cymbeline* is based in part on Holinshed's *Chronicles*, the same source that Shakespeare used in the English history plays, but it is hardly historical. Nor is the play much of a tragedy, despite the fact that it was the last play in the tragedies section of the First Folio, and, in fact, the last play in the book.

Cymbeline is clearly intended as a romantic tragicomedy, with all the implications of the new genre for titillating its audience with dire events. Only Cloten, who as richly deserves his fate as Oswald in *King Lear*, suffers decapitation, but everyone else is revealed, restored, transformed, reunited, and pardoned at the end, except, of course, the witchlike Queen, Cloten's mother, who, "With horror, madly dying, like her life" (5.5.31), confesses all. The happy ending is prepared in the preceding scene, when the god Jupiter *"descends in thunder and lightning, sitting upon an eagle"* (5.4.62 s.d.) to announce to the complaining Ghosts of Posthumus's family that all will be well. Jupiter speaks pedagogically and defensively as he justifies the ways of God to man:

> Whom best I love I cross; to make my gift,
>   The more delayed, delighted. Be content.
> Your low-laid son our godhead will uplift;
>   His comforts thrive, his trials well are spent. (71–74)

This sounds like Prospero stage-managing the romance of Ferdinand and Miranda:

> But this swift business
> I must uneasy make, lest too light winning
> Make the prize light. (*The Tempest* 1.2.451–53)

One of the main purposes of the theophany in act 5, scene 4 is to cheer up the despairing Posthumus and to announce the happy ending of romance. All will be well, and the excessive, heraldic specifications of the oracle that Posthumus reads when he awakens will be fulfilled to the last tittle. The Soothsayer, Philharmonus, does a Derridean turn on the hidden etymology of the oracle at the end of the play:

Thou, Leonatus, art the lion's whelp;
The fit and apt construction of thy name,
Being *Leo-natus*, doth import so much.—
The piece of tender air, thy virtuous daughter,
Which we call *mollis aer* [= tender air], and *mollis aer*
We term it *mulier* [= woman].—Which *mulier* I divine
Is thy most constant wife . . . (5.5.443–48)

This is perhaps an amusing, self-conscious comment on the Byzantine elaborations of the plot, which are all justified and rectified in the final epiphany.

In an echo from *As You Like It*, the pastoralism of Belarius, Guiderius, and Arviragus is celebrated in *Cymbeline*. They are mountaineers and hunters rather than shepherds, but the assumptions are the same. Belarius is a banished courtier, who stole Guiderius and Arviragus, the sons of Cymbeline, when they were infants. They have been raised in the wilderness, but their inherent nobility manifests itself despite their upbringing. This is an important idea in romance.

Although Belarius attacks the corruption of the court, the royal sons complain of the limitations of the life of nature. Like Orlando in *As You Like It*, Arviragus is aware of his cultural deprivation:

When we shall hear
The rain and wind beat dark December, how
In this our pinching cave shall we discourse
The freezing hours away? We have seen nothing.
We are beastly . . . (3.3.36–40)

Belarius concludes from this conversation: "How hard it is to hide the sparks of nature!" (79). The boys speak intuitively from their royal birth, not "meanly":

their thoughts do hit
The roofs of palaces, and Nature prompts them
In simple and low things to prince it much . . . (83–85)

That is why Caliban, by contrast, is "A devil, a born devil, on whose nature / Nurture can never stick" (*The Tempest* 4.1.188–89). Belarius

333

sounds like Prospero on educational topics, emphasizing that royal blood will manifest itself despite environment. He wonders how it is possible that "an invisible instinct should frame them [Guiderius and Arviragus]/To royalty unlearned, honor untaught" (4.2.177–78). Natural instincts are always right.

The most successful character in *Cymbeline* is, without doubt, Iachimo. Although he is developed within a narrow range, Shakespeare seems to have perfect control of his movement. Despite the name he is unlike Iago, even though he echoes Iago's insinuating style. At the end of the play, much is done to make Iachimo seem an Italianate, Machiavellian villain. Posthumus calls him "Italian fiend" (5.5.210), and Iachimo himself, in the confessional mode, boasts that his "Italian brain / Gan in your duller Britain operate / Most vilely" (196–98). It is curiously anachronistic, not at all uncharacteristic of romance, that Iachimo is a Renaissance Italian courtier in a play consciously set in ancient Britain at about the beginning of the Christian era, and the Rome in the play is imagined at around the time of Julius Caesar. But Iachimo is hardly diabolical. He plays the folktale wager for all it is worth in order to win, but he is not thought to be allied with the devil, unlike other Shakespearean villains.

The wager is entirely directed against Posthumus's macho bragging and has little to do with Imogen herself. Iachimo is courtly if not suave, but he enters into the wager fairly and bets the much larger sum of ten thousand ducats against Posthumus's ring. It is a sporting engagement. Iachimo may have a cynical opinion of women's virtue, but Posthumus is foolishly idealistic. From the beginning, Iachimo shows himself a polished courtier, who makes his wager "rather against your confidence than her reputation" and is willing to make the same bet "against any lady in the world" (1.4.116–19). In terms of folklore, we are sure, from reading medieval and Renaissance stories of the testing of a wife or mistress, that Posthumus is certain to lose.

Iachimo first tries to seduce Imogen, but when he fails, he emerges surreptitiously from the trunk to collect incriminating details. He is more interested in winning the wager than in enjoying Imogen, which endows the entire proceeding with a homoerotic cast. The whole matter is an affair between men in which women are only the bait. In his wooing of Imogen, Iachimo's discourse is so overloaded,

so overrich, so excessive and bejewelled that it is hardly connected
with sexual desire at all. It is basically designed to calumniate Posthumus so that Imogen can take her revenge by yielding to Iachimo. But
Imogen cannot follow Iachimo's intricate rhetoric of seduction: "I
pray you, sir, / Deliver with more openness your answers / To my
demands" (1.6.87–89). Like Iago, Iachimo insinuates all sorts of
possibilities for a perfidious Posthumus, but it is so hypothetical that
Imogen is not convinced.

Notice how quickly Iachimo begins his prepared discourse. By his
second speech he is already asking insidious questions: "What, are
men mad?" (1.6.32). Can they not distinguish " 'Twixt fair and foul?"
(38). Iachimo's portrait of Posthumus seems entirely lost on the
innocent Imogen:

> The cloyèd will—
> That satiate yet unsatisfied desire, that tub
> Both filled and running—ravening first the lamb,
> Longs after for the garbage. (47–50)

Imogen, the "lamb," cannot grasp that Posthumus, like Gertrude in
Hamlet, will "prey on garbage" (*Hamlet* 1.5.57). Iachimo finally has to
abandon seduction entirely and pretend that he was just testing
Imogen, who remains "chaffless" (1.6.178) to his fanning or winnowing.

The scene in which Iachimo emerges from the trunk while Imogen
is sleeping is the most exciting in the play, but it represents a fallback
position for Iachimo, who knows that Imogen is unassailable but who
doesn't want to lose the wager. This scene echoes others in Shakespeare. Iachimo, for example, is like Othello in act 5, scene 2, who
comes to murder the sleeping Desdemona in her bed. Iachimo's
"That I might touch! / But kiss, one kiss!" (2.2.16–17) reflects Othello's "I'll smell thee on the tree" (*Othello* 5.2.15) as he kisses Desdemona three times, just as Iachimo's concern with Imogen's breath—
" 'Tis her breathing that / Perfumes the chamber thus" (2.2.18–19)—
picks up Othello's "O balmy breath, that dost almost persuade /
Justice to break her sword" (*Othello* 5.2.16–17).

Imogen has been reading the tale of Tereus in Ovid's *Metamorphoses*—"Here the leaf's turned down / Where Philomel gave up"

(2.2.45–46)—like Lavinia in *Titus Andronicus*, but the mute and hand-less Lavinia uses the book and her staff to accuse Chiron and Deme-trius. Iachimo is conscious of "Tarquin's ravishing strides" (*Macbeth* 2.1.55) as he himself "Did softly press the rushes ere he wakened / The chastity he wounded" (2.2.13–14), which is the subject of *The Rape of Lucrece*. Collatine in that poem is like Posthumus in boasting of his wife's beauty to Tarquin. To complete our catalogue of echoes, Imogen will "Fold down the leaf" (2.2.4) where she has stopped reading, just as Brutus, before the appearance of Caesar's Ghost, asks: "is not the leaf turned down / Where I left reading?" (*Julius Caesar* 4.3.270–71). Also, the bracelet Iachimo takes from Imogen's arm is a fatal love token like the handkerchief in *Othello*.

Iachimo has plenty of "ocular proof" (*Othello* 3.3.257) when he encounters Posthumus in Rome in act 2, scene 4 to collect on his wager. Like a whole series of jealous husbands in Shakespeare—Othello, Leontes, Ford, Claudio—Posthumus is too ready to believe anything that Iachimo has to say. In fact, Iachimo puts him off so that he can enjoy the full satisfaction of his supposed triumph; he doesn't want his performance interrupted by Posthumus's too sudden capitulation. Again, the details relate to Iachimo's triumph over Posthumus rather than over Imogen: "Your lady being so easy" (2.4.47) has the emphasis on *Your* rather than *lady*. Unlike Iago, Iachimo revels in the aesthetic frisson of the naked Imogen in her bed. He is a consummate peeping Tom, which is the voyeuristic point of the whole scene:

> On her left breast
> A mole cinque-spotted, like the crimson drops
> I' th' bottom of a cowslip. (2.2.37–39)

Ars gratia artis. It is interesting that in the earlier scene, Iachimo already seems to be talking to Posthumus as well as to himself, which is why he doesn't want the literal scene with Posthumus to end too quickly.

In act 2, scene 4 Iachimo expatiates fully and imaginatively on the scene he has witnessed in Imogen's bedchamber, and we don't know for sure whether Iachimo invents some of the rich details of interior decoration, although a scene designer is more or less obligated to put everything Iachimo talks about into the setting. Iachimo begins with a detail from *Antony and Cleopatra*, which mimics Enobarbus's report on Antony's first meeting with Cleopatra on the river Cydnus. Imogen's bedchamber

> was hanged
> With tapestry of silk and silver; the story
> Proud Cleopatra, when she met her Roman
> And Cydnus swelled above the banks, or for
> The press of boats or pride . . . (68–72)

Imogen may be Cleopatra, but the Roman Antony she meets is Iachimo rather than the Briton Posthumus. Iachimo elaborates on all the erotic detail of the goddess Diana on the chimney-piece and the two winking Cupids of silver on the andirons, as if Imogen can only be imagined as being herself a work of art.

Iachimo has stolen Imogen's bracelet, but he represents her as giving it to him in the seductive language of Cressida giving Diomed Troilus's sleeve in *Troilus and Cressida* (5,2):

> She stripped it from her arm; I see her yet.
> Her pretty action did outsell her gift,
> And yet enriched it too. She gave it me and said
> She prized it once. (2.4.101–4)

Iachimo has a vivid, visual imagination and he evokes dramatic scenes that have not, of course, occurred, but Posthumus is impressed.

Iachimo's crowning touch is the "mole cinque-spotted" (2.2.38) that he has observed on Imogen's breast. This image is now developed with lustful fullness:

> under her breast—
> Worthy the pressing—lies a mole, right proud
> Of that most delicate lodging. By my life,
> I kissed it, and it gave me present hunger
> To feed again, though full. You do remember
> This stain upon her? (2.4.134–39)

Iachimo again recalls Cleopatra, who "makes hungry / Where most she satisfies" (*Antony and Cleopatra* 2.2.239–40). Posthumus, convinced before, is now in a paroxysm of misogynistic grief, and the stain of Imogen's mole "doth confirm / Another stain, as big as hell can hold, / Were there no more but it" (2.4.139–41).

The next scene (3,5) is a long, antifeminist soliloquy of Posthumus in which he inveighs against all women in a style reminiscent of the mad King Lear: "But to the girdle do the gods inherit, / Beneath is all the fiend's" (*King Lear* 4.6.126–27). He remembers both his mother and his wife as counterfeits. The innocent Imogen in the past tried to mollify Posthumus's furious sexual appetite, which we never hear about, but now it is aroused by images of Iachimo's carnality:

> Me of my lawful pleasure she restrained
> And prayed me oft forbearance—did it with
> A pudency so rosy, the sweet view on't
> Might well have warmed old Saturn—that I thought her
> As chaste as unsunned snow. (2.5.9–13)

Rosy pudency and chastity like "unsunned snow" are powerful images we have of Imogen throughout the play—she is the romantic heroine par excellence.

But now "This yellow Iachimo" (2.5.14) has canceled all chaste thoughts. Yellow is a color strongly associated with Malvolio in *Twelfth Night* and his yellow stockings, but it also connotes natural decay, as in "the sear, the yellow leaf" in *Macbeth* (5.3.23). Posthumus imagines Iachimo, as Hamlet fantasizes Claudius, as a bestial superstud:

> This yellow Iachimo in an hour, was't not?
> Or less? At first? Perchance he spoke not, but,
> Like a full-acorned boar, a German one,
> Cried "O!" and mounted . . . (2.5.14–17)

In his misogynistic hysteria, Posthumus imagines his own sexuality suppressed by the "woman's part" (20) in him and "All faults that have a name, nay, that hell knows, / Why, hers, in part or all, but rather all" (27–28). This is a low point for Posthumus in the play.

Imogen resembles the other young heroines of romance, such as Marina, Perdita, and Miranda. They are all star-struck, innocent, lyrical, yet resourceful young women who understand the over-

whelming power of love. Iachimo knows immediately upon seeing
Imogen that she cannot be seduced:

> If she be furnished with a mind so rare,
> She is alone th' Arabian bird, and I
> Have lost the wager. (1.6.16–18)

The phoenix is a perfect symbol for Imogen, as in Shakespeare's
poem *The Phoenix and the Turtle*. It is a legendary bird associated with
immortality. Only one phoenix exists at any one time, and when it
dies, it flies to Arabia and builds a nest of spices, which it sets on
fire; from its ashes a new phoenix arises.

Imogen in love speaks in a highly metaphoric and free blank verse
that follows the breathless interruptions of thought, as in her speech
to Pisanio:

> Then, true Pisanio,
> Who long'st like me to see thy lord, who long'st—
> O, let me bate—but not like me, yet long'st,
> But in a fainter kind—O, not like me!
> For mine's beyond beyond: say, and speak thick—
> Love's counselor should fill the bores of hearing,
> To th' smothering of the sense—how far it is
> To this same blessèd Milford. (3.2.53–60)

This turns out to be a simple request for directions and for distance.
I quote the sentence in full in order to give an idea of the new kind
of romantic speech that Shakespeare is devising for his heroines.
Unlike Viola, Rosalind, and Beatrice, Imogen is not witty but adora-
tional, and her image of "beyond beyond" thrusts at an infinity of
wishes and aspirations. She seems ideally girllike and much younger
than the heroines of Shakespeare's earlier comedies.

When Imogen learns that she has been rejected by Posthumus,
who wants to kill her through Pisanio, her reaction is like Desdemona's. She cannot believe what is happening to her, yet she seems
more defenseless than Desdemona because the entire action of *Cymbeline*
is much more fictional and much less rooted in psychological probability than that of *Othello*. Imogen seems like a child betrayed by her
dreams, yet we are sure, by the inevitable workings of tragicomedy,

339

that all mistakings will be resolved in the happy ending, which is an assurance we definitely don't have in *Othello*.

Imogen asks a series of incredulous questions that are tender and touching:

> False to his bed? What is it to be false?
> To lie in watch there and to think on him?
> To weep 'twixt clock and clock? If sleep charge nature,
> To break it with a fearful dream of him
> And cry myself awake? That's false to's bed, is it? (3.4.41–45)

The rhythm of the last question is wonderfully colloquial, and we are made to believe that Imogen has no idea at all of what it means to be false. She is cut adrift by her sorrows. Her transformation into the boy Fidele at the end of this scene offers her some solace from her griefs as Imogen, as she prepares to undertake a new and active role in the mountains of Wales. Her mock death in act 4, scene 2 allows her to be reborn in a new role.

The Winter's Tale

The structure of *The Winter's Tale* is odd. Like the sonata form, it is in three distinct parts. The first and longest part takes up acts 1 and 2 and the first two scenes of act 3. All this is set in Sicilia, mostly at the court of Leontes. Act 3, scene 3 shifts to the seacoast of Bohemia—Ben Jonson made fun of Shakespeare for this topographical gaffe—and the action remains in Bohemia during act 4. Meanwhile, there is a sixteen-year gap in the action, announced by Time, the Chorus, who functions like Gower in *Pericles*. Act 5 returns to Sicilia and the court of Leontes, and it is a kind of recapitulation sixteen years later. In Act 5 we see a contrite and repentant Leontes, presiding over a highly romantic action of wonder, the marvelous, restoration, and rebirth. Time is both a destroyer and a healer, which has the power to reconstruct most of the reality broken in the first part.

In the transitional scene of act 3, scene 3, the old counselor Antigonus is eaten by a bear, but his prize, the newborn Perdita, is discovered alive by the old Shepherd, who says to his son, announcing the theme of romance, "thou met'st with things dying, I with things new born" (112–13). It is a romantic assumption that almost nothing is irrecoverably lost. *The Winter's Tale* imitates the double recovery of wife and daughter in *Pericles*, but it concentrates on the revival of Hermione, who dies definitively in Shakespeare's principal source, Robert Greene's *Pandosto* (1588).

The Winter's Tale turns on the fiction of an old tale told in winter, around the fire, perhaps a ghost story, and always in a supernatural, folkloric tone. This is the frame of *The Old Wives' Tale* (1590) by George Peele, and it is explicitly the story that Mamillius, the son of Leontes, is about to tell before he is abruptly taken away by his father: "A sad tale's best for winter; I have one / Of sprites and goblins" (2.1.25–26). All we hear of the tale—and Shakespeare may have had a specific story in mind—is: "There was a man. . . Dwelt by a churchyard" (29–30). This "winter's tale" colors our understanding of the first part of the play, as Mamillius gradually pines away and dies. The whole play is bittersweet, as a romantic tragicomedy should be.

In the last part of *The Winter's Tale*, the events of restoration are all spoken of as an old tale, which, despite probability, now turn out to be true, as if fiction were being converted into reality. The Second Gentleman reports that the oracle is fulfilled and "This news, which is called true, is so like an old tale that the verity of it is in strong suspicion" (5.2.29–31). The Third Gentleman tells his news of Antigonus: "Like an old tale still, which will have matter to rehearse, though credit be asleep, and not an ear open: he was torn to pieces with a bear" (65–68). Thus the events of the play are recalled as if they were entirely fictional, or at least staggered belief. That Hermione is alive is the most incredible detail of all, as Paulina reports: "That she is living, / Were it but told you, should be hooted at / Like an old tale" (5.3.115–17). The narrative elements of *The Winter's Tale* are deliberately steeped in fiction, so that the wonder of the final scenes can be developed.

The dramatic effect of a winter's tale was already clearly laid out in *Richard II*, when the King as prisoner is being taken to the Tower and speaks tragically to his Queen:

> In winter's tedious nights sit by the fire
> With good old folks, and let them tell thee tales
> Of woeful ages long ago betid;

> And ere thou bid good night, to quite their griefs
> Tell thou the lamentable tale of me,
> And send the hearers weeping to their beds.
> (*Richard II* 5.1.40–45)

Mamillius's sad winter's tale is reversed in Shakespeare's play, and the old tale has an unexpectedly happy ending. The foreboding winter mood is lightened, as it is at the end of *Love's Labor's Lost*, when Hiems, or Winter, represented by the owl, sings " 'Tu-whit, / Tu-who!' a merry note" (5.2.914–15).

The jealousy of Leontes echoes the jealousy of Othello, but in some fundamental way it is entirely different. Leontes' jealousy is self-created, and Shakespeare scrupulously avoids giving it any cause—even superficial, rationalizing causes like those cited by Iago. It comes over Leontes suddenly, like a dark cloud, without any psychological development or preparation. Therefore I will not suggest reasons for Leontes' jealousy—there are none—but merely speak about the symbolic context, especially the idea of loss of innocence. The jealousy bursts out in Leontes' aside, "Too hot, too hot!" (1.2.108). Before this, we have a gracious social scene between Leontes and his sworn brother, Polixenes, whom he is trying to persuade to prolong his stay in Sicilia, but when he cannot, he gives the argument over to Hermione, his wife, whom Polixenes cannot refuse. The play opens with a low-key conversation between Camillo, the chief adviser of Leontes, and Archidamus, a lord of Bohemia, who is a confidant of Polixenes. We have then a little more than 150 lines in the first two scenes before the sudden explosion of Leontes' jealousy. What kind of context do these lines establish?

The first scene of the play notes the close friendship between Leontes and Polixenes (or Sicilia and Bohemia, as they are called here). Camillo reports: "They were trained together in their childhoods; and there rooted betwixt them then such an affection, which cannot choose but branch [= flourish] now" (1.1.23–25). Although they are separated by their different kingdoms, they make symbolic gestures to confirm the bond between them: "their encounters, though not personal, have been royally attorneyed with interchange of gifts, letters, loving embassies" (27–30). In this way they annihilate distance: "they have seemed to be together, though absent: shook hands, as over a vast; and embraced as it were from the ends of opposed winds" (30–32). All these hyperbolic assertions of friendship and unity suggest that they are too extreme to be maintained. This is the point of comedy: to challenge superlatives.

Leontes and Polixenes in the next scene enact the expectations of Camillo and Archidamus, and again we feel the perils of such a devoted and unexampled friendship. There is a curious coincidence between the nine months of Polixenes' stay in Sicilia and the advanced pregnancy of Hermione, who appears in this scene as a mother about to give birth. Leontes later makes this link specific. Another connection is with the sons of Leontes and Polixenes, who are mentioned often before Leontes' rage manifests itself. Talk of the children leads Hermione naturally to speak of Leontes and Polixenes when they were boys:

> Come, I'll question you
> Of my lord's tricks, and yours, when you were boys:
> You were pretty lordings then? (1.2.60–62)

This evokes a nostalgic response in Polixenes about the loss of childhood:

> Two lads that thought there was no more behind
> But such a day tomorrow as today,
> And to be boy eternal. (63–65)

Polixenes remembers this time as paradisal in the Wordsworthian sense of the Immortality Ode:

> We were as twinned lambs, that did frisk i' th' sun,
> And bleat the one at th' other; what we changed
> Was innocence for innocence; we knew not
> The doctrine of ill-doing, nor dreamed
> That any did . . . (1.2.67–71)

The lamb is the supremely innocent animal in Christian symbolism as well as in the pastoral, and the children exchange innocence for innocence as if the doctrine of Original Sin did not exist and man were not tainted at birth. Polixenes follows up a specifically Christian point:

> had we pursued that life,
> And our weak spirits ne'er been higher reared
> With stronger blood, we should have answered heaven
> Boldly, "not guilty"; the imposition cleared,
> Hereditary ours. (71–75)

This is a strongly doctrinal statement, which assumes that Original Sin only enters at some point beyond childhood through the operations of sexuality ("stronger blood").

Hermione picks up the sexual suggestion, which implies a reenactment of the fall: "By this we gather / You have tripped since" (1.2.75–76). She speaks wittily, like Polixenes, with an assured sense of social grace beyond any improprieties, but Leontes is silent, and, presumably for an actor, his jealous rage is brewing. Hermione understands intuitively what Polixenes is saying and what its moral implication is because, logically, she and Polixenes' queen have corrupted their totally innocent mates, and the husbands could claim: "Your queen and I are devils" (82). Hermione is still speaking in a bantering tone to match the gracious account of Polixenes, but Leontes changes the subject, which must be painful to him, and continues with husbandly flattery. We are soon shocked by his peremptory aside: "Too hot, too hot!" (108).

The innocence of the newborn babe once more enters into Hermione's trial scene. She too would like to proclaim the baby "Not guilty" (3.2.25) as Polixenes and Leontes did when they were infants (1.2.74)—the two phrases echo each other across the first part of the play. In this homicidal atmosphere, her newborn daughter "is from my breast, / The innocent milk in it most innocent mouth, / Haled out to murder" (3.2.97–99). Leontes' tyranny is represented by the slaughter of the innocents. One of the stipulations of the oracle is that Leontes' "innocent babe" is "truly begotten" (132). The play turns on innocence and guilt and their implications for fathers, mothers, and children. Shakespeare's romances are particularly preoccupied with the fate of children and the absolute necessity to reunite families. Unlike the earlier comedies, which end in marriages, Shakespeare's romances end in the restoration of what has been lost or thought dead, and the reconstitution of families, especially the wonderful reunion of fathers and daughters.

One of the oddest lines in the trial scene is Hermione's claim on Leontes' oneiric powers:

> Sir,
> You speak a language that I understand not.
> My life stands in the level of your dreams,
> Which I'll lay down. (3.2.77–80)

Leontes' dreams are like the "murd'ring piece" spoken of by Claudius in *Hamlet*, which gives him "superfluous death" (*Hamlet* 4.5.96–97). The dreams are an instrument of destruction, and they identify the fantasy aspect of Leontes' tyranny as they do of the sleepless Macbeth. Leontes answers significantly: "Your actions are my dreams" (3.2.80). Is this an acknowledgment, sixty lines before, that Leontes must surrender his fantasies about Hermione, what Paulina calls his "dangerous, unsafe lunes" (2.2.29), or mad fits? Does Leontes mean that he has only dreamt about Hermione's actions but that dreams and reality are now equated? In this psychological quirk, the oppressive nature of tyranny, born out of excessive love mingled with guilt, is clearly shown.

In his mad jealousy, Leontes is highly characterized by his repetitions, just as Shylock is in his first scene in *The Merchant of Venice*. It is as if Leontes' passion is so intense that he can no longer curb his words to reasonable expectations:

> Too hot, too hot!
> To mingle friendship far is mingling bloods.
> I have tremor cordis on me; my heart dances,
> But not for joy, not joy. (1.2.108–11)

What has pumped Leontes up to this intensity of rage? In *Othello* we can attribute the protagonist's change of style to the influence of Iago, whose grossness and broken, insinuating discourse is catching, but in *The Winter's Tale* Leontes serves as his own tempter and betrayer. His mind is overflowing with a kind of pernicious lava.

One way of understanding Leontes is to say that he is extremely histrionic. He suddenly sees reality as if it were a play and he himself an actor, probably a bad one, as Macbeth postulates: "a poor player / That struts and frets his hour upon the stage" (*Macbeth* 5.5.24–25). In the midst of his interwoven repetitions, Leontes arrives at the truth of his histrionic image:

> Go play, boy, play: thy mother plays, and I
> Play too—but so disgraced a part, whose issue
> Will hiss me to my grave . . . (1.2.187–88)

It is interesting that Shakespeare always uses the acting image in a negative way to indicate counterfeiting, deceit, and deception. Leontes stands self-accused in much of his discourse.

In his violent image of the spider in the cup, it is one's knowledge that is self-destructive. Just as the unknowing cuckold partakes of no venom, "for his knowledge / Is not infected" (2.1.41–42), so the drinker. But

> if one present
> Th' abhorred ingredient to his eye, make known
> How he hath drunk, he cracks his gorge, his sides,
> With violent hefts. I have drunk, and seen the spider. (42–45)

Leontes wallows in his own histrionic self-knowledge. He is the most paranoid protagonist in Shakespeare, at least in the first part of the play.

The great Renaissance theme of Art versus Nature figures largely in *The Winter's Tale*, as it does in all Shakespeare's romances. Art is the application of human agency, imagination, learning, and effort to what is given by Nature, but the debate is complicated by the idea that Art perfects Nature and makes what is natural even more natural-seeming through the intervention of human ingenuity and the aesthetic sense. Thus, in cosmetics, which was often at the center of this debate, the natural look of freshness and innocence is achieved with the help of art to remove any natural imperfections. The issues are directly addressed in the Sheep-shearing Scene, in which Perdita refuses to "put / The dibble in earth" (4.4.99–100) to plant any streaked, painted, or pied flowers like "gillyvors" (82) or pinks. They are called "Nature's bastards" (83) because they are the product of art rather than nature, that is, presumably, of cross-breeding and the perfectibility of the horticultural imagination. As Perdita explains, "There is an art, which in their piedness shares / With great creating Nature" (87–88). Their "piedness," or spottedness, is for Perdita a product of human agency.

Polixenes, in disguise, makes an eloquent plea for the necessity of art to perfect nature:

> Yet Nature is made better by no mean
> But Nature makes that mean; so over that art,
> Which you say adds to Nature, is an art,
> That Nature makes. (4.4.89–92)

Grafting is "an art / Which does mend Nature, change it rather; but / The art itself is Nature" (95–97). Perdita remains unconvinced and connects gillyvors with painting, or cosmetics. Art introduces a false note.

The conflict between Art and Nature lies behind the final Statue Scene of *The Winter's Tale*. Paulina's art, like that of Cerimon in *Pericles*, has revived Hermione from the dead, and in this scene she comes alive again as a statue. It is an extraordinary transformation that we see before our eyes and one that we, as audience, were not prepared for, as we usually are by the workings of dramatic irony. We are meant to share Leontes' sense of wonder. Paulina plays on specific terms of art in a way that resembles *Timon of Athens*, in which an actual painter is one of the characters. Here Hermione is a stone statue, artfully polychromed, "newly performed by that rare Italian master, Julio Romano" (5.2.103–5). This is an intriguing anachronism, since Giulio Romano died in 1546 and was best known as a painter. We have no idea what Shakespeare knew of him or whether he had actually seen his works, but in this play he is invoked as a kind of magical artist, who, like Pygmalion, can sculpt statues of women who are so exactly imitated that they have the power to come alive. Throughout Shakespeare, excellence in painting and statuary is measured by its lifelike quality. As Paulina says, "prepare / To see the life as lively mocked, as ever / Still sleep mocked death" (5.3.18–20). In this art context, *lively* always means "lifelike," and the "mocking" of life is a literal reenactment of mimesis or imitation.

348

The key word here is *warm*. Leontes' first reaction is that Hermione is different from what she was, more wrinkled and aged, but Paulina praises "our carver's excellence, / Which lets go by some sixteen years, and makes her / As she lived now" (5.3.30–32). Leontes is comforted and returns to his former thoughts, rejecting the ravages of time:

> Oh, thus she stood,
> Even with such life of majesty—warm life,
> As now it coldly stands—when first I wooed her. (34–36)

The illusion of warm life gradually penetrates Leontes as he thinks that the statue breathes and that its veins "Did verily bear blood" (65). To Polixenes, it is "Masterly done! / The very life seems warm upon her lip" (65–66). Leontes wants to kiss the statue, punning significantly on the word *mock*: "Let no man mock me, / For I will kiss her" (79–80). Art mocks, or imitates, Nature, but it also mocks or ridicules our belief in a material world ruled by cause and effect— "we are mocked with art" (68), as Leontes says.

With a sure sense of dramatic effect, Paulina calls for solemn music as the statue moves and descends from its pedestal. Paulina speaks in lines that are extraordinary for their slowness and multiplicity of caesuras: "Music, awake her: strike. / 'Tis time; descend; be stone no more; approach" (5.3.98–99). Again, we have the contrast between cold stone and warm life, which Leontes acknowledges with his exclamation: "Oh, she's warm!" (109). The scene quickly concludes with this effect of wonder, the marvelous, and the redemption of life. Paulina's practical explanations are put off to some mythical time in the future after the play is done.

The Tempest

he Tempest depends greatly on magic. This is Prospero's "art" that he has learned so assiduously from books. Book learning has cost Prospero his dukedom, as he explains laboriously to Miranda in the long exposition at the beginning of the play. He was so addicted to the study of the "liberal arts" that

> The government I cast upon my brother
> And to my state grew stranger, being transported
> And rapt in secret studies. (1.2.75–77)

"Secret studies" are magic, like the studies of Doctor Faustus, and Prospero's retirement from public life opens the way for his brother Antonio to usurp the dukedom and become "Absolute Milan" (109).

As a contemplative, Prospero recognizes that he neglected "worldly ends, all dedicated / To closeness and the bettering of my mind" (1.2.89–90). Antonio steps in, with the aid of Alonso, King of Naples, when he recognizes that for his brother "my library / Was dukedom large enough" (109–10). Therefore, when Prospero is set adrift with Miranda, the kindly Gonzalo

> Knowing I loved my books, he furnished me
> From mine own library with volumes that
> I prize above my dukedom. (166–68)

It is interesting that Peter Greenaway's new movie about *The Tempest* is called *Prospero's Books* (1991) and focuses on books of medieval and Renaissance learning that Prospero might have used.

Art is a key word for Prospero's kind of white, or benevolent, magic, theurgic magic, which depends upon the close study of the secrets of nature. Theurgy is opposed to goety or necromancy, the black magic that calls upon evil spirits or makes a compact with the devil. In Marlowe's *Doctor Faustus* (1592), we see Faustus passing at the beginning of the play from theurgic magic learned from books to goetic magic derived from selling his soul to the devil. Often there is a thin line between white and black magic, and Prospero is preoccupied with the dangers of his theurgy. The word *art* echoes in Prospero's exposition in act 1, scene 2. The tempest in the first scene, for example, is a product of Prospero's art, as Miranda says in her first lines: "If by your art, my dearest father, you have / Put the wild waters in this roar, allay them" (1–2). We soon see Prospero asking Miranda's help to pluck his "magic garment" from him, and when his robe is off he says: "Lie there, my art" (25). Through the "provision" of his "art" the tempest is "So safely ordered" (28–29) that no one has suffered any harm.

Ariel has "Performed, to point, the tempest" (1.2.194), and this idea that Prospero's art is like Shakespeare's in his ability to create shows, masques, and spectacles is repeated when he speaks about the masque of goddesses that he will present for the wedding of Ferdinand and Miranda. He speaks of it as an important promise that must interrupt all other action:

> I must
> Bestow upon the eyes of this young couple
> Some vanity of mine art. It is my promise,
> And they expect it from me. (4.1.39–42)

It is as if Prospero needs to show off his art for the benefit of his new son-in-law. He explains further that the actors are

> Spirits, which by mine art
> I have from their confines called to enact
> My present fancies. (120–22)

So we know that Prospero, like Glendower, "can call spirits from the vasty deep" (*1 Henry IV* 3.1.52). We also know that, unlike Glendower, he can force them to appear, as he does with the airy spirit Ariel.

Prospero's art goes beyond aesthetic effects and is represented in the play as potent and dangerous. He freed Ariel from the "cloven pine" (1.2.277) in which Sycorax, the mother of Caliban, confined him:

> It was mine art,
> When I arrived and heard thee, that made gape
> The pine, and let thee out. (291–93)

But he threatens to "rend an oak / And peg thee in his knotty entrails" (294–95) if Ariel continues to murmur about his freedom. Caliban knows that he must obey Prospero because he is omnipotent:

> His art is of such pow'r
> It would control my dam's god, Setebos,
> And make a vassal of him. (372–74)

Setebos is a god of the Patagonians that Shakespeare found in the voyage literature, specifically in the account of Magellan's voyage in Robert Eden's *History of Travaile* (1577). We know that Shakespeare also used various accounts of the Bermudas in conceiving his desert island in the Mediterranean between Sicily and Tunis.

In an important moment at the end of the play, Prospero gives up his art as he prepares to forgive his enemies and return to his dukedom in Milan. He reviews at length the marvelous deeds he has done in controlling nature, ending with:

> graves at my command
> Have waked their sleepers, oped, and let 'em forth
> By my so potent art. (5.1.48–50)

But this magical power may have dehumanized him, and he needs Ariel, who is only a spirit of the air, to remind him that his compassionate tears would run freely, like Gonzalo's, "were I human" (19). Prospero vows: "And mine shall" (20). Like Duke Vincentio at the end of *Measure for Measure,* he resolves on mercy and human kindness: "The rarer action is / In virtue than in vengeance" (27–28).

That is why Prospero's conclusion is so important: "But this rough magic / I here abjure" (50–51). He will put aside his magic robes, break his conjuring staff, and, most significant of all, he will get rid of the books on which his art depends: "And deeper than did ever plummet sound / I'll drown my book" (56–57). It is a ritual of simplification, like Antony's disarming at the end of *Antony and Cleopatra.* Once this purgation is accomplished, Prospero can return to his former life in Milan. He may now "want / Spirits to enforce, art to enchant," as he says in the epilogue, but he no longer needs his art.

Actors have always complained about the difficulty of playing Prospero and the problem of controlling the anger written into the part. He is a "heavy" father, like old Capulet in *Romeo and Juliet,* and he doesn't allow Miranda, a professedly free spirit, any room in the play to express her freedom. In his first long scene with his daughter, Prospero speaks, by his own acknowledgment, as "thy schoolmaster" (1.2.172), and he is constantly calling her to attention as if she were an inattentive pupil. This is repeated so often in the action that it functions almost as a tic. At line 66 Prospero interrupts his discourse because he thinks his daughter is not listening: "My brother and thy uncle, called Antonio— / I pray thee mark me" (66–67). Presumably, "I pray thee mark me" is spoken in a tone different from the narrative voice. At the end of this speech another, more importunate break occurs: "Thy false uncle— / Dost thou attend me?" (77–78). The question is startling and Miranda reassures him that she is listening "most heedfully" (78).

In his next speech Prospero asserts even more emphatically: "Thou attend'st not?" (1.2.87), which can be either a question or an exclamation. He begins his next speech with "I pray thee mark me," (88) despite Miranda's strong assurance that she does, and at the end of this speech is a remarkable break: "Hence his ambition growing— / Dost thou hear?" (105–6). It is hard to imagine how Prospero can speak this question with anything less than suppressed rage. After his narration, he puts her to sleep—"I know thou canst not choose" (186)—and awakes her at line 305 after he has transacted his business with Ariel. We can understand Prospero's anger with Caliban, but Prospero's fury at Ariel is more difficult to comprehend. Ariel's moodiness is only to remind his master of his promise of freedom. This seems to enrage Prospero, and he threatens Ariel with new punishments.

Part of Prospero's master plan is to bring the ship with his enemies to his shores after they leave the wedding of Alonso's daughter Claribel in Tunis. Another part of his plan is to wreck Ferdinand, Alonso's son, elsewhere on the island and make him meet Miranda. It is Prospero's assumption that they will immediately fall in love and want to get married. He is a meticulous planner who leaves nothing to chance. His concern for his daughter's welfare goes beyond that of a loving father to that of a rather stern schoolmaster, who observes and supervises every step his pupil takes. His stage-managing of Miranda is excessive from the beginning. As soon as she and Ferdinand have met and fallen in love, Prospero in an aside sets up rules for their courtship:

> But this swift business
> I must uneasy make, lest too light winning
> Make the prize light. (1.2.451–53)

In the next scene between the lovers, Prospero enters from behind, invisible, and makes asides on the action. When Ferdinand and Miranda leave after they have plighted their troth, Prospero remains to comment on the joyous occasion and vows to return to his "book," for he must "perform / Much business appertaining" (3.1.95–96). He is always busy, if not officious.

When he warns Ferdinand against breaking Miranda's "virgin-knot before / All sanctimonious ceremonies may / With full and holy rites be minist'red" (4.1.15–17), he once again rises to a not fully suppressed rage:

> barren hate,
> Sour-eyed disdain, and discord shall bestrew
> The union of your bed with weeds so loathly
> That you shall hate it both. Therefore take heed . . . (19–22)

Why are these dire warnings necessary, unless Prospero takes over a voyeuristic role as the keeper of his daughter's virgin-knot? His little lecture to Ferdinand later in this scene is like Polonius's advice to Ophelia (*Hamlet* 1.3.115ff.):

> Do not give dalliance
> Too much the rein; the strongest oaths are straw
> To th' fire i' th' blood. (4.1.51–53)

Ferdinand protests unnecessarily about his own chastity: "The white cold virgin snow upon my heart / Abates the ardor of my liver" (55–56). The liver is the seat of sexual passion. The "white cold virgin snow" that Ferdinand claims is on his heart is not a strong recommendation for a new husband, but he speaks in rhetorical exaggerations in order to please his prospective father-in-law.

So when Prospero renounces vengeance in act 5, scene 1 and resolves that "The rarer action is / In virtue than in vengeance" (27–28), it is difficult to believe that he has fully abandoned the rage and superiority that magic endowed him with. To his brother Antonio, Prospero is grudgingly forgiving. He technically pardons him his offenses, but he also mentions various reservations: "I do forgive thee, / Unnatural though thou art" (78–79). There is an almost comic limitation in Prospero's later speech:

> For you, most wicked sir, whom to call brother
> Would even infect my mouth, I do forgive
> Thy rankest fault—all of them . . . (130–32)

Prospero goes on to require his dukedom of Antonio "which perforce I know / Thou must restore" (133–34). Antonio wisely does not answer and speaks only a line and a half in this entire scene—Alonso is the spokesman for the conspirators. With Miranda, Prospero is similarly cynical, especially when she is overflowing with wonder at "How beauteous mankind is!" (183). To her exclamation "O brave new world / That has such people in't!" (183–84), her father can only answer with sour world-weariness: " 'Tis new to thee" (184).

Despite Prospero's crustiness—he is not fully humanized at the end of the play, although he is on the way—*The Tempest* enacts the wonders and marvels of romance in its happy ending. The tempest itself was a performance by Prospero with the help of Ariel, like the wedding masque and the other shows of the play, and at the end everything is miraculously restored. The Master and the Boatswain enter at the end to report that their ship "Is tight and yare and bravely rigged as when / We first put out to sea" (5.1.224–25). In other words, the ship shows no signs of having traveled at all but instead looks as fresh and impressive as when it started its voyage from Naples. The Boatswain reports further of the strange events by which everyone was "dead of sleep" and "clapped under hatches" (230–31) before they were awakened and "freshly beheld / Our royal, good, and gallant ship" (236–37).

The miracle of the restoration is already anticipated in act 2, scene 1, where Gonzalo comments over and over again on the freshness of their garments: "That our garments, being, as they were, drenched in the sea, hold, notwithstanding, their freshness and glosses, being rather new-dyed than stained with salt water" (64–67). This alerts us to the inevitable happy ending. Like the ship itself at the end of the play, Gonzalo observes that "our garments are now as fresh as when we put them on first in Afric, at the marriage of the King's fair daughter Claribel to the King of Tunis" (71–74). The good Gonzalo is the only one who is so optimistic, and he interprets his fresh doublet (107) as a sign from heaven.

It is Gonzalo who pronounces the final benediction of the play, as if an oracle had been fulfilled:

> In one voyage
> Did Claribel her husband find at Tunis,
> And Ferdinand her brother found a wife
> Where he himself was lost; Prospero his dukedom
> In a poor isle; and all of us ourselves
> When no man was his own. (5.1.208–13)

This is the "sea change" that Ariel sings about "Into something rich and strange" (1.2.401–2), and it is the essence of the romances that precede The Tempest: Pericles, Cymbeline, and The Winter's Tale. Gonzalo implies further that the sea change involves important discoveries that the characters make about themselves.

After the loose and wandering sense of time in the other romances—there is a fourteen-year gap in the middle of Pericles and sixteen years in The Winter's Tale—it is surprising that Shakespeare should insist so strictly on the unity of time in *The Tempest*. Unity of time is certainly not an idea demanded by a romantic action—only the early *Comedy of Errors* has it. *The Tempest* is something of an experiment in compressing a long action. Prospero and his three-year old daughter, Miranda, were exiled from Milan and set adrift on "A rotten carcass of a butt" (1.2.146) twelve years ago. *The Tempest* begins at the end of Prospero's long-meditated plan, as all his enemies are shipwrecked on his island and brought within his power. The final unfolding of the plot is imagined to occur in the elapsed time of the stage presentation, or at least in several hours.

In the last scene of the play three hours are repeatedly mentioned. Alonso asks Prospero to give him details of his preservation: "How thou hast met us here, whom three hours since / Were wracked upon this shore" (5.1.136–37). Again, Alonso asks his newfound son, with some astonishment: "What is this maid with whom thou wast at play? / Your eld'st acquaintance cannot be three hours" (185–86). Here the time scheme embarrasses us with its lightninglike swiftness. Finally, the Boatswain reports that the ship,

> Which, but three glasses since, we gave out split,
> Is tight and yare and bravely rigged as when
> We first put out to sea. (223–25)

(The "glasses" here are hourglasses and not the nautical half-hour glasses as claimed by the *Oxford English Dictionary*, which cites this passage as its example.)

In other parts of the play, the time references are more indeterminate than exactly three hours. We remember that the prologue to *Romeo and Juliet* speaks of "the two hours' traffic of our stage" (12), as if Elizabethan plays were all roughly two hours. *The Tempest* seems to be projected to take place between 2:00 and 6:00 in the afternoon. In answer to Prospero's question "How's the day?," Ariel answers that it is "On the sixth hour, at which time, my lord, / You said our work should cease" (5.1.3–5). This is in keeping with the time indications early in the play. Prospero asks, "What is the time o' th' day?" and Ariel establishes that it is "Past the mid season" (1.2.239), or noon. Prospero then fixes the time more precisely as "At least two glasses," which is the nautical indication of two o'clock.

Once again, Prospero announces the 2:00 to 6:00 P.M. chronology that Ariel refers to in the last scene of the play: "The time 'twixt six and now / Must by us both be spent most preciously" (240–41). It is necessary for Shakespeare's purposes that Ariel shall be a free spirit shortly after 6:00 P.M. There is something astonishing about these effects of time—especially that they are so exceedingly well calculated—that fits in with the copious sense of wonder, admiration, and miracle in the last scene of the play. Prospero must indeed be a wonder-worker if he can make everything come out so fittingly by six o'clock.

Caliban is something of a puzzle in *The Tempest*. He has been exalted as the hero of the play in a third world, neocolonialist discourse that is far beyond Shakespeare's scope. In the play itself he is a creature of Nature, just as Prospero is a creature of Art. Both virtues and defects stem from Caliban's being natural. He is the son of the witch Sycorax begotten on her by the devil, "A freckled whelp, hagborn" (1.2.283). There is some question in the play as to whether he is actually human or a prodigious monster. Certainly, Trinculo, who finds him in the storm, and later the drunken Stephano are both in doubt about his humanness. Trinculo's first thought is to take him back to civilization and exhibit him in a sideshow:

> Were I in England now, as once I was, and had but this fish painted, not a holiday fool there but would give a piece of silver. There would this monster make a man; any strange beast there makes a man.
>
> (2.2.28–32)

In the unusual list of actors included in the Folio after the epilogue Caliban is described as "a savage and deformed slave." That he is servile by nature is obvious when he is so eager to make Stephano his god and lick his feet. After his unsuccessful conspiracy at the end of the play, when he is driven in by Ariel with Stephano and Trinculo, his first words are to acknowledge Prospero as his master and to flatter him: "How fine my master is! I am afraid / He will chastise me" (5.1.262–63).

Even the gentle and tender Miranda, who has "suffered / With those that I saw suffer" (1.2.5–6), despises Caliban. Prospero explains that he has used him,

(Filth as thou art) with humane care, and lodged thee
In mine own cell till thou didst seek to violate
The honor of my child. (346–48)

Humane care and *honor* are all seignorial terms, and Caliban, the natural man, laughs at Prospero's middle-class rectitude:

O ho, O ho! Would't had been done!
Thou didst prevent me; I had peopled else
This isle with Calibans. (349–51)

Miranda then reviles Caliban in a speech that is much like her father's (and which many editors transfer to Prospero): "Abhorrèd slave, / Which any print of goodness wilt not take, / Being capable of all ill!" (1.2.351–53). Miranda went to great pains to teach Caliban speech, but the only benefit from this instruction was: "I know how to curse" (364). The underlying idea is that Caliban is uneducable, at least to the values of Western civilization. Prospero says this explicitly in a later scene. Caliban is "A devil, a born devil, on whose nature / Nurture can never stick" (4.1.188–89). "Nurture" is education in its largest sense, the product of art and human agency, which cultivates, civilizes, and socializes wild Nature.

The violent savagery of Caliban is evident in his plot against Prospero, where he advises Stephano and Trinculo

with a log
Batter his skull, or paunch him with a stake,
Or cut his wezand [= windpipe] with thy knife. (3.2.93–95)

But above all it is first necessary to seize his books. Caliban also offers the beautiful Miranda to Stephano as his concubine. The upshot of the plotting in this scene is Caliban's lyrical description of the island in its natural state: "the isle is full of noises, / Sounds and sweet airs that give delight and hurt not" (140–41). This is not Caliban speaking out of character for the play, as it were, but Caliban speaking as the natural man, sensitive, like an Aeolian harp, to the spontaneous impulses of nature. This is not Caliban the psychopathic murderer of the previous speeches, but Caliban the poet:

in dreaming,
The clouds methought would open and show riches
Ready to drop upon me, that, when I waked,
I cried to dream again. (145–48)

These two Calibans cannot be separated. The paradox is well phrased by Ariel, who leads Caliban on, with Stephano and Trinculo, "As they smelt music" (4.1.178). In this synesthetic image we have a clue to Caliban's sensitivity to nature.

At the end of the play, the newly humanized Prospero extends to all a judgment tinged with mercy. Caliban is still a "demi-devil" (5.1.272), as Othello calls Iago (*Othello* 5.2.300), but at the close of his speech, Prospero seems to take responsibility for him: "this thing of darkness I / Acknowledge mine" (5.1.275–76). Is Caliban literally a "thing of darkness" because of his dark complexion, like a Moor, or is he dark because of his association with the devil? The latter would seem to be the primary meaning, as Prospero recognizes the dark side of his reality and deals with Caliban as if he were his son (but Caliban, of course, never regards him as a surrogate father, the way the Fool does Lear). After freeing his slave Ariel, Prospero can no longer curse and revile his slave Caliban. He is not only forced to acknowledge that Caliban is a human being and not a monster or beast but also required by the ending of *The Tempest* to surrender his absolute authority over Nature, the island, the conspirators, his daughter Miranda, and especially over his slaves Ariel and Caliban. In the largest sense of the word, he must set free all these persons and powers.

Caliban joins Malvolio, Jaques, and Shylock in being unreconciled to the comic ending. He doesn't return to Milan with Prospero, but once more asserts his political rights over the island: "This island's mine by Sycorax my mother" (1.2.331). If *The Tempest* is the only play in the Folio with a scene location—"The Scene, an uninhabited island"—this location is not accurate, because Caliban inhabited the island before Prospero arrived and he takes it back from him in the end. By acknowledging "this thing of darkness," Prospero also acknowledges Caliban's legal right to repossess his own island.

The Two Noble Kinsmen

*T*he *Two Noble Kinsmen* does not appear in the First Folio. It was first printed in a quarto edition in 1634, written "by the memorable worthies of their time, Mr. John Fletcher and Mr. William Shakespeare." There is strong evidence that the play was first presented in 1613 or early 1614 by the King's Men at the Blackfriars private theater, acquired by Shakespeare's company in 1608. Most critics agree that the play is a collaboration between Shakespeare and Fletcher, his successor as principal dramatist for the King's Men. Shakespeare may also have collaborated with Fletcher on *Henry VIII* and on the lost play, *Cardenio*, performed in 1612. Fletcher probably had the major share in shaping *The Two Noble Kinsmen*, and Shakespeare probably wrote no more than a third of the play, which may be the last in which he had a hand before his death in 1616.

The latest account of the collaboration, in Eugene M. Waith's edition for the Oxford Shakespeare (1989), assigns to Shakespeare all of act 1; act 2, scene 1 (which Waith ends at line 59 in the Signet edition); act 3, scenes 1 and 2; act 4, scene 3; and act 5, scenes 1, 3, and 4. Fletcher's share is act 2, scene 2 (which Waith begins at 2.1.60 in the Signet edition) to scene 6; act 3, scenes

3–6; act 4, scenes 1 and 2; act 5, scene 2; and the prologue and epilogue, but Fletcher may also have rewritten passages in the scenes assigned to Shakespeare.

All in all, the play doesn't seem to me very Shakespearean, especially in its language. It doesn't have the close stylistic relation that one would expect to the romances that precede it: *Pericles, Cymbeline, The Winter's Tale*, and *The Tempest*. It does contain a great many Shakespearean echoes of these plays and earlier plays, such as *A Midsummer Night's Dream* and *The Two Gentlemen of Verona*, but on the whole *The Two Noble Kinsmen* seems much more like Fletcher's play than Shakespeare's. We don't know much about Shakespeare's career after he presumably retired from the London stage to take up his life in his grand, newly acquired house, New Place, in Stratford. The pastoralism of *The Two Noble Kinsmen* might suit this new life better than we can know. In any case, even if the play is only very partially by Shakespeare, it has some wonderful touches in it.

The theme of male friendship corrupted by heterosexual love recalls *The Winter's Tale*. There Leontes and Polixenes as boyhood friends were "as twinned lambs, that did frisk i' th' sun" (1.2.67), innocent and untouched with Original Sin, until their weak spirits are "higher reared / With stronger blood" (72–73), or sexuality (sexual passion was carried by the blood and thought to be seated in the liver). Hermione sees clearly that she and Polixenes' wife are in danger of being called "devils," since "you first sinned with us" (84).

In *The Two Noble Kinsmen*, before Palamon and Arcite both fall in love with Emilia, they are sworn brothers, who speak of each other in the erotic vocabulary of love. Act 2, scene 1, just before they see Emilia, is filled with professions of mutual affection, which are deliberately written up to prepare us for the destruction of male friendship by the sight of the Eve-like Emilia. Palamon and Arcite expect to be prisoners forever, but they have each other, and therefore they do not feel imprisoned. Arcite speaks in the extravagances of Platonic imagery:

> And here being thus together,
> We are an endless mine to one another;
> We are one another's wife, ever begetting
> New births of love . . . (2.1.137–40)

This is not specifically homosexual, although it is certainly homo-erotic, as the tradition of exalted male friendship insists. The assumptions are similar to the first 126 of Shakespeare's *Sonnets*, addressed to a male friend.

It is clear that Arcite does not mean literally "We are one another's wife," but he dwells on the image of wife as an inherent danger for the two noble kinsmen: "Were we at liberty, / A wife might part us lawfully" (2.1.147–48). A wife is therefore conceived of as the chief destructive force of male friendship, which surely predicts what will happen in this scene. Palamon's reply escalates the almost ecstatic nature of their captivity: "You have made me— / I thank you, cousin Arcite—almost wanton / With my captivity" (154–56). Lascivious is the most frequent sense of *wanton*, although it could also mean, more neutrally, frolicsome, sportive, or playful. These assertions reach their climax just before they see Emilia in the garden. Palamon says: "Is there record of any two that loved / Better than we do, Arcite?" (171–72), and "I do not think it possible our friendship / Should ever leave us" (173–74).

Emilia and her woman in the garden below are both conversing wantonly (2.1.206) on the merry, proverbial theme of "laugh and lie down" (Tilley, L92). Emilia's physical beauty smites both the noble kinsmen equally. Palamon says: "Behold, and wonder. / By heaven, she is a goddess," and Arcite can only answer in the almost mute interjection: "Ha!" (191–92). Palamon claims priority because he saw Emilia first, but Arcite insists on the superiority of his claim because it is sexual:

> I will not as you do, to worship her,
> As she is heavenly and a blessèd goddess:
> I love her as a woman, to enjoy her.
> So both may love. (222–25)

The absurdity that "both may love" in their own ways has no possibility of fruition, so the two noble kinsmen fall into deadly enmity. However, nothing convincing in the play proves to us that Arcite wants to love Emilia primarily "as a woman."

Palamon and Arcite alternate throughout the play between their deadly hatred as rivals in love and their tender affection as friends, in a way that challenges credibility and makes them seem like tragi-comic heroes in the paradoxical Fletcherian mode. When Arcite comes *"with meat, wine, and files"* (3.3 s.d.) to succor Palamon, who has been freed from prison by the Jailer's Daughter, we feel that both of the noble kinsmen would be delighted to return to their eternal friendship but are prevented to do so by the chivalric code of love. An air of relaxation fills this scene as the friends drink to each other. Arcite speaks with a newly colloquial ease: "Drink a good hearty draught, it breeds good blood, man. / Do not you feel it thaw you?" (17–18). And even more familiarly: "Is't not mad lodging / Here in the wild woods, cousin?" (22–23). The tone is exactly right, and for the first time in the play (and probably the last) Palamon and Arcite seem like believable human characters.

Under the influence of the wine and the food, Palamon expansively twits Arcite about his relation with the "Lord Steward's daughter" (3.3.29): "She met him in an arbor: / What did she there, coz? Play o' th' virginals?" (33–34). Arcite makes a good-natured double entendre on virginals as a small keyboard instrument like a spinet and a virgin offering love, which inspires Arcite to remember Palamon's affair with the "Marshal's sister" (36), "A pretty brown wench 'tis" (39). These details are all humanizing, and the two friends merrily pledge each other, until Palamon suddenly thinks of Emilia and breaks off "this strained mirth" (43). Unlike the Lord Steward's daughter and the Marshal's sister, Emilia remains abstract and remote in the play, a chivalric ideal rather than a real woman.

Emilia's relation to Palamon and Arcite is studiously formal and correct, and she nowhere indicates any special preference for either, not even during the grand combat of act 5, scene 3. As the passionate object of two knights eager to die to possess her, she is peculiarly unpassionate and uncommitted. In only one place in the play do we see an animated Emilia, and that is when she talks about her childhood attachment to Flavina, who died when she and Emilia were only girls of eleven. Like Leontes and Polixenes in *The Winter's Tale*, they were innocent children who played together and mingled souls. Emilia's narration is tinged with presexual feelings:

> the flow'r that I would pluck
> And put between my breasts, O then but beginning

To swell about the blossom, she would long
Till she had such another, and commit it
To the like innocent cradle, where phoenix-like
They died in perfume . . . (1.3.66–71)

These overwrought pastoral images postulate a time before Original Sin, as in *The Winter's Tale*, when adult sexuality destroys childhood innocence. Emilia concludes with an observation that applies equally well to Leontes and Polixenes as to Palamon and Arcite and to herself and Flavina: "That the true love 'tween maid and maid may be / More than in sex dividual" (81–82). This is not exactly a plea for lesbian love but an expression of dismay at the destructive powers of heterosexuality.

In the religious ceremonies before the final battle, there are three tableaux of equal weight: Arcite prays to Mars, Palamon to Venus, and Emilia to Diana, the goddess of chastity. It is odd that Emilia should make a third in these invocations. She comes as a virgin, "bride-habited, / But maiden hearted" (5.1.150–51), and asks Diana to grant her the husband "that best loves me / And has the truest title in't" (158–59), but she will make no choice of her own. She feels no passionate attraction to either Palamon or Arcite, as she certainly did to Flavina, and is willing to accept the consequences of her non-choice. By this time her personal desires have ceased to matter to the two noble kinsmen, who are remarkably like Valentine and Proteus, the two gentlemen of Verona, who pass the hapless Silvia between them.

But some remarkable things happen in the scene with Emilia. When *"the hind vanishes under the altar"* and the rose tree ascends *"having one rose upon it"* (5.1.162 s.d.), Emilia seems to see a wished-for conclusion:

If well inspired, this battle shall confound
Both these brave knights, and I a virgin flow'r
Must grow alone, unplucked. (166–68)

It is strange to hear Emilia, at this late date, longing to remain a "virgin flow'r" unplucked. The phoenixlike flower reminds us of the celebration of Flavina in an earlier scene. With both her brave knights confounded in battle, Emilia can return to her nonsexual, childhood innocence.

Pirithous and Theseus are another pair of noble friends, parallel to Palamon and Arcite. There are clear distinctions drawn between Theseus as the prospective husband of Hippolyta, a match with echoes from *A Midsummer Night's Dream*, and Theseus as the male friend of Pirithous. We hear from Hippolyta of their great love for each other:

> Their knot of love,
> Tied, weaved, entangled, with so true, so long,
> And with a finger of so deep a cunning,
> May be outworn, never undone. (1.3.41–44)

The love between Hippolyta and Theseus is different from this and, even though Hippolyta is Queen of the Amazons, she cannot compete with the noble friend. She speaks of heroic deeds that Theseus and Pirithous have shared:

> They have skiffed
> Torrents whose roaring tyranny and power
> I' th' least of these was dreadful; and they have
> Fought out together where Death's self was lodged,
> Yet Fate hath brought them off. (1.3.37–41)

Hippolyta cannot share these martial exercises with her husband, and Palamon and Arcite are similarly bonded in warrior values that define their maleness. Emilia does nothing for them but destroy the integrity of their being.

The Jailer's Daughter stands in sharp contrast to Emilia. She appears in many scenes attributed to Fletcher, yet the basic conception seems to be Shakespeare's, based on Ophelia in *Hamlet*, especially in her madness. The Jailer's Daughter, who is frankly and openly sexual, is different from Emilia, who seems to be fleeing from sexuality. The Jailer's Daughter is never named, nor is her suitor, who is simply called Wooer. For that matter, none of the lower-class characters is named in these scenes—neither the Jailer nor the Doctor, who, like the Doctor in *Macbeth*, ministers "to a mind diseased" (*Macbeth* 5.3.40). It is all acted out according to character functions.

The Jailer's Daughter is enamored of her father's noble prisoners: "It is a holiday to look on them. Lord, the diff'rence of men!" (2.1.58–59). She is especially taken with the refinement of their manners. In her report, they sound like lovers of heightened sensibility:

> Yet sometime a divided sigh, martyred as 'twere i' th' deliverance, will break from one of them—when the other presently gives it so sweet a rebuke that I could wish myself a sigh to be so chid, or at least a sigher to be comforted. (42–47)

This touches the Jailer's Daughter's own innate delicacy.

She is developed unusually by a series of long soliloquies, since she doesn't have anyone to confide in. Her first soliloquy shows her already in love with Palamon, but she despairs of any return of her affection because of the disparity in their social positions. She speaks with an attractive forwardness, not subject to the restraints of the chivalric code: "Out upon't, / What pushes are we wenches driven to / When fifteen once has found us!" (2.3.5–7). *Pushes* is a colloquial word for stratagems or shifts. A wench of fifteen, in responding to her sexual stirrings, is driven back to her natural wits and plottings. Later in the play the Jailer's Daughter is said to be eighteen (5.2.30). She is already planning how she can let Palamon know that she loves him, "For I would fain enjoy him" (30). *Enjoy* is a frankly sexual term as in Arcite's confession (2.1.224). She purposes to set him free from his prison, with an anticipation of Lucy Lockit and Macheath in Gay's *The Beggar's Opera* (1728). The release has specifically sexual implications, as the Jailer's Daughter indicates in her next soliloquy: "For use me so he shall, or I'll proclaim him, / And to his face, no man" (2.5.30–31). "No man" is a plain indication of impotence, but it is difficult to imagine Palamon as a full sexual being.

By act 3, scene 2, the Jailer's Daughter is becoming distracted from her long exposure outdoors and from her lack of food and drink. A lyric sweetness in her soliloquies stands apart from the rest of the play:

> I reck not if the wolves would jaw me, so
> He had this file. What if I halloo'd for him?
> I cannot halloo. If I whooped, what then? (3.2.7–9)

We never know exactly why she cannot halloo but can whoop. By her fourth soliloquy, she is definitely mad in the style of Ophelia, and she even echoes some of Ophelia's random phrases and snatches from songs: "Good night, good night, y' are gone" (3.4.11) and the refrain: "Hey, nonny, nonny, nonny!" (21). She ends with a desire that is both proverbial and sexual: "O for a prick now like a nightingale, / To put my breast against! I shall sleep like a top else" (25–26). The nightingale was imagined to press against a thorn in order to stay awake and sing, but the Jailer's Daughter might also be thinking of a different kind of prick.

Act 4, scene 1, is an extensive mad scene much developed from the part of Ophelia. The Wooer has heard the Jailer's Daughter singing various songs, including "Willow, willow, willow" (4.1.80), a song of forsaken love that Desdemona sings in *Othello* (4,3). He also describes her in a setting of a "Thousand fresh water flowers of several colors" (4.1.85) that made her appear "like the fair nymph / That feeds the lake with waters, or as Iris / Newly dropped down from heaven" (86–88). The Jailer's Daughter is being prettified in her madness. We see her with her uncle singing bawdy songs and making gross sexual allusions: "For I must lose my maidenhead by cocklight" (112), or before dawn. This is her big scene in the play. The Doctor / Psychiatrist plays a large role in this play, and he is, incidentally, a great admirer of her mad imagination: "How prettily she's amiss!" (4.3.28) and "How her brain coins!" (40). He diagnoses her condition as not an "engraffed madness, but a most thick and profound melancholy" (50–51) that can be cured. The treatment he recommends to cure her "pranks and friskins" (82) is elaborately detailed, but depends upon the Wooer playing the role of Palamon.

All this is acted out in act 5, scene 2, where the Doctor reveals his secret "appliance" (4.3.103) or stratagem:

> /   Please her appetite
> And do it home: it cures her *ipso facto*
> The melancholy humor that infects her. (5.2.35–37)

The Doctor is overtly sexual in his practical advice, but it doesn't take much to convince the Jailer, and the Wooer has been more than ready to "fit her home" (11). The action of the Jailer's Daughter is developed at great length, probably mostly by Fletcher, who remembers Ophelia in Shakespeare's *Hamlet* quite well, as a counterpoise to the high-toned, chivalric, and nonsexual action of the main plot. Emilia and the Jailer's Daughter are polar opposites, and they balance the play at either end of the spectrum, leaving the humdrum middle unregarded. We need some way to reconcile these two contrary actions: to bring the chivalric love of the two noble kinsmen in touch with the charmingly gross love play of the Jailer's Daughter and her Wooer.

POEMS

Venus and Adonis

*V*enus and Adonis first appeared in a carefully prepared quarto edition in 1593, and it was extremely popular in its own time. By 1617 there were ten editions of the poem that survive and perhaps others that don't. The publication of quarto editions of this poem, and *The Rape of Lucrece* in 1594, has to do with the closing of the London theaters because of plague between August 1592 and April 1594. Both poems are dedicated to the Earl of Southampton, and there is an apocryphal story told by Nicholas Rowe (on the alleged authority of William Davenant) that Southampton "at one time, gave him [Shakespeare] a thousand Pounds." In his dedication Shakespeare speaks of *Venus and Adonis* as "the first heir of my invention" and promises "some graver labor," presumably *The Rape of Lucrece*. In relation to the half dozen or so plays that Shakespeare had already written by this time (none of which was yet published), *Venus and Adonis* sounds like his first important piece of writing, important because it was a proper lyric and amatory poem in the style of Ovid that was presentable to a patron. Shakespeare speaks in his dedication like the mercenary Poet in *Timon of Athens*. Plays were not considered "literary" in the same sense as poems.

Venus and Adonis is clearly an Ovidian poem like Marlowe's fragmentary *Hero and Leander*, probably also written in 1593. Shakespeare's poem is indebted to at least three episodes in the *Metamorphoses*: the story of Venus and Adonis in Book 10, Hermaphroditus pursued by the nymph Salmacis in Book 4, and Narcissus and the nymph Echo in Book 3. The male figure of Adonis who flees from love and lust is very Ovidian. In Francis Meres's miscellaneous "comparative discourse of our English Poets" in *Palladis Tamia: Wits Treasury* (1598), he observes that

> the sweete wittie soule of *Ouid* liues in mellifluous & hony-tongued *Shakespeare*, witness his *Venus* and *Adonis*, his *Lucrece*, his sugred Sonnets among his priuate friends, &c.

From about the same time, Gabriel Harvey notes that

> The younger sort takes much delight in Shakespeares Venus, & Adonis: but his Lucrece, & his tragedie of Hamlet, Prince of Denmarke, haue it in them, to please the wiser sort.

This echoes Shakespeare's own comment that *Venus and Adonis* is "the first heir of my invention," but that *The Rape of Lucrece* will be "some graver labor."

Interestingly, contemporary opinion held that Shakespeare was "mellifluous & hony-tongued" and that he reembodied "the sweete wittie soule of *Ouid*" in his *Venus and Adonis*. This remark is also true of Shakespeare's first tragedy, *Titus Andronicus*, written at about the same time as *Venus and Adonis* and *The Rape of Lucrece*, which uses a similarly ornamented and highly allusive style. Ovid was thought to be "witty" in a much broader sense of the word than our modern usage. *Witty* means ingenious, clever, inventive, imaginative, and intelligent. Readers of *Venus and Adonis* should be impressed by Shakespeare's boldness of style, rhetorical pointedness, brilliance of analogy, provocative eroticism, flashes of the comic grotesque, and vivid exploitation of figurative language. Ovid was admired for an irony, pathos, and high sophistication that Shakespeare aims at in *Venus and Adonis*. Ovid is titillating without being vulgar or obvious.

If *Venus and Adonis* is Ovidian, then it is also dramatic, although not also theatrical in the sense of the plays. Adonis is clearly conceived as a Shakespearean character, and his reluctance to love is both very adolescent and very male, like that of Bertram in *All's Well That Ends Well*. Venus refers to him throughout the poem as a boy—a "wayward boy" (344) and a "silly boy" (467)—and Adonis is not only young but also awkward and petulant:

> "Fie, fie!" he says. "You crush me; let me go!
> You have no reason to withhold me so." (611–12)

Earlier in the poem, Adonis, disguising his emotions "with a heavy, dark, disliking eye" (182), cries: " 'Fie, no more of love! / The sun doth burn my face—I must remove' " (185–86). He is always ill at ease and passive, so his coyness seems to have a strongly physical basis.

His ultimate plea to Venus is that he is too young for love, "unripe" (524) and an "ungrown fry" (526), in other words a fish too small for fishermen to take from the waters. This is best expressed in his touching excuse: "Before I know myself, seek not to know me" (525). Adonis is really embarrassed by Venus's lustful talk, as he makes clear in seven stanzas beginning at line 769. Like Spenser's Red-Cross Knight, he protests against the prevailing uncleanness:

> "Mine ears, that to your wanton talk attended,
> Do burn themselves for having so offended." (809–10)

Venus doesn't resemble any of Shakespeare's heroines exactly, although she has some similarities to the bawdy-speaking Nurse in *Romeo and Juliet*—Beaumont and Fletcher's lustful ladies are much more in Venus's style. She is definitely not an ingénue but more like the experienced Cleopatra, who is "wrinkled deep in time" (*Antony and Cleopatra* 1.5.29). The grotesque disparity in ages between Venus and Adonis endows the entire verse epyllion with comic irony. Venus as the sweating paramour—"By this the lovesick queen began to sweat" (175)—frightens the youthful Adonis, who strongly associates her not with Love but with "sweating Lust" (794), who feeds on "fresh beauty" (796) "As caterpillars do the tender leaves" (798).

The most powerful image is Venus as a bird of prey, represented early in the poem in the Homeric simile of the eagle:

375

Even as an empty [= hungry] eagle, sharp by fast,
Tires [= tears] with her beak on feathers, flesh, and bone,
Shaking her wings, devouring all in haste,
Till either gorge be stuffed or prey be gone—
    Even so she kissed his brow, his cheek, his chin,
    And where she ends she doth anew begin. (55–60)

Later in the poem the ravenous Venus is conceived in terms of "vulture thought" (551):

Now quick desire hath caught the yielding prey,
And glutton-like she feeds, yet never filleth. (547–48)

Shakespeare is thinking of Venus in relation to Jupiter's amours, often in animal disguises, that are recounted in Ovid's *Metamorphoses*.

Desire is a key word in *Venus and Adonis*, also translated as "lust." The poem is titillatingly erotic, designed to please the "younger sort," as Gabriel Harvey observed. It is also didactic, with Venus as an instructor in love for the naive Adonis. She draws important lessons from the escape of Adonis's palfrey in hot pursuit of "A breeding jennet, lusty, young, and proud" (260):

"Who sees his true-love in her naked bed,
Teaching the sheets a whiter hue than white,
But, when his glutton eye so full hath fed,
His other agents aim at like delight?" (397–400)

Venus is an expert commentator on the voyeuristic / exhibitionistic pleasures of "presented joy" (405), and her hendiadys, "naked bed," is typical of the showy rhetoric of this poem. It is the bed in which your true love appears naked, as if this were the only proper stage setting for amorous encounters.

Throughout the poem Venus thinks in conventional erotic imagery, as in the scene of lovemaking as a medieval tournament:

Now is she in the very lists of love,
Her champion mounted for the hot encounter.
All is imaginary she doth prove,
He will not manage her, although he mount her;

That worse than Tantalus' is her annoy,
To clip Elysium and to lack her joy. (595–600)

Manage and *mount* are specifically equine images, and the mythological allusion serves to ensure the artfulness of the stanza. The
conclusion to all this frustration is wittily expressed: "She's Love, she
loves, and yet she is not loved" (610).

Venus flourishes the standard argument of use, but here it is
applied specifically to seduction, as it is in Marlowe's *Hero and Leander*.
The doctrine of use is connected with the familiar *carpe diem* theme:
"Make use of time, let not advantage slip; / Beauty within itself should
not be wasted" (129–30). This is close in spirit to an important motif
in Shakespeare's *Sonnets*: it is essential to defy a self-defeating self-
love like that of Narcissus, especially if you are endowed with beauty
and other heavenly graces:

> "Torches are made to light, jewels to wear,
> Dainties to taste, fresh beauty for the use,
> Herbs for their smell, and sappy plants to bear.
> Things growing to themselves are growth's abuse.
>   Seeds spring from seeds, and beauty breedeth beauty.
>   Thou wast begot; to get it is thy duty." (163–68)

This is close to the language of the *Sonnets* and explains why "Lilies
that fester smell far worse than weeds" (Sonnet 94). Throughout
Shakespeare's comedies, self-love is the enemy of love, as shown by
Duke Orsino and Malvolio in *Twelfth Night* (and Olivia, too, at the
beginning of the play).

Venus's advice to Adonis is to "Be prodigal," like the lamp that
"burns by night" (755) to illuminate the world. To deny the natural
injunction to propagate is to bury your body in "a swallowing grave"
(757) and to destroy one's needful posterity in "dark obscurity" (760).
Venus makes a natural connection between lovemaking and offspring, as in the *Sonnets*, and sexual prodigality is not an end in itself.
In proverbial form, "gold that's put to use more gold begets" (768).
To be niggardly is to be self-destructive. To the proud Adonis, this
is an "idle over-handled theme" (770) and Venus's doctrines about
use are unappealing: "Your treatise makes me like you worse and

worse" (774). In the context of the poem, we forget that we are listening to a goddess and a mere mortal. The poem turns on the irony of Venus's doubleness as the Goddess of Love but also as an aging, anxious, lyrical, and eloquent nymphomaniac. This duality stimulates interest in her as a dramatic character.

The stanzaic form of *Venus and Adonis* is closely connected with the poem's effects. *Hero and Leander*, in iambic pentameter couplets, seems much less patterned and formal than *Venus and Adonis*, which uses an unvarying iambic pentameter six-line stanza consisting of one quatrain (abab) and one couplet (cc). This is related in form to the Shakespearean sonnet, which also ends in a couplet and has three preceding quatrains. The couplet is crucial since it effects a miniconclusion in each stanza. The next stanza then needs to begin again with some proposition in the quatrain that can be answered or commented on in the couplet. Thus each stanza emphasizes a cadenced polarity.

In the first stanza of the poem, an extravagant image of Adonis appears in the quatrain:

> Even as the sun with purple-colored face
> Had ta'en his last leave of the weeping morn,
> Rose-cheeked Adonis hied him to the chase;
> Hunting he loved, but love he laughed to scorn. (1–4)

In the couplet Venus appears as the antagonist:

> Sick-thoughted Venus makes amain unto him,
> And like a bold-faced suitor 'gins to woo him. (5–6)

The narrative and the essential characterization are given in the first stanza, which sets up characters against each other in quatrain and couplet.

Let me look at one more stanza to see how the couplet works as a conclusion to the propositional nature of the quatrain. This is a stanza on which Coleridge commented with memorable acumen in the *Biographia Literaria* (1817):

> With this he breaketh from the sweet embrace
> Of those fair arms which bound him to her breast

And homeward through the dark laund [= glade] runs apace;
Leaves Love upon her back, deeply distressed.
   Look how a bright star shooteth from the sky,
   So glides he in the night from Venus' eye . . . (811–16)

The embarrassed and frustrated Venus of the quatrain, whom Adonis leaves "upon her back, deeply distressed," is poetically distanced in the marvelous couplet of Adonis as a shooting star. This is the last we see of him alive. The rhetorical point is that the quatrain and the couplet in this stanza are sharply contrasted so that the couplet at its best can offer an imaginative solution to the distress of the quatrain. Shakespeare seemed especially fond of the couplet in his earlier works, both dramatic and nondramatic.

Venus and Adonis is a remarkably successful poem in its genre of the comic-ironic verse epyllion in the style of Ovid. It was a perfect poem to present to a wealthy and influential patron in the hope of financial reward, especially at a time when the theaters were closed because of plague. Venus is a powerful creation, related to the strong women of the Minor Tetralogy and to Tamora in *Titus Andronicus.* Shakespeare seemed fascinated early in his career with women who were not only strong but ruthless. Venus wants to use Adonis as a love object without much relation to the manly, sport-loving adolescent's own feelings. Adonis is part of a male culture, strongly developed in the *Sonnets,* that came to Shakespeare through Ovid and through his reading of classical literature. Adonis represents a Greek ideal that is mediated through Latin poetry. He could conceivably have been one of the lords who retire from the world, and especially the world of women, to found the ill-fated Academy of Navarre in *Love's Labor's Lost.* Thus Shakespeare, early in his career, establishes disdain for love as an important comic theme. It is clear that, even without a strong mythological compulsion in stories of Venus and her son Cupid, one cannot flee from love with impunity.

The Rape of Lucrece

The Rape of Lucrece, a companion piece
to Venus and Adonis, was also dedicated to the
Earl of Southampton the following year, 1594.
It is undoubtedly the "graver labor" promised
in the dedication of Venus and Adonis. Both
poems are rhetorical display pieces suitable
for a noble patron but very different in style.
The Rape of Lucrece is linked with Shakespearean tragedy, especially Titus Andronicus, which
was written around the same time.

The poem is written in the rhyme royal
stanza of seven iambic pentameter lines
rhyming ababbcc. This stanza was made famous by Chaucer, who used it in Troilus and
Criseyde, The Parlement of Fowles, and several of
the Canterbury Tales. Spenser also used it in
Fowre Hymnes. It is quite different in effect
from the six-line stanza of Venus and Adonis,
whose quatrain and couplet seem to divide
the stanza into two distinct parts. In The Rape
of Lucrece, the additional b-rhyme in the fifth
line changes the effect of polarization, slows
the stanza down, and prevents the couplet
from functioning like a separate and distinct
piece.

Let us look at the first stanza of the poem:

> From the besiegèd Ardea all in post,
> Borne by the trustless wings of false desire,

> Lust-breathèd Tarquin leaves the Roman host
> And to Collatium bears the lightless fire
> Which, in pale embers hid, lurks to aspire
>   And girdle with embracing flames the waist
>   Of Collatine's fair love, Lucrece the chaste. (1–7)

The enjambment of lines 4, 5, and 6 prevents the couplet from being a concluding unit set against the rest of the poem, as often happens in *Venus and Adonis*. The stanza is much more interwoven than the separable quatrains and couplets of that poem. There is much more assonance and consonance in this poem than in the earlier work, and the striking internal matching of *trustless* and *lightless* is continued in the *hateless*, *priceless*, and *peerless* of the next two stanzas. Everything in this stanza leads to the strong conclusion of the "waist / chaste" rhyme of the couplet. Although the six-line stanza of *Venus and Adonis* seems similar to the seven-line stanza of *The Rape of Lucrece*, its function is entirely different. In *The Rape of Lucrece* the stanza is not a two-part unit in which the parts are often set against each other.

The violated and mutilated Lavinia is allied with Lucrece in the Renaissance ideology of rape, in which the woman is irrecoverably spoiled even though she is totally innocent. When Lucrece kills herself, the blood bubbles from her breast in two slow rivers of radically different colors:

> Some of her blood still pure and red remained,
> And some looked black, and that false Tarquin stained. (1742–43)

As she tells us earlier:

> Though my gross blood be stained with this abuse,
> Immaculate and spotless is my mind . . . (1655–56)

Before Titus kills his daughter Lavinia, he questions whether it was

> well done of rash Virginius
> To slay his daughter with his own right hand,
> Because she was enforced, stained, and deflow'red?
>   (*Titus Andronicus* 5.3.37–38)

Both Lucrece and Lavinia eagerly seek out death as a release from their dishonor.

Tarquin looks forward to Macbeth in his debate with himself about committing the crime and his sense of his inevitable corruption and doom. This is not to say that *The Rape of Lucrece* is dramatic, because Tarquin's speeches are intensely rhetorical and not very psychologically astute in their understanding of criminality. There is a world of difference between Tarquin's "The eye of heaven is out" (356) and Macbeth's "Come, seeling night, / Scarf up the tender eye of pitiful day" (*Macbeth* 3.2.46–47), followed by the extraordinary image of "Light thickens, and the crow / Makes wing to th' rooky wood" (50–51). Tarquin's commitment to Love and Fortune and his facile confidence that "The blackest sin is cleared with absolution" (354) carries no mystery. This is not at all what Macbeth thinks.

Tarquin does try to debate with himself, yet there is a sense in which the matter is already decided as his "servile powers" "Stuff up his lust, as minutes fill up hours" (297). This is a vivid and colloquial touch, rare in the poem, because Tarquin's thinking generally follows the extreme antitheses upon which the poem is based:

> Thus graceless holds he disputation
> 'Tween frozen conscience and hot-burning will . . . (246–47)

The conclusion is foreordained.

The puns on *will* echo the outrageous Sonnet 135, and we are keenly aware that Will is Shakespeare's first name, making Tarquin both an unstoppable rapist and an ingenious player on words. *Will* is a synonym for lust and carnal appetite, but it also includes the male power to enforce one's will. Lucrece's beauty, separated from her person, marks her out as the victim of Tarquin's will:

> Thy beauty hath ensnared thee to this night,
> Where thou with patience must my will abide,
> My will that marks thee for my earth's delight . . . (485–87)

All that is required of Lucrece in this scene is "patience," like patient Griselda, the ideal masochistic woman.

Tarquin knows the obvious arguments that the honey is "guarded with a sting" (493) and that the rose is defended by thorns, "But Will is deaf, and hears no heedful friends" (495). Will and Beauty are inevitably connected. Lucrece's long, moral discourse is antidramatic in the sense that her static and conventional speech cannot possibly be imagined in a play. "Tears harden lust" (560), but we have no way of conceiving Tarquin's lust as a progressive and developing emotion; it is more a fact of the narrative that is intensified by poetic declamation. Lucrece pleads "From a pure heart command thy rebel will" (625), but we are acutely conscious that *will* rhymes with *kill* and *fulfill*.

Shakespeare's imagery is disturbingly conventional in this poem. Lust is expressed most strongly in the military images of Petrarchan poetry. Like Iachimo gazing on Imogen in *Cymbeline*, Tarquin has a voyeuristic feeding-frenzy from the sight of the naked Lucrece in her bed:

> What could he see but mightily he noted?
> What did he note but strongly he desirèd?
> What he beheld, on that he firmly doted,
> And in his will his willful eye he tirèd.
> With more than admiration he admirèd
> Her azure veins, her alabaster skin,
> Her coral lips, her snow-white dimpled chin. (414–20)

Unlike Imogen, Lucrece on her left breast has no "mole cinque-spotted, like the crimson drops / I' th' bottom of a cowslip" (*Cymbeline* 2. 2. 38–39). By pictorial convention her breasts are "like ivory globes circled with blue" (407). This is poetically disappointing, but it allies this poem erotically with *Venus and Adonis*, which is, however, much fresher and more gross.

Tarquin the soldier's "drumming heart cheers up his burning eye" (435) as he leads his hand "unto the breach" (*Henry V* 3. 1. 1):

> His hand, as proud of such a dignity,
> Smoking with pride, marched on to make his stand
> On her bare breast, the heart of all her land;
> Whose ranks of blue veins, as his hand did scale,
> Left their round turrets destitute and pale. (437–41)

We can't help feeling something grotesque, even comic, about this triumphant military / erotic image. Its highly ornamental character is inappropriate for the tragic feeling of rape.

Most of the poem is devoted to Lucrece's extended complaint after she has been raped, like *A Lover's Complaint*, which may or may not be by Shakespeare, and Samuel Daniel's *Complaint of Rosamond*, which appeared just before *The Rape of Lucrece* in 1592. The complaint is essentially a rhetorical exercise, formal and not very personal. Lucrece presents a whole series of apostrophes to Night, Opportunity, and Time, and a long digression on the Troy tapestry, as if she is systematically going through all the possible topics relevant to her misfortune. The only inadvertent dramatic touch is when the narrator says:

> Sometime her grief is dumb and hath no words;
> Sometime 'tis mad and too much talk affords. (1105–6)

We are too ready to agree with the last proposition.

Lucrece's first formal invocation of Night goes on for sixteen stanzas, when she switches to apostrophizing Opportunity. This is all excessively long and ingenious, with Lucrece metadramatically in the position of a poet who must exercise her wits for an astonishing sixteen stanzas. The feeling of Lucrece's straining her poetic invention conflicts with our sense of her as a tragic victim. She opens with a formal catalogue of the poetic properties of Night in the style of Milton's *Il Penseroso* (1632):

> "O comfort-killing Night, image of hell,
> Dim register and notary of shame,
> Black stage for tragedies and murders fell,
> Vast sin-concealing chaos, nurse of blame,
> Blind muffled bawd, dark harbor for defame!
>   Grim cave of death, whisp'ring conspirator
>   With close-tongued treason and the ravisher!" (764–70)

None of this relates much to Tarquin and the events of the poem.

Later stanzas are more touching, especially the lines about the chaste bee:

"My honey lost, and I, a drone-like bee,
Have no perfection of my summer left,
But robbed and ransacked by injurious theft.
　　In thy weak hive a wand'ring wasp hath crept
　　And sucked the honey which thy chaste bee kept." (836–40)

Why does Lucrece consider herself Collatine's (the bee-keeper's) hive, and why is her chastity so lusciously represented by the image of honey, which is like the "jelly" featured in the "Jelly Roll Blues"? This is definitely an erotic touch.

The best lines of the poem are those that evoke nostalgic sweetness, such as "The adder hisses where the sweet birds sing" (871), which echoes Sonnet 73: "Bare ruined choirs where late the sweet birds sang." *The Rape of Lucrece* is much more affecting when Lucrece is interrupted in her endless discourse and the poem shows some semblance of dramatic interest. When Lucrece and her maid weep together, they create a strong scene, even though the stanza looks ahead to the extravagant conceits of Crashaw's poem, "Sainte Mary Magdalene or the Weeper" in *Carmen Deo Nostro* (1652):

A pretty while these pretty creatures stand,
Like ivory conduits coral cisterns filling.
One justly weeps, the other takes in hand
No cause, but company, of her drops spilling.
Their gentle sex to weep are often willing,
　　Grieving themselves to guess at others' smarts,
　　And then they drown their eyes or break their hearts. (1233–39)

In excuse for this emotional scene, Shakespeare says that "men have marble, women waxen minds" (1240). Male devils like Tarquin easily stamp their images in the yielding waxen minds, which cannot be called "the authors of their ill, / No more than wax shall be accounted evil" (1244–45). This is part of the case Lucrece develops in her own mind, before her husband arrives, that she cannot be held responsible for the crime by which her chastity was destroyed. She fully accepts guilt for the rape and is certain that she must kill herself in order to be redeemed, but she wants to assuage the pain in a strongly dualistic mind-body argument.

The long digression on the Troy tapestry (1366–1568) is the most moving section of the poem because Lucrece's abstract grief is able to fasten onto the Trojan War. She identifies with the aging Hecuba "Staring on Priam's wounds with her old eyes, / Which bleeding under Pyrrhus' proud foot lies" (1448–49). Like Lucrece,

> In her the painter had anatomized
> Time's ruin, beauty's wrack, and grim care's reign . . . (1450–51)

Hecuba presents the sympathetic image of "life imprisoned in a body dead" (1456). Although Lucrece rails against Paris for his rape of Helen—"Why should the private pleasure of some one / Become the public plague of many moe?" (1478–79)—she focuses on the "subtile Sinon" (1541) for ten stanzas because he foreshadows Tarquin. Like him, the "perjured Sinon" (1521) comes to the Trojans "With outward honesty, but yet defiled / With inward vice" (1545–46). The enraged and passionate Lucrece "tears the senseless Sinon with her nails" (1564) according to the emotional assumptions of this scene: "Here feelingly she weeps Troy's painted woes" (1492).

As usual in Shakespeare, painting is praised for being lifelike, and the whole "imaginary work" (1422) presents itself as a giant synecdoche. It is the essence of "Conceit deceitful" (1423):

> That for Achilles' image stood his spear,
> Griped in an armèd hand; himself behind
> Was left unseen, save to the eye of mind:
>   A hand, a foot, a face, a leg, a head
>   Stood for the whole to be imaginèd. (1424–28)

Lucrece engages her grief in the Troy tapestry in a much more effective way than in the abstract invocations to Night, Opportunity, and Time.

The Trojan War is the setting of Troilus and Cressida, which uses the war and all its dissentious, cynical, and unheroic themes as a background for the bitter satire of the play. In Hamlet the Dido and Aeneas play, including the Trojan War, is an important analogue of the tragedy, with Pyrrhus closely allied to Laertes as a revenger and old Hecuba linked with Hamlet's own mother, Gertrude. The use of the Troy tapestry in The Rape of Lucrece begins a whole series of allusions to the Trojan War as a paradigm of tragedy, including the important allusions in *Titus Andronicus*. In the prose "Argument" preceding *The Rape of Lucrece*, the political aspect of the poem is made much more explicit. Here Junius Brutus shows Lucrece's dead body to the people of Rome and tells them about Tarquin's vile deed, "with a bitter invective against the tyranny of the King." At this, "the people were so moved that with one consent and a general acclamation the Tarquins were all exiled, and the state government changed from kings to consuls." In a quick sweep, the narrative moves from rape to revolution, ending with the establishment of the Roman Republic. Interestingly, in the poem Brutus is represented like Hamlet, playing the role of a mad and irresponsible idiot until the rape of Lucrece provides the context for his revenge against the Tarquins. He buries "his folly's show" in Lucrece's wound (1810), and "throws that shallow habit by / Wherein deep policy did him disguise" (1814– 15).

The Sonnets

Thomas Thorpe published 154 Sonnets by Shakespeare followed by *A Lover's Complaint* (also said to be by Shakespeare) in 1609. Unlike the texts of *Venus and Adonis* and *The Rape of Lucrece*, the printed text has many obvious errors, and Shakespeare clearly did not proofread it or see it through the press. Although the *Sonnets* seem to have an authoritative manuscript behind them, they were certainly not published with Shakespeare's knowledge or permission. Sonnets usually circulated in handwritten "books" among one's private friends and acquaintances. It was not considered necessary or even desirable to publish them.

The great vogue of sonnet writing was in the 1590s, and we know from Sonnet 104 that three years had passed since the poet first saw his "fair friend," which makes it likely that the writing of the *Sonnets* occupied at least three years in the 1590s, probably the early 1590s. Some of the *Sonnets* may have been written in the early 1600s, but the bulk of them are associated with Shakespeare's ingenious, heavily conceited, and self-consciously rhetorical style of the early and mid-1590s. In 1598 Francis Meres mentions in *Palladis Tamia* Shakespeare's "sugred sonnets among his priuate friends," an obvious compliment to his elegant style, although we may have some doubts about *sugred* as a term of praise. In 1599 two Sonnets, 138 and 144, were printed in a slightly different form in *The Passionate Pilgrim*.

The *Sonnets* were dedicated to "Mr. W. H." as "the only begetter," but it is hard to know whether this is the poet's or the publisher's dedication. It is unlike the formal dedications of *Venus and Adonis* and *The Rape of Lucrece* to the Earl of Southampton, and it may be that Mr. W. H. is the only begetter in the sense that he made his manuscript copy of Shakespeare's *Sonnets* available to the publisher. There has been endless and mostly fruitless biographical speculation about the *Sonnets*, and even more elaborate autobiographical guessing about Shakespeare's own personal relation to the experience described in the *Sonnets* and to characters in the *Sonnets* such as the Friend, the Dark Lady, and the Rival Poet or Poets. There is no independent confirmation in other writing or records of the time of anything factual that is said in Shakespeare's *Sonnets*. We would expect, at the least, some outside confirmation of the Rival Poet's activities: his sonnets to the friend or to the lady, or some account of his love life. It is curious that in the elaborately punning Sonnets 135 and 136 it seems that Shakespeare, the Dark Lady's husband, and the Friend are all named Will. This is convenient because *will* is also a word for carnal appetite and lust.

We know nothing definite about the historical identity of the Dark Lady and the Friend. The *Sonnets* seem to be strongly homoerotic, but in terms of Petrarchan love conventions, the Platonic idea of friendship offers a much higher ideal than heterosexual love, as we can see plainly in the opening sequence between Leontes and Polixenes in *The Winter's Tale* or in the friendship of Palamon and Arcite (and Emilia and Flavina) in *The Two Noble Kinsmen*. Leontes' fiendish jealousy seems to be generated, like Original Sin, from sexuality itself, as Hermione his wife so keenly recognizes. Sexual love is represented repeatedly in the *Sonnets* as a source of grief and enslavement, nowhere more strongly than in Sonnet 129, "Th' expense of spirit in a waste of shame."

Sonnet 20 seems to lay out clearly the distinction between an ennobling love between two male friends and the potentially debasing sexual love between a man and a woman. The Friend has "A woman's face, with Nature's own hand painted" and is "the master mistress of my passion." Nature first created him "for a woman," but then "fell a-doting, / And by addition me of thee defeated." Nature's "addition" seems to be clearly a penis, as we learn from the punning couplet close:

> But since she pricked thee out for women's pleasure,
> Mine be thy love, and thy love's use their treasure.

There is a clear distinction between the noble "love" and the lesser "love's use," or intercourse. We learn later that the Dark Lady has seduced the Friend and engaged him in a sexual relationship (Sonnets 35, 40, 41, etc.). Sonnet 20 makes a sharp distinction between noble friendship and physical love. Sex is excluded from the relation with the Friend.

The Shakespearean or English sonnet is derived from the Earl of Surrey and has three quatrains (rhyming abab, cdcd, and efef) with a concluding couplet (gg) all in iambic pentameter. Most of the sonnets have fourteen lines, although there is one (Sonnet 99) of fifteen, with an introductory first line, and one of twelve (Sonnet 126), which has six couplets. There are vestiges of the Italian sonnet in Shakespeare, in which an octave is set against a sestet. The octave of two quatrains contrasts with the sestet, which consists of a quatrain and a couplet considered as a single unit. These are relatively uncommon in Shakespeare, although Sonnet 18 has the feeling of an Italian sonnet: it has three quatrains and a couplet, but the third quatrain has a different logical movement from the first two. The feeling of a distinct sestet is continued through the triumphant couplet:

> So long as men can breathe or eyes can see,
> So long lives this, and this gives life to thee.

This couplet provides an upbeat ending.

The most problematic feature of the Shakespearean sonnet is the couplet close, which is sometimes disappointing because it is so epigrammatic, so didactic, so much like a neat summary tacked on to a poem that doesn't need it. There are many feeble couplets, for example the one in Sonnet 37:

Look what is best, that best I wish in thee.
This wish I have, then ten times happy me!

This seems like mere filler for a sonnet that is clearly not one of the best, but is nevertheless complex, about a poet "made lame by Fortune's dearest spite," who shares in his friend's "abundance." This certainly doesn't indicate that the poet is literally "lame," and the couplet doesn't do justice to the poetic reasoning of the three previous quatrains.

The couplet works wonderfully well in Sonnet 73, and is generally successful when it has an element of dramatic surprise, like a punch line. In Sonnet 19 the couplet comes upon us as a sudden peripeteia to the irresistible powers of "Devouring Time":

Yet do thy worst, old Time; despite thy wrong,
My love shall in my verse ever live young.

This couplet introduces an alternative with its "Yet" and "despite" that comes upon us as a hidden truth. Sonnet 65 is similar. Against "sad mortality" and his "spoil of beauty" there is no protection, except for the miracle of poetry trumpeted in the couplet:

O, none, unless this miracle have might,
That in black ink my love may still shine bright.

The couplet form lends itself in the *Sonnets* (and in Shakespeare's plays, too, especially scene-ending couplets) to bold and emphatic statement. Sonnet 56 is not particularly memorable, but its couplet ending vibrates with promise and new possibility. The poem is an appeal to "Sweet love" to "renew thy force," presumably in a period of absence or neglect. The "Return of love" is connected syntactically with the couplet:

Or call it winter, which being full of care,
Makes summer's welcome thrice more wished, more rare.

A series of five accented syllables beginning with *thrice* in the last line is driven home with the unusual fourth-beat caesura, or mid-line pause, after *wished*. *More rare* soars in a way that redeems the entire poem.

Time is the most frequently repeated concept and image in the *Sonnets*. This is the pervasive Renaissance theme of mutability, and the poet presents various ways to defy Time. The first seventeen Sonnets constitute the most distinctive unit of the whole sequence, which is arranged more or less logically by similarity of theme. We don't, of course, know who devised the ordering of the *Sonnets* or what relation the sequence has to date of composition. The first seventeen sonnets all urge the young friend to marry and to reproduce his beauty in children. This is the familiar doctrine of use that is part of Venus's argument to Adonis in *Venus and Adonis* and that echoes the often-repeated parable of the talents in Matt. 25: 14–30. Man is the steward, not the owner, of his good qualities and possessions, and he is obligated to put his natural gifts to use for the benefit of others. If you are beautiful, you must make use of your beauty (as money accumulates "use" or interest) by having children on whom to bestow your god-given gifts.

The beginning of the first sonnet announces the immortality of beauty through propagation:

> From fairest creatures we desire increase,
> That thereby beauty's rose might never die.

You are not allowed to be in love with yourself and waste your substance in "niggarding," or hoarding, to be "contracted to thine own bright eyes" and feed "thy light's flame with self-substantial fuel." This is to make "a famine where abundance lies," that is, the potential abundance that comes from creating children to perpetuate one's beauty. Children are like "flowers distilled" (Sonnet 3), or perfume, that defies the tyranny of Time.

Another way to wage war against Time is to write verse, which confers a kind of immortality upon the Friend. This is a repeated theme in the *Sonnets*. Posterity and poetry both do battle against oblivion. Nature is a destroyer of beauty, but poetry is immutable and guarantees that "thy eternal summer shall not fade" (Sonnet 18). In Sonnet 65 there is a series of unanswerable questions about Time, one in each of the first two quatrains, and two in the third:

> O, fearful meditation, where, alack,
> Shall Time's best jewel from Time's chest lie hid?

Presumably, "Time's best jewel" is the beautiful Friend, whom the Poet is trying to conceal from the ravaging hand of Time, who threatens to seize him and put him in his chest. How can "beauty hold a plea" against the rage of Time? The only solution to this "fearful meditation" is the miracle of poetry: "That in black ink my love may still shine bright." The immanence and immortality of poetry are postulated as a defense against the ravages of Time.

Two sonnets dwell specifically on music, 8 and 128, but the musicality of the *Sonnets* as a group is striking. The slow, sad lyrical effects are the most impressive, and they lend themselves to being set to music (as many sonnets have been). Sonnet 30 is best remembered as supplying C. K. Scott Moncrieff with the English title for Proust's *A La Recherche du Temps Perdu*. It is artful in its heavy use of alliteration and its legal / commercial imagery. In the first quatrain, "remembrance of things past" is summoned to appear at the "sessions of sweet silent thought," in which the poet presumably sits in judgment on the events of his own life. The predominance of s-sounds in the opening line immediately establishes a mood of reverie and meditation—the sibilants are associated with sleep, as in the colloquial expression *a few z's*, meaning a short nap. "My dear Time's waste" continues the most repeated theme in the *Sonnets* of Time the Destroyer. The memorializing of the second quatrain presents a mournful threnody for "precious friends hid in death's dateless night," "love's long since canceled woe," and "th' expense of many a vanished sight."

The sonnet is an elegy to death, the expiration of love, and the gradual disappearance of all that is lovely and beautiful. There is a sense in the third quatrain that "grievances foregone" can never be forgotten and that "The sad account of fore-bemoanèd moan" must be paid anew as if it had never been paid before. The music of the three quatrains is an almost perfect elegy for "remembrance of things past," but the couplet is jarring and facile:

> But if the while I think on thee, dear friend,
> All losses are restored and sorrows end.

It is as if a mere thought of the "dear friend" is enough to cancel the previous three quatrains. This is one of the most disturbing and inappropriate couplets in the *Sonnets*. We are soon to learn of many negative and unfavorable aspects of the "dear friend."

Sonnet 73 is similar to Sonnet 30 in its elegiac tone and in its meditation on man's mortality. It does not use such deliberate alliteration, but its prominent caesuras, or midline pauses, slow the rhythm down, especially in the three caesuras of line 2:

> That time of year thou mayst in me behold
> When yellow leaves, or none, or few, do hang
> Upon those boughs which shake against the cold . . .

The numerous accented syllables in the fourth line also slow down the movement of the poem practically to a funeral dirge: "Bare ruined choirs where late the sweet birds sang." "Bare ruined choirs" and "sweet birds sang" are all heavily accented without any intervening unaccented syllables. The autumn of the first quatrain is matched by twilight in the second, with black night and sleep, which is described as "Death's second self." In the third quatrain, the embers of the fires of youth match autumn and twilight as images of death. The fire consumes "that which it was nourished by." In this sonnet, the couplet is a perfect conclusion to the somber mood and adagio movement of the first three quatrains:

> This thou perceiv'st, which makes thy love more strong,
> To love that well which thou must leave ere long.

Love is intimately connected with death, and the idea of mutability and mortality should serve to make love more intense.

The *Sonnets* are obviously related to the plays, but generically there are important differences between lyric and dramatic expression. The wooing sonnet in *Romeo and Juliet* (1.5.95ff.), for example, is a playful and witty part of the early courtship of Romeo and Juliet—they answer each other—but it would be inappropriate later in the play. If we consider specific sonnets in relation to plays, it is clear that Sonnet 66 looks ahead to *Hamlet* in its account of "The slings and arrows of outrageous fortune" (3.1.58), especially in the third quatrain:

And art made tongue-tied by authority,
And folly (doctorlike) controlling skill,
And simple truth miscalled simplicity,
And captive good attending captain ill.

Hamlet's "sea of troubles" includes

the whips and scorns of time,
Th' oppressor's wrong, the proud man's contumely,
The pangs of despised love, the law's delay,
The insolence of office, and the spurns
That patient merit of th' unworthy takes . . . (*Hamlet* 3.1.70–74)

Despite verbal similarities in the catalogues of ills, in Hamlet's "To be, or not to be" speech they are part of an intolerable strain that includes the possibility of suicide. In Sonnet 66 the cry for "restful death" is rejected in the couplet close because it would isolate the poet from his love. The sonnet itself is a self-contained logical unit that ends by rejecting the possibilities of the first three quatrains. It has no relation to a highly characterized speaker or to a specific point in the dramatic action.

Even if radical differences exist between the *Sonnets* and the plays, the best sonnets still use dramatic devices that are similar to those in the plays. The sonnets that are most appealing seem to be those that explore a strong sense of turmoil and perturbation and that consequently offer poignant, often negative, characterizations. Sonnet 94 is powerfully dramatic—not theatrical in the sense of any imagined scenes—in its characterization of the Friend as cold, disdainful, and unattached. Despite all the earlier sonnets on the doctrine of use and the insistence on man's stewardship rather than absolute possession of his beauty, in the octave the Friend ironically claims to be one of those who are "the lords and owners of their faces" rather than "stewards of their excellence." He is "Unmovèd, cold" and husbands "nature's riches from expense." The opening line, "They that have pow'r to hurt and will do none," is so frightening because the powerful Friend is affectless, lacedemonian, and uninvolved. Therefore his beauty is like a flower that suffers "base infection," and that is why, finally, "Lilies that fester smell far worse than weeds." The lily pretends to be a nobler flower than a weed, and hence its possibilities of corruption are more extreme. The Friend is characterized in this and many of the surrounding sonnets as incapable of real love.

A comparably dramatic sonnet is 129 about the Dark Lady, who appears in Sonnets 127–52. She is much more specifically sexual than any of Shakespeare's dramatic heroines, including Cleopatra and Cressida, and she seems to enslave the Poet (and his Friend, too) in an irresistible but shameful intensity of lust, such as Tarquin's self-defeating lust in *The Rape of Lucrece*. Sonnet 129 is not directly about the Dark Lady, but about her demonic effect on the Poet, who doesn't know how "To shun the heaven that leads men to this hell." Active lust involves "Th' expense of spirit," or the expenditure of seminal fluid, "in a waste of shame," which may pun on *waste* and *waist*. Until ejaculation, male lust follows the pattern of Tarquin, who seems to be arguing with another self that he doesn't recognize: lust "Is perjured, murd'rous, bloody, full of blame, / Savage, extreme, rude, cruel, not to trust." The spondaic thrust of the last line carries some of the metrical and phonetic harshness of the meaning. Lust is deceptive and self-defeating: "Enjoyed no sooner but despisèd straight" and "A bliss in proof, and proved, a very woe." The stark alternatives make this a very dramatic sonnet, as if lust is entirely outside a man's power to control. The Dark Lady is therefore both the heaven and the hell of the Poet.

The personal anguish of Sonnet 129 is displaced in the witty, mannered, sexual puns of Sonnet 151, "Love is too young to know what conscience is." It is as if the Poet has finally mastered the "sensual fault" (Sonnet 35) and "Lascivious grace" (Sonnet 40) of earlier poems, and he can proceed to the "sensual feast" (Sonnet 141) without any trepidations or pricks of conscience. The Poet willingly betrays his soul to his "gross body's treason," and "flesh" (specifically the penis) doesn't wait for any further excuses, "But, rising at thy name, doth point out thee, / As his triumphant prize." The double entendres on erection—*reason, rising, pride, stand*, and *rise and fall*—resemble Shakespeare's early comedies. Lust is no longer an excruciating torment, but rather an entertainment. The couplet cadence is playful:

> No want of conscience hold it that I call
> Her "love" for whose dear love I rise and fall.

This is a good example of a couplet that really concludes the three preceding quatrains and seems to answer the opening proposition of the sonnet. I am not offering the ingenious Sonnet 151 as an example of one of Shakespeare's best sonnets, but it does provide a contrast to the ferocious energy and reckless mood of Sonnet 129.

The wittiest sonnet is undoubtedly 130, which is endlessly quoted although it is not at all characteristic of Shakespeare's entire sequence. It stands out because it satirizes the very Petrarchan conventions upon which Shakespeare so firmly depends. Specifically, it ridicules the accepted clichés of a woman's beauty that were made so much fun of in *Love's Labor's Lost* and Shakespeare's early comedies. The Dark Lady, by definition, doesn't fulfill the Nordic criteria of beauty established in the 1590s: exceptionally white skin, brightly rosy cheeks, and brilliantly blonde hair, which standards were met more vividly by cosmetics than by nature. As Hamlet complains to Ophelia: "I have heard of your paintings, well enough. God hath given you one face, and you make yourselves another" (*Hamlet* 3.1.143–45). The Dark Lady, then, has eyes that "are nothing like the sun," presumably in clarity and brilliance. She lacks the classic war between the white and the red in her cheeks:

> I have seen roses damasked, red and white,
> But no such roses see I in her cheeks.

Her lips are not as red as coral nor her breasts white as snow. They are, in fact, "dun" colored, or dark and swarthy, like Cleopatra's, another Dark Lady, who shows a "tawny front" (*Antony and Cleopatra* 1.1.6) and is sunburned, "with Phoebus' amorous pinches black" (1.5.28). The Dark Lady is a practical and seemingly unromantic figure: her breath "reeks," her speaking voice is not very musical, and "when she walks" she is unlike a goddess because she "treads on the ground."

The couplet conclusion, however, is in an entirely different and unexpected tone:

> And yet, by heaven, I think my love as rare
> As any she belied with false compare.

The soaring assertion and affirmation in the couplet is out of keeping with Sonnet 129, "Th' expense of spirit in a waste of shame," that immediately precedes it. This should give us pause about making exact autobiographical claims for Shakespeare's *Sonnets*. We don't know who arranged the poems in their present order—perhaps it was the printer, or perhaps he was only following the sequence of his manuscript—but there are some striking inconsistencies of tone and mood. The Dark Lady is hardly the same figure in Sonnets 129 and 130, nor do her sexual attractions seem to match in Sonnets 129 and 151.

We are struck by Shakespeare's skepticism about his own powers as a poet and a dramatist. He is excessively deferential to the Rival Poet or Poets, who are also writing sonnets to the Friend and the Dark Lady. His "poor rude lines" (Sonnet 32) are "exceeded by the height of happier men"—"happier" in the sense of more gifted. The "proud full sail" of the Rival Poet's "great verse" has "struck me dead" and swallowed up "my ripe thoughts in my brain," as if their womb became their tomb (Sonnet 86). This undercuts in some important way the power of the Poet to confer immortality on the love object through his poetry.

Shakespeare feels himself unable to cope with the newer and more refined style of such poets as John Donne and the Metaphysicals, who wrote what the Elizabethans called "strong lines." In Sonnet 76, Shakespeare complains that his verse is "barren of new pride," "far from variation or quick change," but "still all one, ever the same." He cannot seize the moment and use "new-found methods" and "compounds strange." The explanation is rather facile: "I always write of you," "So all my best is dressing old words new." We feel that the Poet is dissatisfied with the fact that "every word doth almost tell my name," but he doesn't know how to shift into a more innovative style.

The Poet expresses even stronger dissatisfaction with his public career as a playwright and actor, in which he feels trapped. In a striking image from daily life:

And almost thence my nature is subdued
To what it works in, like the dyer's hand. (Sonnet 111)

Like Macbeth's, the dyer's hand is "incarnadine" (*Macbeth* 2.2.61), and "all great Neptune's ocean" (59) cannot change its color. Shakespeare is engaged in a profession to please the public, and "public means" breed "public manners." From this obvious cause comes the fact that "my name receives a brand." In the previous sonnet (110), Shakespeare apologizes to the Friend that he has made himself "a motley," or clown dressed in a motley, parti-colored costume, "to the view," and "Gored mine own thoughts, sold cheap what is most dear." In other words, he has betrayed his innermost thoughts to the public scrutiny of the theatrical public. I am not assuming that this is an autobiographical statement of utmost sincerity, but merely that it is an essential part of the fictional persona (and personas) created in the *Sonnets*. If Shakespeare is the most unrevealing and paradoxical English Renaissance author in his plays, there is no convincing reason to believe that he bares his heart in the *Sonnets*. The very directness of the revelations should put us on our guard.

It is unfortunate that Shakespeare's *Sonnets* have attracted a mass of biographical speculation different from that expended on the plays. Some of the same questions haunt all of Shakespeare's works, both dramatic and nondramatic: the ambiguous nature of art, revealing and concealing at the same time; the tendency to dramatize experience, as if "All the world's a stage, / And all the men and women merely players" (*As You Like It* 2.7.138–39); and, most comprehensively, the fictionalizing of human experience on the assumption that we enact and represent a reality that we create in our minds from our own histrionic imagination. The *Sonnets* share these qualities with Shakespeare's other works, especially those of the earlier 1590s. They can't be dealt with autonomously as if they were written by a poet separate from the man who wrote the plays.

A Lover's Complaint

A Lover's Complaint was included at the end of the volume of Shakespeare's *Sonnets*, published by Thomas Thorpe in 1609. It doesn't seem convincingly Shakespearean in its diction, yet there is no strong reason to deny Shakespeare's authorship. It is a highly conventional pastoral complaint by a forsaken maiden, who bewails her present state. It is written in the same rhyme royal stanza as *The Rape of Lucrece*, which is also mostly a complaint by Lucrece. The poem is very formal and, if it is indeed by Shakespeare, it doesn't show his poetic talent at its best.

The opening scene is poetic pastoral, in which we see a "fickle maid full pale" (5) disposing of her love tokens in the river. Because of her sorrow, she is "The carcass of a beauty" (11), but some beauty still peeps "through lattice of seared age" (14). A stanza is devoted to her hair, which proclaims in her "a careless hand of pride" (30). Some is untucked, but

Some in her threaden fillet still did bide
And, true to bondage, would not break from
     thence,
Though slackly braided in loose negligence.
                                                   (33–35)

While she is throwing in the river various favors from her "maund," or woven basket with handles, a "reverend man" appears to listen to her complaint—an aged man, it would seem, because he slides down "upon his grainèd bat" (64), or shepherd's staff showing the wood grain.

The maiden tells the reverend father of her woes in love, especially of having been deceived by a popular and eloquent young man. A good part of the poem is devoted to the young man's seduction speech. One curious detail is his account of the women he has already seduced, including a nun, "Catching all passions in his craft of will" (126). He is more than willing to present the maiden with the previous tributes that "wounded fancies sent me / Of pallid pearls and rubies red as blood" (197–98), of hair ornaments "With twisted metal amorously empleached, / I have received from many a several fair" (205–6), and also, surprisingly, "deep-brained sonnets" (209). This may be the verbal link connecting Shakespeare's own "deep-brained" *Sonnets* with *A Lover's Complaint*.

The young man is described affectingly:

> His browny locks did hang in crooked curls,
> And every light occasion of the wind
> Upon his lips their silken parcels hurls. (85–87)

Hurls is rather inelegant in this description, unlike the beauty of the young friend of the *Sonnets*. The account of his newly appearing beard is similarly naive and pictorially crude, like a portrait by a primitive artist:

> Small show of man was yet upon his chin;
> His phoenix down began but to appear,
> Like unshorn velvet, on that termless skin
> Whose bare out-bragged the web it seemed to wear. (92–95)

If "termless skin" is skin untouched by the ravages of time, then the youth's bare skin itself "out-bragged" the slight, downlike web of hair upon it. The images are not complex.

Another odd phrase appears in the young man's eager request for her hand:

"O, then, advance of yours that phraseless hand,
Whose white weighs down the airy scale of praise!" (225–26)

A "phraseless hand" is very un-Shakespearean. It is "phraseless" in the sense that it is ineffable—no appropriate phrases could be offered to describe it. It is also grotesque in its suggestion of a mute sign language. Lavinia in *Titus Andronicus* could more aptly be described as having a "phraseless hand."

Another strikingly un-Shakespearean exclamation is:

O cleft effect! Cold modesty, hot wrath,
Both fire from hence and chill extincture hath. (293–94)

"Cleft effect" is divided or double effect, playing with the Petrarchan contraries of hot and cold that are at the heart of amorousness, but the assonance in the phrase is excessive and almost comic. The net effect of the cleft effect is that the maiden succumbs: "There my white stole of chastity I daffed" (297). The homely image of chastity as a "white stole" seems stilted, naive, and crude for Shakespeare.

The poem ends dramatically with the maiden rekindling her passion and her anger at the same time. She asks a telling rhetorical question: "Who, young and simple, would not be so lovered?" (320). *Lovered* is not used as a verb anywhere else in Shakespeare; it seems an oddly passive word. The maiden admits "I fell" (321) but questions what she would "do again for such a sake" (322). The last stanza ends with a revealing, self-defeating statement that the young man's "false fire" (324) and "forced thunder"

Would yet again betray the fore-betrayed
And new-pervert a reconcilèd maid! (328–29)

There is no additional stanza to record the reaction of the reverend father to this surprising admission.

The ambiguity of the ending is in the Shakespearean dramatic mode of divided feelings and the overwhelming force of passion. It recalls Olivia's soliloquy of wonder at a love over which she has no control:

I do I know not what, and fear to find
Mine eye too great a flatterer for my mind.

Fate, show thy force; ourselves we do not owe.
What is decreed must be—and be this so! (*Twelfth Night* 1.5.306–9)

The maiden in *A Lover's Complaint* fears that she will be betrayed again and newly perverted by a false love that she is struggling against. Olivia doesn't fear that Viola will betray her, but she is acutely conscious of the tyranny of love. In *A Lover's Complaint* the maiden is staggered by the possibilities of love, even a false love, which, like the lover's pinch in *Antony and Cleopatra*, "hurts, and is desired" (5.2.296).

The Phoenix and the Turtle

*T*he *Phoenix and the Turtle* is a curious poem,
first printed in Robert Chester's *Loves Martyr:
or, Rosalins Complaint* in 1601 in a quarto edition of only fifty copies, which seemed to be
intended for private circulation. Poems by
Shakespeare, Ben Jonson, John Marston,
George Chapman, and others were ap-
pended to Chester's long poem, which announces its intention in the subtitle: *"Allegorically shadowing the truth of Loue,* in the constant
Fate of the Phoenix *and* Turtle." Shakespeare's
poem grows out of the symbolic and emblematic nature of Chester's poem.

   The Phoenix and the Turtle, written in tetrameter quatrains (rhyming abba) and tetrameter triplets, is divided into three parts: the
assembly of birds to mourn the death of the
phoenix and the turtle, the anthem for the
death of Love and Constancy, and the threnos
(or "threne"), a funeral song made by Reason
"As chorus to their tragic scene." The assembly of birds resembles Chaucer's *Parlement of
Fowles,* but is very short. The screech owl,
"shrieking harbinger" of death, is excluded
from this mourning group as is "Every fowl
of tyrant wing" except the eagle. The "death-
divining swan," who proverbially sings just
before its death (Tilley, S1028) and therefore knows "defunctive music," is to play the

role of "the priest in surplice white." The "treble-dated crow," who was fabled to have an exceptionally long life, is also among the mourners. Shakespeare attributes mystical powers to the crow or raven: "With the breath thou giv'st and tak'st," referring to the belief that this bird was thought to conceive its young and lay its eggs at its bill.

The anthem celebrates the death of Love, represented by the Phoenix (female) and Constancy, represented by the Turtle Dove (male). Shakespeare is already departing from tradition in thinking of the phoenix as female, since the mythical bird was usually considered as combining male and female gender (or as being sexless) and as immortal because it died after a long period and was reborn from its own ashes. The turtle is the familiar turtle dove from love poetry, who is almost always shown as female. The anthem presents various Platonic themes of unity in duality and imitates the metaphysical style of such contemporary poets as John Donne, especially in his *Anniversaries* (1611–12). Number is confounded in the phoenix and the turtle because there are "Two distincts, division none" and "Either was the other's mine." "Property," meaning the appropriateness of each being's attributes to itself (from the Latin *proprietas*, or propriety) "was thus appallèd / That the self was not the same." The image is applied to Elizabethan pharmacology: "To themselves yet either neither, / Simple were so well compounded." "Simples" were medicinal herbs, such as Friar Lawrence gathers in *Romeo and Juliet.* Simples, or single ingredients, were put together in a compound, but here the simple and the compound are equated.

Reason composes the beautiful "threnos," or lamentation, for the phoenix and the turtle that closes the poem in magical triplets. It is a celebration of "married chastity," which has religious connotations. Shakespeare clearly indicates that their lack of offspring was not the result of sterility or impotence: " 'Twas not their infirmity"—an important qualification from the celebrator of procreation in the *Sonnets!* The phoenix and the turtle represent all the poetic qualities and associations of "Beauty, truth, and rarity, / Grace in all simplicity." This includes an extremely wide gamut. Reason ends by calling upon all "That are either true or fair" to "sigh a prayer" for the departed phoenix and turtle.

This is a remarkable poem, unlike anything else that Shakespeare wrote, although resembling some of the songs in his plays. It is homely and specific, yet broad enough in its symbolism to hover on Platonic and metaphysical themes. The tetrameter lines tend to limit the scope of the poem, which, by avoiding longer pentameter lines also refuses to imitate a character talking, as in the plays. The poem is definitely not dramatic. The five triplets of the threnos are the most exciting part of the poem because they seem so songlike. The whole idea of married chastity is steeped in theological and mystical speculation, so that Shakespeare's odd assignment of gender to the phoenix and the turtle is finally nullified. They represent Truth and Beauty, two subjects that Shakespeare is greatly concerned about here, as in the *Sonnets*. One may wonder why Shakespeare chooses to kill off the immortal phoenix; the death of Truth and Beauty suggests a despondent close.

Index

Designer: Susan Clark
Text: Weiss
Compositor: Maple-Vail
Printer: Maple-Vail
Binder: Maple-Vail